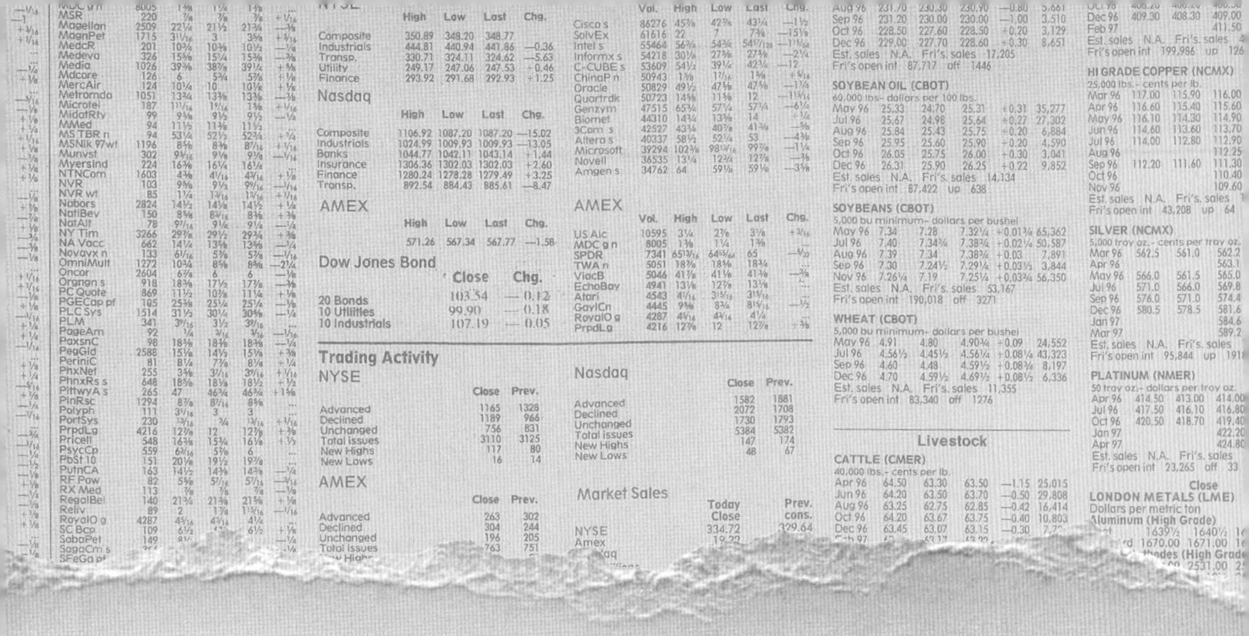

The Development of Rural Finance in China

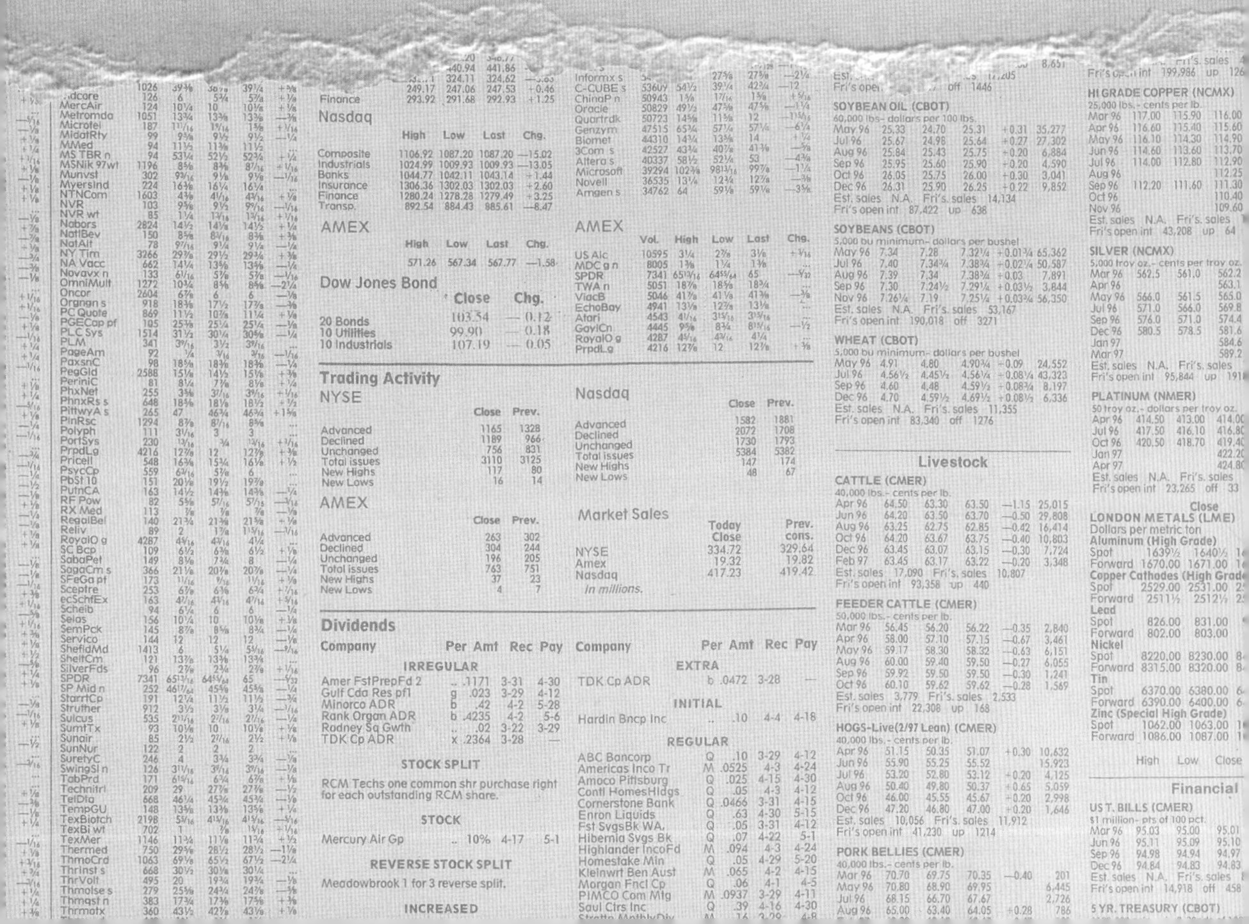

The Development of Rural Finance in China

Chen Yulu and Ma Yong

Enrich Professional Publishing

Published by

Enrich Professional Publishing (S) Private Limited
16L, Enterprise Road,
Singapore 627660
Website: www.enrichprofessional.com
A Member of Enrich Culture Group Limited

Hong Kong Head Office:
2/F, Rays Industrial Building, 71 Hung To Road, Kwun Tong, Kowloon, Hong Kong, China

China Office:
Rm 1800, Building C, Central Valley, 16 Hai Dian Zhong Jie, Haidian District, Beijing, China

United States Office:
PO Box 30812, Honolulu, HI 96820, USA

Translated by Vivien Lee

Edited by Barbara Cao and Glenn Griffith

ISBN (Hardback)	978-981-4332-08-8
ISBN (ebook)	978-981-4332-07-1 (pdf)
	978-981-4332-06-4 (epub)

Enrich Professional Publishing is an independent globally-minded publisher focusing on the economic and financial developments that have revolutionized new China. We aim to serve the needs of advanced degree students, researchers, and business professionals who are looking for authoritative, accurate, and engaging information on China.

Printed in Hong Kong with woodfree paper from Japan

Contents

Foreword vii

Preface xi

Acknowledgements xv

Chapter 1 The Adverse Situation of Rural Finance in China: Past and Present 1

Chapter 2 Rural Households' Behavior in China's Rural Finance 31

Chapter 3 The Agricultural Loan Market in China's Rural Finance 95

Chapter 4 The Government and Financial Institutions in China's Rural Finance 143

Chapter 5 Understanding China's Rural Finance: The Transformation of Rural Households and the Financial Layout 231

Notes 293

References 309

Index 331

Foreword

New China has celebrated its 60th anniversary, and the reform and opening-up policy has been implemented for over 30 years. China's economy has been surging and expanding. Although things change, the issues of rural areas, agriculture, and farmers—referred to as the "Three Rural Issues"—remain as the focus of economic development in China. From the start of the rural reform when the household responsibility system was implemented, to the sudden emergence of rural enterprises in the 1980s, the migration of tens of millions of rural laborers to the urban areas, and the urban-rural integration at the turn of the 21st century, There have been countless milestone events by which the soaring Chinese economy gained extra momentum and the Three Rural Issues are given special status and meaning in the course of socioeconomic reform and domestic economic development.

After more than 30 years of development, China's economic development has achieved many things that have attracted the world's attention. However, as an agricultural nation, China has been lagging behind in the development of a rural economy. The rural areas were both the starting point and driving force of China's reform, but under the ideology of "leading by industrialization and prioritizing urbanization," resources in rural areas are relocated to urban areas, and the agricultural surplus is invested into industrial development. As a result, despite the fact that China has become the third biggest economy in the world, and its development path is regarded as an exemplar for emerging market countries, the problem of imbalanced urban-rural development is still severe. Admittedly, there are many merits in this developmental pathway, but it has undoubtedly posed a major obstacle in China's further economic development.

The history of global economic development tells us that if the development of the rural economy lags behind, it will slow down the pace of the entire domestic economy. The new century signifies a new phase. China's reform in rural areas is at a new starting point in history, and reform and opening-up policy has entered into a critical period: substantial reform in the economic system, fundamental changes in the social structure, considerable adjustment of the state of affairs, and profound changes in the mind and values. At this time, facing the persistent problem of poor rural development, we need to search for an effective way and devise practical plans to break through the bottleneck and activate the rural market where there are vast lands and population. Not only can this way improve the lopsided urban-rural dual structure, but it can also establish a solid foundation for sustainable development of China's economy.

Under the conditions of the modern market economy, to solve the Three Rural Issues requires support from modern finance. This notion, since 2004, has prompted the Chinese government to concentrate on rural finance in the annual first official document (No.1 Document) concerning the Three Rural Issues. These documents have repeatedly had in-depth explanation about rural finance in the hope of promoting financial reform and development in rural areas, and resolving the Three Rural Issues. In the time of economic transformation, China's reform and development of rural finance are provided with unprecedented opportunities.

In recent years, reform of rural finance has become an active research area for scholars. The questions they have raised and the difficulties they have encountered present daunting challenges to traditional thinking and even classic economic theories. Researchers in and outside China have conducted fruitful research in order to salvage China's rural finance. But, due to the face that the problems of China's social economy are special, complex, and long-term accumulated ones, a logical and complete theoretical framework which is accepted by both the economists and the industry has yet to be formed. Further research is required.

While China's rural finance can be studied from different angles and aspects, a theoretical framework must include the following core aspects: First, the characteristics of the economic behavior of the farmers who are the basis of rural microeconomics, and the influence of those characteristics on the effective financial demand. Second, the characteristics of the agricultural credit market which connect the supply and demand sides, and the effect of these characteristics on rural economic resources allocation of those financial resources. Third, the characteristics of financial institutions which act as financial services providers, and their impact on the effective financial supply. Fourth, China, as a traditional country with an economy directed by the government, under the trend of marketization of rural finance, and the ways in which the government should exert its influence. Fifth, rural society is facing continuous transformation, how China's financial system should be developed in order to achieve bidirectional and sustainable development of rural economy and rural finance in the long run. Sixth, with market integration as a background, between the finance related to the Three Rural Issues and how that relates to the urban economy, how to form a system in which the two can cooperate and interact to achieve a win-win situation.

After identifying the core questions, suitable research methods are necessary to support the argument. Drawing on my experience, different from those of many other disciplines, rural financial theories rely more on the conclusion of actual experience. It is the case everywhere in the world. Therefore, rural financial theories are both theoretical and practical. The significance is that while literature review, deduction, and establishing arguments are essential in the study of China's rural finance, our primary job is to step into the actual rural areas. We need surveys on the situations of China's rural areas, agriculture, and farmers; analyses of the effect of industrialization and urbanization on the three aspects; investigation into the ever-changing demand of the Three Rural Issues for financial services; and a scientific conclusion of the rural financial activity. Only on this holistic basis can we determine the direction of future development and propose effective policies.

The special meaning of this book lies here. Based on a series of actual data collected on site, it observes and explains China's rural finance from the angle of dynamic development. The author analyzes and summarizes the characteristics of China's rural households being an entity in the market economy, and looks at economic behaviors of the entity relating to the demand for, and supply of, capital in the framework of nation, society, system, and culture. Therefore, the author's conclusions and proposals are closely tied to the Three Rural Issues.

Professor Chen is the most prominent figure in the middle generation of Chinese economists. In recent years, his books and research have focused on various areas in economics and finance with real insight. Now, he is about to publish new findings of China's rural finance. I believe this book will inspire readers who are interested in that topic.

Professor Chen Yulu invited me to write the preface for this forthcoming book. It is a great privilege for me and I also cherish this opportunity to learn.

Li Yang
Vice President, Academy Member, Chinese Academy of Social Sciences
Deputy President, China Society for Finance and Banking

Preface

Nobel Prize laureate in economics Gunnar Myrdal has said that "it is in the agricultural sector that the battle for long-term economic development will be won or lost." In the past, agricultural growth played an important role in economic development. The positive relationship between the two is supported by a great deal of empirical research. Data from industrial countries and fast-developing countries shows that agriculture can originate in non-agricultural growth and raise economic benefits on the whole: Economic growth driven by agricultural development is especially influential in combating poverty and famine; the rise in the employment rate and the income of the agricultural sector stimulates the demand for non-agricultural products and services and non-agricultural income in rural areas.

China is in the process of transforming to a middle-income country. As urbanization accelerates and the income gap widens, the Three Rural Issues are becoming a strategic problem in reform, and one of the core concerns of administration for the new government in recent years. According to the national policies, the solution to the Three Rural Issues should center on raising farmers' income, nurturing and refining the factor market, promoting the transfer of rural labor force, and maintaining the stable and sustainable development of agriculture. Obviously the Three Rural Issues are dependent on the support and development of rural finance directly or indirectly. However, the current development of rural finance is in a difficult situation: Formal finance is fading out and the left-alone rural credit cooperatives are unable to offer enough support to satisfy the rural financial demand. The adverse situation of rural finance and the sluggish increase in farmers' income are acting on each other, which renders some farmers in distant rural areas as "forgotten corners" of finance.

Recently, as China pays more attention to the Three Rural Issues, the core problem of rural finance has come under the limelight of academics and managerial boards. Rural financial issues are not only part of the reform of the national financial system, it also relates to the financial support for the development of the rural areas, agriculture, and farmers. As such, research on, and reform of, China's rural finance has become more urgent.

Among the current research on China's rural finance, the majority focuses on qualitative studies. Quantitative studies are rare. There is much debate about the credit behavior of rural households, agricultural credit market, and financial support at the level of financial system. In theoretical studies, when research touches on the financial system, the focus is still on whether farmers' credit behavior conforms to the classical economic assumption of rationality (to maximize profits): Some scholars stress the rationality of small farmers, upholding the assumption, while others oppose this by incorporating elements of sociology and history into their analyses, proposing the "survival logic" of small farmers. This kind of debate not only directly touches on the explanation of rural economic behavior, but affects the arrangement of the systems (including the financial system) in both the past and future.

Through incorporating elements of sociology and history, the theory of "survival logic" of small farmers explains their credit behaviors under a relatively less advanced economic situation. It has to be pointed out that when these conclusions from long-term historical research are applied to the studies of China's current rural finance, a few crucial logical aspects require deeper consideration. First, if we say famers still abide by the "survival logic," is this phenomenon a result of culture and tradition as proposed by the studies? Second, much research distinguishes between "rational small farmers" and "surviving small farmers." In a continuous long-term analysis, the clear-cut separation of the two throughout the diachronic analysis would cause problems because of the possibility of the transformation from surviving small farmers to rational small farmers. Once this transformation proves to be real, the long-term conclusion would be different. Third, the studies rely on a lot of historical and cultural understandings to argue that small farmers' "survival logic" has not changed. But, from the perspective of economic research, this kind of understanding lacks convincing empirical evidence.

Moreover, we notice that there are several tendencies and problems in our domestic research which deserve attention: First, they put too much emphasis on the specialty of Chinese rural households and neglect the common economic characteristics of Chinese farmers acting as the economic entity of the market economy. Second, the period of study is too long. They do not offer a reasonable explanation on the logic of continuity. Third, they overstress the incompatibility between the formal financial system and rural economy, which prompted them to adopt a pessimistic perspective on the effort of reforming formal finance to boost farming. We believe that the aforementioned problems require a new objective interpretation on the credit behavior of rural households, agricultural credit market, and financial support at the level of financial system. This interpretation must have a logical theoretical basis and could undergo empirical examination based on China's practical condition. We must proceed from the actual situation in China's rural areas, dissect the micro-economic mechanism in, and constraints on, farmers' economic behavior, and interpret and evaluate objectively the problems of the development of rural finance (including both formal and informal finance).

This would help us in conducting in-depth studies and devising accurate policies regarding rural finance.

The adverse development in rural finance is closely tied to the complexity of the Three Rural Issues. Now, we are at the stage of understanding the problem, and continuous detailed research is needed. In terms of finance, only when the rural financial problem is solved can the distorted dual financial structure be reformed. In terms of economy, only when the income gap narrows, which would be achieved by an increase in rural income, can the long-term, distorted dual economic structure be rectified. In terms of the state, only when the development of urban and rural areas achieves a dynamic equilibrium, can our politics, economy, culture, and society all improve.

Regarding China's issues in rural areas, Liang Qichao (a Chinese intellectual and reformist in the 19th and 20th centuries) once said that "New China must originate from rural areas, and the Chinese must reinvent rural areas before they can reinvent China." When China's economy again comes to the threshold of change, his words can still describe the importance of the Three Rural Issues in the midst of economic transformation. Without a doubt, in the process of breaking through the dual economic structure to achieve a higher growth rate, rural finance is the lever to boost the entire economy.

Chen Yulu

Acknowledgements

This research is the collaborative effort of the Institute for Rural Economy and Finance of Renmin University of China and the Research Centre for Economics and Rural Finance of the Agricultural Bank of China on the topic "Rural Finance in China: Core Questions and Choices of Development." We extend our gratitude to Broad Union Fund of China, the Soon Ching Ling Foundation, and the Renmin University of China Social Sciences Research Projects for financing the research.

1

Chapter

The Adverse Situation of Rural Finance in China: Past and Present

We believe that the most basic and yet effective way to tackle unemployment in developing countries is to curb the bias toward the development of strategic cities.

—Edgar O. Edwards

China's Rural Areas in the Dual Economy: A Macroeconomic Background

In developing countries, there usually exists a dual economic contrast between the traditional and modern sectors, represented by agriculture and industry, respectively (Lewis 1954, Fei and Ranis 1964, Bardhan and Udry 1999). The study of the contributions of, and relationship between, agriculture and industry in boosting national economic growth is one of the core studies in the modern development of economics.

First proposed in the article "Economic Development with Unlimited Supplies of Labor" written by the American economist Arthur Lewis (1954), and subsequently developed by Dale W. Jorgenson, John C. H. Fei, and Gustav Ranis, the dual economy theory states that in areas with a vast agricultural population—South Asia, Southeast Asia, Africa, and Latin America—the co-existence of the traditional agricultural sector and the modern industrial sector is inevitable during economic development: In the traditional agricultural sector, productivity is low, technology is less advanced, and surplus labor exists which brings about zero or even negative marginal productivity. Labor is supplied at a minimum wage and there is an unlimited supply of labor. On the other hand, in the modern industrial sector, there is higher productivity and wages, which attracts the transfer of surplus labor from the traditional sector to the modern sector. This transfer promotes the expansion of the modern industrial sector and raises the marginal productivity in the agricultural sector. Over a period of time, the marginal productivity of the agricultural sector and the industrial sector will equalize, and the dual economic structure will disappear. How to achieve dynamic optimization in a dual economy and a stable transition from a traditional to a modern economy, and avoid the Malthusian Trap, are the core issues in the dual-sector model.[1]

As the largest developing country in the world, China shows an obvious feature of dual economy. As China's economy develops, the adverse effect of the dual economy on long-term economic development is becoming more prominent. Since reform and opening up, China's outstanding economic development has attracted attention from all over the world. However, the conflicts in the dual structure of urban and rural areas are not yet resolved but accumulating. Because of the failure to shake off the long-lasting constraints of the dual economy, a lot of problems are becoming "chronic diseases." Not only does this restrict the transmission of structural reform, but it leaves less room for structural adjustment (Liu Yuanchun and Luo Yübo 2003). To a certain extent, the dual economy has become one of the reasons why China's economic development has reached its bottleneck.[2] Corresponding with the development of the dual economic structure, the income gap between urban and rural areas has been widening since the 1990s (see Fig. 1.1). In 2004, China's income gap was the largest in the world (Li Shi and Yue Ximing 2004).

Fig. 1.1. The income gap between urban and rural residents in China

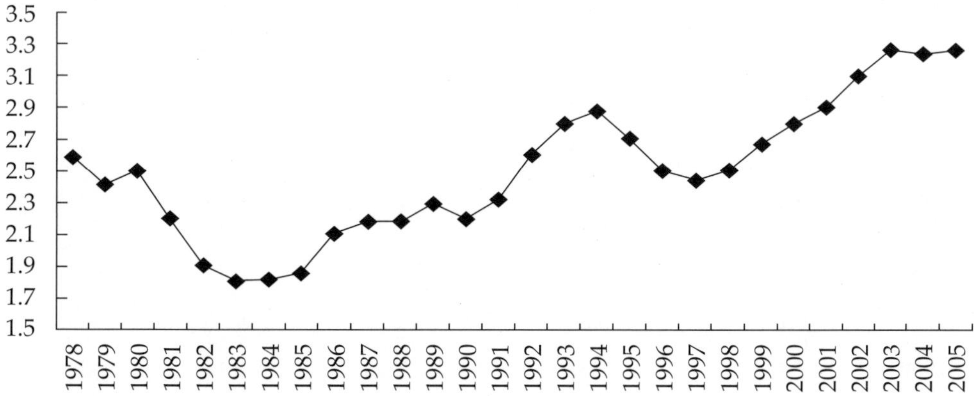

Source: *China Statistical Yearbook* (1978–2005).

To give a quantitative description of the development of China's dual economic structure, we employ some basic indexes used by the international economic academics: the difference in comparative labor productivity, dual contrast coefficient, and dual comparative coefficient. (1) The difference in comparative labor productivity is calculated by the non-agricultural labor productivity minus agricultural labor productivity, which signifies the difference in labor productivity between the two sectors under a certain labor input. The larger the value is, the stronger the duality is. (2) Dual contrast coefficient refers to the ratio of comparative labor productivity of agricultural sector to that of non-agricultural sector. It reflects the degree of difference between agricultural and non-agricultural comparative labor productivities. The smaller the ratio is, the larger the contrast between the two sectors and hence the more prominent the dual structure is. (3) Dual comparative coefficient is the average of the absolute value of the difference between production ratio (production value of either sector to that of the total) and labor force ratio (labor force of either sector to that of the total) of each sector. The smaller the value is, the less prominent the dual structure is. Table 1.1 and Fig. 1.2 present statistic data of the abovementioned indexes.

Table 1.1. The statistical measurement of the transformation of China's dual economic structure

Year	Primary industry's comparative labor productivity	Second and third industries' comparative labor productivity	Difference in comparative labor productivity	Dual contrast coefficient	Dual comparative coefficient (%)
1952	0.60	3.00	2.40	0.20	33.0
1953	0.55	3.20	2.65	0.17	37.2
1954	0.55	3.21	2.67	0..17	37.5
1955	0.55	3.02	2.67	0.17	37.1
1956	0.54	2.93	2.39	0.18	37.4
1957	0.50	3.18	2.68	0.16	40.9
1958	0.59	1.58	1.00	0.37	24.1
1959	0.43	1.94	1.51	0.22	35.5
1960	0.36	2.23	1.88	0.16	42.3
1961	0.47	2.80	2.33	0.17	41.0
1962	0.48	3.39	2.91	0.14	42.7
1963	0.49	3.41	2.92	0.14	42.2
1964	0.47	3.46	2.99	0.14	43.8
1965	0.46	3.38	2.91	0.14	43.7
1966	0.46	3.37	2.91	0.14	43.9
1967	0.49	3.26	2.77	0.15	41.4
1968	0.52	3.16	2.65	0.16	39.6
1969	0.47	3.37	2.90	0.14	43.6
1970	0.44	3.38	2.94	0.13	45.6
1971	0.43	3.25	2.82	0.13	45.6
1972	0.42	3.18	2.76	0.13	46.0
1973	0.42	3.13	2.70	0.14	45.3
1974	0.43	3.03	2.60	0.14	44.3
1975	0.42	2.96	2.55	0.14	44.8
1976	0.43	2.78	2.34	0.16	43.0
1977	0.39	2.77	2.37	0.14	45.1
1978	0.40	2.44	2.04	0.16	42.4
1979	0.45	2.28	1.83	0.20	39.6
1980	0.44	2.23	1.80	0.20	38.6
1981	0.47	2.14	1.67	0.21	36.3
1982	0.49	2.09	1.60	0.23	34.8
1983	0.49	2.04	1.54	0.24	34.1
1984	0.50	1.89	1.39	0.27	32.0
1985	0.45	1.91	1.45	0.24	34.0
1986	0.44	1.86	1.42	0.24	33.8
1987	0.45	1.83	1.38	0.24	33.2
1988	0.43	1.83	1.40	0.24	33.7
1989	0.42	1.88	1.46	0.22	35.1
1990	0.45	1.83	1.38	0.25	33.1
1991	0.41	1.88	1.74	0.22	35.3
1992	0.37	1.89	1.51	0.20	36.7
1993	0.35	1.84	1.48	0.19	36.5
1994	0.37	1.74	1.37	0.21	34.0
1995	0.40	1.66	1.26	0.21	31.3
1996	0.41	1.60	1.19	0.26	29.8
1997	0.39	1.61	1.22	0.24	30.5
1998	0.38	1.62	1.24	0.24	30.9
1999	0.36	1.64	1.29	0.22	32.1

(Cont'd)

Year	Primary industry's comparative labor productivity	Second and third industries' comparative labor productivity	Difference in comparative labor productivity	Dual contrast coefficient	Dual comparative coefficient (%)
2000	0.33	1.67	1.34	0.20	33.4
2001	0.31	1.69	1.38	0.18	34.5
2002	0.31	1.69	1.38	0.18	34.6
2003	0.30	1.68	1.38	0.18	34.5
2004	0.32	1.60	1.27	0.20	31.7
2005	0.28	1.58	1.30	0.18	32.2
2006	0.27	1.87	1.61	0.14	36.3
2007	0.27	1.81	1.54	0.15	34.7
2008	0.29	1.47	1.18	0.19	28.3

Source: *China Statistical Yearbook* (2000–2009).

Fig. 1.2. The trend of the difference in comparative labor productivity, dual contrast coefficient, and dual comparative coefficient

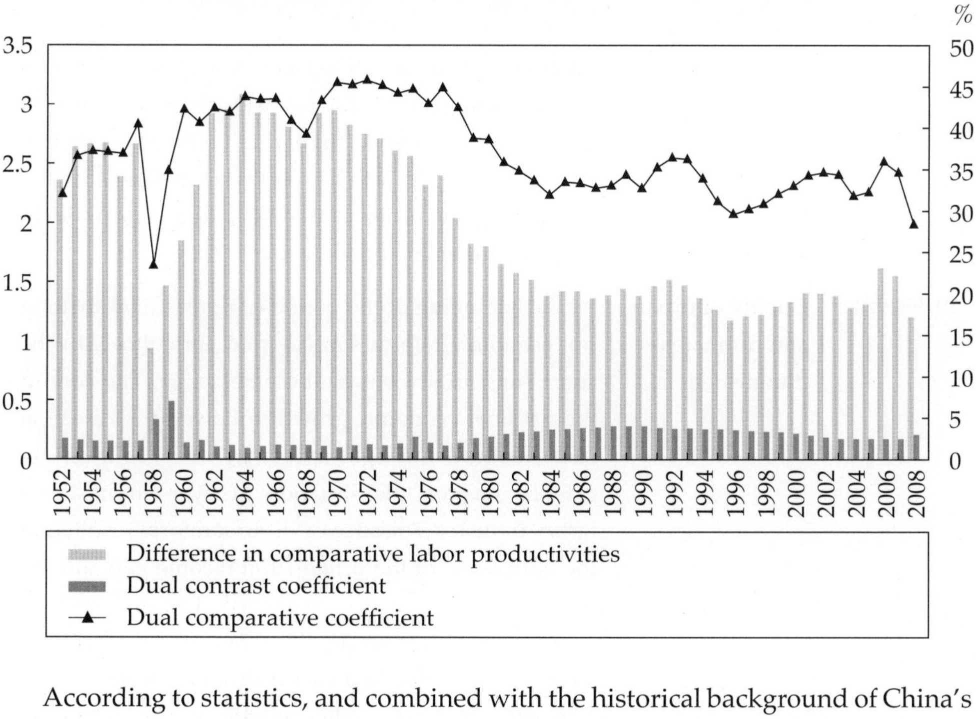

According to statistics, and combined with the historical background of China's socioeconomic development, the transformation of China's urban-rural dual economic structure can be divided into the following phases: (1) Before 1978: the urban-rural dual economic structure was formed and expanded rapidly; (2) 1979–1984: duality of urban and rural areas diminished; (3) 1985–1996: urban-rural dual structure fluctuated; (4) 1997–2002: urban-rural duality was reinforced; (5) after

2003: urban-rural dual economic structure faced disintegration. See Table 1.2 for a more detailed description.

Table 1.2. The phases of the transformation of urban-rural dual economic structure in China

Time	Features	Description
Before 1978	The urban-rural dual economic structure was formed and expanded rapidly	In the early stages of New China, China adopted the strategy of prioritizing heavy industry. It implemented mandatory industrial accumulation through administrative planning to organize and allocate social resources. Rural resources flowed to urban areas by means of "price scissors" to support the urban industrialization. This forging ahead strategy based on the suppression of agricultural development caused the widening of the urban-rural gap, and the deterioration of the urban-rural dual economic structure: The difference in comparative labor productivity between the primary and the other two industries continued to increase and remained high; dual contrast coefficient stayed below 0.2, which was lower than that of the developing countries (0.31–0.45); dual comparative coefficient remained high (above 40%) .
1979–1984	Duality of urban and rural areas diminished	At the beginning of the period of reform and opening up, economic reform started from agriculture. In the short run, rural economy became active. The core of the national economic growth followed the direction of agriculture and light industry, which, to a certain extent, changed the situation of over-emphasis on heavy industry. The success in rural reform resulted in the narrowing of the urban-rural income gap and the dual structure was also weakened: The difference in comparative labor productivity between the primary and the other two industries dropped from 1.83 to 1.38; dual contrast coefficient rose from 0.20 to 0.26; dual comparative coefficient decreased from 38.6% to 32.0%

(Cont'd)

Time	Features	Description
1985–1996	The urban-rural dual structure fluctuated	Since 1984, the focus of reform in China has shifted from rural to urban areas, which triggered rapid economic development in cities for successive years. Reform of the urban economic system was implemented on two levels: the first level is to reform the state-owned enterprises, and the second is to promote the economic development of non-state-owned enterprises. The overheated economy caused severe inflation in the early 1990s, which prompted the Chinese government to adopt "soft landing" economic policies from 1994 onwards. As a result, the expansion of the industrial sector halted, and measures designed to support agricultural development were adopted. The industrial output of the primary industry has weighed more than 20% again since 1994. Under such conditions, the enhancement of the duality of urban and rural areas was temporarily suppressed: Up to 1996, the difference in comparative labor productivity between the primary and the other two industries continued to drop to 1.19, dual contrast coefficient climbed back to 0.26, and dual comparative coefficient dropped to 29.8%
1997–2002	Urban-rural duality was reinforced	In this phase, due to socioeconomic problems, such as deflation and a surging unemployment rate in urban areas, the macroeconomic regulation and control unit provided more support to the urban economy, and the social security system was biased toward the urban sector in order to maintain social stability. Against such a backdrop, since the middle and later half of the 1990s, duality of urban and rural areas grew strong again: The difference in comparative labor productivity between the primary and the other two industries and dual comparative coefficient increased to 1.38 and 34.6%, respectively, in 2002, and dual contrast coefficient continued to decrease to 0.18.

(Cont'd)

Time	Features	Description
After 2003	The urban-rural dual economic structure faced disintegration	The 16th National Congress and the 3rd Plenary Session of the 16th Central Committee of the Communist Party of China (CPC) put the resolving of the Three Rural Issues as the top priority. In order to coordinate the socioeconomic development of urban and rural areas, effort was made to ensure that industry supports agriculture, urban areas support rural areas, and rural areas were took less and were given more with loosened control. The government drafted four No.1 Documents from 2004 to 2007 concerning the Three Rural Issues with distinct themes, namely "Increase Rural Income," "Raise the Overall Agricultural Production Capability," "Promote Socialistic New Rural Constructions," and "Actively Develop Modern Agriculture." The joint research group of the China Rural Labor Association under the Development Research Center of the State Council, planned three stages for China to eliminate the dual economic structure. First stage (2004–2010): gradually and partly suppress the expansion of dual economic structure to achieve overall preliminary structural improvement. Second stage (2011–2020): significantly ameliorate the dual structure. Third (2021–2050): basically disintegrate the dual structure.

Zeng Yinchu (2006) categorized China's industrialization into four periods (1949-1978, 1979–1992, 1993–1996, and after 1997) based on the features of the strategies of industrialization and the changes in background environment. He believed that the effect on the transformation of the dual structure was more prominent during the period of reform and opening up than during the period of the planned economy. If reform and opening up was further divided into three periods, the structural transformation was fastest during 1979–1992, the improvement of the dual structure was fastest during 1993–1996, and industrialization became less effective on the transformation of the dual structure after 1996.

Table 1.3. The comparison of the rate of change of economic structure during different periods

Period	Year	Average annual growth rate of per capita GDP (%)	Average annual contraction in the percentage of agricultural GDP to total GDP (%)	Annual contraction in agricultural employment percentage (%)
1st	1952–1978	3.79	0.83	0.48
2nd	1979–1992	7.99	0.72	0.87
3rd	1993–1996	9.69	–0.16*	1.97
4th	1997–2004	7.43	0.56	0.43

Note: * There was an increase of 0.16% during 1993–1996.

Source: Zeng Yinchu, Renmin University of China's Report on China's Economic Development (Beijing: Renmin University of China Press, 2006).

The above analysis demonstrates that China has a typical dual economic structure. Moreover, it shows differences in different periods. Chronologically, as previously demonstrated, its transformation fluctuated and was repetitive. Regionally, the transformation process was the fastest in the east, followed by the central region, and the west came last. Using the cross-sectional data of China's 31 provinces, municipalities, and autonomous regions as an example, the huge difference exists in dual contrast coefficient among different places: The coefficient was largest in Yuannan and the smallest in Hainan, with an over fourfold difference (see Fig. 1.3). The above facts show that, from east to west, the degree of transformation of the dual economic structure is diminishing, and the degree of contrast is increasing.

Fig. 1.3. The dual contrast coefficient of China's 31 provinces, municipalities, and autonomous regions

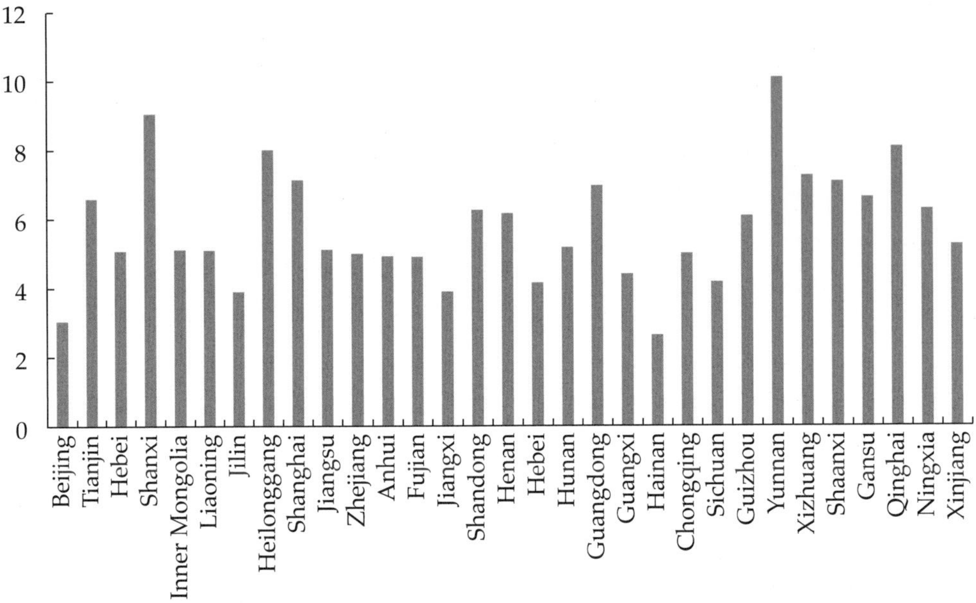

Source: Gao Fan, "Transformation of china's dual economic structure: Track, characteristics, and effect," *Study and Exploration* 6 (2007).

As a whole, the transformation of China's dual economic structure is rather slow. The long-term accumulated problems in the system have brought more problems to the current adjustment of economic structure. Dual economy has indisputably caused many structural complications which has in turn brought negative consequences to the social economy:

(1) In terms of resources allocation, the dual economic structure has caused segmentation of the factor markets. The labor force of the traditional sector cannot work well with the capital of the modern sector, resulting in a double surplus of labor and capital (Wang Jiangui 2002).

(2) In terms of the economic growth mode, the dual economic structure has caused a concentration of capital in the modern sector. Growth in industry was motivated by investments rather than technological advancement. The continual increase in the capital-output ratio justified people's doubts about the sustainability of this type of growth (Hayami 2003).

(3) In terms of regional development, the dual economic structure does not help the regions to be mutually supplementary and dependent. The allocation of capital, labor, technology, and etc., are hardly at best. These two factors lead

to an inter-regional backwash effect instead of diffusion effect, as witnessed since 1978 when the regional gap first closed up before widening again, showing a U-shaped trend (Lin Yifu and Liu Peilin 2003).

(4) In terms of income distribution, the dual economic structure does not allow the market competition mechanism and the wage equalization mechanism to fully function. The modern sector cannot benefit the traditional sector by trickle-down effect. The urban-rural income gap does not quickly close up but expand (Cai Fang 2002).

Moreover, the dual economic structure is self-repetitive and derivative: If the duality of industries is the core of the entire economic structure, it will further "clone" and generate by-products of regional, financial, and technological duality. These by-products interact and reinforce one another, which causes duality to become strengthened and seep into every aspect of the economy. Dual economy is transforming from an issue into a problem.

Urban-Rural Resources Allocation Under the Dual Economy: The Repressed Rural Finance

Capital, as we have learnt in the previous sections, plays an important role in the transformation of the dual economy. It follows that the successful transformation of the dual economy is energized by the capital mechanism. Under the Harrod-Domar model, capital is the crucial factor in economic growth, assuming technology remains unchanged. In fact, Schultz's traditional agricultural model states that reforming traditional agriculture can be through an increase in capital, technology, and institutions, etc., so as to expand the source of agricultural income. Chinese scholar Wen Tiejun also holds that agriculture revived under the Dabaogan, the individual peasant small-holding responsibility system, can be regarded as traditional agriculture. What Schlitz believes is prevalent in traditional agriculture—a lack of capital and technology, and institutions—still holds true in China. What hinders the development of China's rural finance is a serious shortage of capital. Only when the capital shortage is solved can China's rural finance improve.

Many studies have shown that financial intermediaries are at the core of capital formation and allocation (e.g. King and Levine, 1993). In the dual structure, the rural capital shortage implies a misallocation of financial resources. In the theory of financial repression, McKinnon (1988) observes how, in order to promote industrialization, some developing countries suppress the financial sector by heavily regulating interest rates and influencing credit allocation by administrative means. These measures have kept many small and medium–sized enterprises, individual merchants, and rural households from the financial market. Only those modern businesses controlled or favored by the government, large- and medium-sized enterprises and a few of those privileged ones, could obtain capital support. This financial repression directly led to a further imbalance of the dual economic structure.

There is abundant literature about the established fact of the imbalanced credit allocation toward urban areas under the dual economic structure. Some of the representative works include Yang and Zhou (1999), Li Yifu (2002), Zhang Qi (2003), and many others.[3] The World Bank pointed out in its summary of the global experience of developing rural finance: "In many developing countries, the main reason why rural development lags behind is that they favor industry but neglect agriculture; their policies focus on the urban sector but neglect the rural sector. These policies reduce the profitability of agricultural and rural non-agricultural enterprises, and destroyed the rural financial market. Many policies are beneficial to the owners of large farms but not to the owners of small farms or the poor farmers. This worsens the income allocation to the agricultural and rural sector. Countries which discriminate most against agriculture are countries who have the lowest economic growth rate."

And since financial market competition is directed by the price signals, the financial market and the commodity market are closely related. Confusing price signals in the commodity market would cause a misallocation of resources in the financial market. For many years, developing countries have imposed high taxes on the agricultural sector through a series of direct or indirect policies. Those policies, typically favoring the urban sector, severely affected the profitability of agricultural enterprises and non-agricultural rural enterprises.[4] Based on the 1960–1984 data from 18 countries, Schiff and Valdes (1992) estimated that direct and indirect governmental interference caused the domestic agricultural trade to drop 30%, and revenue transfer from agriculture accounted for 46% of the agricultural GDP. This "seizure from agriculture" is very short-sighted because countries with discriminatory policies against agriculture have a very low economic growth rate.

It should be noted that China's dual economic structure has been also shaped by a raft of socio-political, economic, and historical factors. No doubt, the economic perspective, the repression of rural finance, and the resulting outflow of rural financial resources have obviously been strengthening the dual economic structure.

First, in order to prioritize the development of heavy industry—as part of its Forging Ahead strategy—the central government for the longest time has suppressed the interest rate to ensure that capital which was in shortage was allocated to the urban industrial sector first (Lin Yifu et al. 2002). Although after the reform and opening up, the strategy was weakened, the government continued to restrict the fluctuations of savings and loans rates so as to obtain low-cost financial resources to subsidize the urban sectors and national enterprises. China's interest rate has long been regarded as lower than the market clearing interest rate (see table 1.4). Although suppressing savings interest rate would cause a shortage in capital accumulation (McKinnon 1988), the correlation between household savings and interest rate is weak in China's experience (Li Yan 1999). Under the national credit guarantee, the low savings interest rate and the incessant increase in household savings offer a continuous supply of capital to the state-owned enterprises and the urban sectors favored by the government.

Table 1.4. China's urban-rural savings and interest rates (1979–2004)

Year	Urban-rural savings (RMB100 million)	Inflation rate (%)	Savings interest rate (1 year, %)		Loans interest rate (1 year, %)		Interest margin
			Nominal	Actual	Nominal	Actual	
1979	281.0	2.0	3.96	1.96	4.32	2.32	0.36
1980	399.5	6.0	5.40	–0.60	5.04	–0.96	–0.36
1981	523.7	2.4	5.76	3.36	5.04	2.64	–0.72
1982	675.4	1.9	5.76	3.86	7.20	5.30	1.44
1983	892.5	1.5	7.20	5.70	7.20	5.70	0.00
1984	1,214.7	2.8	7.20	4.40	7.20	4.40	0.00
1985	1,622.6	9.3	7.20	–2.10	7.92	–1.38	0.72
1986	2,238.5	6.5	7.20	0.70	7.92	1.42	0.72
1987	3,081.4	7.3	7.20	–0.10	7.92	0.62	0.72
1988	3,822.2	18.8	8.64	–10.16	9.00	–9.80	0.36
1989	5,196.4	18.0	11.34	–6.66	11.34	–6.66	0.00
1990	7,119.8	3.1	8.64	5.54	9.36	6.26	0.72
1991	9,241.6	3.4	7.56	4.16	8.64	5.24	1.08
1992	11,759.4	6.4	7.56	1.16	8.64	2.24	1.08
1993	15,203.5	14.7	10.98	–3.72	10.98	–3.72	0.00
1994	21,518.8	24.1	10.98	–13.12	10.98	–13.12	0.00
1995	29,662.3	17.1	10.98	–6.12	12.06	–5.04	1.08
1996	38,520.8	8.3	7.47	–0.83	10.08	1.78	2.61
1997	46,279.8	2.8	5.67	2.87	8.64	5.84	2.97
1998	53,407.5	–0.8	3.78	4.58	6.39	7.19	2.61
1999	59,621.8	–1.4	2.25	3.65	5.85	7.25	3.60
2000	64,332.4	0.4	2.25	1.85	5.85	5.45	3.60

(Cont'd)

Year	Urban-rural savings (RMB100 million)	Inflation rate (%)	Savings interest rate (1 year, %)		Loans interest rate (1 year, %)		Interest margin
			Nominal	Actual	Nominal	Actual	
2001	73,762.4	0.7	2.25	1.55	5.85	5.15	3.60
2002	86,910.6	–0.8	1.98	2.78	5.31	6.11	3.33
2003	103,617.0	1.2	1.98	0.78	5.31	4.11	3.33
2004	119,555.0	3.9	2.25	–1.65	5.58	1.68	3.33
2005	141,051.0	1.8	2.25	0.45	5.58	3.78	3.33
2006	161,587.0	1.5	2.52	1.02	5.99*	4.49	3.47
2007	172,534.0	4.8	3.33*	–1.47	6.93*	2.13	3.60
2008	217,885.0	5.9	3.33*	–2.57	7.07*	1.17	3.74

Note: * The interest rate was adjusted more than once. The average is adopted here.
Source: *China Statistical Yearbook* (1979–2004) and IMF data (IFS).

Additionally, one of the important factors driving the transformation of China's financial system was the government's heightened need to tap even more social resources—rural finance was not spared. At the initial stages of the reform, China's top-down control of rural financial surplus resulted in a rapid expansion of the state-owned banks in the rural areas. Because a monopolized financial system was better at controlling the cost of issuance of certificate of deposits and expanding the scale of savings (Zhang Jie 2000), the central government, in the early stage of the reform, established the monopoly status for the four state-owned commercial banks in order to absorb as much household savings as possible. In 1998, China carried out a full-scale reform to commercialize the state-owned banks, and further suppressed the already marginalized rural financing in the name of reform. At the same time, the government strengthened the control over rural society and economy, which directly hindered the rural households' resources allocation based on their own strengths. As a result, the tax burden on rural households became heavier and their income growth was impeded; the relative profits from agriculture declined and worsened (Zhang qi et al. 2003) As the rural economic growth slows down and the rural economic surplus slumped, there was a reduction of China's benefits from rural resources. The outcome: national finance quickly retreated from the rural areas (Zhang Jie 2003). In response to this phenomenon, Xie Ping et al (2005) pointed out that supporting the development of the rural areas, agriculture, and the farmers is very important, because the financial sector is no substitute for the state's financial duties. In the past, both Beijing and the local government relied too much on the financial sector without properly defining the sector's role in the rural area. Consequently, the sector shouldered many financial responsibilities: Not only did the finance fail to do the job, but it also caused huge losses. Rural finance shrank, draining the villages of capital, and causing all kinds of moral hazards. According to 1998–2001 data, the number of domestic financial institutions and other business outlets which merged with state-owned commercial banks reached 44,000 (Zhong Hanxiao and Tang Li 2003). The retreat of state-owned commercial banks from rural areas triggered an increase in rural housing savings and capital outflow. The upshot is a vacuum of rural finance, and a squeeze on rural credit.

Fig. 1.4. Rural capital outflow through the financial system (RMB100 million)

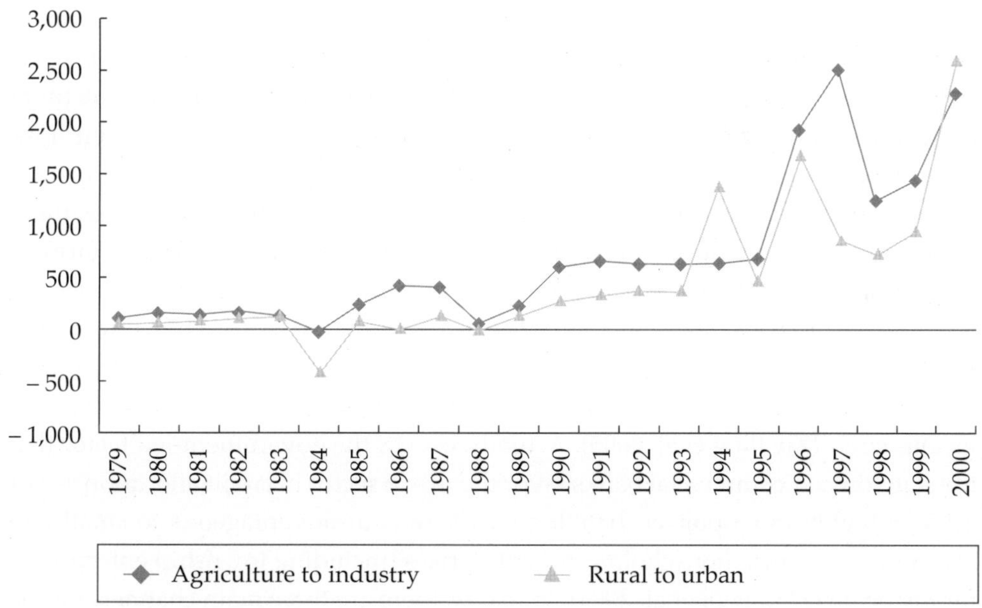

Source: Huang et al. (2006).

Lastly, in terms of the financial structure, after the withdrawal of the four major state-owned commercial banks, the formal finance in the rural financial market left are rural credit cooperatives (RCCs), the Agricultural Development Bank of China (hereinafter known as Agricultural Development Bank), and postal savings banks. Postal savings banks only accept deposits but do not issue loans, which would lead to the outflow of rural capital. The Agricultural Development Bank is a policy bank, which mainly issues loans for purchasing agricultural and sideline products, the construction of production sites for commodity grains, and rural infrastructure construction. It basically does not conduct the business of credit loans with the rural households. Therefore, the only formal financial institution which directly works with rural households in the rural financial market are RCCs. They almost monopolized the rural financial market. But their efficiency as financial intermediaries is low. To RCCs, a transaction of rural microcredit incurs high cost and the credit limit is low. In many mid-western regions, the loss-making RCCs are unable and unwilling to issue loans to rural households. People's Bank of China's reissuance of agriculture-supporting loans is hardly sufficient. Rural households still rely on borrowing money from friends and relatives, and private lending. Interest-free poverty loans issued by the government through the Agricultural Development Bank cannot truly reach the households and the ratio of non-performing loans remains high. This loan cannot actually help the poor. Therefore, solely relying on People's Bank of China, which shoulders fiscal responsibilities to reissue loans and poverty loans, cannot resolve the problems of rural capital outflow and the difficulties in obtaining agricultural loans. Moreover, since the 1990s, under small-scale self-sufficient production mode, the labor productivity of China's rural areas (especially the mid-western regions) has been low. Additionally, the market price of agricultural products remains low and many rural enterprises shut down. Together, these factors contributed to the lack of investment opportunities in rural areas, and a lot of farmers' work in cities and these farmers send money home to the rural financial institutions. However, money in the rural financial institutions flows to the eastern developed areas through purchasing national bonds, inter-bank lending, and capital reserve. This makes it difficult for rural areas to obtain sufficient funds for development. Some areas even enter a vicious circle (Xie Ping et al. 2005). Actually, even if the government-led factor that the state-owned commercial banks favor the urban sector in credit allocation is cast aside, a highly monopolized banking structure is disadvantageous to small and medium–sized rural households and enterprises (including township enterprises) for financing (Zhang Qi et al. 2004). In reality, there are three main channels for the outflow of rural capital: First, after the industrialization reform, the state-owned commercial banks reduced their number of branches. Many rural branches are no longer allowed to issue loans, resulting in capital outflow from rural to urban areas.[5] Second, the interest rate for transferring savings from postal savings banks to the People's Bank of China is too high. Farmers see the opportunity to gain more money. So much rural capital outflows through transfer of deposits. Third, many RCCs purchase national bonds, issue loans to urban customers, and deposits in other banks, which could cause capital outflow to urban areas (see Table 1.5).

Table 1.5. The statistics of rural resources (capital) outflow

Year	Rural credit cooperatives					Postal savings	
	Non-agricultural loans (RMB100 million)	Net loans to financial institutions (RMB100 million)	Bond reserve balance (RMB100 million)	Total savings (RMB100 million)	Percentage of capital outflow* (%)	Total savings (RMB100 million)	Amount of capital outflow** (RMB100 million)
1998	1,919.84	32.60	375.40	12,191.47	19.09	3,202.05	2,241.43
1999	1,998.66	29.70	461.80	13,358.09	18.64	3,815.37	2,670.75
2000	2,332.44	32.60	500.70	15,129.43	18.94	4,579.21	3,205.44
2001	2,596.74	34.40	744.20	17,263.45	19.55	5,908.46	4,135.92
2002	3,216.01	28.32	921.93	19,875.47	20.96	7,363.46	5,154.42
2003	4,225.77	416.13	923.30	23,710.20	23.47	8,985.69	6,289.98
2004	4,792.71	675.47	1,544.58	27,289.10	25.70	10,787.25	7,551.08

Note: 1. *Capital outflow rate = (Non-agricultural loans + Net loans to financial institutions + Bond reserve balance) / Total savings
2. **According to Xie Ping (2005), 70% of postal savings came from rural areas. Therefore, its amount of capital outflow is calculated as 70% of the total savings.

Source: Gu Shen, "Efficiency of China's Rural Finance: Evidence and Analysis," *Journal of Xi'an Jiaotong University* 9 (2006).

From the changes in the arrangements of China's rural finance, it is clear that the existing institutional arrangements cannot resolve the shortage of rural capital. Not only can rural formal finance act as the principal part in promoting rural financial development, but it also becomes a channel for capital outflow. Zhong Hanxiao and Tang Li (2003) estimated that, during 1979–2000, the total amount of capital outflow from agriculture to industry and from rural to urban areas were RMB148 billion and RMB103 billion, respectively, and the tendency for rural capital outflow became stronger. In terms of regional economy, rural capital outflow to urban areas through financial channels amounted to at least RMB4.5 trillion in 2005 (Chen Jianbo 2007). Marketized financial institutions and the small-farmer economy can hardly adjust to each other. The supply of agricultural capital and the rural households' demand do not match. Financial institutions cannot provide sufficient all-round and effective services or offer sufficient funding. The conflicts caused by the allocation of the already insufficient rural capital are sharpened. The shortage of capital worsens. Without a doubt, the past financial reform did not improve the basic structure of China's rural finance, which is evident in the following aspects: (1) Local governments still control rural finance. The commercialization of financial institutions still faces restrictions by policy loans and the low interest rate. (2) The constituents of the rural financial market remain unchanged. The Agricultural Bank and RCCs still monopolize the rural credit market. (3) The performance of financial institutions has not been improved, which contrasts to the rocketing development of the entire economy, especially the rural economy (Xie Ping et al. 2005).

It is not difficult to see from above analysis that the repressed rural finance and the resulting rural financial resources outflow are the main reasons why China's dual economic structure is continuously reinforced. We believe that to break through from the dual economic structure which has structural defects and systematic constraints, the nation should first understand rural finance, revive, and reestablish capital support as the link and compass in the development of rural finance. Xie Ping et al. (2005) also hold that reform of rural finance cannot wait: "If we say China's traditional rural financial system once supported the development of China's rural economy, this kind of 'overdrawn' financial support can hardly continue. When reform of rural finance lags behind, it cannot continue supporting the development of the rural financial system, and its low efficiency may even become an obstacle. Therefore, reform of the current traditional rural financial is of great urgency."

In terms of the structural characteristics of the financial system, the coexistence of formal finance and informal finance is common among developing countries. The duality of China's financial system is especially conspicuous in the repressed rural financial system. There are two mainstream theories that explain the dual financial structure: First, the financial repression hypothesis which claims that the government's restrictions on the interest rate and other control policies constituted the emergence of informal finance; second, the new structuralism which explains credit market segmentation through the difference in selection, supervision, and contract costs.

Notable scholars advocating the financial repression hypothesis include McKinnon (1973), Fry (1983, 1988), Roe (1990), et al. They believe that government's control policies are the main reason why dual financial structure exists in developing countries. Government's excessive intervention caused inefficiency and repression of the financial system. Restriction on the interest rate stimulates the demand for capital but hinders capital formation. Excess demand for capital forces financial institutions to allocate capital through means other than the interest rate. Moreover, the informal finance, which is not restricted by the interest rate, gains room to develop, resulting in a dual financial structure. Under the conditions of a dual financial structure, some of the economic entities receive government's subsidies at a low cost. The remaining has no choice but to seek informal finance at a high cost (e.g., usury).

Representative scholars of new structuralism include Stiglitz and Weiss (1981), Stiglitz (1990), Hoff and Stiglitz (1993), etc. New structuralists, based on asymmetric information, the difference in selection, supervision, and contract costs, concentrate on the structural and systemic characteristics of the formation of the dual financial structure in developing countries. They think that because of asymmetric information and high contract cost, market failure caused by moral hazard and adverse selection would disrupt the running of the financial market, which would let the interest rate level interfere with the risk component of the financial asset portfolios. After considering the risk factors, a creditor facing excessive demand for credit could employ credit rationing strategy instead of raising the interest rate. Under asymmetric information, even if there is no restriction on interest rate, credit rationing could ensure market equilibrium.

Although the coexistence of formal finance and informal finance is common among developing countries, in the situation which rural finance is repressed for a long time, China's dual financial structure has some unique and distinct characteristics. These characteristics formed under the influence of economy, system, policies, history, society, and culture. This will be discussed in later chapters or sections, and the internal characteristics and actual performance of the duality of China's rural finance will be explicated.

Adjustment and Evolution of the Dual Economy: Structural Transformation and Financial Support

With reference to the dual-sector model, agriculture plays a very important role in the transformation of a dual economic structure into a single economic structure. Ranis and Fei suggested that it is impossible for any countries which try to accelerate industrialization without first, or at the same time, carrying out reform of the agriculture sector. Therefore, any standard that focuses only on labor force absorption in the industrial sector is just an indicator. It implies the ability of the agriculture sector to release labor force." Therefore, we can borrow a simple dual-sector model in development economics to generally explain the logic.[6]

Assume there are two sectors in the economy: Agricultural sector S and industrial sector M. The two sectors employ different methods of production. The industrial sector employs capital and labor force to product while the agricultural sector only employs labor force. Assuming that there are increasing returns to scale in the industrial sector and considering the "learning by doing" and technological spillover, the production function of the industrial sector is as follows:

$$M = A(\overline{K})^{\mu} K^{a} L_M^{1-a} \qquad (1\text{–}1)$$

$\overline{K}$ represents the average capital deposit of the whole economy, K represents the capital input of the industrial sector, L represents the labor force of the capital sector, $(\overline{K})^{\mu}$ represents the external returns of the average capital deposit of the whole economy $\overline{K}$. Therefore, at equilibrium, $\overline{K} = K$, with the assumption that $a + \mu < 1$.

There is much excess labor in the agricultural sector. Before the excess labor force is transferred to the industrial sector, the production function of the agricultural sector is as follows (L_s being the labor input):

$$S = S_o,\ L_s \geq L_o \qquad (1\text{–}2)$$

When all excess labor force is transferred, there is decreasing marginal returns of labor force in the agricultural sector. The production function is as follows:

$$S = L_s^{1-b},\ L_s < L_o \qquad (1\text{–}3)$$

C_S and C_M represent the consumption of agricultural and industrial products respectively, p_s and p_m represent the prices of agricultural and industrial products respectively, P is the profit of the industrial sector, and S_{π} is the savings rate of the industrial sector (the agricultural sector does not save). The price of consumer goods is as follows:

$$p_s C_S + p_M C_M = w_s L_s + w_M L_M + (1 - S_{\pi}) P \qquad (1\text{–}4)$$

Therefore,

$$P = aM = \frac{a}{1-a} w_M L_M \qquad (1\text{–}5)$$

Assume the rate of substitution between industrial and agricultural products is a constant (h is the elasticity of substitution):

$$\frac{C_M}{C_S} = B\left(\frac{P_S}{P_M}\right)^h \qquad (1\text{–}6)$$

Market clearing requires the following:

$$S = C_S \qquad (1\text{–}7)$$

Assume the labor market is in perfect competition, the wage in the industrial sector is that of the agricultural sector plus premium (the premium is for compensating the higher cost of living for those who work in the industrial sector). w_M represents the wage in the industrial sector, and w_S represents the wage in the agricultural sector:

$$w_M = f w_S,\ L_s \geq L_o \qquad (1\text{–}8)$$

Therefore, the marginal returns of capital are as follows:

$$r = aAK^{a+\mu-1} A^{\frac{1-a}{a}} K^{(1-a)(1+\frac{\mu}{a})} (1-a)^{\frac{1-a}{a}} (w_M)^{\frac{a-1}{a}} = aA^{\frac{1}{a}} K^{\frac{\mu}{a}} \left(\frac{1-a}{w_M}\right)^{\frac{1-a}{a}} \qquad (1\text{–}9)$$

From (1–9), it can be derived:

$$\frac{d\log r}{d\log K}=\frac{\mu}{a}-\frac{1-a}{a}\frac{d\log w_m}{d\log K} \tag{1–10}$$

As it is assumed that the labor market is in perfect competition, therefore:

$$w_S=\frac{p_s S}{L_S} \tag{1–11}$$

From (1–2), (1–3), (1–7) and (1–11), the wage in the labor market is as follows:

$$w_S=\frac{p_s S_o}{L_S}, \quad L_s \geq L_o \tag{1–12a}$$

$$w_S=p_S L_S^{-b}, \quad L_s < L_o \tag{1–12b}$$

Therefore,

$$\frac{w_M}{p_M}=f\left(\frac{C_M}{BC_S}\right)^{\frac{1}{h}}\frac{S_o}{L_S}, \quad L_s \geq L_o \tag{1–13a}$$

$$\frac{w_M}{p_M}=f\left(\frac{C_M}{BC_S}\right)^{\frac{1}{h}}L_S^{-b}, \quad L_s < L_o \tag{1–13b}$$

From (1–1), (1–4), (1–5), (1–7) and (1–13), the following can be derived:

$$\text{When} \quad L_s \geq L_o, \quad \frac{C_M}{C_S}=\frac{1-S_\pi a}{1-a}\frac{w_M}{p_M}\frac{L_M}{S_o} \tag{1–14a}$$

$$\text{When} \quad L_s < L_o, \quad \frac{C_M}{C_S}=\frac{1-S_\pi a}{1-a}\frac{w_M}{p_M}\frac{L_M}{L_S^{1-b}} \tag{1–14b}$$

Put (1–14) into (1–13):

$$\frac{w_M}{p_M}=f\left[\frac{1-S_\pi a}{B(1-a)S_o}\frac{w_M}{p_M}L_M\right]^{\frac{1}{h}}\frac{S_o}{L_S}, \quad L_s \geq L_o \tag{1–15a}$$

$$\frac{w_M}{p_M}=f\left[\frac{1-S_\pi a}{B(1-a)L_S^{1-b}}\frac{w_M}{p_M}L_M\right]^{\frac{1}{h}}\frac{S_o}{L_S}, \quad L_s < L_o \tag{1–15b}$$

Take (1–15a) as an example, the logarithm is as follows:

$$\log\left(\frac{w_M}{p_M}\right)=\log f+\frac{1}{h}\log\left(\frac{1-S_\pi a}{B(1-a)S_o}\right)+\frac{1}{h}\log\left(\frac{w_M}{p_M}\right)+\frac{1}{h}\log L_M+\log S_o-\log L_S \tag{1–16}$$

The derivative of $\log(\frac{w_M}{p_M})$ is:

$$\frac{d\log L_M}{d\log(\frac{w_M}{p_M})} = \frac{\frac{L_S}{L}}{\frac{1}{1-h} + \frac{L_M}{L_S}}, \qquad L_S \geq L_o \tag{1–17}$$

If $L_M = 1 - \frac{L_S}{L}$, the elasticity of the labor supply in the industrial sector is as follows:

$$e = \frac{d\log L_M}{d\log(\frac{w_M}{p_M})} = \frac{1 - L_M}{L_M + \frac{1}{h-1}}, \qquad L_S \geq L_o \tag{1–18a}$$

By the same principle,

$$e = \frac{d\log L_M}{d\log(\frac{w_M}{p_M})} = \frac{1 - L_M}{bL_M + \frac{1}{h-1}}, \qquad L_S < L_o \tag{1–18b}$$

Based on profit maximization of the manufacturers, the following can be derived:

$$L_M = A^{\frac{1}{a}} K^{1+\frac{\mu}{a}} (1-a)^{\frac{1}{a}} (\frac{w_M}{P_M})^{\frac{-1}{a}} \tag{1–19}$$

If $P_M = 1$, then:

$$\frac{d\log w_M}{d\log K} = \frac{1}{e}\frac{d\log L_M}{d\log K} \tag{1–20}$$

The derivative of (1–20) is:

$$\frac{d\log w_M}{d\log K} = \frac{a+\mu}{a} - \frac{1}{a}\frac{d\log w_M}{d\log K} \tag{1–21}$$

Put (1–21) into (1–20):

$$\frac{d\log w_M}{d\log K} = \frac{1+\frac{\mu}{a}}{e+\frac{1}{a}} \tag{1–22}$$

Put (1–22) into (1–10):

$$\frac{d\log r}{d\log K}=\frac{\mu}{a}-\frac{1-a}{a}\frac{d\log w_M}{d\log K}=\frac{\mu}{a}-\frac{1-a}{a}\frac{1+\frac{\mu}{a}}{e+\frac{1}{a}} \tag{1–23}$$

$$\frac{d\log r}{d\log K}\geq 0 \Rightarrow e\mu+\mu+a\geq 1 \tag{1–24}$$

According to (1–24), when $e\mu + \mu + a \geq 1$, there is increasing marginal returns for capital. This signifies that when the number of employment is higher in the agricultural sector (when e is larger), the condition can be satisfied, and so that there is increasing marginal returns for capital; as there is transfer of labor, e moves toward zero, and the marginal returns for capital become decreasing. This is to say that as capital deposit increases, the marginal returns for capital will first rise and then fall.

At economic equilibrium, $S_\pi r = \delta$ (1–25)

Put (1–9) into (1–25):

$$w_M^* = A^{\frac{1}{1-a}}(1-a)\left(\frac{S_\pi a}{\delta}\right)^{\frac{a}{1-a}}K^{\frac{\mu}{1-a}} \tag{1–26}$$

$$\frac{d\log w_M^*}{d\log K}=\frac{\mu}{1-a} \tag{1–27}$$

From (1–22), the following are known:

When $L_M \to 0, K \to 0, e \to h-1, \frac{d\log w_M}{d\log K} \to \frac{a+\mu}{ah-a+1}$ (1–28a)

When $L_M \to 1, K \to \infty, e \to a, \frac{d\log w_M}{d\log K} \to a+\mu$ (1–28b)

Therefore, the following can be derived: When $\frac{a+\mu}{ah-a+1}<\frac{\mu}{1-a}$ and $\frac{\mu}{1-a}<a+\mu$ are valid at the same time, there would be multiple equilibria in the process of economic development. From these two inequalities, the conditions for multiple equilibria can be easily derived:

$$\mu h + a > 1 \text{ and } \mu + a > 1 \tag{1–29}$$

The situation with multiple equilibria is shown in Fig. 1.5.

Fig. 1.5. Multiple equilibria in a dual economy

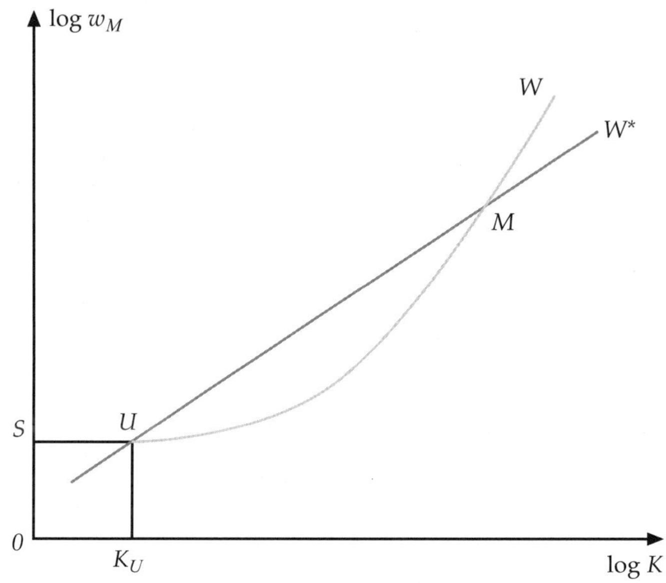

From Fig. 1.5, when $\mu h + a > 1$ and $\mu + a < 1$, there are three equilibrium points in the economy: low level equilibrium point *S*, unstable equilibrium point *U*, and high level equilibrium point *M*. At *S*, there is only the agricultural sector, income per capita is very low, and capital deposit per capita is zero; at *M*, the industrial sector dominates the economy, income per capital is higher, and capital deposit per capita is larger. *U* is an unstable equilibrium because when capital deposit per capita is smaller than K_U, the market clearing wage is lower than the market equilibrium wage, the accumulation rate of the whole economy is smaller than the depreciation rate, the capital sector contracts, and economy drops back to *S*. Similarly, when per capita capital deposit is larger than K_U, the market clearing wage is lower than that at the market equilibrium, the accumulation rate of the whole economy is larger than the depreciation rate, the capital sector expands until the economy reached *M*. Low level equilibrium and unstable equilibrium exist because the rate of return on capital is too low. Only when per capita capital deposit is larger than K_U, can the rate of return on capital be larger than the depreciation rate. The economy can then escape from the "development trap" and start to grow.

In the dual-sector model, the key factors to realize the transformation from a dual economic structure to a single one are the reform of, and support from, the agricultural sector. The development of the agricultural sector is closely related to the dynamic accumulation of capital: Extremely low rate of return on capital and per capita capital deposit could keep the economy in the "development trap" for a long time. In other words, to transform the dual economy from low level equilibrium to high level equilibrium, we must pay attention to the effect of capital mechanism.

Under modern economic conditions, the capital mechanism cannot work without the support from financial mechanism. According to Saint Paul (1992), there are multiple layers of equilibrium in the relationship between financial development and economic growth. The inspiration of this conclusion to the Three Rural Issues is how to direct the economy to attain a higher level of equilibrium growth through the development and restructuring of rural finance, so as to break through from the "development trap." Furthermore, the importance of rural financial support also lies in: when rural economic development cannot receive corresponding financial support for a long time, there exists the risk of the economy falling to a lower level.

In the study of the financial support and the corresponding reform plans concerning the Three Rural Issues, it is essential to delve deep into the initial conditions for the reform. Economists of rural development Swinnen and Rozelle pointed out that the effect of reform is different in different countries. It mainly depends on the initial conditions for reform (Swinnen and Rozelle 2006). The implication is that the study of China's rural financial problems should be carried out based on China's real situation. We cannot rely on the simple deduction from theoretical models or directly take the international experience without thinking. This is also one of the standpoints of this study, namely, based on the reality of China's rural households, agriculture, and rural areas to conduct our analysis.

Although many scholars (such as Lin Yifu, 2004) have pointed out that the transformation of the dual economic structure is the key to resolving the Three Rural Issues, we are not going to stop here. We believe that while the dual economic structure has strongly affected rural finance, there is an internal characteristic of dynamic transformation in the dual economy. For example, the traditional analysis of the rural financial market is based on a urban-rural dual economy—the economy is segmented into two sectors which are the same in essence (the rural sector and the urban sector), and it is assumed that the rural sector is engaged solely in agricultural production while the urban sector is engaged in non-agricultural production (Fei and Ranis 2001). Yet, if we look at the whole picture of China's rural finance, the duality of China's economy is also seen in the fact that in some developed areas, there are many industries in rural areas. But, those industries differ from the industries in the urban sector in terms of technology and organizational form. This signifies that "double dualism" as proposed by some scholars could be a more suitable background in the macroscopic studies of rural finance. The first is the duality between the urban sector and the rural sector. The second is the duality between the rural agricultural sector and the rural industrial sector. If we take into account the actual course of economic development after China's reform and opening up, one thing is clear: In many rural areas where there is a huge industrial sector, those areas were engaged in agricultural production before transformation. In other words, if we look at China's rural development and transformation as a continuous process, there is a dynamic transformation of traditional rural areas to "new rural areas" (represented by the industrialization of the rural sector or modern agricultural production).

In addition, an in-depth analysis of the internal dynamic transformation mechanism of the dual economy would help us evaluate the current issue of regional difference from the perspective of development. This issue will be further discussed from a dynamic and continuous perspective in later sections.

A deep understanding of the problems of China's rural financial development requires a dynamic, continuous, and all-round perspective based on the macroscopic analysis, and also calls for a detailed study of the specific features of different aspects. As pointed out by the World Bank (2002), rural poverty is different in nature. A certain method may have different effects under different social and economic conditions. To China, the rural financial issues are very complex. This is not only due to the unbalanced regional and industrial structures, but also the path dependence resulting from the long-time political and economic constraints. Certain special economic activities deeply influenced by history and culture also add to the complexity. Those intertwining factors are the origin of the complexity of China's rural finance and the starting point of, and initial conditions for, our correct understanding of the current situation.

Major Conclusions and Policy Implications

(1) To realize the transformation from a dual economic structure to a single economic structure requires support from, and transformation of, the agricultural sector, and the development of the agricultural sector is closely related to the dynamic accumulation of capital: Extremely low rate of return on capital and per capita capital deposit could keep the economy in the "development trap" for a long time. In other words, to transform the dual economy from low level to high level equilibrium, we must pay attention to the effect of capital mechanism.

(2) To reform traditional agriculture is to expand the source of income of agriculture through increasing the supply of capital and technology, and institution. What Schiltz believed as a common occurrence in traditional

agriculture—a shortage of capital and technology, and institutions—is a truth in China. And the most significant obstacle hindering the development of China's rural finance is the heavy shortage of capital.

(3) Under modern economic conditions, the capital mechanism cannot work without the support from financial mechanism. The inspiration of this conclusion to the Three Rural Issues is how to direct the economy to attain a higher level of equilibrium growth through the development and restructuring of rural finance, so as to break through from the "development trap." Furthermore, the importance of rural financial support also lies in: when rural economic development cannot receive corresponding financial support for a long time, there exists the risk of the economy falling to a lower level

(4) In the study of the financial support and the corresponding reform plans for the Three Rural Issues, it is essential to delve deep into the initial conditions for the reform. A deep understanding of the problems of China's rural financial development requires a dynamic, continuous, and all-round perspective formed on the macroscopic analysis, and it also calls for a detailed study of the specific features of different aspects.

(5) The complexity of China's rural finance not only lies in the unbalanced regional and industrial structures, but also the path dependence resulting from the long-time political and economic constraints. Certain special economic activities deeply influenced by history and culture also add to the complexity. Those intertwining factors are the origin of the complexity of China's rural finance and the starting point and initial conditions of a correct understanding of the current situation.

Feature 1–1
Urban-Biased Policies and Fallacies of Balancing Policies

Eight major urban-biased policies

Influenced by the theories of dualistic economic development and the experience of wealthy industrial countries, policy makers of developing countries see industry, but not agriculture, as a tool for achieving economic growth. Agriculture is usually heavily taxed through price and budget mechanism in order to subsidize the expansion of industries. In the development process, there are many urban-biased policies and public investment priorities. This is caused by rapid industrialization and the political pressure stemmed from the urban residents' request to lower the food price. Below shows eight major urban-biased policies:

(1) The exchange rate is overestimated.

(2) The price of agricultural products is very low, controlled, and not adjusted along the changing of the season.

(3) The effective rate of protection of domestic industries is too high, and all the industrial outputs result from the inputs of agriculture.

(4) Budget for infrastructure in urban and rural areas is not in proportion (highways, electricity, and water supply).

(5) Investment in urban and rural labor resources is not in proportion (health and education).

(6) Usury law (it excludes agricultural loans that have a small credit limit, high risks, and high cost)

(7) Relatively incomplete laws and legal structure regarding the land rights and asset mortgage right in comparison to those in urban areas

(8) Over taxation in agricultural exports

For the past few decades, these policies have hindered agricultural and rural development in many developing countries. To eliminate these urban-biased policies and public investment priorities is very important in raising the living standards of the majority in the world.

Fallacies of balancing policies

In order to eliminate the negative impact brought about by urban-biased development strategies on agriculture, many countries adopted corresponding balancing policies. Through subsidy, tax reduction, control over the interest rate, credit guide, and the establishment of state-owned rural financial institutions, they try to improve the stagnant situation of the agricultural sector. While many policies are intended for the best, the actual results are often unsatisfactory.

(1) Subsidy. To offset the negative effect of the urban-biased policies, the government offers credit subsidy to the agricultural sector and assigned specific state-owned rural financial institutions to the task. The government also subsidizes agricultural inputs, such as fertilizers, pesticides, seeds, water, and electricity. However, reality shows that these compensations are not effective in a malignant policy environment. The intention of policies-makers may be to compensate the farmers who are heavily taxed though providing credit subsidies. Actually, those who are rich and have social connections receive a large part of the subsidies. Only a very small part of the subsidies can reach farmers who are most in need of capital. Schiff and Valdes (1992) studied the agricultural subsidies of 18 countries and found that during 1960–1984, income brought about by the transfer of subsidies on average accounted for 2% of the agricultural GDP, while indirect interference in the agricultural sector accounted for 15% of the agricultural GDP through negative transfer. Credit subsidy can only compensate a small part of the agriculture producers' loss incurred by discriminatory urban-biased policies, usually less than 30%.

(2) Control over the interest rate. As part of the financial repression policies, in some countries the government imposed a fixed interest rate on loans of many banks, especially agricultural loans, through administrative means. This kind of intervention may be harmful because the signaling mechanism of the interest rate is a crucial factor in mobilizing and allocating resources. The interest rate is determined by the market, which is a basic factor in a competitive financial market. In reality, the government's control over the extent and ways for financial institutions to be involved in the rural financial market, because the imposed interest rate on directed rural lending is usually lower than the market interest rate. In such a situation, the undifferentiated excessive control over the interest rate represses savings and hinders the formal financing of rural households and small-sized agricultural enterprises.

(3) Specific credit guidance (policies). For various reasons, such as the need for balanced growth and social political pressure, the government may adopt specific credit guidance or credit policies as a part of agricultural industry supporting policies. In reality, many similar credit guidance or policies cannot achieve the expected results. In Mexico, state-owned agricultural development banks and nationalized commercial banks set up more than 500 agricultural bank outlets and input several billion U.S. dollars to do credit guidance. A

study of the World Bank discovered that only 8% of rural enterprises could obtain formal credit and only 1% can obtain direct loans from the government. Furthermore, the mandatory credit policies which provide benefits to some particular enterprises or sectors would shift the burden onto the financial system. As a result, the tax on the financial sector is higher than that of other sectors, which increases the future cost of growth (Giovannini and de Melo 1993, Levine 1994).

(4) State-owned rural financial institutions. When private financial institutions refuse to engage in rural finance, it is easiest to arrange state-owned financial institutions set up by the government to execute credit supporting plans or provide financial services. However, intertwined with politics and economic benefits, together with the central government's tendency of "paternalism," state-owned rural financial institutions are often treated with privilege—the government runs them as a capital dispenser, not as individual financial institutions, resulting in poor performance of the rural financial institutions. But due to the high political and economic costs of shutting down a state-owned rural financial institution—a lot of employees would be out of work, and the number of pensions without a source of capital increases—the government could be put into a dilemma.

2 Chapter

Rural Households' Behavior in China's Rural Finance

Credibility is like a mirror. Once there is a crack, it is not a whole piece.

—Amir

Rural Financial Demand and Decision-Making

Characteristics of China's rural financial demand

Since the 1990s, as agricultural production and the rural economy continue to develop, the amount of rural households' savings and loans showed an increasing trend, but the growth rate of savings was much higher than that of loans (see Table 2.1). With respect to the financial services, the financial demand concentrated on the basic business of savings and loans and investments in other financial products such as stocks and bonds were very limited. The demand for loans still dominates China's rural finance.

Table 2.1. The trend for rural households' financial demand (RMB/household)

Year	Savings	Loans	Bonds	Stocks
1995	2634.57	1012.67	3.70	12.74
1996	3453.91	1403.85	4.12	19.29
1997	4328.90	1478.67	4.91	26.71
1998	4638.97	1519.14	6.80	22.25
1999	4997.60	1740.43	14.27	69.69
2000	5771.56	1703.24	8.17	49.93
2001	5549.54	1709.31	2.25	20.98
2002	6608.07	1751.04	2.97	114.43
2003	7252.04	1742.64	2.95	115.32

Source: Statistics from the fixed-site rural survey system (1995–2003) from the Ministry of Agriculture of China.

Although the national statistics of the frequency for loans in rural areas is yet to be obtained, many studies reveal that rural households' demand for loans has become larger and more frequent. For example, Shi Qinghua (2002) surveyed 745 rural households in Shanxi Province, and discovered that the percentage of families who borrowed money increased from 29.6% in 1996 to 40.7% in 2000. Zhu Shouyin et al. (2003) presented his findings from a 1999–2001 survey on 217 rural households in Anhui Province that the percentage of families who borrowed money rose from 31% to 51%, the amount of loans increased from RMB278,000 to RMB697,000, and the number of loans borrowed per family increased from 1.57 to 2.05.

The main sources of loans in rural finance can be classified as formal and informal in regard to the nature of the creditor. The former includes loans from Rural Credit Cooperatives (RCCs), as well as other financial institutions such as Agricultural Bank of China, the Postal Savings Bank of China, and rural banks. The latter broadly includes private lending, loans from credit foundations, Rotating Savings and Credit Association (ROSCA), private banks, and usury.

Rural households show a multi-level financial demand with respect to the lending quota. Microcredit can only satisfy the financing demand of rural households with low living standards. In 2006, Tsinghua University and Hong Kong and Shanghai Banking Corporation Limited (HSBC) conducted a survey on rural households in 29 counties (cities and districts), with 1,523 questionnaires returned qualified for analysis. The statistics showed that rural households which required loans of less than RMB3,000, RMB3,000–10,000, RMB10,000–25,000, RMB25,000–50,000, and more than RMB50,000 were 21.2%, 36.4%, 16.1%, 12.8%, and 13.5% respectively. Qian Shuitu (2006) obtained similar results in his survey on rural households in Jiezhang Province. The surveys suggested that most of the rural households considered the credit offered by credit cooperatives too small. Microcredit was no longer able to satisfy their need to carry out large-scale investments or expand their scale of production. This is especially true for the farm villages which are now better off. They have varied financial demand during agricultural industrialization and urbanization. A multi-level rural financial system is required to satisfy the financial demand of rural households in areas with different levels of economic development.

Taking RCCs as an example, the total amount of agricultural loans[1] increased from RMB845.17 billion in 2004 to RMB1,085.30 billion in 2007. Among them, rural household loans increased steadily from RMB473.12 billion to RMB642.17 billion; rural microcredits rose from RMB167.84 billion to RMB189.09 billion; rural household joint-guarantee loans fluctuated considerably, first dropping from RMB138.94 billion in 2004 to RMB82.78 billion in 2005, then rising to RMB92.42 billion in 2006 before reaching RMB103.99 billion in 2007 (see Fig 2.1).

Fig. 2.1. Agricultural loans in RCCs

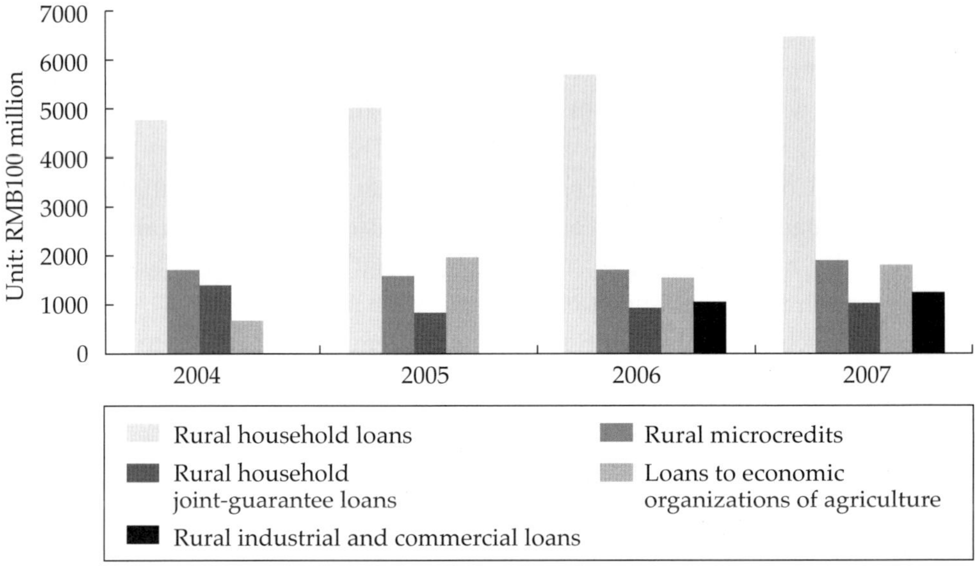

Since 1999 when Rural Credit Foundations were abolished and replaced, private loans have become the major source of informal loans. According to statistics from the fixed-site rural survey system (1995–2003) of the Ministry of Agriculture of China (see Table 2.2), the average amount of private loans obtained by rural households during this period was RMB948.5 per person, 95.7% of informal loans; after 1996 the percentage remained over 90%, up to 97% in 2002–2003 when the Rural Credit Foundations had been shut down. Although the amount of interest-free loans between friends and families was more or less the same as the amount of loans with interest rates (or with high interest rates) for informal loans, the former showed a downward trend. In 1995–2003, loans without interest fell by 10% while loans with an interest rate shot up from 39% to 51%, showing a growth of 12%. As urbanization accelerates in rural areas, rural households' attitude towards financing is gradually adapted to the market economy, which allows the interest rate in the market to be more influential.

Table 2.2. The composition of the sources of informal loans in rural areas (RMB/person, %)

Year	Rural credit foundations		Private loans				Others	
	Amount	Percentage (%)	With an interest rate	Without interest	Total	Percentage (%)	Amount	Percentage (%)
1995	59.85	7.29	354.32	380.02	734.34	89.44	26.85	3.27
1996	44.48	4.63	428.83	463.03	891.86	92.87	24.03	2.50
1997	35.70	3.82	396.01	468.15	864.06	92.53	34.17	3.65
1998	45.33	4.31	496.30	489.02	985.32	93.62	21.78	2.07
1999	50.74	4.62	491.87	516.69	1008.56	91.83	39.99	3.55
2000	6.65	0.65	475.46	520.09	995.55	96.94	24.75	2.41
2001	11.66	1.11	518.26	501.92	1020.18	96.80	22.00	2.09
2002	7.13	0.68	476.87	543.99	1020.86	97.20	22.25	2.12
2003	7.09	0.68	474.58	541.38	1015.96	97.20	22.15	2.12

Source: Statistics from the fixed-site rural survey system (1995–2003) from the Ministry of Agriculture of China.

The characteristics of rural financing demand can be summarized as follows:

(1) Loans for agricultural production are highly seasonal and periodical. It is typical of agriculture activity to be seasonal and periodical, so agricultural financing accords with the characteristics of agricultural production. According to statistics, farmers' expectation for the acquisition of loans does not follow the calendar year. Their calendar for demanding loans starts from somewhere between March and May until the same period of the next year. This suggests that loans granted at the beginning of the year would take 15–18 months to better match the agricultural production cycle. Of course, it must be pointed out that the more focused on agriculture the farmer, the more seasonal his financing demand is. And when rural households start to run other businesses or completely abandon farming and work in the industrial or commercial sector, their financing demand would become less seasonal. In other words, in traditional agricultural areas rural financing demand may be seasonal and periodical, while in urbanized and marketized non-agricultural areas these characteristics are much less obvious.[2]

(2) Most agriculture-related financing demand is timely. In most cases, rural household's financing demand has stronger timeliness. Not only is this decided by the agricultural production cycle, but it also generally permeates every stage of agricultural economic activities. For example, fruits and

vegetables must enter market circulation once they are ripe. When they start to rot, they lose value; mature livestock must be sold in time, or else any additional material and time costs for maintaining them would generate extra net expenditure which brings about no marginal revenue. Therefore whether it is in the production cycle or market circulation, the opportunity cost for rural households to acquire loans is very high. The surveys conducted by us in many rural areas of Western China manifest that the long waiting time and complicated procedures of loan review and issuing are the major obstacles preventing most rural households from choosing the formal financing. Qian Shuitu and Lu Hui (2008) conducted a questionnaire survey in rural areas of Wenzhou and discovered that it could take more than one month for rural households to obtain loans from formal financial institutions, 90% of the rural households had to wait one to 10 days, and only 8% of them were granted loans immediately. In comparison, rural households did not have to wait when they borrowed informal loans. This correlates with the reason why private loans are mostly popular in "acquaintance society"—in a society where people know one another inside-out and the information everyone has is highly symmetric, the risk from asymmetric information is bypassed.

(3) The use of loans is closely related to the economic foundation. Agricultural loans can be categorized with respect to their uses as production loans, maintenance loans, and special loans. Loans for production can be further classified as agricultural or non-agricultural. In the less developed traditional rural areas of Western China, the static distribution of the total amount of loans shows that maintenance loans account for a much larger part than production loans. The trend analysis suggests that the use of loans is closely related to the economic foundation and the labor capital of different regions. For instance, Qian Shuitu and Lu Hui (2008) discovered that the motivation behind the rural financing demand in Wenzhou had shifted from "non-productive and response to natural risk" to "production and investments," and commercial financing activities accounted for a major part. Moreover, rural labor capital should be taken into account. Even in the less developed rural areas in Western China, studies have found that rural households are more inclined to make production loans as their educational level rises. A study of the World Bank (2002) had similar findings: The poorest borrowers used their loans in activities such as consumption or low-risk production technology while most borrowers who lived above the poverty line usually used their loans in high-risk, high-return investments such as technology transfer. The above findings demonstrate that the use of agricultural loans is

dynamic, which implies that the analysis of the trend is more important than the analysis of static distribution at any time.

(4) The transaction cost is high. The cost for rural financing includes not only explicit cost of interest as the dominant cost, but implicit transportation, menu, and relationship costs. Statistics show that to successfully obtain a loan, a farmer needs to visit the formal financial institution for two to three times. It generally takes three to four hours for each visit and costs a total of RMB36 on transportation for each loan. In some remote areas where transportation is inconvenient, the transportation cost can add up to 5–10% of the loan. Furthermore, considering the fact that some farmers are poorly educated, the complicated loan application form will bring about a menu cost that cannot be neglected. Also requiring attention is the expensive relationship cost. Regardless of formal financial institutions or private parties, borrowers have to pay for meals and buy gifts before obtaining the loan and pay another sum of money as a token of gratitude afterwards. In many cases, the lower the interest rate, the higher the implicit cost the borrowers have to bear. From our interviews with rural households in rural areas of Western China, it can been seen that if rural households borrowed loans from credit unions, the money they had to pay to village cadres, township leaders, and the staff of RCCs amounted to around 10% of the loan, which was higher than the interest rate over the same period.

(5) A lack of conventional collaterals. Undoubtedly, rural households lack the collaterals accepted in city, industrial, and commercial loans. According to Rome (1996), an ideal collateral should be: (1) appropriable,[3] (2) salable,[4] (3) able to incur the feeling of loss on the borrower,[5] (4) durable,[6] (5) able to incur a transaction cost on the borrower.[7] Normally, the more these features an asset possesses, the more easily it can be accepted as collateral by financial institutions. Obviously, assets of rural households hardly possess those features, as manifested by the absence of a market for collateral disposal, high disposal cost, and the fact that the assets cannot be stored for a long time. Under these conditions, collateral substitutes, such as social capital, group loans on the basis of joint debts, and internet-based trading, have become the major way out for alleviating the shortage of collaterals for rural households.

It needs to be pointed out that there is a lack of systematic statistical data collected by a formal statistics department, and national statistical data are unavailable. Previous studies had to rely on informal social surveys. Because of the difference in samples and perspectives, related studies are different in kind and point of views. Table 2.3 shows some of the typical studies on the demand for rural financial services.

Table 2.3. Typical studies on the demand for rural financial services

Researcher/Research department	Subjects	Basic conclusions
Lin Yifu (1989)	Survey on rural households in Gongzhuling of Jilin Province, and Tai County and Jurong County of Jiangsu Province in 1987 and 1988	Formal loans were used mainly for production. Most non-productive projects relied on informal loans to support the expenditure.
Xu Xiaobo (1994)	Sample survey of the borrowing behavior of more than 10,000 rural households by the Agricultural Bank of China in 1990	Only about 40% of the formal loans was production loans, of which only about 50% was actually used for production purpose. Private loans were mainly maintenance loans.
Wen Tiejun (2001)	Case studies of 15 provinces, 24 counties, and 41 villages in eastern, central, and western regions from Fixed-site Rural Survey System	After reform and opening up, loans from formal rural financial institutions were mainly used in production and business operation. In the later part of the 1990s, the proportion of maintenance loans rose. Private loans were mainly used in daily consumption.
Zhu Shouyin et al. (2003)	A questionnaire survey on 217 rural households in 18 villages in Fuyang and Bozhou, Anhui Province	During 1999–2001, more than 70% of the sample rural households borrowed loans. The rate of loans to rural households rose from 31.0% in 1999 to 59.3% in 2001. In 414 issuances of private loans, 90% were interest-free loans, there were only 27 issuances (6.5%) of interest-bearing loans, of which 11 (2.6%) were low-interest loans.
Wang Sangui et al. (2004)	Study of 446 rural households in six national poverty-stricken counties of six provinces	Loans from formal financial institutions were mainly used in production while informal loans in daily life. Poor rural households might use loans to maintain life.

(Cont'd)

Researcher / Research department	Subjects	Basic conclusions
Asian Development Bank (2005)	Survey of 720 rural households in six counties in Tonren, Guizhou Province	Loans were mainly used in large-scale farming and animal husbandry, and developing industry and commerce. The main sources of repaying debts were income from animal husbandry and labor wages. Limited and unstable income was the main reason why rural households could not repay debts on time.
He Guangwen and Li Lili (2005)	Study of rural households in Zhejiang Province and Ningxia Hui Autonomous Region in 2003	Production loans were a lot more than consumption loans. Agricultural production loans were larger than non-agricultural production loans.
Luo Jianchao (2005)	The first statistics (1986–2003) from the Office of the Fixed-site Rural Survey System, The Ministry of Agriculture of China	The basic features of rural borrowing behavior were short-term, small in amount, and had a high interest rate. Loans were mainly maintenance (survival) loans. Physical and monetary credits coexist. Borrowing is highly dependent on private loan market.
Chen Xiwen, Han Jun, and Zhao Yang (2006)	Investigations of grassroots and sample analysis of rural households in 18 counties of 12 provinces	Only 20% of rural households could receive loans, and 20% of them was responsible for 80% of the borrowing amount from rural financial institutions.
University of Witten* (2006)	Joint project of rural finance	Private finance with rural cooperative financing as its core would be an effective supplement to rural formal finance.
People's Bank of China (2006)	Surveys of Qianjiang, Dianjiang, Nanchuan, and Fuling in Chongqing	Insufficient demand of rural financial services was evident. Small guaranteed loan was effective in alleviating the demand for loans of rural households. Yet, limited variety of agricultural loans, difficulty in mortgage guarantee, and other problems required improvement.

(Cont'd)

Researcher / Research department	Subjects	Basic conclusions
People's Bank of China (2006)	Investigation on 2,486 rural households in rural areas of Guiyang	Of the various problems that the sample rural households encountered during application for loans, the short loan period was the main one, which accounted for 51%. Rural households expected a loan period to last for an average of 31 months, which was much longer than the actual loan period of 12 months. Second, about 46% of the rural households thought the credit limit could not satisfy the demand for capital. They expected the amount of loan to be on average RMB21,972. Third is the high interest rate. About 35% of the rural households considered the interest rate of loan too high. They expected the annual rate to be 5.28%.
Research Group of China's Rural Financial Demand and Reform of Rural Credit Cooperatives (2007)	Questionnaire survey on 1,962 rural households of 29 provinces in 2005, of which 773 were in the east, 483 in the middle, and 706 in the west.	As agricultural and rural industrial structures were continuously adjusted and daily expenditure was increasing, rural households have an expanding demand for capital, and the average amount of production loans was much greater than that of maintenance loans. Rural households' demand for investment in production was more elastic. Once they face credit constraints, their demand for production loan (especially the demand for expanded reproduction) would be first repressed.

(Cont'd)

Researcher / Research department	Subjects	Basic conclusions
Zhang Jie, Xie Xiaoxue, and Zhang Shumin (2005)	Surveys in Nandong village, Beidong village, Sangpo village in Mengzhou, Henan Province, and Ertang village in Shapingba District, Congqing.	In the economically underdeveloped areas or for the low-income rural households, the demand for maintenance loans was major. In the economically advanced areas or for the rural households with higher income, the demand for production loans was obviously larger. Of the demand for production loans, the demand for non-agricultural production loans increased while that of agricultural production loans decreased. Particularly in the economically advanced areas, rural households' demand for production loans grew, and started to become the basis for the institutional arrangements of rural commercial credit.
Qian Shuitu and Lu Hui (2008)	Questionnaire survey on fifteen villages of Cang'an, Rui'an, and Yueqing in Wenzhou, Zhejiang Province	The financing purpose of rural households had changed from the traditional "non-production and response to natural risk" to "production and investments," and commercial financing activities (e.g. running business and factories, purchasing properties) accounted for a major part.

Note: * quoted in Cao Yuequn, Wang Zhengpan, and Liu Xiandi, "Review and Prospect of the Demand for Rural Financial Service," Working paper of Chongqing University (2007).

The types of rural households' financial demand

Judging from the economic conditions and production state, current rural households in China can be categorized into three types: poor rural households, general rural households, and marketized rural households. These three types of rural households differ in capital deposit, production mode and capability, thus forming different types of financial demand and financing methods (see Fig. 2.2).

Fig. 2.2. Features of different types of rural financing demands

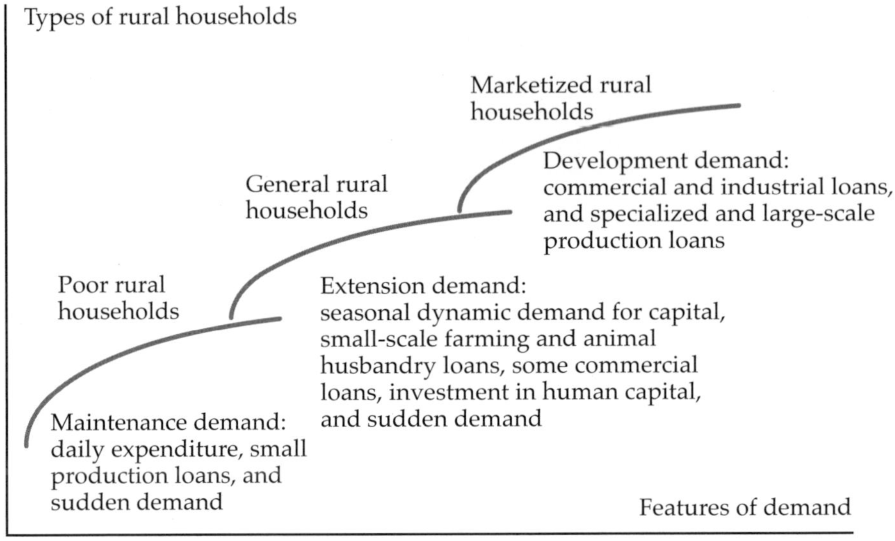

Poor rural households are at the bottom of the rural household hierarchy. Their disadvantaged living conditions, lack of capital, and inefficient production determined that their financing demand must be mainly for maintenance: Borrowing itself is not motivated by the production expansion or capital appreciation, but mainly by the maintaining life and production. The aforementioned features determined that poor rural households' loans are high-risk and low-return. Their demand for loans is not motivated by profit maximization, which means that they are not suitable for the service of commercial financial institutions. The current situation is that poor rural households' financial demands are satisfied by the following ways: small private loans, fiscal poverty alleviation funds, preferential policy loans, international organizations' funds, and assistance from foreign Non-Governmental Organizations (NGOs). With limited financing sources, once there is demand caused by force majeure and emergency (illness, plagues, natural disasters, etc.), these poor rural households with low standards of living and production have no choice but to seek usury.

General rural households refer to those who have been extricated from extreme poverty and have certain production capability. They can maintain life and carry out smallholder farming production as a family. They mainly engage in small-scale and conventional farming and animal husbandry, and may run simple business during the slack season of farming. On the basis of small-scale peasant economy, these households bear the traditional concept and awareness of debt. They generally borrow money prudently within their ability to repay debts and want to preserve their reputation. Because these households have matching creditability with their economic capability, agricultural financial institutions[8] have started to issue microcredit to them.[9] Different from maintenance demand of poor rural households, the demand for credit of general rural households shows the feature of extension demand: Except for the conventional seasonal demand for agricultural capital, there is also the demand for expanded reproduction, commercial loans, and human resources investment (mainly the education investment of children). Apparently, compared with maintenance demand, expansion demand represents improvements in demand orientation, production methods and capital accumulation, and the demand shows a tendency toward marketization and the need of self-development. Currently, the level of technology, capital accumulation, and production method do not meet the market requirements. The average rate of return is still low, which implies that loans to the general rural households are not attractive to large commercial financial institutions.

Marketized rural households are at the top of the rural household hierarchy, representing the future transformation direction of rural households. These households have accumulated some human and physical capitals. They can carry out market-oriented, specialized and technical production in scale. They are the representatives of advanced agricultural production and leaders of getting rich in the local areas. Because this kind of household has gradually been extricated from the constraints of traditional low-efficiency agricultural production, their capital demand shows a stronger feature of development demand, and the risk they are facing is changed from natural risk to market risk. As the production scale increases and technology advances, their demand for capital is vastly greater than that of the general rural households. However, because of the shortage of sufficient collateral and guarantee, bank loans can only satisfy parts of their demand. In such a situation, marketized rural households still depend on the accumulation of their owned capital and generally seek private loans.

In current rural areas of China, poor, general, and marketized rural households form an olive-shaped social structure (large in the middle, small at both ends): General rural households are dominant, while poor and marketized rural households are relatively few. Features of different types of rural financing demands and sources are shown in Table. 2.4.

Table 2.4. Features of different types of rural financing demands and sources

Types of rural households	Features of financing demands	Basic sources of loans
Poor rural households	Maintenance demand: daily expenditure, small production loans, and sudden demand (illness, plagues, natural disasters)	Private loans (including usury), anti-poverty funds, microcredits (occasionally small commercial loans)
General rural households	Extension demand: seasonal dynamic demand for capital, small-scale farming and animal husbandry loans, some commercial loans (e.g. small business during slack season of farming), investment in human capital (children education), and sudden demand (illness, plagues, natural disasters)	Owned capital, private loans (including usury), loans from financial institutions (mainly microcredit from credit cooperatives), and a few commercial loans.
Marketized rural households	Development demand: commercial and industrial loans, and specialized and large-scale production loans	Owned capital, private loans (including usury), loans from financial institutions, and commercial loans.

Rural households' financing preference and influencing factors

Whether rural households' financing preference is specific

In many studies of rural financing, rural households' financing preference is assumed to be specific. From this, a deduction is made: For various reasons (historical, cultural, or social), Chinese farmers who strictly prefer relationship finance are "genetically incompatible" with a formal financial system. After a thorough literature review, we found that the studies needed to be clarified in the following two ways: First, if we say rural households in China have a specific preference for financing, it is logically an argument based on contrast rather than self-verification. In other words, whether rural households' financing preference is specific should be concluded based on the contrast with that of the non-rural households (urban households). Second, financing preference is different from the actual financing order. The former is a desired financing order. Under external constraints, the desired financing order is not always the actual financing order. This implies that it is inappropriate to substitute the rural households' financing preference with the financing order observed.

Based on the understanding above, we conducted a sampling survey on the financing preference of 300 urban residents in the urban areas of City A[10] and 330 rural households in the 11 counties of City A via questionnaire. There were two objectives in this survey: First, to determine the subjects' financing preference from their primary inclination for loans, instead of from the actual financing order which could be affected by external environmental constraints. Second, to determine whether rural households' financing preference is specific through contrasting with that of the urban residents. This can be judged from two aspects: Whether rural households prefer relationship finance, and whether their financing preference is more obvious than that of urban residents.

In order to answer the questions above, we designed the following question in the questionnaire: "When you or your family needs to borrow money, where or who first come to mind?" Form the statistics of 330 rural households, 53% of them chose "banks (RCCs)," 21% chose "relatives," 13% chose "close friends," and the remaining 13% chose "acquaintances (colleagues)." From the statistics of 300 urban residents, 53% of them chose "banks (RCCs)," 33% chose "relatives," 10% chose "close friends," and the remaining 4% chose "acquaintances (colleagues)" (see Fig. 2.3).

Fig. 2.3. The financing preference of rural households and urban residents

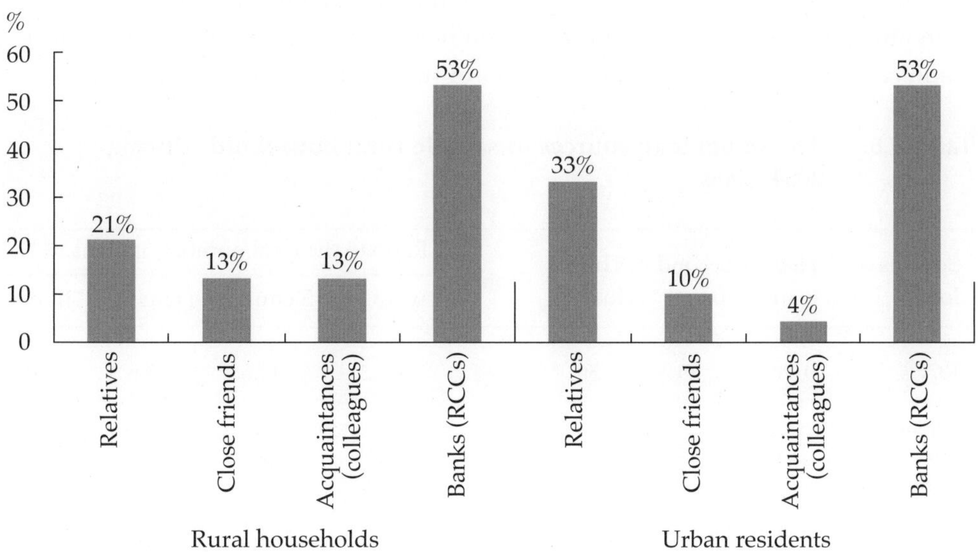

From the comparison and contrast of financing preference between rural households and urban residents, it can be seen that distinct differences and high similarity coexist. The order of preference of both groups is as follows: Banks

(RCCs), relatives, close friends, and acquaintances (colleagues). From the analysis of the financing preference of rural households, it is clear that most of the surveyed households prefer borrowing from financial institutions than relationship finance. This implies that the assumption that rural households prefer relationship finance does not stand. At the same time, the order of preference for relationship loans—relatives, close friends, acquaintances (colleagues)—matches Fei Xiaotong's concentric zone theory. This implies that when formal finance is impossible, the order of relationship loans of rural households is based on blood relation and closeness in relationship.

It should be pointed out that while rural households' financing demand declines in formal loans, due to the difference in the possibility to obtain formal credit, the actual financing order may vary in different regions. For example, a study by the Research Group of Research Center of *The Chinese Banker* (2007) found that although the use of formal financial institutions is the main channel for rural financing,[11] due to the difference in the accessibility of loans from RCCs in different regions, the actual financing order may vary to a larger extent: Sample rural households in Jilin Province had the highest ratio of loans issuance from RCCs to total issuance of loans, reaching 89%, and loans are mainly relied on formal financial institutions. In Henan, 73.6% of the rural households borrowed from friends and relatives, and only 25.6% of the total loans was from RCCs (see Table 2.5). It is worth noting that the ratio of loans obtained from formal financial institutions rose as the local economy improved. This explains from another side that the accessibility of formal credit can affect the actual financing order of rural households.

Table 2.5. The actual loan sources of sample rural households during 2004–2006

Sources of loans	First loan	Second loan	Third loan	Total	Ratio to the total number of loans (%)			
					Average	Sichuan	Henana	Jilin
RCCs	165	89	50	304	62.3	44.6	25.6	89.0
Friends and relatives	118	44	9	171	35.0	51.3	73.6	8.1
Others	6	5	2	13	2.7	4.1	0.8	2.9
Total	289	138	61	488	100.0	100.0	100.0	100.0

Source: Research Group of the Research Institute of *The Chinese Banker*, "Financial demand in traditional rural areas and the distribution of institutions" (2007).

The major factor that influences rural households' financing preference

In order to study the major factor that influences rural households' financing preference, we designed the following question: "What is the most important factor when you decide where to borrow money?" Out of 330 rural households surveyed, 52% chose "convenience and easiness," 27% chose "mutual trust," 11% chose "negotiable and extendable loan period," 10% chose "interest-free or a low interest rate." The results demonstrate that the convenience and easiness in obtaining loans is the major factor that influences rural households' financing preference.

In order to see whether the major factor that influences rural households' financing preference is specific, we asked urban residents the same questions. Out of the 300 urban residents, 54% chose "convenience and easiness" as the major factor that affects their financing preference, 21% chose "mutual trust," 12% chose "negotiable and extendable loan period," 13% chose "interest-free or a low interest rate." Obviously, through the comparison between the results of a survey on rural households and urban residents, it can be seen that the convenience and easiness in obtaining loans is also the major factor that influences urban residents' financing preference.

Fig. 2.4. Factors which influence financing preference

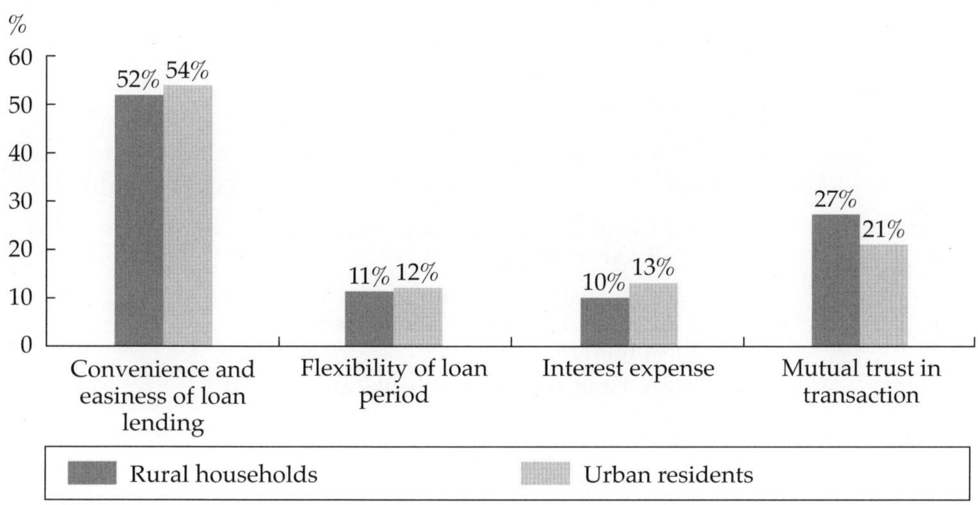

It is worth noting that the availability of rural finance (whether rural households can easily obtain services from financial institutions) plays an important role in the choices of rural financing and financial services of rural households. To most traditional rural areas, as the basic financial facilities are less advanced, the time, transport, and other indirect costs in obtaining financial services could discourage rural households.[12] The influence of convenience and availability on rural households' behavior are also reflected in other studies. For example, in the study by the Research Group of the Research Center of *The Chinese Banker* (2007), the statistics of the answer to the question—"If a formally registered cooperative financial organization founded by a local resident is built in your village but you were not a shareholder or member, are you willing to deposit money in that institution?"—show that of the rural households who were willing to deposit money in the new institution, 71.7% were motivated by convenience. It fits the principle of convenience in providing and purchasing financial services, and also explains the necessity of setting up financial institutions that are close to rural households.

Table 2.6. The attitude of sample rural households toward depositing money in a new rural financial institution

Are you willing to deposit money in the new cooperative financial institute? / Percentage	Reasons	Number of households	Ratio (%)
Yes / 51.66%	(1) Villagers are trustworthy	14	6.0
	(2) It is convenient in the village	167	71.7
	(3) It is safer than other unregistered private lending institutions.	9	3.9
	(1) and (2)	39	16.7
	Others	4	1.7
	Total	233	100.0
No / 40.13%	(1) If I kept my savings there, every villager would know.	3	1.7
	(2) It is risky and unprotected to deposit money in such institutions.	63	35.2
	(3) RCCs and state-owned banks are safer.	102	57.0
	(4) The interest income is higher for deposits in private lending institutions.	1	0.6
	Others	10	5.6
	Total	179	100.0
I will decide after observing for a period, 6.9%			
I will deposit money if I can obtain loans, 1.3%			

Source: Research Group of the Research Institute of *The Chinese Banker*, "Financial demand in traditional rural areas and the distribution of institutions" (2007).

Rural households' sensitivity to the interest rate of financing

The afore-mentioned results show that the burden of interest is not a major factor which influences rural households' financing preference, but due to the importance of the interest rate mechanism in the operation of rural finance, it is necessary for us to conduct an individual study on the influence of interest rate variation. Therefore, we designed the following question in our questionnaire: "If the loan interest rate rises to a small extent, how will you change the loan volume?" 53% rural households chose "Loan volume will remain unchanged," 39% chose "Loan volume will decrease significantly," and 8% chose "Loan volume will increase significantly." When the respondents were questioned "If the loan interest rate rises to a large extent, how will your loan volume change?", only 25% chose "Loan volume will remain unchanged," 66% chose "Loan volume will decrease significantly," and the remaining 9% chose "Loan volume will increase significantly." The results show that rural households are insensitive to the changes in lending rate, but obviously less tolerant toward a high loan rate.

Fig. 2.5. Rural households' sensitivity to the loan interest rate

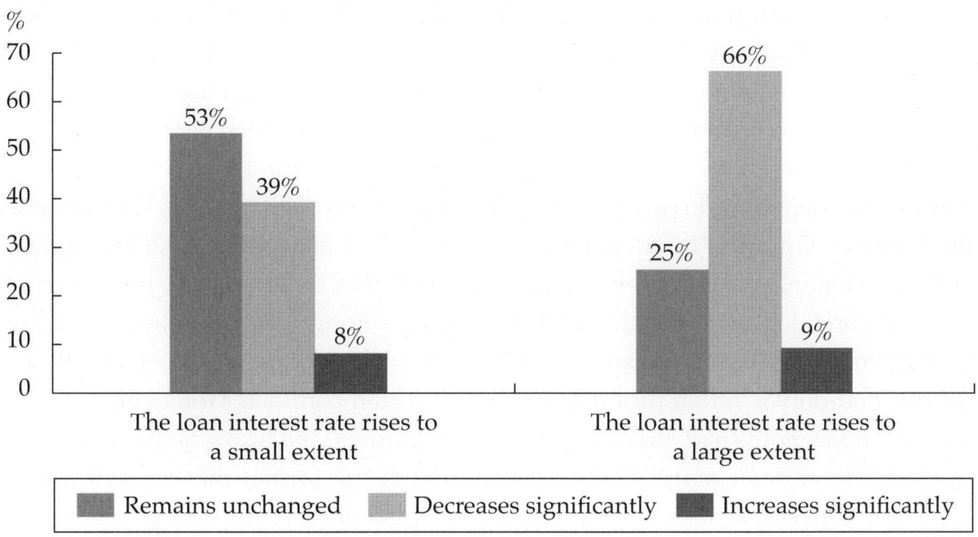

To compare the sensitivity to the loan interest rate, we designed the following question to both rural households and urban residents: "When you need to borrow money, how does the loan interest rate affect you?" 44% of rural households chose A (be more sensitive to the loan interest rate, will compare different ways of borrowing and chose the way that charges less interest), 40% chose B (be insensitive to the loan interest rate, mainly consider the convenience and quickness in obtaining loans), and 16% chose C (depend on the loan volume and total amount of interest: if the loan is small, the higher interest rate is acceptable; if the loan is large, the high interest rate is unbearable). In the same survey on urban residents, 51% chose A, 29% chose B, and 20% chose C. The comparison between the sets of data shows that rural households were less sensitive to the loan interest rate than the urban residents.

Guarantee in relationship loans: Contractual or social constraints

When signing a financial contract, if the verification and execution of the terms of the contract by both parties of the transaction is realized by a formal written contract, the financial transaction is protected by market-based contractual constraints. On the contrary, if both parties of the transaction have not drawn up a formal written contract but only based on a verbal promise, the transaction is mainly protected by non-market-based social constraints.[13]

In the questionnaire survey on 300 rural households, we designed the following question: "When you borrow money from relatives, friends, neighbors, or other people, would you write a receipt for a loan (IOU)?" 76% chose "Usually no, only a verbal promise," only 24% chose "Yes, and will have an agreed interest rate and loan period." This obviously supports the basic conclusion that agricultural loans are less contractual, and relationship loans mainly rely on social constraints.

Other studies have provided supportive evidence for the lower degree of contractual constraints in private loans in traditional agricultural areas. For example, the Research Group of the Research Institute of *The Chinese Banker* (2007) studied Sichuan, Henan, and Jilin provinces. It was found that there was less protection of the credit and debt relationship in the borrowing among rural households. During 2004–2006, of 185 sample rural households who had lent money to others, three-fourths had only a verbal promise without a written contract. Moreover, 97.3% of the rural households had no credit protection measures, and 82.6% of the borrowing did not have a loan period. Of course, although the formal market contractual mechanism is not well-established, at least, up to now, social constraints in the rural network still perform well the supervision and safeguard functions. In Table 2.7, we can see that 87.8% of the rural households who had lent money out could collect their debts when they needed. The occurrence of arrears was just 12.2%.

Table 2.7. The status of contract and credit protection in borrowing among rural households

Question		Ratio to the total number of sample (%)			
		Average	Sichuan	Henan	Jilin
Was there an IOU?	Yes	25.4	29.8	10.8	40.7
	No	74.6	70.2	89.2	59.3
Was there a guarantee or collateral?	Yes	2.7	3.6	0.0	5.6
	No	97.3	96.4	100.0	94.4
Was there a loan period?	Yes	17.4	31.5	5.5	17.9
	No	82.6	68.5	94.5	82.1
Could you collect your debts on time when needed?	Yes	87.8	94.7	78.1	94.1
	No	12.2	5.3	21.9	5.9

Of course, it needs to be pointed out that the above conclusion that rural households have a lower degree of contractual credit is based on the study of traditional rural areas. If we analyze the details of Table 2.7, we could find that in Sichuan, Henan, and Jilin provinces, the status of contract was highest in Jilin, which had the best economic development; the degree of contractual credit in rural borrowing behavior was significantly lower in the less economically developed Henan Province; the degree was moderate in Sichuan Province, whose economic development was average. This tends to show that as an economy develops, more and more rural households will adopt the marketized measure of standard contract to sign a financial contract.

Is the current financial demand of China's rural household effective?

In 1936, John Keynes proposed the concept of "effective demand," which is defined as follows: the demand which the buyer is not only willing but also able to pay is considered effective. If we extend this definition to the rural financial demand, it can be said that a financial demand is effective when there is a desire for loans and the ability to repay debts. Under current circumstances, agricultural production incurs relatively high risks, and rural households lack suitable guarantees or collaterals. Therefore, many scholars regard rural financial demand as ineffective. The credit techniques of most formal financial institutions, which are based on the trade-off relation of "risk-income," are treated as modern credit techniques, such as mortgage, guarantee, and cash flow analysis. This makes most formal financial institutions regard rural financial demand as ineffective—as most rural households want loans but cannot satisfy the borrowing terms required by the suppliers (financial institutions). There is no basis for realizing the transaction.

If we only look at the standardized credit technologies which formal financial institutions now are using, the financial demands of most ordinary households (especially poor households), who are living in the traditional agricultural areas, are rejected by the financial institutions because they cannot satisfy the terms of loans. These rural households lack self-owned dominant capital, and their primitive accumulation of capital is slow. Being incompatible with the modern credit techniques, their demand cannot be transformed to effective demand and corresponding financial supply. It needs to be pointed out that those rural financial demands are regarded as ineffective not because they are not real, but difficult in contracting—the crucial factor is the judging standard of the financial institutions as the suppliers. In other words, do these rural households have the ability to repay debts to support their financial demand? Simply using the judging standards of modern credit techniques, the demand for rural credit without a guarantee or collateral should be considered ineffective. However, is no guarantee or collateral equivalent to no credit (ability)? Apparently, of those rural households who have no guarantee, collateral, or credit record, many are capable of repaying debts. Their demands are considered as ineffective only because the demands are judged by modern credit techniques. We stated in the study of Nanchung MicroCred[14] in Sichuan Province that through developing microcredit techniques and financial services which suit the low-end market (such as rural households, owners of workshops, small traders, craftsmen), many debtors who were "abandoned" (their demands are regarded as ineffective) by formal financial institutions were able to repay debts and the default rate was extremely low.[15] In Nanchung of Sichuan Province, we interviewed many clients of Nanchung MicroCred. Many of them belong to the group of people who have no collateral, no guarantee, and no credit records. Many local formal financial institution networks were in close proximity, but these rural households could not obtain loans from the institutions. When they obtained loans from MicroCred, their potential financial demand and good credit record were released.

The case study of MicroCred shows us that (1) Simply using the status of dominant capital such as no guarantee and no collateral as the criteria to judge the ability of repaying debts, or the effectiveness of demand, is the main reason for formal financial institutions failing to reach the low-end market; (2) Modern credit techniques based on the analyses of mortgage, guarantee, and cash flow do not suit the low-end rural market,[16] and specific credit technologies and services need to be developed for the credit supply and financial services in the low-end rural credit market; (3) As the competition of financial supply is insufficient, formal financial institutions which are used to applying traditional credit technologies to issue loans have certain innovation inertia and no motivation to actively develop specific services for the low-end market. In Feature 2–1 at the end of this chapter, we introduced how MicroCred developed microcredit technologies targeting the low-end market.

It can be seen that to determine whether rural credit demand is effective, financial institutions need to break through from the traditional criteria for credit, and explore extensively the characteristics of the low-end market, so as to recognize and satisfy the potential effective demands. In many of our studies on the low-end rural credit market, it is clearly that the large amounts of potential credit demands of many rural households are real and effective. This suggests that the current judgment that the credit demands of many rural households are ineffective has neglected some potential effective demands. Thus, the key question is whether the financial institutions possess the ability, techniques, and activeness to recognize the potential demand.

Rural Households' Credit Behavior and Investment Preference

Recent studies of rural credit and rural finance mostly focused on the financial system, but the studies on microeconomic behavior are relative insufficient. This section intends to dissect the rural households' credit behavior and investment preference through empirical analysis. The discussion will revolve around three basic variables: (1) the determinant of rural households' borrowing needs; (2) the factor for rural households to decide the financing channel; (3) the deciding factor of rural households' investment preference.

Basic theories

In current studies of rural finance, one of the disagreements is whether rural households' behavior follows the economic assumption of rationality. The different answers determined two different directions of research: rational small farmers and moral small farmers. The theory of rational small farmers holds that rural households, same as all capitalist entrepreneurs, are rational economic players in economic activities. They act according to the principles of a rational investor, and target profit maximization. In general, traditional famers are efficient but poor. If new inputs are not introduced, productivity of traditional agriculture cannot be improved. When small farmers are stimulated by economic benefits, they will become more innovative in order to gain more profit, and traditional agriculture will be reformed. In contrast, the theory of moral small farmers stresses that small farmers produce to support their families, capitalist calculation of profit is not applicable to family farms (because this type of farm does not rely on employing labor, the annual labor input of the family is difficult to be counted as the per unit cost of labor). Family farms produce to satisfy family consumption, not to maximize profit.

It should be pointed out that the theory of moral small farmers (and the theories developed from it) has a certain explanatory power over the system through the inclusion of long-term factors such as history, culture, and tradition in the economic studies. However, we believe that once an economic theory becomes integral to the 1,000-year study of small farmer economy, it will inevitably be strongly influenced by the long and rich history and culture.[17] Recent studies of rural finance have shown some tendencies and raised questions which are worth noting: First, there has been too much emphasis on the distinctiveness of Chinese rural households and a neglecting of their general economic features as market entities. Second, the period of analysis is too long, and reasonable explanation cannot be offered on logical continuity. Third, there is an overemphasis on the incompatibility between the formal financial system and China's small-scale peasant economy, and the explanation of the logic mechanism is unsatisfactory.

Based on the understanding above, with our several studies about China's rural households and rural areas, we believe the following: (1) Rural households' economic behaviors follow the traditional assumption of rationality. Their motivation to seek profit maximization directs their basic economic behaviors. (2) The conclusion of irrationality of rural households' behaviors proposed by previous studies cannot be applied unconditionally to the current studies on rural households (under market economy conditions) since after reforming and opening up, their behaviors have undergone fundamental changes.

With these definitions, we need not bother to choose between surviving small farmers and rational small farmers. Rural households should be regarded as the market entity who seeks profit maximization.[18] The decisions and behaviors of the rural households, who are the basic microeconomic organization in China's rural areas, are the logical starting point of the studies of rural finance. According to general economic theories, rural households' demand for loans is mainly based on transaction demand, precautionary demand, and investment demand; at the same time, as a rational economic man, rural households make the financing decisions (on whether to go for financing and how to finance) based on the "feasible set"—the fundamental economic consideration is still the trade-off between risk and return.

Of course we must see that under the specific market conditions, China's rural household's credit behavior and investments preference are also specific; these constraints must be carefully considered in the search for a solution to the problem of China's rural finance. For example, due to limited financial services, there is a higher cost for rural households to participate in financial activities. As a result, many market transactions (for example, sale on credit) will take place to substitute financial activities in rural areas. Besides, under the poor social insurance system, savings is the dominant method of rural households to satisfy their precautionary demand. When the returns of the basic traditional agricultural production of rural households become saturated, there would be a reduction in borrowing and lending and the capital outflow will be in the form of savings.[19]

Undoubtedly, the factors which influenced rural households' actual credit behavior and investment tendency are complicated. Some of them are hard to observe. From the viewpoint of economics, we believe that of the influential factors, the rural households' capital deposit, human capital, knowledge, technology, and the economic conditions cannot be neglected. These form the theoretical basis for our following positive analysis of rural households' credit behavior and investment tendency.

Positive analysis

The design of model and the explanation of variables

In order to conduct an all-round study of rural households' credit behavior and investment tendency, our model is designed as follows:

Model 1: $Y_1 = C_1 + \alpha X_i + \varepsilon_i$, where $i = 1, 2, 3, \ldots, 10, 11, 12$

Model 2: $Y_2 = C_2 + \alpha X_j + \varepsilon_j$, where $j = 1, 2, 3, \ldots, 10, 11, 12$

In our model, there are two explained variables: (1) Rural households' loan preference (Y_1). If rural households borrow private loans, it is assigned the value 0. If rural households borrow from banks (RCCs), it is assigned the value 1. (2) Rural households' consumption or investment preference (Y_2). If the remaining capital is used for consumption or saved in banks (RCCs), it is assigned the value 0. If rural households use their remaining capital on production expansion or commercial investment, it is assigned the value 1. Regarding the nature of explained variables, we employ ML-Binary Logit regression analysis. The correlation between variables is determined by the sign of correlation coefficients.

The variable indexes considered during the selection of explanatory variables include the following: regional classified index (X_1), total assets index (X_2), per capita arable land index (X_3), income of agricultural production (X_4), income from non-rural jobs (X_5), ratio of labor force to household members (X_6), educational level (X_7), level of agricultural technology and knowledge (X_8), other technology and techniques (X_9), social relationship capital (X_{10}), and understanding towards the policies of agricultural loans (X_{11}). It should be noted that rural households' consumption or investment preference (Y_2) would affect whether rural households borrow loans (Y_1). Therefore, in the first regressive analysis, Y_2 is regarded as an explanatory variable. Similarly, there exists an internal logical relation between rural households' loan preference (Y_1) and rural households' consumption or investment preference (Y_2). Therefore, in the second and third regressive analyses, Y_1 and Y_2 are explanatory variables with respect to each other.

The above explanatory and explained variables are based on the indexes assigned and data from 1,100 questionnaires on information of rural households. Table 2.8 shows the identifier and the assignment of the value of each variable.

Table 2.8. The explanation of the treatment of data of the variables

Variable	Identifier, value assignment, and its explanation
Regional classified index (X_1)	With respect to the actual situation of the sample regions in the studies, rural residential areas are divided into dam area and mountain area. In general, the economic conditions of dam area (such as economic development, commercial trade, transportation, etc.) are better than those of mountain area. A higher assigned value represents a more developed economy.
Total assets index (X_2)	Calculated according to the total assets of rural households, including savings, properties, livestock, economic fruit, agricultural machines, etc.
Per capita arable land index (X_3)	Based on the per capita arable land owned by the rural household. Farmland is a long-term stable capital of rural households which could continuously generate income.
Income of agricultural production (X_4)	Calculated based on the income of agricultural production of the entire household, which includes the incomes from grain crops, cash crops, and animal husbandry.
Income from non-rural jobs (X_5)	Calculated based on the total income of the entire household earned through working away from hometown.
Ratio of labor force to household member (X_6)	In rural areas, every household is a production unit. The labor force of each household is the basic human resources for agricultural production, which is at the same time the major human resources source for generating non-agricultural income.
Educational level (X_7)	Educational level is recognized by many studies as the foundation for the accumulation of human capital. We assign the value according to the highest educational level in each household. A higher value represents more human capital.

(Cont'd)

Variable	Identifier, value assignment, and its explanation
Level of agricultural technology and knowledge (X_8)	It is the dominant factor in raising agricultural productivity. The introduction of agricultural production technology (especially advanced technology) can significantly increase the production and development capabilities. We assign the value according to whether the household has participated in agricultural technological training (including self-learning). A higher value represents a higher level of agricultural knowledge and technology.
Other technology and techniques (X_9)	It is a supplement to agricultural technology. Non-agricultural technology can increase the sources of income of rural households as well as become the main source of income for those who are transforming into commercialists. We assign the value according to whether the rural households know other technology (which can increase income). A higher value represents more advanced non-agricultural production technology.
Social relationship capital (X_{10})	Three factors are considered in the assignment of value: Is any family member a village cadre, or a member of the Communist Party, or is there a relative living in the urban area. The value we assigned to social relationship capital is the sum of the three factors' values. In rural areas, village cadres, whether elected or recommended, generally have better connections. Their social network is significantly larger than that of general households. Similarly, those who are in the Communist Party have generally had access to more privileges in life and are potentially less likely to need loan services. To those who live in less advanced rural areas, having a relative in the urban area (implies higher income level and broader horizon) means more potential sources of capital, information, technology, and development opportunities. A higher value represents a higher level of social relationship capital.
Understanding of policies of agricultural loans (X_{11})	The value is assigned according to the rural households' understanding towards the nation's policies of agricultural loans. A higher value represents a better understanding towards the agricultural loan policies of the nation (RCCs).

Note: The data from the table were obtained from our study of rural households in 11 counties in City A (those households and their production had the economic features of small farmers). We gave out 1,300 questionnaires and received a total of 1,100 effective questionnaires, 100 from each county (so there were 1,100 rural households in total). This survey considered carefully the issue of sampling coverage and avoided the flaws of many previous studies—relying on insufficient data (or merely typical case studies) to draw general conclusions.

Results of positive analysis

We analyze rural households' loan preference (namely, where did the borrowing come from, banks or private lenders?) using ML-Binary Logit regression. Results are shown in Table 2.9.

Table 2.9. The ML-Binary Logit regression analysis of rural households' loan preference (Y_1)

Variable	Correlation coefficient	z–statistical value	Probability
Constant (C)	−1.147229**	−2.382368	0.0172
Regional classified index (X_1)	0.181614	1.064678	0.2870
Total assets index (X_2)	0.277568***	3.549315	0.0004
Per capita arable land index (X_3)	−0.028888	−0.447353	0.6546
Income of agricultural production (X_4)	0.068552	1.155154	0.2480
Income from non-rural jobs (X_5)	−0.203322**	−2.480404	0.0131
Ratio of labor force to household member (X_6)	1.325966**	2.472277	0.0134
Educational level (X_7)	−0.091373	−1.320191	0.1868
Level of agricultural technology and knowledge (X_8)	−0.234207***	−2.123727	0.0337
Other technology and techniques (X_9)	0.000584	0.004490	0.9964
Social relationship capital (X_{10})	0.053647	0.860413	0.3896
Consumption or investment preference (Y_2)	1.149341***	6.947059	0.0000
Understanding of policies of agricultural loans (X_{11})	0.374949***	3.075413	0.0021
Probability (LR stat)	0.000000	McFadden R-squared	0.100116

Notes: * indicates being significant at 10% confidence level, ** significant at 5% confidence level, *** significant at 1% confidence level.

From the above empirical results, it can be seen that the factors which influence rural households' loan preferences include the following: total assets of the households, income from non-rural jobs, ratio of labor force to household member, level of agricultural technology and knowledge, consumption and investment preference of the households, and the understanding of policies of agricultural loans. In particular, the z–test values for the four variables (total assets of the households, level of agricultural technology and knowledge, consumption and investment preference, and the understanding of policies of agricultural loans) are significant at 1% confidence level. This suggests that (1) households with greater total assets are more willing to borrow money from banks (RCCs); (2) households with a higher level of agricultural technology and knowledge are more willing to borrow private loans; (3) households who have a higher tendency to borrow (or a lower tendency to save or consume) are more inclined to borrow from banks (RCCs); (4) households who have a better understanding of policies of agricultural loans are more willing to borrow from banks (RCCs). Moreover, the z–test value of income from non-rural jobs of rural households is significant at 5% confidence level and the coefficient is negative. It represents that as income from non-rural jobs increases, rural households would borrow less from banks (RCCs). The z–test value of labor force to household member ratio is significant at 5% confidence level and is positive, which suggests that households with a higher ratio are more likely to borrow from banks (RCCs).

At last, we apply ML-Binary Logit regression analysis to rural households' consumption or investment preference. Results are shown in Table 2.10.

Table 2.10. The results of ML-Binary Logit regression analysis of rural households' consumption or investment preference (Y_2)

Variable	Correlation coefficient	z–statistical value	Probability
Constant (C)	−2.093780***	−5.114777	0.0000
Regional classified index (X_1)	0.052071	0.384137	0.7009
Total assets index (X_2)	0.271517***	3.949215	0.0001
Per capita arable land index (X_3)	0.045190	0.868253	0.3853
Income of agricultural production (X_4)	−0.003351	−0.088428	0.9295
Income from non-rural jobs (X_5)	0.047445	0.700242	0.4838
Labor force to household member ratio (X_6)	−0.028121	−0.086186	0.9313
Educational level (X_7)	−0.222820***	−3.912842	0.0001
Level of agricultural technology and knowledge (X_8)	0.237806***	2.658380	0.0079

(Cont'd)

Variable	Correlation coefficient	z–statistical value	Probability
Other technology and techniques (X_9)	–0.083137	–0.775258	0.4382
Social relationship capital (X_{10})	0.097816**	1.969908	0.0488
Loan preference(Y_1)	1.151171***	6.962270	0.0000
Understanding of policies of agricultural loans (X_{11})	0.091244	0.930076	0.3523
Probability (LR stat)	0.000000	McFadden R-squared	0.076262

Notes: * indicates being significant at 10% confidence level, ** significant at 5% confidence level, *** significant at 1% confidence level.

The above results show that the factors influencing rural households' consumption or investment preference include the following: total assets of the households, educational level, level of agricultural technology and knowledge, social relationship capital, and loan preference. The z-test values of total assets, educational level, level of agricultural technology and knowledge, and loan preference are significant at 1% confidence level. This indicates that (1) households with more total assets are more willing to expand production or make commercial investment; (2) households which have a higher educational level are more willing to save or consume; (3) households with a higher level of agricultural technology and knowledge are more willing to expand production or make commercial investment; and (4) households which show a stronger loan preference to financial institutions (mainly from banks, i.e. RCCs) are more inclined to expand reproduction and involve in commercial investment. In addition, the z-test value of social relationship capital is significant at 5% confidence level and is positive, which shows that as rural households' social relationship capital increases, they would tend more to expand production or make commercial investment.

Conclusions

In this section we examine the credit behavior and investment tendency. More precisely, we answer the following two basic questions: (1) whether rural households tend to borrow from formal financial institutions or private lenders, and (2) whether they save, consume, or expand reproduction or make commercial investment (the latter represents a stronger tendency toward investment) when they earn profit (namely, they have excessive capital).

Regarding the first question, in our model, factors deciding whether rural households borrow from formal financial institutions or private lenders include the following: total assets of the rural households, income from non-rural jobs, labor force to household member ratio, level of agricultural technology and knowledge, consumption or investment preference, and the understanding of policies of agricultural loans. Those who have more family assets, a stronger tendency to invest, and a better understanding of national agricultural policies are more likely to borrow from formal financial institutions. Those who have better agricultural technology and knowledge and higher non-agricultural income (from non-rural jobs) tend to obtain private loans. We discovered in our field study that the reason behind this is that the rural households having better agricultural technology and knowledge and higher non-agricultural income are those who are more well-informed and have better relationship resources. These households have established their credibility, which reduces their cost and raises their chances of obtaining private loans. In such a situation, compared to the complicated and trivial process of borrowing from formal financial institutions, it is easier and quicker for those rural households to obtain private loans.

Regarding the second question, in our model, the following factors influence rural households' consumption and investment preference: total assets of the households, educational level, level of agricultural technology and knowledge, social relationship capital, and loan preference. Those households with more family assets, a higher level of agricultural technology and knowledge, and a higher tendency to borrow from formal financial institutions are more likely to expand reproduction or make commercial investment by using their excessive capital. Those with a higher educational level are less likely to make investment. Instead, they tend to save or consume more. It should be noted that rural households' investment tendency increases as social relationship capital increases. This demonstrates that when rural households have broader relation resources, their incentives and opportunities to invest grow. We discovered from our further interview that rural households' commercial awareness and horizon, acceptance of new things, and their thirst for fortune, are enhanced significantly as relation resources expand.

Through answering the two questions we now have a basic understanding of rural households' credit behavior and investment preference. There is a logical clue behind these conclusions: To a large extent the initial resources (including environmental resources, material resources, knowledge resources, etc.) determine the rural households' demand for loans—when there is a demand for loans of rural households, the choice between formal finance or private finance in financing depends on the relation resources and relative information advantage that they have. Once rural households obtain capital surplus, the material resources and relation resource they already have further determines whether would invest again. Conversely, we have a more direct conclusion: What represses rural households' demand for credit is the initial resources. What affects the choices of financing channels is the balance of cost and benefit. What prevent reproduction expansion are the opportunities and abilities to invest.

Rural Households' Formal Credit: Debate and Evaluation[20]

Rural credit can be categorized as formal credit and informal credit. In normal situations, we call the credit funds issued to rural households by licensed banks and similar financial institutions formal credit. In 2006, Muhammud Yunus was awarded the Nobel Peace Prize for his work in establishing rural banks and issuing microcredit for poverty alleviation. Relying on credit to raise the benefits of small farmers has then become a recommended policy in relevant studies. Yet, Yunus's work in microcredit for poverty alleviation and formal rural credit is not the same. He targets the poorest and favors females. Most relevant studies focus on gender, credit control, and the degree of poverty (Goetz 1996, NaRanong 1998, Fletschner 2005).

On the whole, studies of formal rural credit can be categorized into three types. The first type takes rural households as their subjects. They analyze the influence of formal credit on rural households and then estimate the efficiency of credit. The second type discusses the problems from the perspective of the nation and analyzes the effect of formal credit on the nation. The third type focuses on rural financial institutions, which empirically examines the productivity of the rural financial system, analyzes the risks of formal credit for rural households, or explores these technical measures of the reform of rural financial institutions. The conclusions of the studies are very different. There are two major contradictions. First is the effect of formal credit on rural households: Some studies claimed that formal credit cannot affect the production and consumption of rural households, while the other claimed that it can significantly improve the production conditions and benefits. Second is about the effect of formal credit on rural financial institutions: Some studies suggested that the risks of formal credit for rural households are high due to asymmetric information. Rural financial institutions cannot be market-oriented regardless of the organizational framework. But some other studies listed part of the efficient rural financial institutions and believed that those organizational frameworks are universal.

There are many comprehensive studies of formal rural credit in China, but the existing literature focuses on the discussion of informal credit. There are few normative studies of rural formal credit. With the above consideration, we will review the relevant studies of formal rural credit and evaluate the research paradigms, quantitative methods, and institutional backgrounds of the studies.

Debate and methodology

There are two different viewpoints on the effects of formal credit on rural households. One is that while the cost of formal rural credit is high, it can still significantly improve the benefits of rural households. Khandler (1988) evaluated the effect of the rural credit of Agricultural Development Bank of Pakistan (ADBP). The conclusion was that although more than 69% of rural households who had no land and could barely survive only received 23% of the national agricultural loans, formal rural credit still significantly alleviated poverty in the entire rural area. Zaman (2004) studied the use of microcredit of the Grameen Bank in Bangladesh. He believed that microcredit reduced the fragility of families in Bangladesh and significantly improved the social welfare index in rural areas. He also believed that the small-scale financing system in Bangladesh can be duplicated and applied to other countries. Some Chinese scholars agree with this view. Lin Yifu (2000) analyzed the rural credit situation in three counties (cities) in China. He concluded that formal credit could affect the fixed assets for production of rural households, and informal credit could not replace formal credit, but the volume of formal credit in the sample areas was low, and there existed general credit constraints.

Another viewpoint is more prudent. Siamwalla (1990) summarized the experience of the Thai government in promoting agricultural loans since 1966. The conclusion showed that despite the fact that the government imposed regulations on banks to support agriculture—rural credit must take up a stipulated proportion in the outstanding loans of commercial banks and rural savings are granted as loans only in rural areas—the banking sector had not solved the problem of asymmetric information of rural credit and the relative inefficiency of formal credit in comparison with informal credit. Besley (1994) analyzed the effect of the credit market on agricultural production. He believes that formal rural credit is an intervention of the nation in the credit market, which would result in moral hazard and monopoly in the sellers' market. This seriously lowers the efficiency of credit fund allocation. Under these premises, formal credit cannot promote agricultural production. Abiad (1988) in his study proposed that the land owned by the rural households, the position of the land, and the volume of household consumption are the key factors which determine the efficiency of loans. He quoted the example of the Philippine government as evidence that relaxing the regulations on credit could not raise the efficiency of agricultural loans. Kochar (1997a, 1997b) examined the performance of formal rural credit using land leasing data of India during 1981–1982. The results showed that even though rural households could obtain formal credit, it will not help in improving the benefits of rural households. Thus, formal rural credit is ineffective as a whole.

Regarding the quantitative method, before the 1990s, foreign literature mostly employed OLS method, which is the most commonly used method of positive analysis. In the research on credit efficiency, Levine (1998) referred to it as "Barro's growth analysis," which utilizes economic growth as the dependent variable and multiple factors involving credit as the variables in regression analysis so as to determine the relationship between the two by the regression coefficient. Employing OLS method to examine formal rural credit usually requires the introduction of multiple variables. For example, in the study by Ellinger and Neff (1993), they included seven variables in their examination of rural credit efficiency. Although multivariable regression can refine the precision of the model, it will cause problems, such as multicollinearity, resulting in unstable results.

Rousseau (1990) employed a vector error correction (VEC) model in his research. Although his VED model was not free from "Barro's growth analysis," and included only two variables (economic growth and rural credit), it carved out a new way of thinking in the study of rural formal credit. Different from other macroeconomic models (e.g., VAR model), constraints are introduced in VEC model. Its higher precision makes it popular in dealing with many economic issues. However, VEC model can only examine bivariate causality. Regarding this, Owoye (1995), Vamvoukas (1997), and Darrat (1998) introduced trivariate into the framework of VEC model based on the theory of general-to-specific (GTS) of the London school of quantitative analysis, and proposed the refined trivariate Granger causality test and error correction model, which compensates for the shortcomings of VEC model. This method eliminates intermediate transmission and can capture the direct relationship between time series.

In the late 1990s, Kochar et al. (1997a) created the two-stage method on the foundation of Heckman's (1977) theory of latent variance, which has become the major estimation method nowadays. The core idea of the two-stage method is that actual data cannot express the latent variable—before the loans to be obtained by the rural households, the output after loans cannot be represented. It would make the random disturbance term nonzero in estimation. General quantitative examination cannot deal with the biased estimation. Heckman solved this problem by introducing the inverse Mill ratio (IMR) into OLS: given that the random disturbance term does not equal zero, unbiased estimation can be achieved by using the mean correction method. Kochar utilized the latent variable techniques in measuring the efficiency of formal rural credit and formulated the maximum-likelihood function of formal rural credit. The biggest advantage of the two-stage method is that it can estimate both the reduced form and structural form, and systematically estimate the simultaneous equation of latent (truncated and filtered) dependent variables (Wang Shaoping 2001). In the presentation words of the Nobel Memorial Prize in Economic Sciences, latent variance estimation method and the two-stage method were regarded as "the most influential contributions to micro-econometrics and an innovation in the combination of Development Economics and econometric methods." The economic idea behind the two-stage method is that rural households would consider whether they opt for formal credit on the basis of economic rationality. As long as the production status of the rural households who have a desire for loans but are neglected by formal financial institutions can be estimated, the efficiency of formal rural credit can be known. Barro's growth analysis only considers the production status of the rural households who can obtain credit capital, to deduce the efficiency of formal rural credit. Apparently the two-stage method has come a long way since Barro's growth analysis. Inspired by Kochar, Diagne (2000) used inverse recursion to design a dynamic game model of rural households and rural financial institutions. He studied from the viewpoint of credit constraints. He calculated by using inverse recursion the agreed loan amount between rural households and rural financial institutions. The difference between the two parties is defined as credit constraint. The core idea of inverse recursion is to express the current status through several previous status; deduce the credit strategy of rural households given their assets; under the given optimal output conditions, deduce the reasonable debt level by inverse recursion and hence the credit constraints. The efficiency of formal rural credit is obtained by estimating the effect of credit constraint on rural household income.

Discussion on national utility

In many developing countries, disadvantaged rural households take up a considerable proportion of the total population. In the early 1980s, some scholars proposed that because disadvantaged rural households lacked saving capability, they should receive financial support, and the interest rate for formal rural credit should be lowered. This point of view is called the theory of rural credit subsidy in China. The theory is not the mainstream. In the evolution of development economics, there is little literature which recommended subsidizing rural households by way of credit. In the famous collection of articles about development economics, *Pioneers of Development Economics*, no article mentioned the support of finance to agriculture (Meir 1984). However, the theory of rural credit subsidy seem to be well-received by many countries when devising national policies. Many countries attempt to design a rural credit system which promotes small-farm production and improves the benefits of small farmers. China's rural cooperative financial institutions, Thailand's Bank for Agriculture and Agricultural Cooperatives, Unit Desas of Bank Rakyat Indonesia are rural credit organizations with a national background.

Regarding national utility, formal rural credit has begun to get a broader theoretical foundation. From the perspective of new institutional economics, the state theory becomes an essential component of relevant studies. Only when we master the state theory can we evaluate the relevant literature on formal rural credit. Weber (1915) proposed a unique theory that the tax base of traditional countries is family instead of fortune, and small farmers are the basis of those countries. This theory was further developed by Scott (1976). In the *Moral Economy of the Peasant: Rebellion and Subsistence in Southeast Asia*, James C. Scott suggested that the stability of Southeast Asian countries depends on the how much the country takes from the little surplus of the rural households. There is a long history of the government promoting rural credit in China, from the Xin Dynasty of Wang Mang, the Southern and Northern Dynasties, to the Qing Dynasty. Although countries in different times are different, they all intend to promote rural credit: they hope they can raise the production ability of small farms with their limited financial ability (or without the use of fiscal capital).

Duara (1988), Skinner (1972), and Huang (1985) directly studied China's small farmer issues. Their studies did not touch on rural credit, but their conclusions can be generalized and applied to formal rural credit. The core idea of Duara was state involution. When technology and economy are in stagnation, the state should increase their fiscal revenue via penetration in society, not by promoting economic growth or supplying public services. Institutions controlled by the state are becoming profit-oriented brokers, which are not in the same accord with the national utility function. Any effort made to promote state development in the mode of profit-oriented brokers is debatable. Current rural financial institutions in China differ from Duara's paradigm in both connotation and denotation, but the rural households faced by China's rural financial institutions are a technologically and economically less advanced group. Skinner (1972) is a prominent figure in the studies of China's rural market features. He analyzed China's rural households from the viewpoint of the market, suggesting that their scope of economic activities is much larger than in the villages. Their own economic activities cannot satisfy survival needs. To study small farmers, one must study the scope of the standard market. Skinner's samples were China's rural areas during 1964–1965. In the information age, the scope of economic activities of China's rural households undoubtedly has been expanded, but it could not break through the restrictions built thousands of years ago in merely a few decades. The scope of the standard market can still explain China's small-farmer economic activities. The current design of China's rural financial system is evidence for Skinner's scope of the standard market. The state assigns the duty of agricultural loan services to rural financial institutions but not the state-owned commercial banks which have branches in various areas. Huang (1985) studied economic activities of rural households in North China and the Yangtze River Delta, and proposed production involution: Under the pressure from capital shortage, large population, and survival needs, China's rural households continue to input agricultural labor, which in the end would result in the decreasing of marginal productivity to zero. However, external marketization cannot dissolve the rural social structure, or put an end to production involution of the agricultural labor force. Rural households rely on marketization to compensate for the insufficient income of agriculture, which will give rise to the "crutch logic"—compensating agricultural income with non-agricultural income. Huang offered a simple explanation to the phenomenon: Non-agricultural income of rural households from modern marketization does not allow them to maintain life. They must continue to rely on the agricultural labor force. The production characteristics of rural households have persisted for thousands of years and will not simply disappear. They imperceptibly affect current households. Formal rural credit is operating in such an external environment.

Zhang Jie (2004) included the institutional factors mentioned in the literature above into his research of China's rural credit. He believes that due to the issue of the "cost of face," China's rural households only borrow money when their income cannot maintain life. The actual borrowing order is as follows: formal credit, informal credit, usury. In his later study (2005a), he delved into this problem by adopting a long-term perspective. He regarded formal rural credit as a product by which the state gets and maintains small surplus from small farmers. In contrast, endogenous informal credit is path-dependent and reasonable. Therefore, formal rural credit cannot replace informal credit or raise the production ability of rural households. With respect to the direction of development, China's efficiency of rural credit depends on rural economic development and the increased income of rural households. Simply changing the framework of rural financial institutions would not yield any actual effect on the efficiency of formal credit. As a whole, Zhang's studies concentrated on analyzing the borrowing order of rural households but did not make a specific analysis on the formal credit.

Unfortunately, studies of formal rural credit regarding national utility are still at the stage of theoretical analysis. Few have analyzed the actual data or made positive analysis. National utility cannot be quantified and economists of the public choice school have deeply explored national utility. Research on national utility function, officers' code of conduct, and budget-maximizing has emerged. Judging from the credit policies to boost agriculture in various countries mentioned in relevant studies, licensed banks often issue rural credit under the supervision of the state. Public choice theory is a valuable reference to national utility.

Discussion on rural financial institutions

Apart from rural households and the state, financial institutions are an important participant in formal rural credit. Literature about rural financial institutions touches on more topics. Main focuses are on the productivity of rural financial institutions, risks of formal rural credit, and the direction of development of rural finance.

One of the focuses of foreign literature on rural financial institutions is performance appraisal. Before the 1990s, foreign studies mostly employed Frontier Production Efficiency (FPE). FPE treats rural financial institutions as general production enterprises. The FPE of rural financial institutions is the maximum profit per unit of input. The FPE of rural financial institutions emphasizes financial indexes such as cost and net profit. Financial indexes are not the only reason why states promote formal rural credit, and rural financial institutions enjoy more financial subsidies. Therefore, FPE cannot completely evaluate the effect of formal rural credit on rural financial institutions. The study of Yaron and Benjamin (1998) to a certain extent overcame the shortcomings of FPE. They proposed that the productivity of rural financial institutions should be analyzed both microscopically and macroscopically. In the macro analysis, they included factors such as legal and political environment and the cost for market withdrawal in their research framework; in the micro analysis, they added credit terms and technological advancement. The weakness of their study was that it did not examine the effect of formal rural credit on social benefits such as fair allocation, the gap between rich and poor, etc.

Another focus of the studies is to evaluate the risks of rural credit. In the late 1990s, many modern credit risk-measurement models were developed from the Value at Risk theory (VaR), such as KMV, CreditMetrics, CreditRisk+, and CreditPortfolio View. Perhaps because rural credit has a different institutional background to other credit products, current studies do not follow the train of thought of research on modern credit risk. Osborne (2006) examined rural credit risk from a dynamic perspective. He found that rural credit risk depends on self-production and consumption features. Therefore, the fundamental way to lower rural credit risk is to reinforce self-production and consumption ability. Udry (1994) surveyed the status of rural credit risk in north Nigeria, and included factors such as the age structure, land assets, residence time, rural households' techniques, and village credit checking, and investigated the risk-pooling of the rural credit market under both perfect and imperfect information. Udry believed that even when there is perfect information in the credit market, mutual insurance between rural households and credit checking are essential in order to avoid risk. When there is imperfect information, state-contingency is the key question which determines the information cost and risk-pooling at this time has not been resolved. Rural credit risk would be determined by the information transaction cost, social system, and other priori factors.

There is a debate about the developmental direction of rural financial institutions. Some studies claim that since rural credit cannot improve rural households' benefits (Khandler 1988, Zaman, 2004), grafting the framework of modern financial institutions onto those of rural areas would not be efficient. Kellee (2004) quoted China and India as examples to explicate that although the states intended to repress the high interest rate of private loans or improve rural benefits by formal rural credit, the problem of imperfect information faced by both China and India determined that licensed rural financial institutions cannot replace informal credit. Kellee addressed the reforms of China's rural financial institutions since 2003, which is similar to the studies of Zhang Jun (2005) and Zhang Jie (2006). He believed that the only way out for China's rural finance was to incorporate informal finance into licensed financial institutions, and the reform since 2003 was an "exogenous grafting of the financial system." On the contrary, The World Bank (2001, 2004) stood by their view that parts of the frameworks of rural financial institutions were efficient. In a series of research reports, it listed three efficient modes of formal rural microcredit: Thailand's Bank for Agriculture and Agricultural Cooperatives, Unit Desas of Bank Rakyat Indonesia, and Grameen Bank in Bangladesh. It claimed that these modes of operation should be promoted globally.

It can be seen from the development of foreign literature that the biggest flaw of the relevant studies is that they fail to employ national utility to evaluate the performance of, or comment on, the outlook for rural financial institutions. Apparently in many countries, rural households do not borrow loans for achieving financial profit, and if national utility is included in the analysis, the conclusion may be different.

Conclusions

Three parties can benefit from formal rural credit: rural households, the state, and rural financial institutions. Current foreign literature focuses on rural households and many scholars hold the view that formal rural credit does not significantly affect the production of rural households. Some scholars in China have studied rural credit, such as Lin Yifu (2000), Liu Minquan (2006), Li Rui (2004, 2007), etc. However, they used combined data of formal and informal rural credits. Because of sample selection bias, the data cannot be used in the estimation of the efficiency of formal rural credit. On the basis of the works of Scott (1976), Skinner (1972), Duara (1988), and Huang (1985), Zhang Jie (2004, 2005a) studied institutional factors in China's rural credit and how these factors come into being. As the samples lack comparability, no study is carried out from the perspective of national utility when discussing the formal rural credit. And there is also no consensus on the follow-up development of rural financial institutions.

Form the evolution of viewpoints and quantitative methods of relevant studies, the analytical framework of formal rural finance is being refined, and the results of empirical analysis reflect reality more closely. China's rural financial institutions are under reforms. Therefore, the theoretical discussion about formal rural credit has become more meaningful in reality, not only because agricultural loan is the major business of rural financial institutions, but more importantly, because using credit to boost farming is a realization of national utility. On the one hand, the productivity of China's rural household is low and they lack capital; on the other hand, rural financial institutions need to face the market and earn profit. In this dilemma, is there a cut-point solution between boosting farming with credit and financial marketization? Is the current reform of rural financial institutions feasible? These are the major research questions in studying the issues of China's formal rural credit.

Rural Households' Credibility and Risk Preference: From the Structural Perspective of Society, Market, and the State

Do Chinese farmers value credibility? Is their "internal credit mechanism (constraints on themselves)" different from their "external one (trust in others)"? How does their credit structure affect their economic behavior? The answers to these questions are related to the economic behavior of the rural households and directly affect the reform of rural finance which is at the stage of exploration. While the previous literature has tried to explain rural households' credibility in the scope of economics, social sciences, cultural studies, etc., very little has addressed the issue (including its origin, development, and evolution) within the framework of society, market, and the state.

Given the above considerations, this section attempts to explain rural households' credibility and risk preference based on reality in China and from a structural perspective. We will not only examine the features and basis of rural households' credibility, but delve into how credibility is maintained and its developmental mechanism. We especially investigate the influence and effect of price (market), authority (the state), and credibility (social network)[21] on the rural credit mechanism, and explicate the complexity of rural households' credibility during social transformation.

Rural households' personal credit: Moralization of social capital

Fei Xiaotong (1985) summarized the interpersonal network in China's rural areas as "Differential Mode of Association": the social network is like the ripple with "the self" at the center. The Chinese society was formed around the "differential relations" of unitary selves, like the ripples formed from a stone thrown into a lake, each circle spreading out from the center becomes more distant and at the same time more insignificant...The most important relationship in our society is kinship which in nature resembles the concentric circles of ripples. Kinship is the social relation based on the facts of birth and marriage...(Whereas geographical relations are merely) the space projection of kinship." The trust of Chinese is not the general trust built on the faith community, but a special trust built on kinship. This view has been verified by many scholars.

Fig. 2.6. Differential mode of association of rural social relationship system

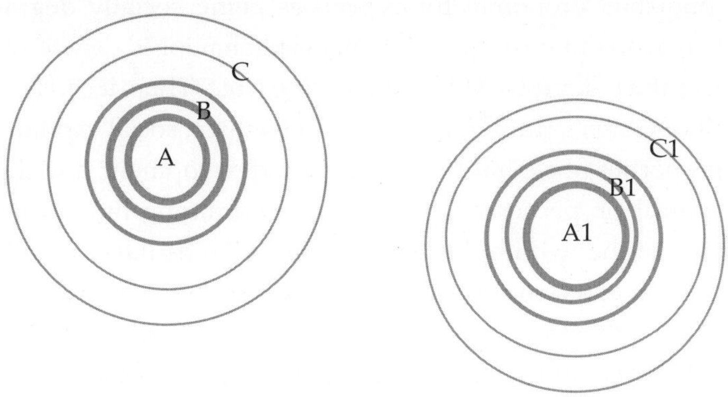

Note: On the left is the order which *A* begins transactions. It assumes a concentric pattern with *A* being the center. The further away, the weaker. Kinship circles which are closer to the center represent the kinship *A* knows better. On the right are *B*'s kinship circles. Assume *A* and *A*1, *B* and *B*1 are rural households with the same level of risk. As there is the differential mode of association, if the relationship circle of each of them is very distant, or they are not in the core of the relationship circle of each other, *A*'s order of transaction would be *B*>*C*>*A*1, and *A*1's would be *B*1>*C*1>*A*.

Obviously, credibility founded on kinship is a kind of relation credibility, but not contact credibility. The latter is generally regarded as the basis for regulating economic behavior, reducing transaction cost, and expanding the room for transaction in market economy. Then, what role does relationship credit play in economic activities and how does it influence rural households' economic behavior?

Unlike the urban social structure, the rural area system is a typical "acquaintance society." As villagers live in the same geographic community, everyone can accumulate perfect information of one another. Therefore, information asymmetry generally does not exist among rural households. In addition, their belief of the timely return of a loan, which makes it easier to borrow a second time, and the commonly acknowledged moral factors such as face, gratitude, relationships, etc., strongly guide and constrain rural households' behavior.[22]

China's rural households have special trust influenced by traditional culture, which reinforces the build-up of personal credit: they are no longer just individual economic men, but social men in the midst of human relationships and moral evaluation. Genetic and emotional closeness and psychological identity, resulting from relationship credit, resemble the physical property of kinship, which are encoded in the genes of rural households. Once rural households appear as a social man in economic activities, their economic behavior would be regarded as part of their ethics and personality, which would in the end be internalized as social evaluation of individual value. From the perspective of economics, to China's rural households, personal ethical credibility is the basic requirement in a transaction, and they also bear the high cost of betraying ethics: Any dishonest behavior which incurs a breach of promise is treated as an exemplification of the failure of ethics. One will be punished economically as well as being socially degraded. At the same time, in an acquaintance society, dishonest behavior is easy to discover. This further increases the risk probability of betraying trust. Thus, it can be said that the personal credit of China's rural households is an ethical social capital,[23] which has not only the properties of capital for production, development, and accumulation, but also the ethical properties of guiding and restraining human behavior. The combined effects of the two imply that rural households have to highly preserve their personal credit and also spontaneously take up the responsibility of debts.

Without a doubt, the acquaintance community keeps community members in a confined geographic community. The immobility of society—as they live there their whole lives—places them in the repetitive gaming, and, together with the concept of "son paying father's debt," makes the economic activities of rural households not only repetitive gaming but eternal gaming. In such a situation, a participant in a relationship cannot extricate him- or herself from an "embedded" relationship, which gives rise to mutual trust and honesty (Qiu Jianxin and Tong Xing 2006).

This credit mechanism which is deeply rooted in acquaintance society can also work between rural households and financial institutions. The process of rural households' obtaining loans from financial institutions is a long-term repetitive gaming. The transaction is not one-off but repetitive. The process will eventually find an equilibrium solution, which enables both parties to obtain maximum benefits—to long-term partners, fulfilling commitments is a better strategy than betrayal. Only when commitments are fulfilled can there be cooperative surplus. Breaching promise can lose the opportunity to borrow. One would have to bear heavy psychological pressure and be regarded as having little credibility, and even the next few generations may suffer (Kuang Yuanpei and Li Ruifen 2002).

Much empirical research supports the notion that China's rural households are credible. For example, Chinese scholar Mao Yushi expressed in many articles that rural households value credibility most.[24] In August 2005, Pro. Wang Shuguang led the research team of rural cooperative finance of Beijing University to Linfen, Shanxi Province. The staff at the local RCCs held the same point of view: Rural households value their credibility, and as long as they have the ability, they would repay debts. According to our data of 250 RCCs front-line loan officers (those who have direct contract with rural households) in 11 counties of City A, we drew the same conclusion: Over 95% of the loan officers thought that "arrears are not common with rural households." When we asked the loan officers about the sources of risks to issue loans to rural households, many of them quoted Force Majeure and agricultural weakness. Only 7.73% of the loan officers believed that rural households have a "natural tendency to avoid repayment" (see Table 2.11).

Table 2.11. The sources of risk of repayment of agricultural loans

Options	Percentage of loan officers who chose the option
(1) Rural households have a natural tendency to avoid repayment. (Refuse to repay debt even though they are financially capable)	7.73%
(2) The rate of return of agricultural production is low. It is difficult for rural households to repay loans with interest.	21.45%
(3) The agricultural production cycle is long and therefore an easy victim of natural disasters. The possibility of investment failure is high.	44.18%
(4) Rural households who borrow are those with low income and without ability to repay debts.	12.91%
(5) Rural households borrow loans to use in high-risk activities with unstable returns.	13.73%

Note: Data based on a survey of 250 front-line loan officers at RCCs.

In a questionnaire survey on the intention to repay debts of 1,000 rural households conducted in the same period of time, 85% of the rural households expressed the intention to repay debts on time, half of which said they would try to make earlier payments (see Fig. 2.7). From several interviews, we found that many rural households bear heavy psychological burden when they borrow money, which prompts them to repay debts before the loan period ends, and only when the debt is clear can they feel relieved—apparently this idea has been a part of the utility function.

Fig. 2.7. Rural households' intention to repay debt

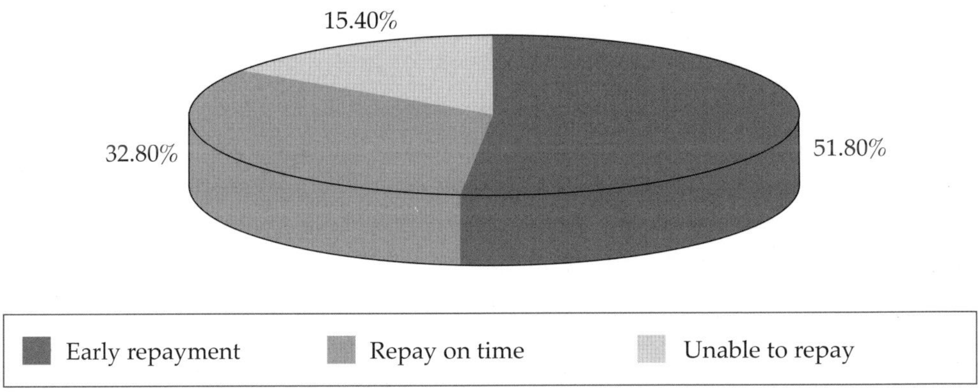

Note: "Unable to repay" refers to the inability to repay on time due to all kinds of reasons, not only deliberately delayed payment.

The above theoretical analysis and empirical results demonstrate that the personal credit of rural households is a kind of moralization of social capital, which reinforces instead of weakens the individual credibility. Therefore, it can be said that rural households, as debtors, have strong credit constraints and willingness to pay.

It should be pointed out that we make the personal credit of rural households a separate discussion because we intend to differentiate that with rural households' social trust. The latter manifests more the intention and ability of credit to extend with the individual and family at the center. This will be discussed in detail in the following section.

Rural households' social credibility: Limited cooperative intentions

We pointed out in the previous section that China's rural households' personal credit as ethical social capital is reinforced in the social relationship network and constraint mechanism. So, can this reinforced individual credibility as self-constraint of rural households evolve into general trust among people? In other words, can individual credibility evolve into general social trust relationships and significantly promote cooperative intentions. The answer is negative.

In China, the trust among rural households is typically "strong inside, weak outside": trust built on the inherited kinship is stronger than that of acquaintance society which is significantly stronger than that among strangers—it is very difficult for China's rural households to extend their trust beyond kinship, and the trust relationship becomes more fragile as risk increases, which represses many external contacts (especially economic activities which are extremely sensitive to transaction cost). To this, Zheng Yefu pointed out that the scale of the social trust system is an important variable that affects trust. The expansion of the trust circle is inversely proportional to the degree of trust. The smaller the scale of the trust system, the stronger the trust among individuals and vice versa.[25] In other words, the strong credibility of China's rural households is only confined to personal level and self-discipline. Since this credit mechanism lacks human interaction, it is based on the self-centered "inward convergence" rather than on the "outward extension" Of mass cooperation. Simply put, the core logic of China's rural households towards credibility is as follows: "I do not violate a contract, but I suspect others would. Therefore, I do not form any contract with others."

Of course, there are complex historical, cultural, and social reasons behind the low social trust of rural households. Weber (1915) pointed out that, in China, trust, as a basis of the buyer-seller relationship, is built on kinship or a kinship-like personal relationship. Because of authoritative dictatorship, conventional dishonesty, and the emphasis of face as advocated by Confucianism, people are generally incredulous. At the same time, the establishment of political and economic organizations relies entirely on individual relationships. All common behavior is surrounded and constrained by pure personal relationships, especially kinship. This skeptical attitude impedes all the credit and business operations. As a result, economic resources are divided into countless small segments. Interactive flow or combination cannot be realized due to high transaction cost. Society cannot enjoy the huge benefits stemming from the extension of cooperation and exchange scope.

Studies have confirmed that incredulity typical among Chinese (Weber 1915). In reality, in a lot of literature such as Smith's *Chinese Characteristics,* Weber's *Confucianism and Daoism,* Gao Weiding's *Chinese Capitalism,* and Fukuyama's *Trust: The Social Virtues and the Creation of Prosperity,* all regard China as a country with low credibility.

In order to gain a general understanding of Chinese rural households' social trust and cooperative intentions, we conducted a survey on the cooperative behavior of rural households in 11 counties in City A. We found that rural households produced with a family as a unit. Joint production was rare even among relatives and much rarer among non-relative families. The same conclusion was reached in our survey of 250 RCC front-line loan officers in 11 counties in City A (see Table 2.12).

Table 2.12. Rural households' cooperative intentions

Question and options	Percentage of loan officers who chose the option
Question: In your county, is there any self-organized cooperative production (e.g., joint farming and animal husbandry, joint contract, joint business, etc.) among rural households?	
(1) Universal	6.00%
(2) Quite a number	8.00%
(3) A small number	55.09%
(4) Almost none	30.91%

Note: Survey results are from 250 loan officers.

Arrow (1962) believed that interpersonal general trust is the lubricant of the construction and operation of society and economy, and an essential factor in transaction. The lack of trust can explain the suffering economies in many places around the world. Fukuyama (1995) categorized culture/society into high credibility and low credibility: In the culture/society with high credibility, self-initiated social contact is common. There are man organizations which are at the middle of society. Large-scale organizations with high centripetal force can be developed by citizens without the help of the government. In contrast, in the culture/society with low credibility, people rarely initiate contact. Without the powerful and centralized government, citizens can hardly develop efficient large-scale organizations. Clearly low social trust among China's rural households directly caused low cooperative intentions. Any economic behavior within the cooperative framework faces a very high cost of organization and coordination. In this situation, low social trust and low cooperative intentions inevitably cause the following: Either cooperative organizations cannot be set up or they would go bankrupt. This situation determines the restrictions of extending the "horizontal credibility" initiated and promoted by rural households. The cooperative financial organizations deriving from rural households or rural economy would be an extremely long process, if not impossible.

So, under such a situation, can we rely on external force, such as the powerful state, to accelerate the growth of "horizontal credibility"? In China, there are two typical cases: First is the RCCs and second is the co-guarantee agricultural loans. The former is a result of compulsory institutional arrangement of government. RCCs are not initiated by members who see the need of cooperative credit, and rural households are "forced" to cooperate. Therefore, RCCs eventually suffer "triple denial"—rural households do not acknowledge RCCs as their organizations, the government does not recognize RCCs as official financial institutions, the staffs of RCCs do not acknowledge RCCs as organizations of rural households (Han Jun 1998). Xie Ping (2001) stated in his study that rural households have never regarded RCCs as their cooperative financial organizations, but a government department or affiliated institution of the national banks. From the day when the RCCs were established, they have not been cooperative in nature. Co-guarantee loans had garnered international success before being introduced into China. Initially, there were high hopes on these, but in the end it was much said and little done. It did not solve China's rural financial problem as expected. Many studies reported that rural households were not active in participating in the co-guarantee group. In He Guangwen and Li Lili's (2005) survey of rural households, only 38.56% of rural households were willing to join the co-guarantee group, and 61.44% were unwilling. Those who were reluctant to join were mainly afraid that other members of the group were untrustworthy and they themselves would suffer—of the 427 households who were unwilling to participate, 309 chose this option. This cannot be simply interpreted as the unreliability of rural households, and one important reason was rural households were pessimistic towards receiving repayment on time. Actually, we stated in many of our field surveys (seminars) in western areas (Yunnan, Guizhou, and Sichuan Provinces) that both rural households and RCCs were not enthusiastic toward co-guarantee loans. (Micro-)Credit directly targeted to individual rural households was more popular.[26] National statistics of the actual amount of loan also support the claim (see Table 2.13).

Table 2.13. Balance of loans of RCCs' agricultural loans, rural micro-credit, and co-guarantee agricultural loans

Year	Agricultural loans (RMB100 million)	Rural micro-credit (RMB100 million)	Co-guarantee agricultural loans (RMB100 million)
2002	3,237.67	745.70	253.33
2003	3,649.75	972.86	385.19
2004	4,731.21	1,678.35	1,389.36
2005	4,989.69	1,578.54	827.67

Source: *China Statistical Yearbook* (2002–2005).

Rural households and the government: Sense of inferiority and strong dependence

Weber (1915) pointed out that in China's development process, the sharpest contrast with the West is the characteristics since the 18th century. Unlike England, the population engaged in agriculture did not reduce but grew and, unlike large-scale agricultural operation in East Germany, the scale of agriculture was small. These two characteristics determined the situation of the rural areas. Obviously, in vast rural areas in China, for a long time, the inherited dispersed family production has led to a dispersed allocation of socioeconomic force. Rural households lack both negotiation and co-guarantee ability.

Undoubtedly, the inefficient social relationships among rural households which are based on small-scale production weaken farmers' negotiation ability to express their desire as an interest group. The ubiquitous power of the government penetrates into the production and life of every household as bureaucracy expands. In modern and contemporary ages, political (administrative) power further destroyed clan force—the only power that can resist the government under feudalism. As a result, a special social structure emerged: Rural households directly face the state, and the state directly controls rural households. In such a situation, even with the smallest desire in economics, the rural households have no choice but to passively seek help from the government (state).

As small farmland operation is continually divided, family structure tends to be smaller. Although the total number of rural households continues to rise, due to the weakening of horizontal contact mechanism among rural households, millions of individual households are surrounded and restricted by ubiquitous administrative force, and they as individuals are so weak and negligible.[27] Against this background, the lack of a unified understanding and tendency towards self-interest and collective actions further weakens their ability in expressing their will as a group. In the social structure, where rural households directly face the state, the continuous weakening of the force of rural households and the constant enhancement of the administrative force eventually lead to the sense of inferiority of Chinese rural households: The government (state) is ubiquitous and supreme and it logically is the natural defender of self-interest.

It should be pointed out that the sense of inferiority of rural households endogenous to China's special political and social structure is manifested as strong dependence on the credit mechanism of the state: Rural households always rely on, or wait, for external help to improve their situation—Chinese rural households always await the help of the government. They reckon it is only logical to wait and hope.

In a questionnaire survey of 1,100 rural households, we asked the subjects to rank the most trustworthy and dependable units (the state, central government, local government, township government, village committee, and production team). Over 80% of them ranked the state or the central government first, when they were asked to rank the most helpful units. Only 60% ranked the state or the central government the first (about 40% ranked the village committee and production team the first). The results seem to support the following fact: The help and care from the state could be disappointing, but Chinese famers still show immense reverence for the supreme political authority and bestow the greatest trust upon the state (central government) even though sometimes the concept of the state is too vague, not as concrete as the production team.

Table 2.14. The results of the survey of 1,100 rural households on the trustworthiness of the state

Questions and options	Percentage of rural households who chose the option
Question: Rank the most trustworthy and dependable units in descending order.	
(1) The state (central government), local government (township government), village committee (production team)	57.8%
(2) The state (central government), village committee (production team), local government (township government)	25.8%
(3) Village committee (production team), local government (township government), the state (central government)	16.4%
Question: Rank the most helpful units in descending order.	
(1) The state (central government), local government (township government), village committee (production team)	44.0%
(2) The state (central government), village committee (production team), local government (township government)	15.4%
(3) Village committee (production team), local government (township government), the state (central government)	40.6%

In the new era, the sense of inferiority and strong dependence on the government of China's rural households created by long-term dependence remained unchanged. The wish that the government will come to their aid and improve their lives still lives in the hearts of many. This strong sense of dependence hinders marketization and business operation to a certain extent, as anything which involves the government would stimulate the wish of governmental aid of rural households and hence create expectation.

From our studies of towns and counties in Western China, many policy loans failed in the past. Although deliberately delayed repayment and incautious use of loan commonly exist, the cause of failure is not what some scholars claim – farmers' withholding of capital caused inherent flaws, or that credibility is extremely low. The key is that any capital (loan, subsidy, or relief fund) issued by the state (governments at various levels) is treated the same by rural households—to those who have a strong sense of dependence, it is a "gift" from the government, and it needs not be repaid.[28] In our studies, one Township Secretary of the Communist Party who had witnessed multiple failures of policy loans pointed out: "Loans to rural households cannot be done through government at various levels. As long as loans are issued from the government, rural households treat them as subsidies, use them without much consideration, and refuse to repay regardless of their financial ability."

Of course, to rural households who are constantly in lack of material capital, the strong sense of dependence gives rise to a wish for national financial aid. Once the expectation of national capital need not be repaid, many rural households will take corresponding actions. Regardless of the actual usage condition of the capital, it would become a bad debt. The intriguing thing is that whatever reasons that have caused collective arrears of the rural household, in the end, the state would grant exemption.[29] As a result, the wish of rural households is realized, and national loan fails to perform its duty. It is clear that in a social structure, where rural households directly face the state, the inferior rural households have a strong and natural tendency to depend on the state, and the superior state develops a tendency to help the rural households. With both tendencies, the national agricultural loan could "mutate" from loans that have to be repaid to bad debt that can be exempted—in nature, a transfer payment of capital from the government to the rural households.

Rural household's risk-bearing: Demonstration effect

In the long history of agricultural civilization, typical small farmers in China started learning the popular agricultural expertise at a very young age. They internalized the basic knowledge of agricultural economics which is passed down through generations as their own human capital. In the process, they relied on mechanical imitation to form their knowledge, which gradually became deeply rooted in their cognitive system. This cognition concept was passed down through generations and externalized as habits, dominating everyday farming and social interactions.

On the basis of the lack of material capital, the conservative mind, together with old habits and the inherited knowledge, strongly influences the behavior of China's rural households. This is especially noticeable in their decision-making process in accepting new knowledge (technology): under asymmetric information, human behavior is externalized as habits. The motivation to adopt new technology is heavily repressed; when rural households are not sure whether new technology would bring them profits, they generally wait and observe, instead of actively taking risks.

In such a situation, self-motivated technological innovation is almost entirely repressed. Any new technology would require demonstration before being adopted: Only when some rural households have received significant economic benefits by using the new technology, will others follow in their footsteps, which in turn slowly reforms agricultural technology and expands reproduction. We call this the demonstration effect among rural households. Apparently, the demonstration effect is a self-initiated risk-relief mechanism emerging from low risk-bearing ability.

In order to conduct an initial empirical study of the demonstration effect among rural households, we set the following questions in our questionnaire: "In the same village, if some households receive high returns through investment (e.g., planting or nurturing a new product), other households will: (1) Learn from the experience and follow suit; (2) Continue with their own production (never mind the low returns); (3) if only a few households receive more returns through new production, others will observe for the time being; if more and more households receive more returns through the same new production, almost every household will imitate." Options (1) and (3) manifest the demonstration effect among rural households, while option (2) does not.

Our results obtained from the survey of 250 RCC front-line loan officers in 11 counties in City A, 48.47% chose (1), 46.53% chose (3), and only 5% chose (2). The results support the notion that demonstration effect exists among rural households.

Fig. 2.8. The demonstration effect among rural households

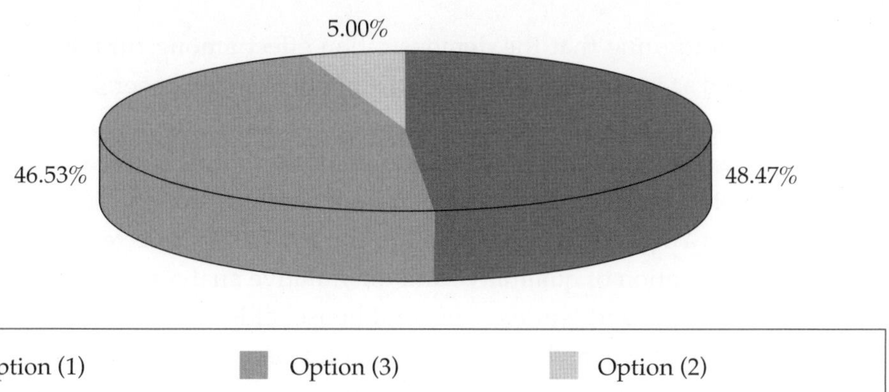

It is worth noting that while both options (1) and (3) represent the tendency to follow and imitate (demonstration effect), there are differences between the two, as (3) implies a rational and meticulous decision, not mere imitation. According to this, we can further classify the demonstration effect: option (1) represents direct imitation, and option (3) careful imitation. Clearly, compared to direct imitation, careful imitation represents a more rational investment decision. Using the above classification, we discovered in our further study that in regions where there was a better social credibility system, the proportion of subjects who chose careful imitation is higher than direct imitation (see Fig. 2.9). This signifies that as regional social credibility develops, rural households would be more rational in their decisions of production and investment.

Fig. 2.9. The social credibility level and the imitation mode of rural households

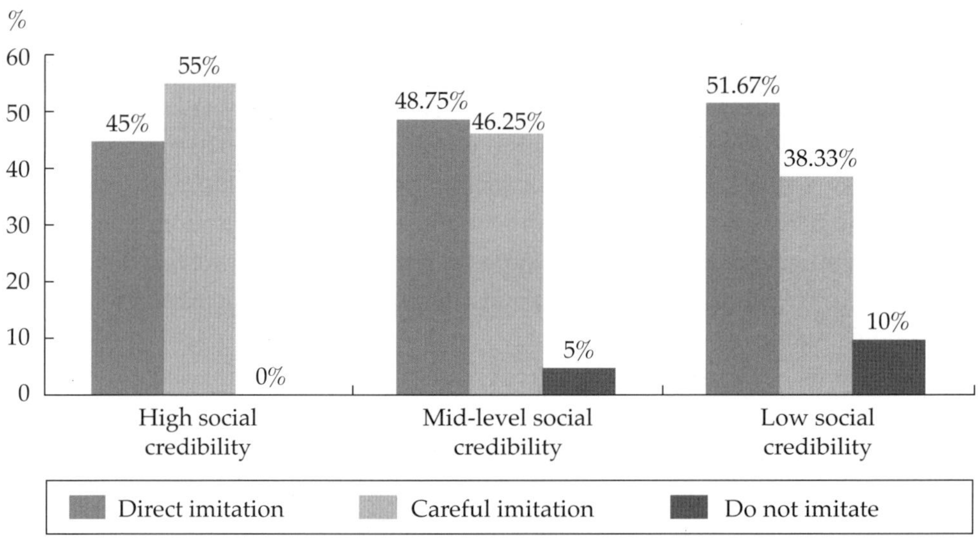

It is very intriguing that the demonstration effect among rural households is also manifested as the power of example. Different from the general demonstration effect, the "example effect" based on typical role model can be realized by a single person or organization with good reputation and exemplary force. The example effect commonly exists in agricultural production and the daily life in China's rural areas. Tan Ying, Wang Dehai, and Xie Yongcai (2004) collected firsthand data using the combination of qualitative and quantitative analyses, and evaluated the information channel and tendency of rural households in China, especially those in mid-west regions where the economy was underdeveloped. The results showed that rural talents (opinion leaders) play an important role in the transmission of scientific information—although rural households can receive scientific information from mass media, many relatively better-off households (opinion leaders) can influence or even determine the attitudes toward scientific information of general households (low- and middle-income households). The results also showed that opinion leaders of a village (rural talents) usually have a more stable income and are financially better-off, such as village cadres, rural households of large-scale production or cultivation, heads of rural enterprises, businessmen, etc.

Fig. 2.10. Results of participatory rural appraisal

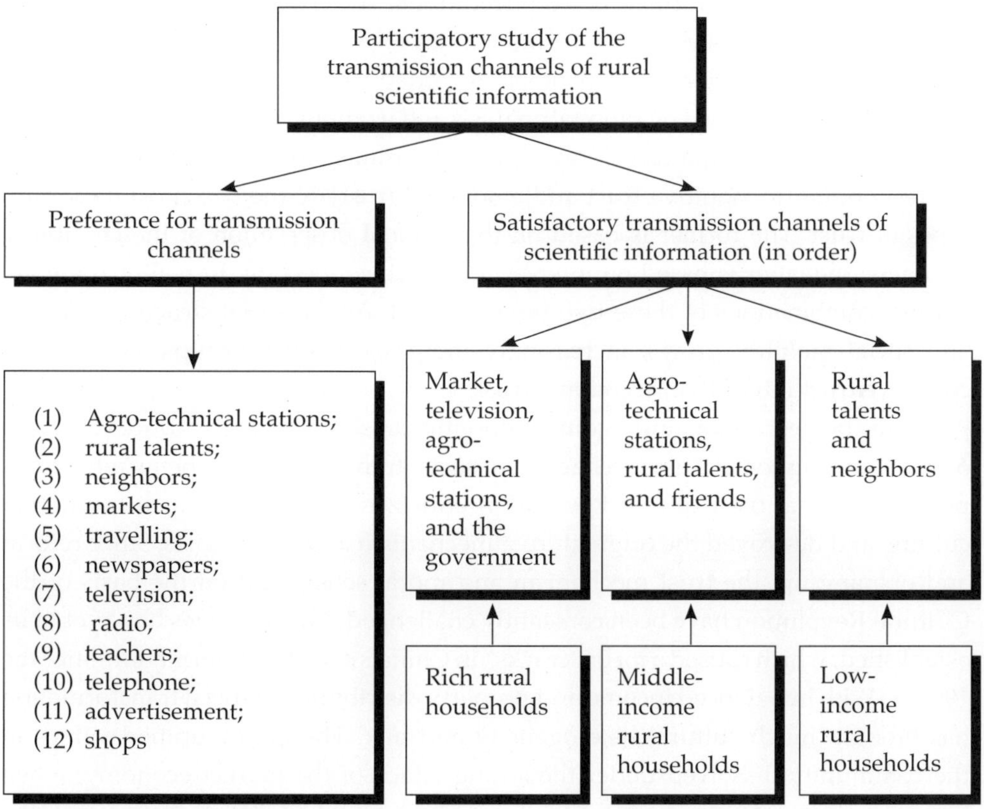

Source: Tian Yin et al. (2004).

Rural households' credibility in a transforming society

Summarizing the analyses of previous sections, the following are the typical structural attributes of trust relationships in China's rural society as they have evolved over the years: (1) Social relations are built on the basis of self-interest. (2) Kinship dominates and constrains trust relationships. The closer to the central kinship, the higher the degree of trust is. (3) Social trust concentrates around kinship. Outside the core circles of friends and relatives, high credibility among members is replaced by low credibility.

We repeatedly stress that high credibility exists between the small realms of kinship and is difficult to extend, but interpersonal relationships are more than kinship. Many complex relationships are formed around kinship. According to Huang Guangguo (1998), interpersonal relationships can be categorized into expressive ties, mixed ties, and instrumental ties. Generally speaking, in traditional society, expressive ties play the main role; in market economy, instrumental ties dominate; in the transformation from traditional society to market economy, the interactions of expressive and instrumental ties give rise to a variety of mixed ties. J. D. Lewis, A. Weigert, and many others regarded trust as interpersonal attitudes, which are co-determined by rational analysis and irrational emotions. They thought that rationality and emotions are two important dimensions of interpersonal trust. Correspondingly, cognitive trust and emotional trust are the two most important types of trust. The former is based on the rational observation of the credibility of others; the latter is based on intense emotional connection. In reality, there are various combinations of these two types of trust. As the social structure changes and social mobility grows, increasingly more social relationships are built on cognitive trust rather than emotional trust.

As the biggest nation undergoing economic transition, China also faces the issue of restructuring social trust mechanism in social transformation. Zheng Yefu (2001) pointed out that the Cultural Revolution criticized and denied much traditional culture, and destroyed the original trust mechanism and moral basis. Since reform and opening up, the trust mechanism and moral sense built on the basis of the Cultural Revolution have been constantly challenged. The new ones have yet to be established, which caused a lot of "cracks" in China's social transformation since the 1990s.[30] With imbalanced income and property distribution,[31] social transformation has brought much cultural heterogeneity and mix. The highly unified values in the community dissolved under the strong attack of the market economy; when the restructuring of society is driven by interest, people neither identify with the original social structure and its cultural norms, nor are they prepared to accept the new social structure and norms (Qiu Jianxin and Tong Xing 2006). Many facts showed that society in China is in the midst of complex mixed ties, which signifies the middle phase of transition. It implies that changes are brewing and underway.

Then, what changes are expected of the credibility of rural households as social transformation continues to deepen?

As part of social transformation, it is impossible for rural society to not be affected. In reality, "anonymous society" brought about by market development rocked the traditional "acquaintance society": As interpersonal trust in rural areas depends, to a large extent, on the long-term stable relationships in the village, changes brought about by the continuous development of the market economy – high mobility of population, globalization of commercial relationships, increasingly complicated transactions – have broken down the traditional social structure in rural areas. The originally smooth-running interpersonal trust mechanism faces unprecedented challenges. In such a situation, on the one hand, the strong and stable interpersonal relationships of rural households in the acquaintance network may dissolve and trust relationships revolving around kinship may be weakened as families are separated or migrate. On the other hand, if contract credit, growing along with the market mechanism, can develop and progressively expand its application, it can compensate for the absence of institutions as relationship credit weakens, and a new form of credibility based on contract can emerge. Here, we must pay attention to the following: the realization of contract credit relies heavily on institutional mechanisms, which include expert system, formal institution, and legal system. Yet, given the mixed ties of a transforming society, institutional mechanisms are usually flawed. This signifies that changes on traditional values and interpersonal network brought about by a drastic transformation of society may corrode and impair social trust which is founded on long history and traditions. The personal credit of rural households and social trust simultaneously weaken, and the overall social credibility drops.

To look at the changes of social credibility in a transforming society on a broader level, social credibility based on the interpersonal network can effectively compensate for market failure and government failure. Together with the price (market) and authority (the state), it can also form the basic mechanism which ensures the smooth running of society and encourages economic development. In the transformation from planned economy to market economy, as individual freedom expands, government power diminishes, and market force (price mechanism) is gradually enhanced. As the structural constraints of family and institutional monitoring of the state give way to the market, there would be open variations which lead to the restructuring of personal credit and social trust in a transforming society. In this process, if the credit mechanism which neutralizes conflicts and encourages cooperation cannot operate smoothly, the friction coefficient will grow. The transaction cost of the market participants will rise, leading to low efficiency and distortion of resources allocation.

Summarizing the current situation in China, we believe that although China's rural households have high personal credit and low social trust, as social transformation deepens and market force expands, the transition from kinship credit to contract credit is inevitable. Before the transition ends, high personal credit based on kinship may weaken and be in disorder before a new credit mechanism (such as contract mechanism) is found. At the same time, the social trust of rural households, which is originally constrained by the kinship system and thus difficult to extend, will develop along the track of contract credit motivated under the driving force of the market. But, whether contract credit can replace relationship credit and become a practice deeply rooted in the hearts of rural households requires further observation.

Conclusions about rural households' credibility and risk preference

Summarizing the analyses in previous sections, we arrive at the following basic conclusions about rural households' credibility and risk preference:

(1) China's rural households are self-constrained regarding their personal credit. In rural finance, the risk of a breach of contract is usually due to the agricultural vulnerability. There is no evidence to support the notion that the risk of rural financial operation is mainly from the moral hazard of rural households.

(2) Because general social trust can hardly extend effectively, China's rural households have little intention to cooperate, which constitutes the origin of role dilemma (e.g., RCCs becoming uncooperative) and operation dilemma (e.g., difficulties in forming co-guarantee groups). It is expected that there will be cooperation dilemma in the development of rural finance before the concept and practice of contract credit is rooted in the mind of rural households. In addition, the lack of social trust has negative effects on general social cooperative activities (including economic activities).

(3) In the social structure, where rural households directly face the state, the inferior rural households have developed dependence on the state, while the state has developed a tendency to help rural households. When both tendencies interact, the national agricultural loan could "mutate." Therefore, loans and relief funds must be distinguished in rural finance: on the one hand, agricultural loans (regardless of the source of capital, including policy loans) should be managed and issued by special financial institutions, instead of the governments at various levels. On the other hand, rural households should be educated about discount policy loans which are different as the national relief funds. They are not supposed to be used in an arbitrary and non-refundable way. It is important to cultivate the concept of loans needing to be repaid and used with caution, or else policy loans would continue to fail.

(4) The lack of human capital of China's rural households is great, and their risk-bearing ability is very low. Therefore, the self-motivation to reform agricultural technology is almost entirely repressed, and any promotion of

new technology requires demonstrations. The demonstration effect is a self-initiated risk-relief mechanism emerging from low risk-bearing ability. Under the constraint of low risk-bearing ability and little self-motivation to reform, it is worth exploring whether agricultural technology would be developed faster by the external force of demonstrations (this is equivalent to actively taking up the risk of trying of rural households in the face of uncertainties).

(5) As a whole, China's rural households have high personal credit and low social trust. As social transformation deepens and market force expands, the transition from kinship credit to contract credit is inevitable. In this process, the key to the transformation of rural households' credibility is to effectively direct and promote the expansion and deepening of contract credit.

Major Conclusions and Policy Implications

(1) The character of rural financing demand can be summarized as follows: Loans for agricultural production are highly seasonal and periodic; most agriculture-related financing demand is timely; the use of loans is closely related to the economic foundation; the transaction cost is high; and collaterals are unconventional.

(2) Rural households prefer formal loans in financing. However, due to the difference in the accessibility of formal credit, the actual financing order may vary in different regions. The convenience and ease in obtaining loans is a major factor that influences rural households' financing preference.

(3) Rural households are insensitive to the changes in loan interest rate, but are obviously less tolerant toward a high loan interest rate.

(4) Contract receives a low status in borrowing among rural households, and relationship loans rely mainly on social constraints. Although the formal market contractual mechanism is not well-established, at least, up to now, social constraints in the rural network still well restrain and protect the credit and debt relationship. Further analysis shows that as the economy develops, more and more rural households will adopt the contractual measures which are marketized and standard.

(5) Simply using the level of dominant capital, such as no guarantee and no collateral, cannot judge the ability of repaying debts, or the effectiveness of demand, which is the main reason why formal financial institutions cannot reach the low-end rural market.

(6) Modern credit techniques, based on mortgage, guarantee, and cash flow do not suit the low-end rural market. Specific credit technologies and services need to be developed for the credit supply and financial services in the low-end rural credit market.

(7) Empirical research showed that what represses rural households' demand for credit is the status of initial resources; what affects the choices of financing channels is the balance of costs; what prevents production expansion are the opportunities and abilities to invest.

(8) China's rural households have strong personal credit, and the default risk is mainly resulting from the agricultural vulnerability. There is no clear evidence to prove that the financial risk in rural areas is due to moral hazard.

(9) The high personal credit of China's rural households does not extend outward, which constitutes low social cooperation incentive. The lack of social trust has negative effects on general social cooperative activities (including economic activities).

(10) To develop rural finance, loans and relief funds must be distinguished: Agricultural loans (regardless of the source of capital, including policy loans) should be managed and issued by special financial institutions instead of governments at various levels. Moreover, rural households should be educated about discount policy loans which are different from the national relief funds. The former are not to be used in an arbitrary and non-refundable way. It is important to cultivate the concept that loans need to be repaid and used with caution.

(11) As there is a shortage of material capital, rural households are not sure that new technology would bring them in return, so they generally wait and observe, and seldom actively accept risk. The demonstration effect is a self-initiated risk-relief mechanism emerging from low risk-bearing ability. This implies that the government, social organizations, or rural talents may play a special role in the technology diffusion in rural society.

(12) As the structural constraints of family and institutional control of the state give way to the market, there will be open variations which lead to the restructuring of personal credit and social trust in a transforming society. In this process, the key to the transformation of rural households' credibility is to effectively direct and promote the expansion and deepening of contract credit.

Feature 2–1
The Development of Credit Techniques Specific to the Low-End Market—A Case Study of Microcred

On December 15, 2007, MicroCred Nanchong (otherwise known as MicroCred) opened as the first foreign-owned microloan company. Located in Guangcai Market in Jialing District of Nanchong, Sichuan Province, MicroCred is a non-financial institution which is invested in, and established by, enterprise legal persons and other social organizations. The company does not accept deposits and is a limited company specializing in microloans.

(1) Structure of shareholders. France's MicroCred Group (holding 67% of the shares)[32] was the main sponsor. Together with International Finance Corporation (holding 15% of the shares) and Germany's KFW Bankengruppe (holding 18% of the shares) established MicroCred China Limited in Hong Kong. MicroCred China fully sponsored the setting up of "MicroCred" with HKD55 million in registered capital. According to regulations on foreign investment administration, capital funds must be collected within two years. By the end of June 2009, "MicroCred" had HKD48.6 million of capital.

(2) Administrative structure. Abiding by international custom, "MicroCred" set up a board of directors and a board of supervisors. Both boards have practical experiences in microcredit and are therefore able to offer professional guidance and make decisions on the sustainable development of the company. The management team has practical experience in international finance, microcredit, and company administration and operation. "MicroCred" adopts a vertical organizational structure (Fig. 2.11). They plan on setting up 11 departments, including strategic development planning, operations, product development, and risk management departments. The company is at the initial stage of development, and the scale of operation is small. To minimize administrative cost and guarantee the efficiency of administration, eight major departments (including accounting, risk control, credit, and legal departments, etc.) have been set up to satisfy the initial administration needs.

Fig.2.11. Administrative structure of MicroCred

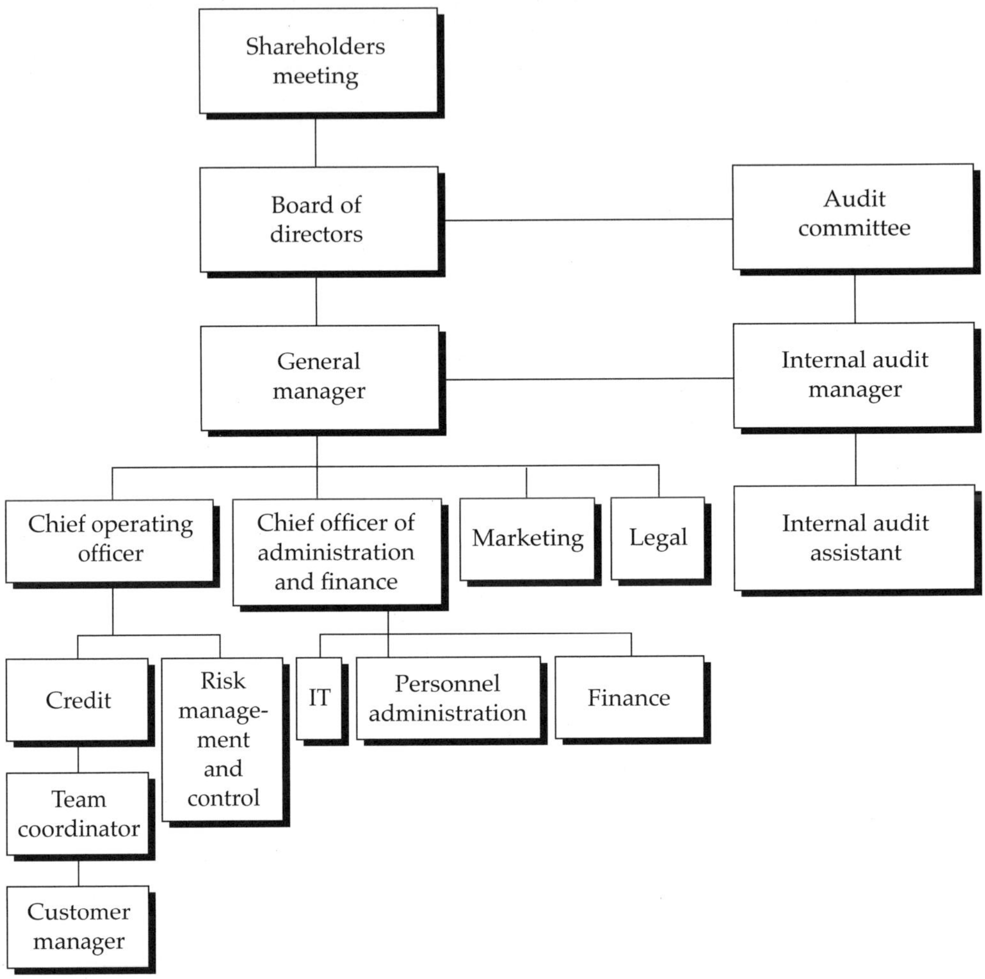

(3) Human resources management. By June 2009, there were 55 employees at "MicroCred," of which 3 were senior managers and 31 were customer managers. Apart from the management team and independent internal auditors, who were assigned by the headquarters of MicroCred in France, other employees were employed through open recruitment (90% were employed in Nanchong). Newly employed customer managers are required to undergo basic training for three months. They learn administrative techniques of microcredit, and cultivate communication skills and team-based cooperation skills. Those who pass the exam would take part in a one-month internship. Afterwards, those who do not acquire satisfactory market development ability, coordination and communication skills, and team-based cooperation

skills would be eliminated (about 20%). Those who pass the exam would form teams of 5–6 people and develop business in different sub-areas. After the tough training and selection process, the customer managers are generally equipped with learning ability, execution ability, and team spirit. MicroCred regards them as the basis of the development of the microcredit business.

(4) Design of incentive scheme. The incentive scheme of MicroCred was formed by three basic parts. First is incentive pay. The salary of customer managers is made up of fixed wage and floating wage. Floating wage is determined by the growth of microcredit sales and the volume of microcredit under one's management. That means a growth in microcredit or the number of clients can lead to a higher salary; the other way round, a growth in credit risk would harm one's salary and chances of promotion. The income level of customer managers is relatively high in the local area, which motivates them to work hard. Second is occupational planning. It adopts staff level management at three levels: junior, middle, and senior. Sales are considered in the annual appraisal, in which promotion and salary are reviewed. Titles of employees are categorized into technical and managerial ones. Employees of different characters both have development space. Third is the team spirit. The business of MicroCred is developed by a team in every sub-area. Communication and cooperation among customer managers contributes to better customer identification and risk management. Every month there is a budget for developmental training for all employees. Annual appraisal focuses on team rewards. The above measures cultivate team spirit and prompt employees to communicate.

(5) Service scope and price. MicroCred offers two types of loans: microloan and small enterprise loan. The microloan limit is RMB5,000–75,000, while the small enterprise loan limit is RMB100,000–300,000. The loan period lasts from three months to eighteen months. It provides working capital and investment capital (for investment in fixed assets). Currently, MicroCred offers four credit products: monthly matching of the repayment of principal and interest, and repayment of principal on the due date with monthly repayment of interest, quarterly repayment of principal with monthly repayment of interest, and parallel loan. Compared to traditional financial services, these products are more specific. The procedure to obtain loans is quick, simple, and flexible. MicroCred follows market price principles in determining the interest rate which covers the risk and cost. Amortizing loans account for 80% of the balance of loans. Using equal repayment of principal and interest, there is a higher efficiency of cash flow. The interest rate for this type of loan is 1.1%. At issuance, a one-off administration fee accounting for 1% of the total amount

of loan is required. The actual annualized interest rate reaches 23.06%. The single-repayment loans account for 20% of the balance of loans. The monthly interest rate is 1.6%, and the actual annualized interest rate is 19.2%.

(6) Credit risk management. Microcredit has the following features: readily available, broad business scope, huge total volume, and small credit line. The major risks include credit risk, moral hazards, and operational risk. In order to effectively manage and control risks, MicroCred implemented an all-round risk management system. First, it pays attention to the development and application of Management Information System (MIS). It monitors the actual loan quality of customer managers and the repayments of clients, which effectively raise the operation efficiency and risk management quality of the company. Second, the system is used to recruit a professional team of customer managers. Those who have passed the tough training program and selection process have mastered basic microcredit techniques and acquired learning ability. They can accurately determine the clients' repayment ability, identify and select clients, and effectively control credit risk. Third the system separates the loan approval from the loan administration. Customer managers are responsible for loan sales and track management. Credit approval is the responsibility of the risk management department. Three-tier management is carried out based on the loan volume with the adoption of one ticket veto. Fourth is the regulation of after-loan management. Risk management officers and customer managers would issue a notice of loan repayment and collect repayments at clients' homes. The legal department keeps track of the entire credit operation process and offers legal advice to lower legal risk. The legal department assists in the collection of the repayment of loans that have been overdue for 25 days. It will issue a letter of loan repayment or a letter of legal advice. The legal department takes legal actions against clients who deliberately delay repayments to ensure that all loans are collected.[33] Fifth, the system is used to adopt conservative financial management strategies. Late payment of one day is considered as a non-performing loan. Late payment of more than 180 days is considered a bad debt. These bad debts are offset by reserves and profits. The actual financial situation and assets are reflected to guarantee the stable operation of the company.

(7) Internal control unit. Following the management principles of well-established international firms, MicroCred set up an independent internal control unit. First there is the vertical organizational structure of internal audit. The headquarters of France's MicroCred Group set up an audit committee, which reports directly to the Board of Directors. The committee appoints internal audit assistants to MicroCred. They are responsible for

supervising and auditing the daily operations of the company. They report directly to the committee. Additionally, the committee appoints an audit team to Nanchong to conduct a special audit of the operation of the company. Second, there is a professional external audit. The Board of Directors employs professional accounting firms to conduct an external audit on MicroCred. The report is shared with shareholders. Third there is a continuous refinement of the internal management system. MicroCred has established various internal management systems, which are refined according to the actual situation. For example, the paid-leave system requires employees who have been employed for more than six months to take annual leave every year. General employees are granted five days and managers nine days of annual leave. This measure can relieve the pressure on employees as well as reveal the existing problems in the employees' work.

As a whole, MicroCred targets the clients who are ignored by formal financial institutions and adopts a differentiation strategy. It identified the entry point in the market and has an all-round management structure and an internal control structure. Adopting commercial operations, it does not enjoy any tax reduction or preferential policy, thus it is able to sustain its development. In summary, the success of MicroCred is due to certain unique features which make the company different from traditional financial institutions:

(1) MicroCred targets clients who are regarded by traditional financial institutions as risky and unsuitable for loans, and specializes in developing credit techniques specific to that market. The techniques focus on evaluating the risk of the client and implementing real-time dynamic risk management of a large number of minor client groups. These credit techniques used in developing the low-end market are clearly different from those used by the general financial institutions, which should be seen as "specific credit techniques." Currently, most financial institutions (including rural and village and township banks, loan agencies, cooperatives, and many newly set up rural financial institutions) have not mastered or developed such systems and credit techniques.

(2) Marketing, management, and services tailored to the clients. MicroCred encourages customer managers to promote loans at the clients' doorstep. They analyze the clients' future cash flow and evaluate the clients' ability to repay, rather than demanding collateral or guarantee. Moreover, they provide comprehensive services which include financial consultation and market analysis in order to connect with the clients. Credit management is treated as continuous follow-up, which is different from that of traditional financial institutions which just focus on three key steps: pre-loan assessment, issuance of loan, collection of loan.

(3) The organizational structure in which members get deeply involved into the market. Of the 55 employees of MicroCred, there are 31 customer managers who directly work with the prospective borrowers and only 3 senior managers, contrary to the ever-growing number of senior managers and administrative officers in the traditional financial institutions. The international experience with microcredit shows that a professional microcredit officer can manage more than 200–250 clients. Currently, a customer manager of MicroCred on average can manage 120 clients, and the best one can manage around 160 clients. Unlike the managers at traditional financial institutions, these customer managers visit villages very often rather than sit in the office to manage loans.

(4) Active to achieve independent sustainable development. Without policy subsidy, MicroCred not only maintains its break-even status, but also gains continuous profit. Under a suitable system and good management, rural finance can attain commercial sustainability. There are international examples that many microcredit banks do not need government subsidy. They even manage to obtain high profits. The rate of return of the top 10 microcredit or small-scale financial banks is much higher than that of the best commercial banks in the world. According to the statistics of International Finance Corporation, as of the end of 2007, a single loan on average amounted to between USD288 to USD1,164. From 2002 to 2007, the growth rate of the number of borrowers rose from 10% to 25%.

3

Chapter

The Agricultural Loan Market in China's Rural Finance

An effective and all-round market system guarantees an increase in rural income... An effective rural financial market can allocate capital to the project with the greatest potential in production. The reason behind the failure of many rural financial projects can be summarized as the lack of understanding or misinterpretation of the rural financial market, such as asymmetric information, market segmentation, and high risk.

—The World Bank

The Demand-Supply Relationship in the Agricultural Loan Market

The study of the demand and supply relationship in China's agricultural loan market should be against the backdrop of the dispersed small-scale peasant economic structure and with a focus on the economic behavior, internal connections, and conflicts between the supply and demand sides. In this section, we try to construct a basic theoretical framework and reexamine the issue of financial support for China's agricultural development, rural households' credibility, and the agricultural loan market. Apart from including a logical theoretical basis, the study is also supplemented with empirical analysis that is applicable to China.

Classic theories

The analysis of the rural households and their behavior in the small-scale peasant economy is essential to the study of rural households' credibility and the agricultural loan market.[1] From the theoretical point of view, the mainstream schools include Chayanov's Labor-Consumption Equilibrium theory, Neoclassical Economics, and the China Question.

Chayanov's Labor-Consumption Equilibrium theory is essentially social agricultural study,[2] advocating that peasant economy is not the same as the capitalist economy. The former is based on the household labor practicing subsistence farming with a household as the production unit. The farmers carry out farming to achieve the equilibrium between hard work and satisfying the household's consumption needs. Therefore, classical economics is not applicable to the peasant economy. Chayanov was the earliest to abandon the assumption that farmers are economic men and adopted methods of cultural anthropology and economic anthropology to study the practical farmer issues.

The central figures of neoclassical economics in studying small-scale peasant economy are Arthur Lewis, Theodore Schultz, Peter Timmer, etc. Lewis proposed the dual-sector model (agriculture and industry), which regards agriculture as lagging behind. Nobel Prize laureate Theodore Schultz (1964) followed the assumption of economic men and held that agriculture can contribute enormously to economic growth. However, in traditional agriculture, agricultural technology is stagnant, and the marginal returns of the production factors are extremely low. Most labor force is restricted to the simplest labor to maintain lives. Therefore, the key to the issue is how to reform the traditional agriculture. In the discussion of economic reforms, Timmer used Hayami Yujiro and Ruttan's data to illustrate three different pathways for technological reforms: those of Asia, Europe, and America. Newbury and Stiglitz (1974) adopted a new perspective on small-scale peasant economics by taking into consideration the risks and uncertainties in agricultural production.

The school of the China Question refers to scholars who obtain relevant conclusions through field studies. The central figures are Mazar, Tony, Wagner, Ramon Myers, Philip Huang, etc. As one of the most influential Chinese scholars, Huang (1992, 1994) proposed the theory of involution under the premise of overpopulation. He believed that production factors (land and capital), apart from labor, are in shortage. Under the immense pressure of population, the aim of the behavior of China's rural households is to maintain lives instead of maximize profit.

Studies prior to the 1990s have touched on the issues of rural households' credibility and the agricultural loan market in China's rural financial system, but they were rather sporadic and unsystematic. In the past decade, as financial reform accelerates and the Three Rural Issues become more urgent, research on rural finance has become more distinct. In the beginning, research was all about the commercialization of rural financial institutions. Gradually, research touched on rural households' credibility and the system of the agricultural loan market. Representative studies include Lin Yifu, Feder, Lau Juen-yee and Luo Xiaopeng (1989), Xie Ping (2001), Zhang Jun (1999), Wen Tiejun (2004), Zhang Jie (2004, 2005), etc.

Zhang Jie (2005) attempted to offer a long-term perspective on China's agricultural loan system and its difficult development in the thousands of years of China's continuous transformation. The research methodology and theoretical starting point demonstrated that Zhang Jie had abandoned the assumption of economic men of neoclassical economics and developed the Chayanovian idea of survival small famers. According to Zhang, the tradition and culture[3] ingrained in small famers can actually deter the effective combination of rural households with any modern financial systems (especially the commercial formal finance), and the determination and effort of the deciding-making body to reform the current agricultural loan system is doomed to fail.[4]

Theoretical model and deductions

In order to establish the internal connection mechanism which promotes the development of rural households (income rise) among rural households' credibility, the agricultural loan market, and financial support in rural development, we need a basic analytical framework. First, we borrow McKinnon's (1973) model to give some basic descriptions. The model expands the Fisher separation theorem and states that under the condition that the inseparability of investment cannot be neglected, poverty and the lack of financing ability would hinder the innovation of agricultural technology. As internal accumulation is insufficient, external credit can boost consumption and stimulate productivity.

Fig. 3.1 is a two-period Fisher diagram. It sheds light on the problem of allocation of inter-temporal investment and consumption.[5] To explain the inseparability, McKinnon assumed that the internal investment of producers is limited to two different kinds of technology: T_1T_1' represents traditional agriculture technology (investment returns start to diminish at T_1); T_2T_2'represents new technology (technological innovation). Before any product is produced using new technology, there exists an income gap due to the investment needs (T_1T_2), which is related to the early inputs of initial production facilities in order to introduce new technology. Once such an investment is made, the returns of farming will become very high. The returns only diminish progressively when it moves into the second quadrant along T_2T_2'.

Fig. 3.1. McKinnon's model: Traditional investment, technological innovation, and credit support

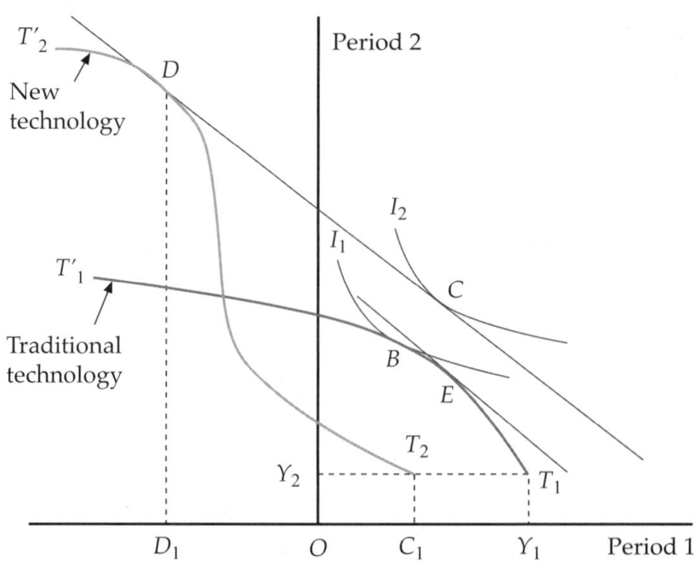

Notes: 1. T_1T_1' represents that a rural household cut down on consumption in period 1 in order to consume more in period 2, under the condition that there has not been an important technological innovation.
2. Y_1 represents the initial capital of the rural household, which includes the left-over consumable capital and the income from period 1. Y_2 represents the natural rise in income of period 2, without deliberate improvement in other areas. The distance from the center axis to Y_1 or T_1 represents the corresponding investment level of initial capital. The slope of T_2T_2' represents the investment returns per USD in the growth of consumable income of period 2 (the extension of the investment into the second quadrant only represents that the opportunities to invest are greater than the capabilities of the current capital of the enterprise).

If producers (rural households) are restricted to internal capital accumulation, with limited initial capital, the choice of technology will deviate. In Fig. 3.1, only when producers employ traditional technology, the values for consumption of both periods 1 and 2 are positive at equilibrium *B*. In contrast, if advanced technology is used in economies of scale, consumption in period 1 must be negative, which is economically impossible. The concave I_1 and I_2 represent the consumption indifference curves of producers. The values of consumption must be positive in both periods. It can be expected that this consumption constraint is severely restricted in an impoverished economy. In the situation represented by Fig. 3.1, the consumption constraint and limited capital confine producers at *B*, at which the technological level is low.

If external loans are obtained, producers at *D* can employ new technology to produce with a higher quality. With improved consumption at *C*, they can breakthrough from traditional production. This is to say that if producers can obtain a desired amount of capital at an interest rate denoted by the slope of line *DC*, this sum of external capital would allow investment in new technology as denoted by Y_1D_1 and increase consumption in period 1. The growth in personal and social productivity would allow the producers to repay the debts on time in period 2. The loan rate represented by the slope of *DC* is greater than the marginal productivity at *B* under the conditions of traditional technology.

It can be seen that McKinnon's model confirms that when inseparability is taken into account, the interactions of the consumption constraint, credit constraint, and stagnant technology would keep rural households at the low-level equilibrium for a long time, at which income, technology, and credibility are low. We can deduce the following from McKinnon's model:

(1) Low income and low credibility interactively lead to the shortage of initial capital and investment of rural households.

(2) A rise in technological level is the key to raising rural households' income. But new technology must be financed by sufficient capital. When rural

households face a shortage of internal capital, obtaining external capital is crucial.

(3) To those rural households who have been investing in technology at a low level, external credit capital can effectively improve their consumption and productivity. So, an increase in agricultural loan can help raise the income of rural households.

(4) Rural households' credibility and the accessibility of external credit (such as the credit from RCCs) are mutually enhancing: Once rural households have solved the problem of initial capital shortage and gradually raise their income level, the continuously increased capital and cash flow would raise their credibility, which results in a virtuous cycle.

We will provide a systematic analysis based on the above deductions from McKinnon's model in the following section.

Empirical analysis

The source of data and assignment of indexes

To avoid the common problems of small sample size and uneven distribution which exist in many early domestic studies, this research satisfies the scientific requirements of statistics in terms of sample size and random sampling. Regarding data collection, basic data were gathered from an actual survey of rural households in City A. We distributed over 1,300 questionnaires, of which 1,100 were returned and qualified for use. Regarding sampling coverage, the qualified questionnaires were evenly distributed among 11 counties, 100 questionnaires from each. So, this study obtained considerable objective and real information with a reasonable sample size and sampling coverage.

From the data we collected, the following variables are mainly used: regional classified index (X_1), total assets index (X_2), arable land per capita index (X_3), income of agricultural production (X_4), income from non-rural jobs (X_5), labor force to household member ratio (X_6), educational level (X_7), level of agricultural technology and knowledge (X_8), other technology and techniques (X_9), loan preference (X_{10}), social relationship capital (X_{11}), consumption or investment preference (X_{12}), and the understanding of policies for agricultural loans (X_{13}). The value of loan preference (X_{10}) is assigned based on the borrowing behavior of rural households in the past three years. If rural households have a stronger preference to borrow loans from banks (RCCs) over private loans, it will be assigned a higher value. The value of consumption or investment preference (X_{12}) is determined by the fund uses. If they utilize more in investment and production expansion rather than savings at banks (RCCs) or consumption, it will be assigned a higher value. The definitions and assignment of values of other variables are stated in Table 2.8.

The results of empirical analysis

We first analyze whether rural households borrow loans (which represents the demand in the agricultural loan market) and the factors which affect their decision. With respect to the duality of explained variables (if rural households have borrowed, it will be assigned value 1; if not, value 0). We employ ML-Binary Probit regression, and the results are shown in Table 3.1.

Table 3.1. The results of regression analysis of the demand in the agricultural loan market

	Whether to borrow money (Y_1)	Whether to borrow money(Y_1)	Whether to borrow money(Y_1)	Whether to borrow money(Y_1)
Constant (C)	–1.218164*** (–4.139892)	–1.258458*** (–4.228992)	–1.431910*** (–4.682996)	–1.585548*** (–5.009396)
Regional classified index (X_1)	0.332911*** (3.189307)	0.335095*** (3.208193)	0.367181*** (3.409300)	0.351204*** (3.246274)
Total assets index (X_2)	0.049407 (0.988785)	0.049442 (0.989410)	0.003322 (0.064440)	–0.015206 (–0.290982)
Arable land per capita index (X_3)	0.049583 (1.274960)	0.053154 (1.358774)	0.046268 (1.163363)	0.027348 (0.668581)
Income of agricultural production (X_4)	0.094392** (1.959063)	0.098631** (2.027738)	0.094520** (1.936464)	0.086434* (1.798732)
Income from non-rural jobs (X_5)	0.038121 (0.730877)	0.040991 (0.784373)	0.024743 (0.461993)	0.027155 (0.507529)
Labor force to household member ratio (X_6)	0.188752 (0.681562)	0.178855 (0.652969)	0.214008 (0.715847)	0.253636 (0.830098)
Educational level (X_7)	–0.188399*** (–4.783078)	–0.179140*** (–4.406210)	–0.169432*** (–4.169421)	–0.182825*** (–4.434823)
Level of agricultural technology and knowledge (X_8)	–0.103671 (–1.630394)	–0.091104 (–1.400360)	–0.143558** (–2.166086)	–0.173794** (–2.550555)
Other technology and techniques (X_9)	0.106255 (1.308116)	0.112098 (1.377092)	0.089322 (1.072834)	0.078332 (0.940291)

(Cont'd)

	Whether to borrow money (Y_1)	Whether to borrow money(Y_1)	Whether to borrow money(Y_1)	Whether to borrow money(Y_1)
Loan preference (X_{10})	0.653442*** (12.72598)	0.657209*** (12.73591)	0.624045*** (11.98348)	0.621007*** (11.91185)
Social relationship capital (X_{11})	—	–0.033221 (–0.893801)	—	—
Consumption or investment preference (X_{12})	—	—	0.236248*** (6.098050)	0.238816*** (6.133186)
The understanding of policies for agricultural loans (X_{13})	—	—	—	0.161806** (2.150058)
McFadden R^2	0.215255	0.215981	0.251437	0.255690

Notes: 1. The bracketed value is the z-value.
2. *at 10% confidence level, **at 5% confidence level, ***at 1% confidence level.

The above results show that apart from educational level which has a negative effect on rural households' demand for loan, other factors including the type of regional economy, income of agricultural production, loan preference, consumption or investment preference, and the understanding of policies for agricultural loans all have a positive effect on the demand for loans (the significance level of most variables is higher than 1%). The results illustrate that the probability to borrow is higher when the following occur: (1) the rural households is in a better regional economy; (2) a higher income of agricultural production exists; (3) a higher rank of formal financial institutions in the desired financing order of rural households; (4) a larger part of loans invested in production expansion or commercial investment; and (5) a better understanding of the policies for agricultural loans. But the higher the educational level is, the lower the borrowing probability.

In the following, we will analyze the supply side in the agricultural loan market (factors which affect the line of credit of banks). The results of OLS regression analysis are shown in Table 3.2.

Table 3.2. The regression analysis of the supply in the agricultural loan market

	Actual line of credit (Y_2)	Actual line of credit (Y_2)	Actual line of credit (Y_2)	Actual line of credit (Y_2)
Constant (C)	–0.173390 (–0.731905)	–0.397526 (–1.557338)	–0.204516 (–0.797064)	–0.228760 (–0.887996)
Regional classified index (X_1)	0.336221*** (3.964069)	0.334517*** (3.951835)	0.322032*** (3.836096)	0.322293*** (3.839369)
Total assets index (X_2)	0.340546*** (8.143563)	0.323360*** (7.629930)	0.314311*** (7.473887)	0.307290*** (7.216399)
Arable land per capita index (X_3)	0.105691*** (3.356365)	0.107036*** (3.405384)	0.090140*** (2.872755)	0.089819*** (2.862519)
Income of agricultural production (X_4)	0.056375** (2.291147)	0.053807** (2.189004)	0.052040** (2.135691)	0.052526** (2.155333)
Income from non-rural jobs (X_5)	0.162277*** (3.827631)	0.167891*** (3.961659)	0.157549*** (3.745139)	0.156273*** (3.713435)
Labor force to household member ratio (X_6)	–0.218898 (–1.054635)	–0.249848 (–1.203719)	–0.250204 (–1.216153)	–0.250448 (–1.217397)
Educational level (X_7)	0.158781*** (3.721416)	0.161418*** (4.721116)	0.123603*** (3.540993)	0.129089*** (3.629848)
Level of agricultural technology and knowledge (X_8)	0.102263* (1.935741)	0.104875** (1.988761)	0.051634 (0.963699)	0.047024 (0.874749)
Other technology and techniques (X_9)	0.227153*** (3.422549)	0.221708*** (3.345201)	0.187227*** (2.831044)	0.186501*** (2.820048)
Loan preference (X_{10})	—	0.106203** (2.328916)	0.097976** (2.165859)	0.090665** (1.980947)
Social relationship capital (X_{11})	—	—	0.138615*** (4.520981)	0.136955*** (4.461085)
Consumption or investment preference (X_{12})	—	—	—	0.030811 (1.048697)
Adjusted R^2	0.201560	0.204791	0.218749	0.218821

Notes: 1. The bracketed value is the z-value.
2. *at 10% confidence level, **at 5% confidence level, ***at 1% confidence level.

From the results above, it can be seen that the line of credit given to rural households by banks (RCCs) is significantly and positively affected by the type of regional economy, total assets of the household, arable land per capita, income of agricultural production, income from non-rural jobs, educational level, level of agricultural technology and knowledge, other technology and techniques, loan preference, and social relationship capital. According to the results of regression analysis, it can be seen that the actual line of credit granted to rural households will rise when the following happen: (1) A better regional economy; (2) greater total assets of the households; (3) greater arable land per capita; (4) higher income of agricultural production or on-rural job; (5) a higher educational level; (6) a higher level of social capital; and (7) higher ranks of formal financial institutions in the desired financing order of rural households. It should be noted that the effect of the knowledge of other technology / techniques (X_9) is significant and stable on the line of credit. But the effect of the knowledge of agricultural technology / techniques (X_8) is unstable. This explains the probable tendency toward non-agricultural production loans when banks (RCCs) decide on the line of credit.

Based on the analyses of the supply and demand sides in the agricultural loan market, we further investigate whether the supply and demand relationship would affect the actual income of rural households. We include Y_1 (whether to borrow) and Y_2 (the actual line of credit) as the explanatory variables of model 3, and apply OLS regression. Results are shown in Table 3.3.

Table 3.3. Regression results of the effects of supply-demand relationship in rural credit on rural households' income

	Annual household income Y_3	Annual household income Y_3	Annual household income Y_3	Annual household income Y_3
Constant (C)	0.168669 (1.084300)	0.071648 (0.449272)	–0.045798 (–0.280444)	–0.053367 (–0.342852)
Regional classified index (X_1)	0.251480*** (4.609835)	0.237793*** (4.350799)	0.221895*** (4.229731)	0.151483*** (2.882737)
Total assets index (X_2)	0.480928*** (17.87988)	0.468665*** (17.21223)	0.460091*** (16.87642)	0.392483*** (14.66193)
Arable land per capita index (X_3)	0.091044*** (4.453659)	0.077899*** (3.710754)	0.075726*** (3.619401)	0.055243*** (2.757042)
Labor force to household member ratio (X_6)	0.157688 (1.172047)	0.164557 (1.226174)	0.141382 (1.055993)	0.172265 (1.349539)
Educational level (X_7)	0.094654*** (4.148699)	0.089104*** (3.899218)	0.100156*** (4.347131)	0.072854*** (3.294581)
Level of agricultural technology and knowledge (X_8)	0.031237 (0.888491)	0.012874 (0.360088)	0.019387 (0.543447)	0.007615 (0.223813)
Other technology and techniques (X_9)	0.155653*** (3.601422)	0.143604*** (3.312884)	0.137863*** (3.190047)	0.095208** (2.300194)

(Cont'd)

	Annual household income Y_3	Annual household income Y_3	Annual household income Y_3	Annual household income Y_3
Social relationship capital (X_{11})	0.086771*** (4.315505)	0.084709*** (4.221110)	0.084802*** (4.242400)	0.055612*** (2.888348)
Understanding of policies of agricultural loans (X_{13})	—	0.104422*** (2.626105)	0.095842** (2.413935)	0.093857** (2.480094)
Loan preference (Y_1)	—	—	0.206889*** (3.099695)	0.191212*** (3.004798)
Consumption or investment preference (Y_2)	—	—	—	0.196382*** (10.51524)
Adjusted R^2	0.366383	0.369792	0.374735	0.431943

Notes: 1. The bracketed value is the t-value.
2. *at 10% confidence level, **at 5% confidence level, ***at 1% confidence level.

From the results above, all factors have a significant effect on the annual income of the households apart from the proportion of labor force in a household and the level of agricultural knowledge. All explanatory variables we included in the model show obvious statistical significance (significance level at 1%). The results answer our question of whether the rural households' demand for loans and their ability to obtain loans can explain the difference of income among households: the stronger the demand, the greater the line of credit, which would help raise the income level.

Further discussion and comments

We systematically examined the various factors affecting the supply and demand in the agricultural loan market through evaluating rural households' credibility and its effect on their income level. The results illustrate the following:

(1) The status of the regional economy (including the overall degree of economic development, development of commercial trade, convenience of transactions, and rural households' awareness of marketization) not only exerts influence on the households' demand for credit but the actual supply of credit from banks (RCCs). In regions with a better economy, the income level of households is generally higher. This shows that improving the overall regional economy can raise the credit and income level of rural households.

(2) The income level of rural households (including both agricultural and non-agricultural income) affects the households' demand for credit. But in contrast, its effect is more significant on the line of credit granted by banks (RCCs). This demonstrates that banks (RCCs) are very concerned about rural households' ability to generate cash flow (this means that those who can generate larger and more stable cash flow will receive more credit support). This also proves that when the aggregate supply of rural finance is insufficient, rural households who are financially better off can more easily obtain credit support from banks (RCCs) during credit allocation.

(3) The total assets of the rural households greatly affect the actual line of credit, but only insignificantly the households' demand for credit. This shows that banks (RCCs) are very concerned about the households' assets, collaterals, and guarantee when they issue credit. The degree of richness or poverty of the households has little relation to their demand for credit.

(4) The arable land per capita index significantly affects the banks (RCCs)' supply of credit and the income level of rural households. This again proves that when there is a serve shortage of capital, land is still a very important form of asset and capital of rural households.

(5) Compared with the level of agricultural technology and knowledge, non-agricultural technology and knowledge would significantly help rural households obtain larger lines of credit and receive more income. This is to say that the main channels for households to increase credit and income are to extricate themselves from the inefficient traditional agricultural production and increase the returns of non-agricultural production. The results also show that banks (RCCs) are biased toward non-agricultural loans when they determine the line of credit for rural households.

(6) When there is a shortage of dominant capital deposit, potential capital of rural households may influence their credit. We discovered from empirical analysis that social relationship capital can significantly affect the ability of the households to obtain credit and their income level. This shows that to gradually extricate from the constraint of the concentric zone[6] and expand the relationship resources of rural households would help them obtain higher credit and earn higher income.

(7) As rural households are becoming better educated, banks (RCCs) increase their line of credit. However, the borrowing tendency of rural households drops. This may be saying that farmers who are better educated have a smaller dependence on credit resources.

(8) Rural households' demand for loans and their ability to obtain loans can explain the difference in income levels among rural households. This indicates:

First, their demand for credit is motivated by profit, and this motivation can help increase their income; second, banks (RCCs) actively support rural credit, which raises rural income through improving the financing and the production of rural households.

Policy recommendations

It can be easily seen from empirical analysis that the four basic deductions we proposed earlier are confirmed. Therefore, it can be concluded that McKinnon's model and our deductions based on the model can explain rural households' credibility and the agricultural loan market in current China.

Based on further study of the results shown in the previous section, we make the following policy recommendations:

(1) At the initial stage of poverty alleviation, national policy-related agricultural loans or fiscal subsidies should be immensely effective. Empirical analysis shows that the low income level and the shortage of capital deposit (total assets) are the major reasons why it is difficult for rural households to obtain formal commercial credit. This demonstrates that under asymmetrical information, to improve the services offered by formal financial institutions to rural households requires the demand side (rural households) to raise their credibility such as having stable cash flow and greater amount of total assets. There is a practical problem that to those who are in particular poverty, the over-low initial credibility level creates a dilemma: to breakthrough from poverty, they need credit to develop a new form of production; the banks find it difficult to manage risk so that they do not issue credit to those who have low credibility. Apparently the dilemma is the reason why many rural households have low income and low production level for a long time. We believe that those households who face the dilemma need a sum of initial capital to realize their production transition. When they are unable to accumulate capital or obtain external commercial loans, national policy agricultural loan or fiscal subsidies should come to their aid.[7]

(2) To encourage commercial finance to support the new form of agricultural production. Suitable policy guidance and privileges can be offered. The rise in the income level of rural households depends on the sustainable development of agricultural development, in which process technological advancement (introducing new technology) is crucial. Therefore, the state should on the one hand encourage rural households to develop a new form of production; on the other hand it should guide the financial institutions to provide more credit support and other financial services to this type of production. From

our survey, the adoption of new technology (e.g., to develop cash crop) to produce by rural households can raise the economic efficiency, and the average returns can cover the principal and interest of the loan. From this point of view, this type of loan is economically possible.[8] Moreover, it needs to be pointed out that as the development of the technological ability is constrained by the existing knowledge base (Cohen 1990), as well as the barrier from tacit knowledge (Winter 1982, Kim 1999).[9] Therefore, as China's farmers have a low level of knowledge, both explicit and tacit knowledge must be taught to them in a suitable way, and support must be given to their development of new technology for transforming production. We discovered from our study that in rural China the most effective way to promote technology is to offer the chance of technological imitation to rural households.[10]

Establish and develop "regional financial ecology" with respect to local conditions. We have seen from empirical analysis that the health of the regional economy which the rural households are in can affect the households' demand for credit as well as the actual credit supply of the financial institutions. This illustrates that a better regional economy can help raise rural households' credit and income. We believe that the establishment of regional financial ecology to the benefit of the sustainable development of credit can significantly alleviate the problem of asymmetric information among rural households and RCCs, and lower the transaction costs between market entities. In ecology of regional finance which includes rural households, financial institutions, and the government, the three entities are supplementary, and they actively promote the natural expansion of rural households' credit and the agricultural loan market. Attention should be paid to the role that the government plays.[11] Based on our field studies, we believe that the government should not merely apportion its responsibilities or voice their demands in the form of commands. Rather, it should shoulder and extend its responsibilities as a public service provider, imposing macroeconomic regulation and control, offering technological guidance and information consultancy.[12] Only when the entities—financial institutions, rural households, the government, and enterprises—coexist and are supplementary to each other, can there be an interest-oriented incentive structure. So, the internal resources coordination and allocation of the financial ecological system will be in orderly operation.

The Determination of the Interest Rate in the Agricultural Loan Market

Judging from the existing studies, there is relatively abundant literature on financial support on agriculture, the system of the agricultural loan market, etc., but microeconomic research on the agricultural loan market is severely lacking. So far there has been no systematic economic study on the determination of the interest rate and its mechanism which is crucial to the demand and supply relationship in the market. Regarding this situation, the section aims to offer an initial economic discussion about the mechanism of the determination of the interest rate in the agricultural loan market. The discussion is based on our study of rural households and RCCs in 11 counties of City A.

The basic structure of the current rural financial system

The basic structure can be categorized into formal and informal finance. The former includes the Agricultural Bank of China, the Postal Savings Bank of China, the Agricultural Development Bank, the Rural Commercial Bank, Rural Credit Cooperatives (RCCs), village banks and other new forms of the financial institutions. The latter includes loans from rural cooperative foundations, rotating savings and credit associations (ROSCAs), pawnshops, private banks, private loans, and usury (see Fig. 3.2).

Fig. 3.2. The basic structure of the current rural financial system

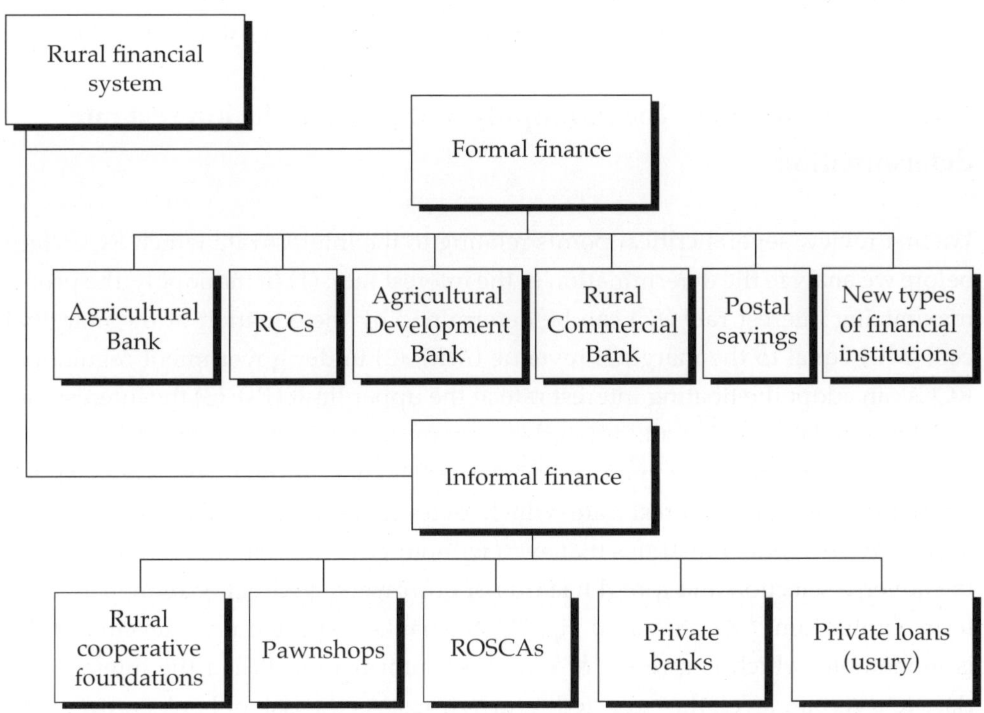

Currently, after RCCs and the Agricultural Bank separated, the formal market was co-dominated by RCCs, the Agricultural Bank, and the Agricultural Development Bank. However, in recent years, as the Agricultural Bank follows in the footsteps of the other three state-owned commercial banks (the Industrial and Commercial Bank of China, Bank of China, China Construction Bank) to gradually withdraw from the rural credit market. And the Agricultural Development Bank as a policy bank could only take on acting for the Ministry of Finance to give out grain subsidies and to purchase loans,[13] without being involved in direct credit relationships with individual rural households. Also, postal savings and new forms of financial institutions can hardly become a reservoir of rural capital in a short period of time. It is not surprising that RCCs monopolize the formal rural financial market.

Since 1999, more than 1,000 rural credit foundations around China closed down in the informal rural finance market. The economic service and financial departments similar to credit cooperatives were outlawed. Overall, private finance is in its infant stage. It can only provide simple financial services to farmers and the rural economy through a limited business network. The demand for rural finance cannot be satisfied.

We draw two conclusions from the analysis above: (1) RCCs are monopolizing the formal rural financial market; (2) the informal rural financial market is underdeveloped, and cannot satisfy the financial demand of rural households.

Rural formal finance: The monopoly of RCCs and the interest rate determination

We first review several critical points relating to the interest rate which RCCs face before we analyze the determination of the interest rate: (1) In monopoly, the profit-maximizing interest rate (R^*) can be determined by the equation of the marginal cost (MC) equal to the marginal revenue (MR); (2) under government regulation, RCCs can adopt the floating interest rate at the upper limit (R_2); (3) the interest rate is determined by the demand for and supply of capital in the local market (R_m).

Apart from the three indexes mentioned above, Stiglitz and Weiss (1981) proposed using the interest rate which determines credit rationing (R_h). The Stiglitz-Weiss model illustrates that even without government intervention, due to the adverse selection and moral hazards of borrowers, credit allocation is in long-term equilibrium.[14] As shown in Fig. 3.3, the banks' expected revenue curve $E(\rho)$ is monotonic, which is a result of imperfect information: When the interest rate rises to a certain level, the expected return drops. As the risk of banks grows with the rising of the interest rate, and banks cannot evaluate the risk status, they opt for credit rationing. This implies that the banks would not choose an interest rate higher than the optimal interest rate in credit rationing.

Fig. 3.3. Stiglitz-Weiss model (1981)

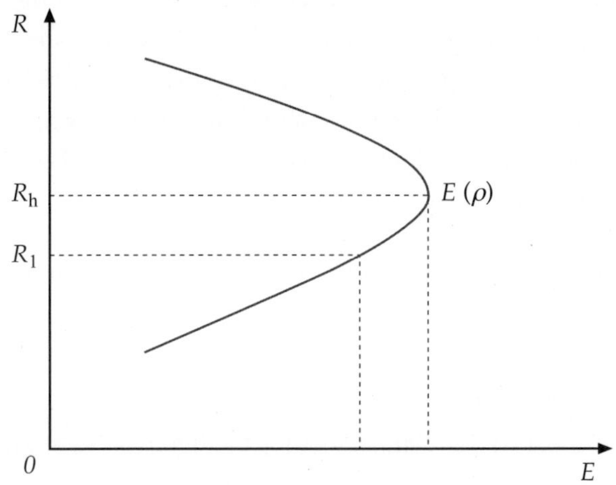

In Fig. 3.4, we assume that the current interest rate of RCCs is R_1. When $R_1<R_2<R_m<R_h<R^*$, once the state relaxes the regulation on the interest rate and raises the upper limit (i.e., R_2), revenue-maximizing RCCs would raise the current interest rate from R_1 to R_2. In other words, when the interest rate which RCCs adopt is lower than the market interest rate, as long as the regulation relaxes, their rational choice is to raise the interest rate to the maximum. The profit of RCCs expands from R_1R_0FG to R_2R_0EK.

Fig. 3.4. The determination of interest rate of RCCs in monopoly

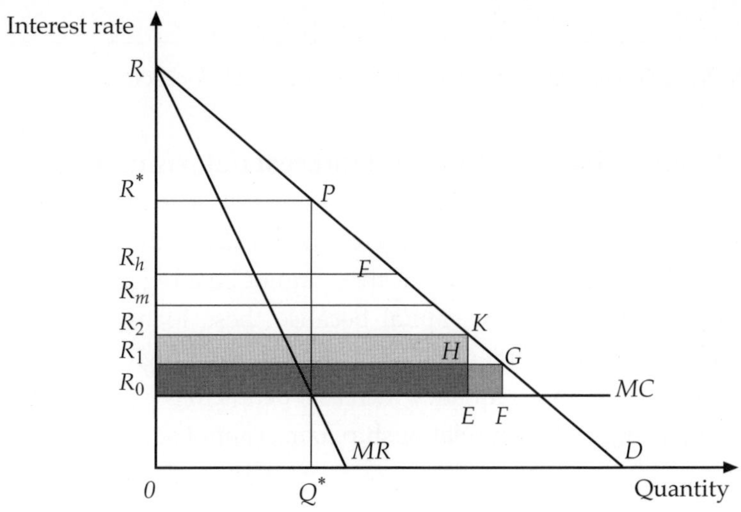

Then the questions become: Does the current market situation satisfy $R_1<R_2<R_m<R_h<R^*$? Do RCCs raise their interest rates to the maximum when the government regulation relaxes? According to the *Fourth Quarter Report on the Implementation of Monetary Policies 2006* published by the People's Bank of China, the answer to the second question is positive (see Table 3.4). Feng Bangyan and Chen Binrui (2003) suggested that the formation of price mechanism lags behind the relaxation of regulation, and many pilot RCCs do not set up a pricing mechanism based on the demand and supply relationship, risk evaluation, and time cost. Instead, they adopted an indiscriminate increase of interest. Lu Lei (2008) held the same opinion in his research.

Table 3.4. The proportion of loans in the floating bands of interest rate (%) in the fourth quarter of 2006

Financial institutions	Fall	Benchmark	Rise				
	0.9–1	1.00	Total	1.0–1.3	1.3–1.5	1.5–2.0	2.0 above
Total	25.81	26.63	47.56	27.90	7.32	10.63	1.71
State-owned banks	31.52	29.96	38.52	35.48	2.54	0.49	0.02
Joint stock commercial banks	40.75	30.21	29.03	28.56	0.42	0.05	0.00
Regional commercial banks	24.34	18.37	56.93	41.60	10.71	4.20	0.43
Policy banks	26.43	72.15	1.42	1.42	0.00	0.00	0.00
Urban-rural cooperatives	1.51	4.62	93.86	17.16	23.67	45.49	7.55

Source: *Fourth Quarter Report on the Implementation of Monetary Policies* 2006.

Rural informal finance: Private loans and interest determination

Relationship and friendship loans (usually interest-free) exist in the "relationship circles" described by Fei Xiaotong (1985), but they cannot be a regular and stable source of production and investment capital because these loans are small in amount and are requested in emergencies (e.g., illness, weddings, funerals). In addition, when the loan limit and frequency increase, people have to consider the "cost of face" (Zhang Jie 2004). When relationship loans cannot satisfy the regular financing demands of rural households, and the supply of formal finance in the agricultural loan market is in shortage, rural households would turn to informal private loans since formal financial institutions (RCCs) fail to grant them full credit.

The interest rate of private loans has the following features: (1) it is high; (2) it is not synchronized with that of the formal financial institutions; (3) it is agreed on by the creditor and debtor in the contract. According to our study of 1,100 rural households and 150 front-line loan officers in City A, the interest rate of private loans is generally four to ten times that of formal financial institutions. 78.82% of the subjects believed that there was no direct connection of interest rate between formal and informal institutions, and only 21.18% thought the opposite.

The term structure of interest rate of private loans is special. We found from field studies of 11 counties in City A that the term for usury was mostly below six months. The shorter the term is, the higher the weighted annual interest rate is. Although a small amount of this type of super-short-term usury is borrowed for handling emergencies, most of it is for commercial reasons. For example, when a rural household sees an opportunity to invest (the investment cycle takes about one to four weeks), he must turn to usury,[15] because formal financial institutions (RCCs) cannot offer loans with such a short loan period. Otherwise, he would miss the investment opportunity. Private lending is less active in a six- to twelve-month period. As the term of either rural microloans or the credit issued by RCCs is mainly within one year, capital is easier and more convenient to obtain during this time limit. The probability of rural households taking private loans will be lower. Correspondingly, within that time limit, the difference of the interest rates between private loans and formal finance is the smallest. As the loan period exceeds one year, the risk of capital use and the number of rural households who borrow significantly increases, and the difference in the interest rates between private loans and formal finance also expands.[16] As shown in Fig. 3.5, the typical term structure of interest rate of private loans shows a U-shape. The difference of interest rates between the formal and informal institutions is significantly larger in super-short-term and mid- and long-term loans. The difference is smaller in short-term loans (six to twelve months) when the accessibility of loans from formal financial institutions is high.[17]

Fig. 3.5. The U-shaped term structure of interest rate of private loans

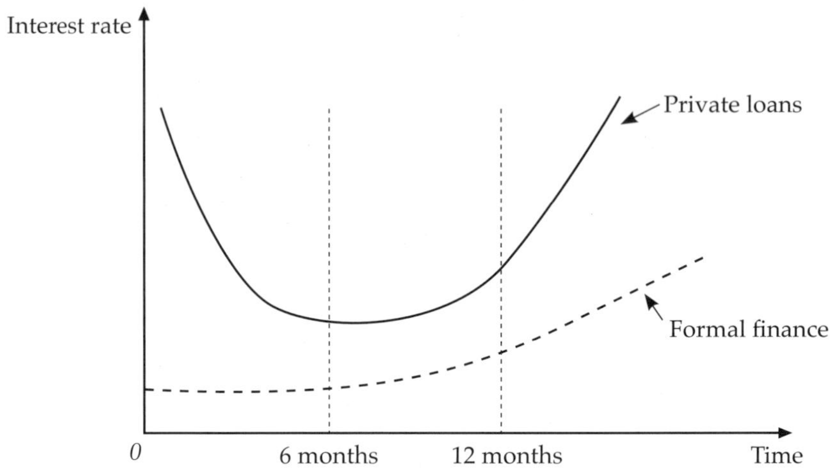

With respect to our continuous field study of rural private lending, we discovered that the demand for high-interest private loans can be classified into the following types: (1) sudden demand, (2) production demand, and (3) short-term investment demand. The lending behavior has the following characteristics: (1) Line of credit of relationship loans and formal finance is too small. (2) The time to obtain relationship loans and formal loans is too long. Besides, private loans also require collaterals that are worth the amount of loans. Those collaterals are different from those used in formal finance. They need not be a tangible asset. They can be (1) tangible objects or assets such as houses, land, cows, machines; (2) future cash flow which would be generated by the harvest of cash crop and grain crop;[18] or (3) human capital (repayment in form of labor).[19] Generally speaking, tangible objects or assets are preferred over future cash flow, and future cash flow over human capital.[20]

To those rural households who have little asset deposit and capital, when there is a sudden demand, and relationship loans and formal financial resources cannot be obtained, private lending becomes the only way out. In this sense, informal loans (private loans) in rural finance possess some features of monopoly: Facing a capital shortage, if rural households are shunned by monopolistic RCCs in formal finance, and other financing methods (e.g., relatives and relationship loans) cannot satisfy their demand, they can only turn to private lending and accept the high interest rate. According to our study of private lending in 11 counties of City A, in some of the rural areas where there were not enough RCCs, there were usurers. They were distributed among villages and there was lack of competition. This implies that private lenders are monopolistic. Because of the small number of private lenders (usually there is only one lender in a few villages), the capital suppliers are under little market competition. Eventually it is the suppliers who determine the interest rate, which is an important reason why the interest rate of private loans remains high for a long time. Virmani (1982)[21] pointed out in his study of the exclusiveness of information in rural financial markets: "Even when there is good local information about the actions or characteristics of certain people, that information may not be widely available outside the community. Limited access to information can lead to the segmentation of financial markets into 'islands of information.' Information about rural areas with few infrastructure links to the wider economy is especially likely to be limited. Under such circumstances local creditors with information better than that available to lenders outside the community can extract monopoly rents from their clients."

Interest rate mechanism in rural finance: Monopoly supply and market segmentation

It can be seen from the analysis above that in China's rural finance in which the small-scale peasant economy is the core, whether formal finance is dominated by RCCs or informal finance is dominated by private lending, both possess characteristics of monopoly. When the financial supply is inefficient, the financial demand of rural households is inelastic. The suppliers dominate the market and hence control the pricing of loans. The pricing of agricultural loans has two characteristics: first, the interest rate of RCCs directly moves up to the maximum; second, interest-bearing private loans show the features of usury.

If we say the monopoly of suppliers can explain the high interest rate in the agricultural loan market, why does the difference in the interest rate between formal and informal finance remain significant? The interest rates of formal and informal finance cannot converge. It cannot be explained by the difference in risk premium, but the segmentation of the agricultural loan market.

(1) Interest-free relationship loans are limited to relatives and friends. The boundaries of the relationship loan market are drawn within the "relationship circles." Although there is no interest, borrowers still have to bear cost. In reality, apart from the "cost of face," they owe the creditors a favor, which they have to return anytime in the future. The actual cost of relationship loans is implied in their future duties, such as providing similar financial assistance when the creditors require.

(2) As a monopoly in the formal financial market, RCCs can set their interest rate at the maximum with respect to the government policy, but after all it is still under government control and cannot directly equal its interest rate

with that of private loans. Even if the state withdraws their control over the interest rate, RCCs as financial institutions still face the issue of asymmetric information as suggested by Stiglitz and Weiss (1981). To minimize adverse selection and moral hazards, RCCs would follow the Law of Large Numbers to determine the investment in loans and the corresponding interest rate. This signifies that RCCs cannot differentiate its interest rate with respect to individual households like private lenders. The interest rate is determined by the risk-revenue equilibrium.

(3) Creditors involved in informal finance in the form of interest-bearing private loans are usually not large-scale organizations but individuals. They are more like self-employed or private enterprises and face a market no bigger than several villages. They are well-informed of the situations of every household. So, their small scope of business allows them to differentiate between households or between requisitions for loans during price-setting (This is also the reason why there is no benchmark but great variation of the interest rate of private loans). It should be noted that private loans with a high interest-rate are ranked last in the financing order of rural households. When relationship loans and formal finance can satisfy their demand, they would not turn to usury. So, informal finance can only exist in the "leftover area" of formal finance. Therefore, there is no competitive substitution relationship between formal and informal finance—the market is segmented.

Rural market segmentation and the determination of interest rates are summarized in Fig. 3.6.

Fig. 3.6. The structure of market segmentation of rural households' loans and the determination of interest rate

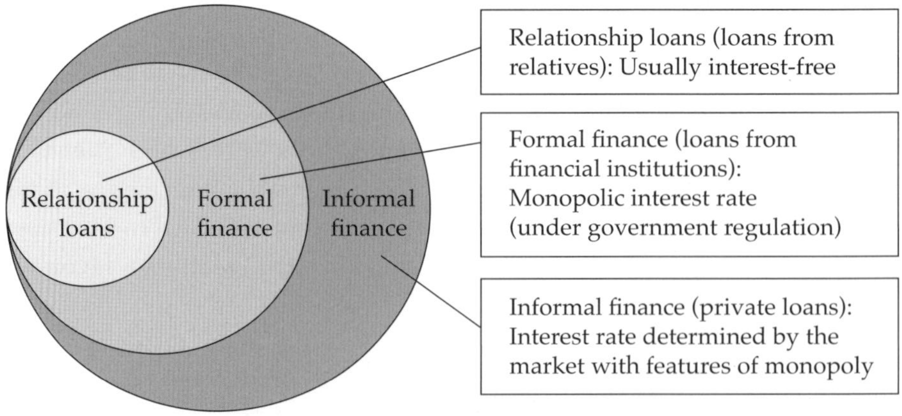

Notes: The dotted line represents the segmentation of the financial market, and the area of the three circles represents the weighting of the three sources of capital in the total financing of rural households.

The above conclusion is drawn from rural areas with typical features of traditional small-scale peasant economy. When rural households become entrepreneurs and rural areas start to urbanize, the segmented market would start to merge with improved market information and automatically increased financial supply. In the merging financial market, a unified benchmark interest rate would emerge in the formal and informal markets, and interest-free relationship loans would be gradually substituted by interest-bearing ones. These features exist in areas with advanced economic development in the Jiangsu and Zhejiang provinces.

Conclusions

The analysis of the current agricultural loan market and interest rate determination mechanism demonstrates that market segmentation results from suppliers' monopoly and insufficient aggregate supply. The segmented market leads to multiple equilibrium interest rates: Relationship loans remain nominally interest-free, and the interest rates are separately determined in the formal and informal financial market. High spreads between the two markets commonly exist, which inevitably leads to the following:

(1) Crowding-out effect resulting from the difference between interest-rates. McKinnon pointed out in 1973 that a high-interest rate absorbs savings and leads to a flow of financial resources to the corresponding sector. When the interest rate of informal finance is much higher than that of formal finance, part of the capital will flow to the former. When rural households do not deposit their surplus capital in RCCs but, whether directly or indirectly, let it flow into the hands of usurers, economic and civil disputes will continue to emerge with an incomplete regulation of private financing. Besides, the capital flow to usury will aggravate the shortage of deposit of RCCs in regions where the economic aggregates are small. To maintain the break-even operation of a RCC, there should be at least RMB2.5 million deposits. Therefore, in some poor villages, the threats of informal finance to RCCs should not be underestimated, especially when the high interest rate of informal finance exerts its "crowding-out effect" on RCCs. When the RCC cannot break even, without external subsidy, they have to close down the branch and withdraw from the market.

(2) Rent-seeking arbitrage. In market segmentation, a huge gap between the interest rates seems to present an opportunity for arbitrage. However, as the aggregate supply of capital is insufficient, the gap between interest rates will not close up due to the arbitrage. Market segmentation does not encourage an effective flow of resources. The opportunity to perform arbitrage is more

often realized as seeking rent—the opportunity is only available to those who have more relationship resources and information advantages. We discovered in our research that some enterprises and individuals attempted to seize the credit capital from RCCs and lend it to rural households who urgently needed money in the form of usury. They received a large sum of interest spread income.[22] In such a situation, the effect of market segmentation and insufficient aggregate supply are the prerequisites for capital arbitrage. This kind of arbitrage does not promote effective resources allocation.

Multiple equilibrium interest rates and the huge difference between the interest rates of formal and informal financial markets are inevitable under market segmentation and supply monopoly.[23] When rural households' financing demand remains substantial, and the aggregate supply of formal credit is insufficient, the market situation would not change. On the one hand, informal finance though having a high-interest rate compensates for insufficient financial supply; on the other hand, the huge difference between the interest rates of formal and informal finance could "crowd-out" formal finance and encourage rent-seeking behavior. Therefore, regulation and control are needed. In short, there are two ways to solve the problems brought about by market segmentation: (1) adopt the strategy of guidance instead of prohibition;[24] (2) increase the credit supply in the rural financial market to alleviate the shortage. The key lies in the latter one, and as to how to increase the effective supply in the rural financial market, it requires further exploration.

Financial Ecology, Increase in Rural Income, and Agricultural Development

Financial ecology was proposed on the basis of the English ecologist Tansley's concept (1935) of an ecosystem. The internal structural arrangement and developmental order of the financial system show some structural and functional features of synecology, which forms the basis of the study of the financial system from the perspective of ecology. The financial system is not an independent system which creates financial products or provides financial services. Its operation involves and relies on environmental factors such as politics, economy, culture, and legal system in the area.[25]

Generally speaking, financial ecology and economic development interact and are mutually dependent: The goal of optimization of financial ecology is to accelerate economic growth; and the optimization is also beneficial to the "low-lying land effect" which accumulates capital for economic growth. Optimal financial economy is required for the development of the financial industry as well as overall economic development. Because the basic conditions and environment for financial operation closely relate to the development of regional economy, a better financial ecology can help reduce the regional gap (including the urban-rural gap), and promote a balanced development of regional economy.

The concept of ecology introduced a new perspective into the study of the problems of financial development. A vast amount of literature emerged afterwards to provide the building blocks for the theoretical system of financial ecology. Many studies of the relationship between financial ecology and agricultural (rural) development only focus on one or a few particular areas. Few have studied the topic at the national level. Although there are many studies of financial ecology and regional development, they are all oriented towards urban areas. Few have focused on the relationship among regional financial ecology, income of rural households, and agricultural development. In this section, we will examine the relationship based on data collected across provinces.

Literature review

In China, the first person to propose the concept of financial ecology was Zhou Xiaochuan (2004), the governor of the Bank of China. He said that "financial ecology is metaphorical. It does not refer to the internal operation of financial institutions, but the external environment, which is a prerequisite for financial operation." After further theoretical study of financial ecology was conducted, the term now refers to an array of factors which affect the survival and development of the financial industry. It includes factors such as politics, economics, laws, and credibility, which are also affected by the development of finance; Also, internal factors of the financial system such as financial market and financial instruments are included. In this system, factors interact with and influence each other through the multi-dimensional network formed by capital and credit chains.[26]

Literature about financial ecology concentrates on the following issues: (1) the entity (Xu Nuojin 2005, Du Zhaoyun and Wang Lina 2006, Li Xiaoxi 2006), (2) the environment (Zhou Xiaochuan 2005, Su Ning 2005, Sheng Junfeng 2006, Xie Taifeng 2006), (3) the establishment of a regional financial ecology (Xiao Anfu and Xu Yanfei 2005, Li Ying 2006), (4) and the evaluation (Li Yang, Wang Guogang, and Liu Yuhui 2005, ibid. 2007). One of the representative studies was Xu Nuojin's research (2005) of China's financial ecology from the aspects of the entity, adjustment, and environment. Lin Yongjun (2005) used system theory to analyze the relationship among sub-systems in financial ecosystem and the factors which determine China's financial ecosystem. Li Yang et al. (2005) distinguished financial ecosystem from financial ecological environment. They defined the former as comprising financial entities and the financial ecological environment which depends on it. The mutual dependence and influence give rise to a dynamic balanced system.[27]

Kuang Jianguo (2005) suggested that financial ecological environment includes hard environment and soft environment. The former refers to the political, economic, and legal systems with formal regulations (written and mandatory); the latter refers to social customs, habits, culture, traditions, values, morals and beliefs, which constitute the underlying rules (unwritten). Financial ecosystem defines the room for choices of the entity of financial ecosystem and the institutional structure which governs the choice. Yi Xianrong and Lu Ting (2006) analyzed the relationship between financial entity and financial ecology from the perspective of institutional economics. They pointed out that the institution is decisive in the formation of a financial ecology: the institution determines the behavior, constraints, and choice boundaries of every financial entity, which in turn determines the relationship among them. Financial entities alter the institution to reform financial ecological environment in order to improve the entire financial ecology. Pi Tianlei (2006) agreed that financial ecology is formed under the political, economic, and legal systems, and culture. Its structure bears institutional features.

Institute of Finance and Banking (IFB), the Chinese Academy of Social Sciences published the *Evaluation Report on the Urban Financial Ecological Environment in China.* Fifty large- and medium-sized cities were evaluated and ranked with respect to their financial ecological environment by using nine indicators.[28] In *Evaluation of Regional Financial Ecological Environment in China* (2006–2007), with reference to the features of a transition economy, the nine indicators were combined and reduced to four: The dominance of government in economy, the operation of regional economy, the development of regional finance, and the infrastructure and institution of financial credit.

Optimal financial ecology can encourage and constrain financial entities. It can lubricate the market mechanism and hence reduce the transaction cost and raise the efficiency. Using the indicators employed by the IFB (2007), we empirically analyze the relationship among the regional financial ecology, the income of rural households, and agricultural development, explore the relationship between the current regional financial ecology and the Three Rural Issues, and recommend policies which can promote rural income and agricultural development.

Empirical analysis and examination

Sampling and the model design

Cross-sectional data were collected data from 30 provinces (including autonomous regions and municipalities)[29] in 2007. The objective of this analysis is to find out whether the development of financial ecology can raise the income of rural households and promote agricultural development. So, in the model, the explained variables (Y) include income of rural households and agricultural development while the explanatory variables (X) include the development of financial ecology.

Four sets of data are represented by substitution variables: income of rural households is substituted by per capita annual income of rural households (Y_1); agricultural development by added value of agriculture (Y_2), total power of agricultural machinery (Y_3), and gross output value of agriculture, forestry, animal husbandry, and fishery (Y_4).[30] The indicators for development of financial ecology include the following indexes: composite index for financial ecology (X_1), government dominance in economy (X_2), operation quality of economy (X_3), development of regional finance (X_4), and the infrastructure and institution of financial credit (X_5). The composite index for financial ecology (X_1) is the weighted average of X_2, X_3, X_4, and X_5. To better monitor the economic features of different regions, we included development of social credit (T)[31] and the rural population to total population ratio (P)[32] as control variables. The model is designed as follows:

$$\text{In}Y = C + \alpha X + \beta T + \gamma P + \varepsilon$$

The statistical characteristics of variables are shown in Table 3.5 and the indexes of financial ecology in different regions are shown in Table 3.6.

Table 3.5. The statistical characteristics of variables

Variable name	Minima	Maxima	Mean	Standard deviation
Per capita annual income of rural households (Y_1)*	3.51	4.05	3.76	0.15
Added-value value of agriculture (Y_2)*	1.74	3.40	2.78	0.48
Total power of agricultural machinery (Y_3)*	1.99	3.93	3.14	0.46

(Cont'd)

Variable name	Minima	Maxima	Mean	Standard deviation
Gross output value of agriculture, forestry, animal husbandry, and fishery (Y_4)*	1.90	3.59	3.02	0.46
Composite index for financial ecology (X_1)	0.26	0.83	0.48	0.17
Government dominance in economy (X_2)	0.18	0.86	0.50	0.20
Operation quality of economy (X_3)	0.23	0.75	0.48	0.16
Development of regional finance (X_4)	0.19	0.87	0.48	0.18
Infrastructure and institution of financial credit (X_5)	0.26	0.97	0.46	0.20
Development of social credit (T)	2.70	218.90	38.14	52.63
Rural population to total population ratio (P)	0.11	0.68	0.53	0.15

Note: *Data in logarithm.

Table 3.6. The indexes of financial ecology in different regions

Province/ autonomous region/ municipalities	Composite index for financial ecology (X_1)	Government dominance in economy (X_2)	Operation quality of economy (X_3)	Development of regional finance (X_4)	Infrastructure and institution of financial credit (X_5)
Chongqing	0.54	0.57	0.45	0.70	0.47
Zhejiang	0.83	0.86	0.75	0.87	0.84
Yunnan	0.41	0.40	0.31	0.56	0.39
Xinjiang	0.31	0.23	0.31	0.28	0.36
Tianjin	0.72	0.77	0.61	0.69	0.82
Sichuan	0.46	0.55	0.50	0.46	0.33
Shanghai	0.81	0.68	0.74	0.84	0.97
Shaanxi	0.38	0.42	0.30	0.46	0.33
Shanxi	0.40	0.39	0.37	0.46	0.37
Shandong	0.66	0.82	0.59	0.60	0.63
Qinghai	0.29	0.09	0.32	0.39	0.37

(Cont'd)

Province/ autonomous region/ municipalities	Composite index for financial ecology (X_1)	Government dominance in economy (X_2)	Operation quality of economy (X_3)	Development of regional finance (X_4)	Infrastructure and institution of financial credit (X_5)
Ningxia	0.37	0.18	0.36	0.59	0.36
Inner Mongolia	0.37	0.35	0.39	0.29	0.45
Liaoning	0.51	0.51	0.58	0.52	0.43
Jiangxi	0.36	0.46	0.42	0.35	0.22
Jiangsu	0.77	0.84	0.74	0.70	0.82
Jilin	0.32	0.36	0.43	0.19	0.32
Hunan	0.40	0.45	0.51	0.33	0.30
Hubei	0.41	0.58	0.39	0.33	0.36
Henan	0.41	0.55	0.46	0.37	0.26
Hebei	0.46	0.59	0.41	0.37	0.49
Hainan	0.44	0.55	0.34	0.40	0.47
Guizhou	0.33	0.25	0.23	0.45	0.38
Guangxi	0.38	0.46	0.41	0.38	0.27
Guangdong	0.69	0.82	0.75	0.67	0.52
Gansu	0.26	0.19	0.28	0.30	0.27
Fujian	0.64	0.71	0.65	0.59	0.63
Beijing	0.69	0.50	0.69	0.74	0.81
Anhui	0.45	0.46	0.52	0.42	0.40
Heilongjiang	0.34	0.41	0.50	0.17	0.27
Average	0.48	0.50	0.48	0.48	0.46

Source: Liu Yuhui, *Evaluation Report on the Urban Financial Ecological Environment in China* (2006–2007) (Beijing: China Financial Publishing House, 2007).

Empirical results

First, we analyze the effect of financial ecology on the income of rural households. Adopting per capita annual income of rural households (Y_1) as the explained variable and composite index for financial ecology (X_1) as the explanatory variable, the OLS regression function of the cross-sectional data is as follows:

$$Y_1 = 3.44 + 0.67\ X_1$$

The regression coefficient is significant at 1% confidence level, and X_1 can explain 57% of the variation of Y_1. This signifies that the level of development of financial ecology is directly proportional to the total income of rural households. Fig. 3.7 shows the scattered diagram. Further details of the data of regression analysis are shown in the first row of Table 3.8.

Fig 3.7. The correlation between financial ecology and income of rural households

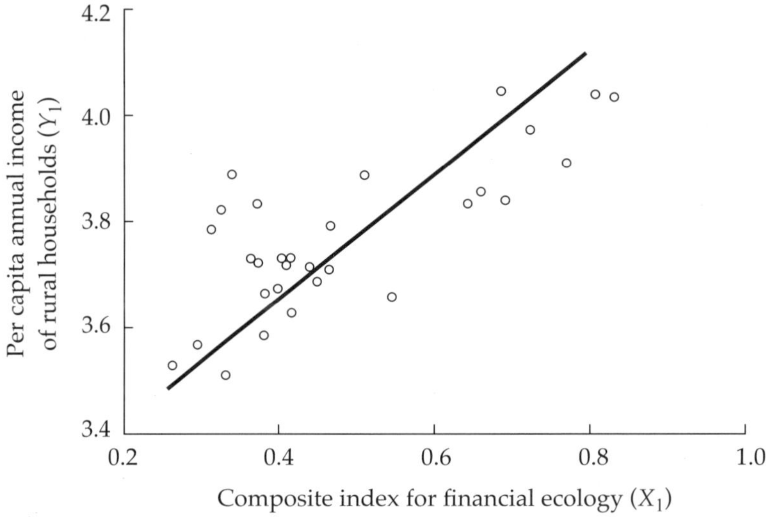

Through the indexes of government dominance in economy (X_2), operation quality of economy (X_3), development of regional finance (X_4), and infrastructure and institution of financial credit (X_5), we further research the relationship between financial ecology and income of rural households. We adopted OLS regression analysis to examine the cross-sectional data (see Table 3.7).

Table 3.7. The OLS regression analysis of financial ecology and the increase in income of rural households

Variable name	Per capita annual income of rural households (Y_1)	Per capita annual income of rural households (Y_1)	Per capita annual income of rural households (Y_1)	Per capita annual income of rural households (Y_1)
Composite index for financial ecology (X_1)	0.674568*** (6.291558)	—	—	—

(Cont'd)

Variable name	Per capita annual income of rural households (Y_1)	Per capita annual income of rural households (Y_1)	Per capita annual income of rural households (Y_1)	Per capita annual income of rural households (Y_1)
Government dominance in economy (X_2)	—	–0.075765 (–0.713827)	–0.077243 (–0.682190)	0.046208 (0.460183)
Operation quality of economy (X_3)	—	0.713073*** (4.455598)	0.717052*** (3.857095)	0.447108** (2.725184)
Development of regional finance (X_4)	—	–0.398729*** (–3.199084)	–0.398388*** (–3.126316)	–0.327663*** (–2.962899)
Infrastructure and institution of financial credit (X_5)	—	0.483285*** (3.817374)	0.486341*** (3.328859)	0.259212* (1.960166)
Development of social credit (T)	—	—	–2.15E–05 (–0.044818)	—
Rural population to total population ratio (P)	—	—	—	–0.429691*** (–3.039937)
Constant (C)	3.443907*** (63.34115)	3.434470*** (80.80553)	3.432581*** (56.75495)	3.793196*** (30.68254)
Adjusted R^2	0.570902	0.784937	0.775995	0.838256
F-statistic	39.58370	27.46107	21.09227	31.05910

Notes: 1. The bracketed value is the t-value.
2 *at 10% confidence level, **at 5% confidence level, ***at 1% confidence level.

It can be seen in Table 3.7 that operation quality of economy (X_3), development of regional finance (X_4), and infrastructure and institution of financial credit (X_5) significantly affect the per capita annual income of rural households. The effect of government dominance in the economy (X_2) is insignificant. Together with the signs of the regression coefficients, the analysis illustrates the following: (1) The operation quality of a region has a positive effect on the growth income of rural households; (2) Infrastructure and the institution of financial credit is directly proportional to the income of rural households. That is to say, better infrastructure and institution could lead to higher per capita annual income of rural households. The regression analysis shows that the income level of rural households lowers as regional finance develops. This confusing result can be explained by the fact that the indicators employed by IFB (2007) were developed from overall data of each province, which include urban finance and rural finance. Furthermore, considering that urban finance is much more developed than rural finance, the negatively proportional relationship can be understood in the following way: In imbalanced urban-rural development, financial resources flow toward the urban area in the regions where the economy is more developed. The dual structure has an unfavorable effect on the growth of income of rural households, widening the urban-rural income gap. As the fallout from the control variables, the rural population to total population ratio (*P*) is negatively proportional to rural households' income.

Below we examine the relationship between the development of financial ecology and that of agriculture. The substitution (explained) variables for agricultural development includes added-value of agriculture (Y_2), total power of agricultural machinery (Y_3), and gross output value of agriculture, forestry, animal husbandry, and fishery (Y_4). The explanatory variables remain to be X_2, X_3, X_4, and X_5. OLS regression analysis is shown in Table 3.8.

Table 3.8. The OLS regression analysis of financial ecology and agricultural development

Variable name	Added-value of agriculture (Y_2)	Total power of agricultural machinery (Y_3)	Gross output value of agriculture, forestry, animal husbandry, and fishery (Y_4)
Government dominance in economy (X_2)	1.658587*** (4.758456)	1.140900** (2.319915)	1.628789*** (5.462556)
Operation quality of economy (X_3)	1.363752** (2.310901)	1.406735* (1.689488)	1.354514** (2.683075)
Development of regional finance (X_4)	−1.239528*** (−3.256151)	−1.119244** (−2.083864)	−1.279732*** (−3.929799)
Infrastructure and institution of financial credit (X_5)	−0.649030 (−1.375907)	−0.302319 (−0.454242)	−0.783631* (−1.941957)
Development of social credit (*T*)	0.002095 (1.447105)	0.000858 (0.420148)	0.002961** (2.390617)
Rural population to total population ratio (*P*)	2.410027*** (4.803577)	2.445595*** (3.454809)	2.196111*** (5.116822)
Constant (*C*)	0.893367** (2.113182)	1.301419** (2.181830)	1.318533*** (3.645870)
Adjusted R^2	0.796556	0.586419	0.834630
F-statistic	19.92419	7.853226	25.39405

Notes: 1. The bracketed value is the t-value.
2. *at 10% confidence level, **at 5% confidence level, ***at 1% confidence level.

From Table 3.8, the following can be seen: (1) Government dominance in economy (X_2) and operation quality of economy (X_3) positively affect the added-value of agriculture (Y_2), total power of agricultural machinery (Y_3), and gross output value of agriculture, forestry, animal husbandry, and fishery (Y_4). As the government becomes more dominant or the operation quality of economy increases, agricultural development improves. (2) Development of regional finance (X_4) has a negative effect on Y_2, Y_3, and Y_4. As the regional economy develops, agricultural development slows down. (3) Infrastructure and institution of financial credit (X_5) shows no statistical relationship with agricultural development. It only negatively affects Y_4 at 10% confidence level. (4) As the fallout of control variables, the rural population to total population ratio (P) positively affects Y_2, Y_3, and Y_4. (5) Development of social credit (T) does not affect Y_2 and Y_3, but is directly proportional to Y_4.

Extensive analysis

From the analysis above, it can be seen that the rise in income level of rural households is a concept of unit, while the substation variables of agricultural development are concepts of total quantity. We employed comparison and contrast to analyze the effect of the development of financial ecology on the unit efficiency and aggregates to understand better the empirical results.

(1) Table 3.7 and 3.8 show that the development of regional finance is in indirect proportion to agricultural development. To a certain extent, it signifies that the urban-biased development of regional finance has a crowding-out effect on rural households' income and agricultural development. When the development of regional finance is still dominated by urban finance, agricultural and rural development will be suppressed and lag further behind.

(2) Financial infrastructure and institution is directly proportional to the per capita annual income of rural households, but not in proportion with the level of development of agriculture. This shows that infrastructure and institution of financial credit is efficiency-oriented. While it does not raise the total output of agricultural aggregates, it does raise the income level of rural households.

(3) Government dominance is in direct proportion to the aggregates of agricultural development (added-value of agriculture, total power of agricultural machinery, and gross output value of agriculture, forestry, animal husbandry, and fishery), but its relationship with per capita annual income of rural households is not significant. This demonstrates that the goals of the local governments' dominance in the economy still focus on the scale and total value. This form of scale-motivated government dominance can increase the

total output of agriculture but not income. In other words, the current form of government dominance may concentrate too much on aggregates and neglect efficiency per unit.

(4) The operation quality of regional economy is in direct proportion with the rural income rise in agricultural development. The improvement of the former has scale effect and unit efficiency. When the regional economy develops to a stage where there is a unified market, the improved operation quality can transform agricultural production, which would be directed by market efficiency, and raise the agricultural efficiency through channels such as improving the fluidity of production factors.

(5) Rural population to total population ratio is indirectly proportional to per capital annual income of rural households, but directly proportional to agricultural development aggregate (added-value of agriculture, total power of agricultural machinery, and gross output value of agriculture, forestry, animal husbandry, and fishery). As China's current agricultural production is stagnant at the stage of extensive development, the rise of the aggregate needs to rely on the growth of labor, and the earning capacity of unit labor is dropping.

Conclusions

Based on data collected across provinces, we analyze the relationship between financial ecology, rural income, and agricultural development. The four indexes of financial ecology—government dominance in economy, operating quality of economy, development of regional finance, and the infrastructure and institution of financial credit—have different effects on rural income rise and agricultural development. We can draw the following conclusions:

(1) Operating quality of regional economy. In regions with higher operation quality of economy, not only are the aggregates of agricultural development larger, but also the unit efficiency is greater. Correspondingly, the income level of rural households is higher. According to the general economic principle, an improvement in the operation quality of the economy, whether it originates from the urban or rural sector, would benefit both rural areas and agriculture through market spillover effect. Especially under the policy of "urban-rural integration and linkage," the unification of the urban and rural markets would help the price-setting of the factor market and raise the agricultural rate of return. As urban-rural integration accelerates, and

agricultural transformation and transfer of labor occur, the unit efficiency of agricultural production will increase. The improvement in the operation quality of the regional economy is essential to the construction of the financial ecology. It implies that local protectionism should be abandoned to form a unified market with an efficient flow of factors. The market mechanism would run to its full potential, the price mechanism would be fairer, and resources allocation would be more efficient. These improvements would significantly reduce the urban-rural gap, liberate the long suppressed rural economy, and accelerate rural development which would result in the catch-up effect. Given that financial ecology can promote agriculture and rural development, to transform an imbalanced urban-rural economy to a balanced one is not only a sign of the improvement of the operation quality of the regional economy, but also a motivation for the improvement.

(2) Regional financial development. It has been confirmed in much literature that the relationship between economic growth and regional financial development is in direct proportion. The relationship is, however, different between rural development and regional financial development. Many empirical analyses have found out that the net outflow of rural finance is detrimental to rural and agricultural development. Our analysis also illustrates that regional financial development cannot promote, but is in indirect proportion with rural households' income and rural development. As previously pointed out, this situation occurs as regional financial development is still urban-biased. When most financial resources are concentrated in urban areas, regional finance can hardly boost the rural economy. If the incremental parts of financial development favor the urban sector more than the rural sector, urban-rural duality would be reinforced. This urban-biased development of regional finance would eventually sacrifice rural and agricultural development, causing a further lag of rural households' income and agricultural development.

(3) Financial infrastructure and institutions. According to our selection of indexes, financial infrastructure and institutions include market intermediary organizations (legal service, accountancy, audit, and notary), cultivation of credibility (local credibility culture and credit information system), legal environment (copyright protection, judicial enforcement, protection of bonds), social security (old-age, medical, and unemployment insurances), etc. Our analysis shows that financial infrastructure and institutions are directly proportional to per capita income levels of rural households. The construction of financial infrastructure and institutions displays the feature of

positive externalities. The formation is not only beneficial to the sustainable development of the entity of the financial industry, but also extends the positive economic effects to the objects of the financial service. Better financial infrastructure and institutions would improve rural households' income.

(4) Government dominance in economy. A core characteristic of China's financial ecology is resources allocation through government administration. After the reform of the revenue-sharing system, the local government has become an individual interest entity. The political power behind China's economic growth has changed from the central government to the local government.[33] Due to the institutional defects and the competition regarding the GDP across regions, the local governments influence or even control financial resources allocation through various means to achieve a specific economic growth. Especially under the current quantity-oriented performance appraisal system, the local governments aim at enlarging the scale and increasing the aggregates of regional economy, but pay little attention to the quality of economic development. As previously mentioned, this type of scale-motivated government dominance could cause the local governments to focus too much on raising the aggregate indicators but neglect economic efficiency. The result is that the total output level of agriculture will increase, but the income level of rural households shows no significant growth.

The implications of the above conclusions are clear. In order to set up a better financial ecological system to improve rural households' income and agriculture development, the operation quality of regional economy must be raised, financial infrastructure and institution must be improved, and the urban-biased financial resources allocation mechanism must be corrected. The local governments must be guided and regulated so that their focus would change from quantity to economic efficiency and quality in promoting economic growth.

Financial Ecology, Information Discrepancy, and the Demonstration Effect in the Agricultural Loan Market

In information economics, information can discover and create value. As information increases, credibility improves, and financial ecology can be set up and develop. The value relationship of financial ecology includes both internal and external factors. The target function of the analysis of the financial ecology is value maximization. Good financial ecology is essential to the functioning of the financial market—allocating resources, lowering transaction cost, promoting healthy economic development.

From the viewpoint of economics, we believe that the financial ecology intends to set up a sharing platform for economic entities—the institutionalized economic and social environment allows the smooth transmission of signals, lowers information processing cost, and raises the efficiency of production and transaction. So, the economic sense of financial ecology and information discrepancy (asymmetric information and incomplete information) are closely linked.

The current financial ecology in China is at its exploration stage and far from the ideal status as theoretically predicted. Still, from the initial status, we can observe the internal operation mechanism and generalize common factors. This is the value of case study in economics.

Financial ecology and information discrepancy in local agricultural loans: "Credit Villages and Towns Scheme" in City A

City A is a pilot point of "Credit Villages and Towns Scheme (hereinafter as 'Credit Scheme')" which has shown some effects. Compared to the traditional plan for co-guarantee scheme, Credit Scheme is more adaptable and easier to promote. Take County K1[34] of City A as an example, Credit Scheme has advantages in reducing transaction cost and information asymmetry, and promoting the development of financial ecology in the region.

(1) Transaction cost is significantly lowered. After rural households qualify as credible households, when they borrow loans, they do not need to be assessed by loan officers (loan officers are mainly responsible for credit investigation for new borrowers and chasing overdue debts). They can bring their loan notes, identification card, and stamp to the RCC to apply for loans. It only takes a few minutes to obtain loans at the agency. The old procedure of going to the agency a few times to fill in the application form, find guarantee, and gain approval from loan officers is abandoned.

(2) Incentive and constraint scheme under reputation mechanism. In order to cultivate better credit culture, preferential credit is given to households who uphold their credibility, and credit sanctions to those who do not. Through annual loan note review, those who have better credit standing and greater ability to repay are given a larger line of credit; those who do not pay interest or repay debts on time have to repay their loans immediately and lose their loan notes. This procedure motivates rural households to preserve their credibility

and reputation. They become active in repaying their loans. Queues to pay interest or debts can be seen at RCCs.[35]

(3) Cooperation mechanism from the viewpoint of financial ecology. To promote the setting up of county financial ecology, County Joint Association and relevant departments in the county government assembled the Assessment Committee for Credit Villages. The members are the leaders or relevant staff from the local governments, the county branches of the People's Bank of China, county-level General Office of China Banking Regulatory Commission, and County Joint Association. The Committee is responsible for assessing and managing all credit villages. There is a general office at the County Joint Association under the Committee. There is an assessment team in every county (township) which gives a preliminary assessment of the credit villages. Rural households in credit villages can enjoy the following privileges: priority to obtain credit, a larger line of credit, and a preferential loan rate. Moreover, RCCs offer an incentive scheme to village committees to motivate the local authorities (village committees can receive RMB3,000–20,200 if they achieve a certain credit standard). The measures cultivate rural households' awareness towards credibility and motivate all parties. The rural households can enjoy benefits while RCCs can develop, resulting in a win-win situation.

(4) Dynamic management to ensure smooth feedback. The grading of credit villages is conducted by the local RCC every month, and reviewed by the Assessment Committee for Credit Villages in County K1 with respect to relevant indicators to ensure that adjustment can be made in time.

We can see that through institutional construction the Credit Scheme activates the interactions among RCCs, rural households, the government, and financial departments. County financial ecology is the core of the scheme. In the process, rural households' spontaneous reputation mechanism works and is reinforced. Village committees are more active in the role of facilitating and monitoring the transmission of signals. The production, transmission, and information feedback run more smoothly. As a result, transaction cost is reduced. RCCs improve the diseconomies of scale, through "double credit granting" (i.e., granting credit to individual households as well as the village at the same time, enhancing the mutual monitoring among households, and between the village committee and households). Information expansion and the reputation mechanism in the Credit Scheme are illustrated in Fig. 3.8.

Fig. 3.8. Information expansion and the reputation mechanism in the "Credit Villages and Towns Scheme" in City A

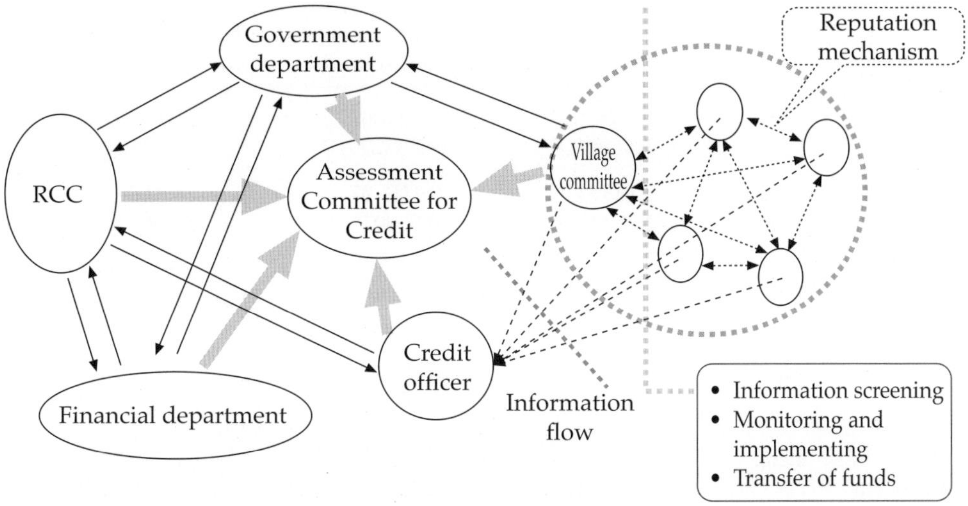

Note: The unmarked small circles represent individual households, and the circle in dotted line represents a natural village (credit village).

County financial ecology and rural financial development: Empirical analysis of City A

We believe that a healthy regional financial ecology should promote financial development in the following aspects: (1) to satisfy rural households' effective demand for finance and promote income growth; (2) to effectively release the financial supply of financial institutions and to improve benefits on this basis; (3) to promote interactive development between the regional financial ecology and the overall economy.

Below we evaluate the performance of the Credit Scheme in City A from the perspective of the development of the regional economy and the supply-demand in the rural financial market.

First, we analyze the effect the scheme has on the demand and supply in rural finance at the county level by regression analysis. The number of rural households in the region, economic development in the county (per capita GDP), and the living standards of rural households (using Engel coefficient as the substitution variable) are controlled variables. We apply regression analysis to the effect of financial ecological development (the implementation progress of Credit Scheme) on the balance of rural microcredit, per capita income of rural households, and the non-performing loan ratio in RCCs.[36]

Table 3.9. Regression analysis: the effect of county financial ecology on the demand and supply in the agricultural loan market

	Balance of rural microcredit	Per capita income of rural households	Non-performing loan ratio in RCCs
Constant	–154767.6 (–2.442081)**	3.525661 (9.735299)***	–10.08064 (–2.575048)**
The number of rural households in the region	0.148143 (2.783397)**	9.11E–07 (0.569039)	4.61E–05 (2.666095)**
Per capita GDP of the county	38634.03 (2.237798)**	—	—
Engel coefficient	—	–0.006518 (–1.105083)	0.342909 (5.378176)***
Degree of financial ecological development	6331.252 (2.727987)**	0.105934 (2.153463)*	–2.329207 (–4.380244)***
Adjusted R^2	0.684141	0.391366	0.789557

Notes: 1. The bracketed value is the t-value.
2. *at 10% confidence level, **at 5% confidence level, ***at 1% confidence level.

The balance of rural microcredit can be viewed as the satisfaction degree of the rural households' financial demand, and the per capita income of rural households and the non-performing loan ratio in RCCs represent the economic effects of financial ecological development on the demand and supply sides in the agricultural loan market. So, the above results demonstrate that at 1%, 5%, and 10% confidence level, the implementation progress of Credit Scheme significantly affects rural households' financial demand, and the economic benefits of the demand and supply sides in the agricultural loan market. Rural households in counties with a higher level of implementation of Credit Scheme have more financial resources (a larger credit balance), a higher income level, and RCCs have assets of better quality (a significant drop in the non-performing loan ratio). The empirical analysis shows that the construction of financial ecology can actively promote rural finance at the county-level economic development.

Below we contrast the different economic performances as affected by different financial ecologies across counties. Since reforms in 2002, the overall non-performing loan ratio of RCCs in City have been dropping. However, in the later development, the development degree of RCCs varies across counties. Take late

2007 as an example, the RCC in County K1 had the lowest non-performing loan ratio at 0.94%, the one in County K11 had the highest at 10.12%. Fig. 3.9 shows the non-performing loan ratio of RCCs across counties in City A during 1998–2008.

Fig. 3.9. Comparison of the non-performing loan ratio of 11 counties in City A

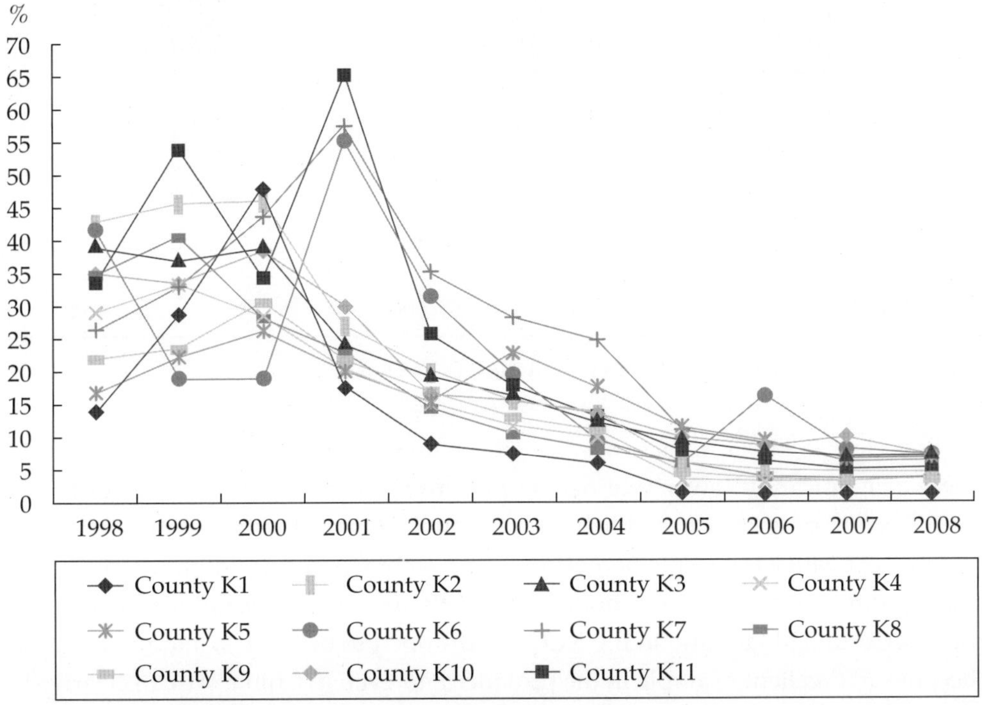

Note: Data in 2008 were collected up to the end of May.

We can see from Fig. 3.9 that there is a huge difference in the quality of assets of the RCCs. We are interested in the questions: whether the difference is a manifestation of the difference in the progress of establishing the financial ecologies; and whether there is a systemic relationship. With reference to our questionnaire survey of 250 RCCs front-line loan officers, we classified the 11 counties in City A to three grades according to their degree of financial ecological development (counties in the same grade are the closest in scores): First grade (K1, K2, K3), second grade (K4, K5, K6, K7, K8), and third grade (K9, K10, K11). The higher the grade is, the higher the degree of development is.[37] Fig. 3.10 shows the average non-performing loans ratio of RCCs in the three grades.

Fig. 3.10. The non-performing loans ratio based on the degree of financial ecological development

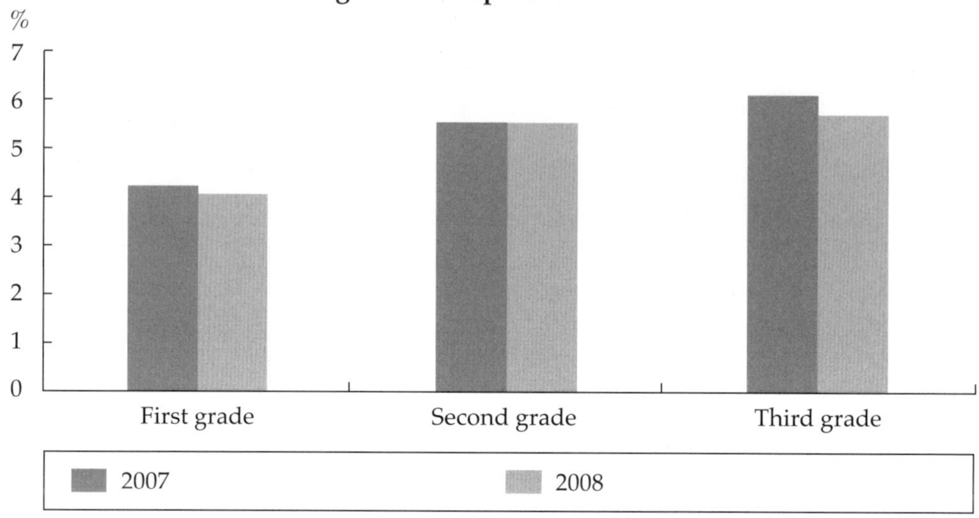

Note: Data in 2008 were collected up to the end of May.

It is clear in Fig. 3.10 that counties whose financial ecology is better developed have a significantly lower rate of non-performing credit in RCCs. Out of the 11 counties, the progress of establishing a Credit Scheme is the fastest in County K1. A few years after the implementation of the scheme, the rural finance in County K1 is entirely different. Rural households' income has significantly increased, the non-performing loan ratio in the RCC has dropped to below 1%, and the RCC has become an excellent example in the province and even in China. We can clearly see the benefits of establishing and developing financial ecology at the county level. Table 3.10 is a brief analysis of the situation before and after the setting up of the financial ecology in Count K11.

Table 3.10. The changes in the credit balance and credit quality before and after the establishment of financial ecology in County K1[38]

Unit: RMB10,000

Time	Deposit balance	Credit balance	Balance of rural microcredit (as part of credit balance)	Non-performing loan ratio (%)
T - 4	9338	5943	5348	14.13
T - 3	9899	6659	5993	28.49
T - 2	10560	7345	6610	47.75
T - 1	13888	10801	9720	17.62

(Cont'd)

Time	Deposit balance	Credit balance	Balance of rural microcredit (as part of credit balance)	Non-performing loan ratio (%)
T	15798	18480	12936	9.17
T+1	17108	21368	14958	7.92
T+2	18122	19052	13335	6.26
T+3	44715	32350	12940	1.29
T+4	51468	40305	15278	0.91
T+5	60575	47536	17853	0.94

Note: T = year 2002.

The empirical analysis above shows that setting up financial ecology can motivate the development of rural finance (both demand and supply). Fig. 3.8 displays the overall picture of the county's financial ecology, in which the information expansion among each subject and the spontaneous formation of reputation mechanism serve important functions. But we still have the following questions: Is government participation in the establishment of financial ecology important? In the financial ecological system where the accessibility to credit resources is not a problem, how could rural households improve productivity (and hence the economic benefits)?

We discovered from our survey of 250 RCCs front-line loan officers in City A and several field studies that in counties with better financial ecological development, the demonstration effect among rural households is evident. When some rural households employ new technology and use credit to obtain economic benefits, others will imitate them, which results in a self-organized technological reform and production expansion in financial ecology. Thus, the promotion of a new form of production through credit resources is an important endogenous mechanism in the financial ecological system. Government participation can speed up technological reforms. As shown in Table 3.11: (1) Counties which have better financial ecological development have a higher degree of government participation. (2) The demonstration effect among rural households exists. In counties with better financial ecological development, imitation (including both "prudent imitation" and "direct imitation") is common, which is not the case in counties whose financial ecology is less developed. Interestingly, in counties with better financial ecological development, significantly more households chose "prudent imitation" over "direct imitation," which implies that as the county-level financial ecology develops, rural households become more rational in production and investment decisions.

Table 3.11. Government participation and the demonstration effect in financial ecology

Financial ecology grading	Government participation	Demonstration effect among rural households		
		Direct imitation	Prudent imitation	No imitation
First grade	84.33%	45.00%	55.00%	0%
Second grade	79.17%	48.75%	46.25%	5%
Third grade	38.33%	51.67%	38.33%	10%

Note: The data of the demonstration effect were collected by asking the following question: "In the same village, if some household(s) receives high returns through investment (e.g., planting or nurturing a new product), other households will: (1) Learn from the experience and follow suit; (2) Continue with their own production (never mind the low returns); (3) if only one household receives more returns through new production, others will observe for the time being; if more and more households receive more returns through the same new production, almost every household will imitate." Option (1) is classified as "direct imitation," option (2) as "prudent imitation," and option (3) as "no imitation."

Conclusions and further thoughts

From theoretical and empirical analyses, we draw the following conclusions:

(1) It is important to establish financial ecology. On the macro level (country level), it should be standardized and coordinated; on the micro level (county level), it should be feasible. Our research of City A shows that in those counties with better financial ecology, rural households had a higher income level and RCCs had more assets of higher quality. This strongly suggests the setting up of a financial ecology at the county level can benefit the development of rural households and RCCs. We believe that setting up regional financial ecology, which is beneficial to the sustainable development of credit, can significantly alleviate the problem of asymmetric information in the agricultural loan market and lower the transaction cost among market entities. A regional financial ecology which includes rural households, financial institutions, relevant enterprises, social organizations, and the government would allow the entities to supplement one another and promote the development of rural credit and the expansion of the agricultural loan market.

(2) Information production and technology diffusion give rise to lower cost and an increase in return. It is an endogenous mechanism in financial ecology to promote economic development. In modern finance, information is valuable. As there is more useful information, information discrepancy inside the financial ecosystem would be improved, which leads to credit increase. A self-initiated credit increase mechanism would appear inside the financial ecological system. A good financial ecology can utilize the function of information discovery to the fullest and reduce the cost. Technological development is constrained by accumulation of knowledge, as well as the barrier of tacit knowledge (Kim 1999).[39] Therefore, as China's farmers have a low level of knowledge, both explicit and tacit knowledge must be taught to them in a suitable way, and support must be given to their development of new technology for transforming production. We discovered from our study that the demonstration effect exists in rural China. Thus, the most effective way to promote technology is to offer the chance of technological imitation to rural households. The financial ecological system offers an incentive-compatible operation mechanism.

(3) In financial ecology, financial institutions, rural households, the government, and enterprises should be supplementary to one another while their functions must be reasonably defined. In the financial ecological system, with the introduction of RCCs, borrowing is no longer restricted to within the village. It becomes easier to obtain loans and thus lower the capital threshold of rural households. Production scale expands which motivates technological innovation. The reputation mechanism provides the basis for credit culture. The demonstration effect helps with the diffusion of production improvement directed by credit capital. In the ecological chain, enterprises link together every production and sales stage, assisting in industry consolidation and refreshing market information. The economic effect in the financial ecology is extended to the broader external market. The role the government plays in financial ecology is worth noting. Based on several field studies, we believe that the government should not delegate its responsibilities or voice its demands in the form of commands. Rather, it should shoulder more responsibility as a public service provider, imposing macroeconomic regulation and control, offering technological guidance and information consultancy. Only when entities such as financial institutions, rural households, the government, and enterprises have formed an identical interest-oriented incentive structure, can the internal resources coordination and allocation of the financial ecological system work in an orderly way.

(4) The long-term development of the financial ecology requires the interplay among three types of stabilizing strategies, which are, on the macro level, as follows: (1) The natural selection stabilizing strategy (Darwin), which claims that revenue maximization is done through natural selection. (2) Cultural stabilizing strategy (Hayek), which advocates the use of imitation and replication to achieve equilibrium. (3) Developmental stabilizing strategy, which claims that specific types of behavior can be learnt by trial and error (Try Out Method). During reform and opening up, China adopted developmental stabilizing strategy. We believe that due to the internal features and mechanism of the financial ecological system, the long-term development of the financial ecology should gradually transform from adopting only developmental stabilizing strategy to the optimal combination of three types of strategies. The natural selection stabilizing strategy implies that the natural resources allocation and coordination in the financial ecosystem should not be interfered with by the external forces but we should follow their internal rules and tendency; cultural stabilizing strategy implies that the diffusion of knowledge and information are required to promote the expansion of the radiation area of the financial ecology; developmental stabilizing strategy implies that innovation would be encouraged by trial and error, and error correction mechanism.

Major Conclusions and Policy Implications

(1) Empirical analyses show that rural households' demand for and ability to obtain credit can convincingly explain the difference in income level. Their credit level is determined by the regional economic conditions, capital deposit, production and income ability, social relationship capital, etc.
(2) China's market segmentation results from supply monopoly and insufficient aggregate supply. The segmented market leads to multiple equilibrium interest rates: Relationship loans remain the nominal zero interest, and the interest rates are separately determined in the formal and informal financial markets.
(3) The huge difference between the interest rates of formal and informal financial markets inevitably leads to the following results: the crowding-out effect and rent-seeking arbitrage.
(4) In order to set up a better financial ecological system to improve rural households' income and agriculture development, the operation quality of regional economy must be raised, financial infrastructure and institution must

be improved, and the urban-biased financial resources allocation mechanism must be corrected. The local governments must be guided and regulated so that their focus would change from quantity to economic efficiency and quality in promoting economic growth.

(5) On the macro level (country level), the construction of the financial ecology should be standardized and coordinated; on the micro level (county level), the construction should be operable. In counties with a better financial ecology, rural households have a higher income level and RCCs have more assets of higher quality.

(6) Setting up regional financial ecology, which is beneficial to the sustainable development of credit, can significantly alleviate the problem of asymmetric information in the agricultural loan market and lower the transaction cost among market entities. A regional financial ecology which includes rural households, financial institutions, relevant enterprises, social organizations, and the government would allow the core entities to supplement one another and promote the development of rural credit and the expansion of the agricultural loan market.

(7) The establishment of financial ecology should originate from the cultivation of rural households' contract credibility. The greatest risk in the transformation of China's rural areas is that as relationship credibility weakens along with the dissolution of the rural system, if contract credibility cannot fill in the absence of relationship credibility, the overall credibility level of rural society and households would drop.

4

Chapter

The Government and Financial Institutions in China's Rural Finance

In a functioning market economy, sometimes the state needs to take action. Some government intervention can be beneficial to the market economy. As long as the government action accords with the standards of an effective market, market economy can accommodate more such actions... The quality is what matters, not quantity.

—Friedrich Hayek

There is no single formula for a successful rural financial institution. The most appropriate modes of operation will be determined by the needs and socioeconomic characteristics of the target clientele, as well as by the physical, economic, and regulatory environment.

—The World Bank

The Government's Role in Rural Finance

In both the old subsidized credit paradigm and the new financial development paradigm, how to direct financial resources to the low-income group in rural areas and nurture the rural households' ability to sustain self-development is an unresolved and complex issue. The issue is difficult to resolve as the allocation of financial resources is profit- and efficiency-driven, which is incompatible with the high-risk and low-return characteristics of rural finance; the issue is complex because the efficiency of financial resources allocation is not only constrained by the developmental ability, but also the special economic and cultural structure of rural society. Therefore, rural finance is concerned with the allocation of cost and risk, the dynamic balance of efficiency and fairness, and the accurate positioning of the government's role in the development of rural finance.

A review on the relationship between the government and the market

The debate about the relationship between the government and the market has been lasting for a few centuries. In the West, there are several developmental stages of market economy. Different schools of economic theories were adopted by government in different eras. The theories can be classified into two categories: economic liberalism (Laissez-faire and schools which advocate appropriate intervention in supply) and economic interventionism (mercantilism, Keynesianism).

The theoretical studies of the relationship between the government and the market were conducted from the following angles:

(1) Free-market economy. From classical economics to neoclassical economics, scholars have advocated laissez-faire and minimizing government intervention. General equilibrium theory has confirmed that under perfect

competition, government intervention is unwarranted.

(2) Regulatory economics. The development of monopoly in the 20th century gave rise to regulatory economics. It advocates that the government should regulate monopoly and allow the market competition mechanism to function in order to raise economic efficiency.

(3) Property rights economics. The Coase Theorem explains the importance of law and property rights. Well-defined property rights and a sound legal system guarantee an effective market. What property rights economics is most concerned about is the relationship between property rights and the efficiency of resources allocation. It advocates privatization, free enterprise, and free market.

(4) Transition economics. During reform, the economy transformed from a planned economy to a market economy; from Washington Consensus to post–Washington Consensus and then Beijing Consensus; from neoliberalism economics which stress stabilization, liberalization, and privatization, to the notion that only with a sound government can the efficiency of property rights improve. Freedom without constraints would bring injustices and instability.

In mainstream economics within the framework of neoclassical economics, the government is regarded as the "night-watcher," which implies that if the market operates normally, government intervention is redundant or even unwarranted. This puts the government in the position where it is only needed when there is market failure, which minimizes government intervention in the market. In other words, only when the invisible hand loses its effect will the visible hand come into play.

In mainstream economics, when the market price mechanism cannot fully function, which leads to the failure of achieving optimal allocation of social resources, government intervention is required. Generally speaking, there are four major factors which cause market failure: public goods, externalities, monopoly, and information asymmetry. Regardless of the cause, market failure implies that the market mechanisms have failed to make effective adjustments. Once the market becomes inefficient, the government becomes essential to salvage the market. Government intervention can effectively increase the supply of public goods and market transparency, and resolve the issues of unfair allocation, vicious competition, monopoly, information asymmetry, and negative externalities during economic development. When the government intervenes in the market, it must adopt policies and measures accordingly with respect to the reason behind market failure in order to tackle the problem of low efficiency in resources allocation. Of course, government intervention may not be the most effective way to salvage the market. Preference, the quality of officials, rent-seeking behavior of interest groups, and information asymmetry are some reasons why governments' intervention fails. It should be pointed out that if government regulation is not standardized, short-term action and speculation of market entities would appear in the market, further encouraging the unstandardized behaviors.

Table 4.1. The motivations for and methods of government intervention and reasons for the failure

Motivations	(1) Unfair social income; (2) vicious competition and monopoly; (3) information asymmetry; (4) social problems caused by negative externalities; and (5) insufficient supply of public goods.
Methods	Different methods are used to handle market failure caused by different reasons. (1) Public goods: whether to supply public goods and how much they should supply; (2) externalities: tax and subsidies, internalization policy, define property rights, administrative measures; (3) monopoly: anti-monopoly law, government regulation; (4) information asymmetry: impose measures to resolve adverse selection and moral hazards.
Reasons of failure	(1) Government bias; (2) the quality of officials; (3) rent-seeking behavior of interest group; (4) information asymmetry; (5) difficulties in determining the cost and revenue of government intervention; and (6) the law and regulations for government intervention are rigid that the government cannot act according to the change in economy in time.

There has been an ongoing debate about market imperfections and government intervention. Stiglitz (1993) believed that the government should influence the market, which results from the spread of market failure. Without a doubt, market failure in developing countries is more severe than the one in developed countries. If a market is more constrained in developing countries than in developed countries, many people would regard this as a constraint on the government. But the government should consider these constraints when they devise policies. Apparently, no promise of liberalization of the financial market can be made simply from economic theories or large-scale test of practice. In contrast, Besley (1994) is incredulous. There are good reasons for government intervention such as market failure. However, when they are analyzed in detail, we gradually realize that there is no absolute answer to the current situation. No one can determine whether intervention in the financial market is correct. If the development in the operation of the rural financial market and the policies is in sync, empirical research can predict the next challenge.

In *World Development Report* 1991, the World Bank summarized the experience of 40 years. It analyzed the relationship between the government and the market, and proposed the developmental strategy of the "friend of market."[1] Unless it is confirmed that in a specific area government intervention can raise efficiency, the market should not be interfered with. When the private sector can operate normally, the government should not intervene. The government, however, should intervene accordingly to control the expenditure on public goods such as education and infrastructure, population control, poverty relief, and environmental protection. When the market does not function to its fullest, the government should devise suitable policies and essential regulations for the development of the market, as well as strengthening property rights and tightening market constraints. As the market has its own laws and regulations, the government should not tamper with the price signals for a long time. Government intervention should be simple, transparent, and bounded by principles. It should not be arbitrarily decided by officials. Later, in *Rural finance: Issues, design, and best practices,* the World Bank (1997) explained the status of the government:

> *Government intervention should aim at removing the causes of market failure or poverty. For example, market failure caused by imperfect information can be addressed, where appropriate, by providing seed capital for the establishment of rural financial institutions in remote areas. The high transaction costs associated with the small loan and deposit amounts of the poor can often be lowered through subsidies sharing a portion of the transaction costs on a declining basis, or by assuming the costs of training staff in modes of operation known to reduce transaction costs.*
>
> *Interventions should always aim to complement, facilitate, or improve the market over the long term. The management of a state-owned rural financial institution requires full autonomy and should be accountable: no special privileges should be accorded to such an institution, and competition from private rural financial institutions should be encouraged.... The cost of an intervention should be monitored continuously in order to assess the cost-effectiveness of the intervention while maintaining a level playing field among participating financial intermediaries, irrespective of their ownership.*

As economics develops, the relationship between the government and the market has evolved from oppositional to compatible, and the issue has changed the suitable positioning of effect areas of the two under different conditions. As Hayek said, in a functioning market economy, sometimes the state needs to take action. Some government intervention can be beneficial to the market economy. As long as the government action accords with the standards of an effective market, market economy can accommodate more such actions. But, government actions which conflict with the basic principles of a free system should be eliminated. Otherwise, the system cannot function...The quality is what matters, not quantity."

Government intervention in rural finance: Debate and evaluation

Ohio critique

The Ohio school should not be missed in the discussion about how to promote rural financial development in developing countries. Not only did it initiate criticism of government, but it also affected the World Bank's policies of rural finance. It holds that government's policy of cheap credit causes a difficult situation in rural finance. Subsidized development financial institutions (DFIs) tamper with resources allocation and generate negative incentives, resulting in a high probability of breach of contract, and the dependence on subsidy and unsustainable development of financial institutions. As market constraints loosen, DFIs fall into the trap of subsidy-dependence and fail to extricate themselves from the situation. Moreover, the excess demand under government rationing gives rise to rent-seeking behavior. Subsidies are seized by the small group of high-income households in rural areas and cannot reach the low-income group and the impoverished. The Ohio school, which is against government intervention, advocates that DFIs should be eliminated. Under liberalism, informal rural financial institutions would spontaneously form a bottom-up rural financial system and provide efficient financial services.

Without a doubt, the Ohio school contributed substantially to the formation and development of the financial market, and the analysis of unwarranted government intervention. However, liberalism based on general equilibrium theory usually fails in the rural market which has special characteristics. On the one hand, the market is either monopolistic or segmented, which does not allow enough competition. The price mechanism cannot operate smoothly. On the other hand, the special information and risk distribution in the rural financial market incurs increasingly high marginal cost on the private financial sector when it expands its services. This suppresses the development of private finance and its ability to expand the market. Furthermore, low production ability does not allow self-development, especially in impoverished areas. In the situation which the retention rate of return required by private finance cannot be satisfied, the private financial market cannot evolve by itself. Pioneer institutions should be the first to bear the pioneer cost. The success of pioneer institutions lays the foundation for the private financial market. In other words, when positive externalities exist, private finance cannot internalize profit and loss. Corresponding pioneer institutions should bear the risk of being the first to enter the market—once they succeed and positive externalities function, private finance would enter the market and a competitive financial market would emerge. The Ohio school neglects the special features of the rural financial market and regards it the same as other general markets, which causes them to be disappointed with government intervention and have false hopes for the market mechanism. Hulme and Mosley (1996) termed the worship of the liberal market "market illusory": "The theory of the Ohio school is more like a developmental theory in the former generation than a policy statement. When they talk about the government's role in the rural financial market, they are always vague."

Three-pronged theory

The three-pronged theory was proposed by the Asian Development Bank. Centered on the government's function, there are three points of emphasis in the theory.

First, in order to promote the development of rural finance, there needs to be a healthy and sustainable policy environment. The prevalent financial suppression policy such as interest rate control, access control, business rationing, and competition suppression should be altered. Broader policies of rural areas and the rural market such as price control on agricultural products, unreasonable import subsidies, and distorted policies on the exchange rate and terms of trade also exert an adverse effect on the development of rural finance. These distorted policies worsen the rural financial environment and render the development of rural finance unsustainable. McKinnon and Xiao (1973) pointed out: For a long time, intermediaries in rural finance are troubled by the twisted policies. The intermediaries cannot serve marginal clients, and rural financial transactions are far more complex than the problems endogenous to the market which we expected. The research of the Asian Development Bank (2006) indicated that financial suppression policies such as interest rate control prevent financial institutions from obtaining enough revenue to compensate for the cost of loans, high reserves requirements do not benefit savings mobilization, and restrictions on the expansion of financial institutions and their branches further suppresses the competition among rural financial institutions. A stable macro-economy is desirable for the sustainable development of the policy environment in rural finance.

Second, to refine financial infrastructure. Infrastructure in rural finance includes laws and regulations, the information system, institutional system, and regulatory system, which directly affect financial transactions, as well as the communication network and transport system, which affect the cost and convenience of financial transactions. In many developing countries, the development of rural financial infrastructure is lagging behind in the economy and is sluggish compared to that of urban financial infrastructure, which is manifested in the following aspects: the lack of law and regulations reduce the efficiency of preparing and executing contracts; poorly defined property rights cause the difficulties in the circulation of collaterals and guarantee; financial regulation fails to regulate or promote the development of financial institutions, or keep up with the development of new forms of financial institutions; rural issues are entangled with political ones, which causes a sluggish development of market credit and hence many problems with repayment. Asian Development Bank (2007) suggested that well-established financial infrastructure should benefit the entire financial system instead of particular organizations for the former has more externalities.

Third, to promote the development of financial institutions. Under the conditions in which the policy environment and infrastructure have met the basic requirements, as market entities practicing micromanagement, financial institutions cannot achieve sustainable development. Especially in the early stages of marketization, there is a shortage in both capital (including human capital) and funds. Financial institutions lack the ability, channels, and initiative to experiment and innovate. They are unable to expand their scope of services, which leads to insufficient financial supply. As the innovation of information, technology, and products typically generate externalities, the initial market supply can hardly satisfy social expectations (social-benefit maximization). The government as the producer of public goods should intervene and bear the initial cost. Considering that these initial inputs can bring about huge externalities, through supplying information, technology, capital and human resources to support the development of financial institutions and the expansion of financial services, in the long run the government function can be maximized.

Externalities and pioneer cost

Regarding how externalities hamper the development of financial intermediaries, Stiglitz et al. (1993, 1994, 1996) hold that information has the characteristics of externalities as a public good, the marketing school overestimates the effect of competition in the early stages of rural financial development, to encourage financial institutions to expand their services requires access and contingent rent. As there are many externalities in the initial stages of the development of the rural financial market, the market may freeze and cannot be activated: with little information of the risk status, use of loans, and the collaterals and guarantee of borrowers, financial institutions need to select clients and offer extra financial services (e.g., educate clients on the financial system and regulations, develop new loan products) before issuing loans. This is the pioneering process. Only when the process succeeds can financial services expand. Yet, the pioneering financial institutions would realize that as the number of competitors increases, their initial pioneer cost would become sunk cost: Institutions who enter competition later can enjoy the externalities brought about by the time-consuming and costly effort the pioneers—client information—without a cost. Pioneer cost and revenue can hardly be internalized. As a result, the incentive for financial institutions to enter the undeveloped rural financial market will diminish. Hulme and Mosley (1996) discovered from the studies in Indonesia, Bangladesh, Bolivia, Kenya, Sri Lanka, etc., that the private sector is unwilling to expand the scope of financial services because it requires early investment in various aspects relating to the information of borrowers.

Due to the externalities, the financial institutions do not want to get involved in the immature rural financial market. The process of pioneering cannot be operated through market. Herderson and Khambata (1985) believe that the commercial operation measures such as monopoly and a high interest rate cannot resolve the problem in the early stages of the development of the rural financial market. A possible solution is to call for government intervention in the form of subsidy.[2] Subsidy serves two functions in the rural financial market with many externalities: First, to compensate the pioneering institutions and private organizations for the high risk and cost they bear, and increase the incentive to act as pioneers. Second, to control the loan rate at a level which is tolerable to the agricultural rate of return, promote production through loans, and minimize the effect of adverse selection and moral hazard incurred by the high interest mechanism.

When rural financial institutions cannot internalize their cost and revenue, market failure occurs. When externalities and public goods coexist, there will be potential benefits which cannot be obtained through private transactions. Greenwald and Stiglitz (1986) believe that while both the government and the private sector face the problem of insufficient information, the government can enjoy more benefits by internalizing its social cost and revenue. Without sufficient information, the financial market cannot function. At the same time, problems of externalities and incentive linked to information (e.g., free-riding, adverse selection, moral hazards, etc.) can also lead to market failure. As pointed out by Besley (1994), if everyone waits for others to make the first attempt, it is ineffectiv e. Some agricultural technology is slowly promoted because no one wants to make the first move. Therefore, the government should intervene by subsidizing those who welcome the change. For example, the Grameen Bank in Bangladesh should be subsidized for their experiment of a new system. Subsidy should be given to new creations only and withdrawn gradually as the creations develop.

Evaluation of government intervention in rural finance

Research has been vague on whether government's decision on the flow direction of credit is better than that of the private market (Thomas 1987). However, state divestiture and market divestiture are commonly observed in the transformation of rural finance in many countries. In Socialist countries such as the former Soviet Union, financial liberalization has not brought about the development of the private financial sector. In many countries in Asia, Africa, and Latin America, as DFIs and specialized financial organizations retreat, there is a "vacuum" in the rural financial market. The low-income group which urgently needs aid is utterly neglected. International Monetary Fund (2001) points out that state divestiture and market divestiture are prevalent because when the government disinvests, the "vacuum" is not filled by the development of the private financial system or its dependent systems. As state divestiture and market divestiture reflect the lack of market response, when the development of private financial institutions cannot substitute government finance effectively, the government should not over-restrict its functions. Especially when the development of the private financial market is seriously constrained, government intervention in the rural financial market is essential and practical.

In fact, before the effective private financial supply forms, the rapid contraction of the scope of financial services caused by a large-scale government withdrawal may further destroy the basis for the incubation and development of private finance. Under free market competition, a feasible plan is to coordinate the rate and area of government retreat and the follow-up rate of private financial capital in the area. The government functions in rural finance can be expanded through the expansion of the scope of financial services or supporting the development of private finance.

We believe that inappropriate government intervention certainly cannot achieve expected results, but eliminating the government from rural finance is as undesirable. When the development of rural finance is seriously constrained and distorted, it would take a tremendously long time for the market to perform self-repair and improvement. The process is difficult and incurs unbearably high transition cost. Therefore, the question to ask is not whether the government should intervene in the market, but how it should intervene and maintain the efficiency after intervention.

To those who believe in economic liberalism, how to ensure the efficiency of government intervention is trivial as they believe efficiency would be low. However, while there are cases where the efficiency is low after the government intervention in rural finance, there is a lack of convincing and logical support for the claim that low efficiency is caused by government intervention. It should be taken into account that the use of agents is inevitable in executing any policies. Carefully devised policies could go wrong during execution. Under such conditions, the effectiveness of government intervention could be criticized because part of the policies has not been executed. From this perspective, in evaluating the effectiveness of government intervention, conflict of interest of various parties in every part in the process of intervention should be considered in order to ensure that the policies would be correctly executed.

The balance between government intervention and private factors: Cultural constraints and institutional development

To explain the choice of financial systems, Zhang Jie (2005b) constructed a two-dimensional space of private factors and government factors for analysis based on the DGLLS framework (see Fig. 4.1).[3] In this effective combination of institutions formed by private factors and government factors, both factors are market factors. Different types of market economy have a different ratio of government factors to private factors in terms of their weighting and balance of power. The steeper IPF_1 represents a market economy dominated by the private sector;[4] the flatter IPF_2 represents a market economy dominated by the government.[5] The two institution utility curves IU_1 and IU_2 intersect with the two system probability curves at point E_1 and E_2. These two points represent the most effective combinations of private factors and government factors in the two types of market (The weighting of both private and government factors are in the best ratio). The two straight lines which originate from O (SCP_1 and SCP_2) with a positive slope represent two different pathways of social cooperation: SCP_1 represents the bias toward the system in which the private sector is more eager to cooperate and more capable; SCP_2 represents the bias toward the system in which the private sector is less eager to cooperate and less capable.

Fig. 4.1. Effective combination of institutions

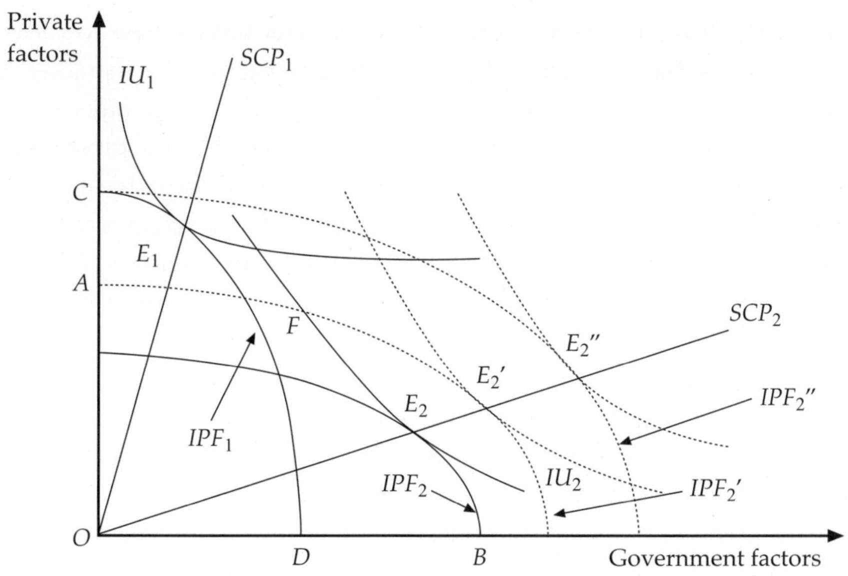

Fig. 4.2. Paths of social cooperation and targets for reform

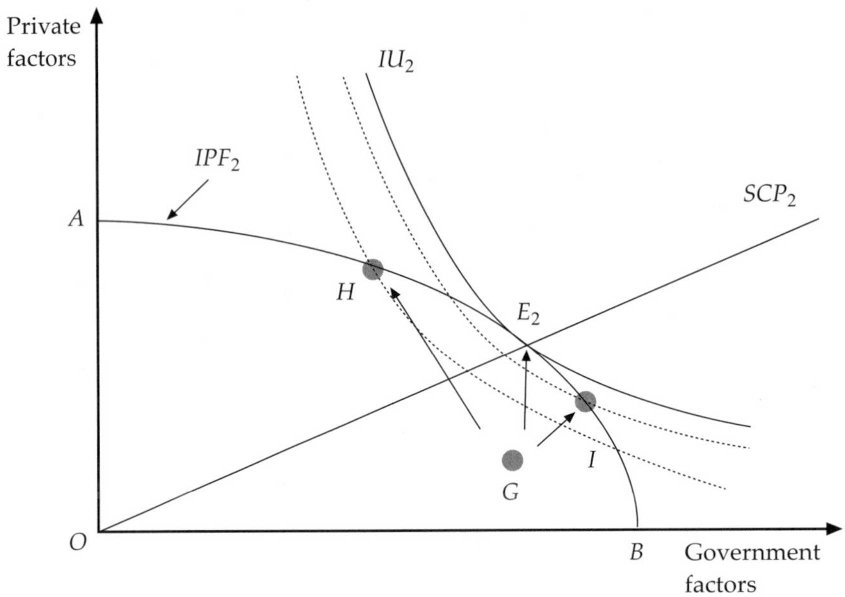

Based in the model above, Zhang further analyzed the balance between private and government factors in China's choice of financial system. As shown in Fig. 4.2, assume G is the starting point of China's economic reform. G is to the left of IPF_2 and close to the x-axis, which signifies that the weighting of government factors is too much and the economic choices for private factors are limited. As economic reform progresses, the institution combination point would gradually moves towards E_2. During this process, the weighting of the private sector gradually increases. It is only an adjustment and restoration of the weighting which is originally too small. It does not imply a bias toward a market economy dominated by the private sector. As the effective institution combination point closes up to E_2, due to the constraints of cultural factors (SCP_2), the weighting of government factors cannot reduce and that of the private sector cannot increase. According to this logic, as long as the starting point of economic reform is to the left of IPF_2, as the reform progresses, the effective institution combination point would move toward E_2. Under such conditions, the growth in the share of the private sector and the reduction in the government share would raise the efficiency of the system. If G does not move toward E_2 but in other directions (i.e., toward H or I), it cannot achieve an effective combination of institutions, only a possible combination of institutions. Regardless of whether the private sector (at H) or the government (at I) has too much weighting, economic reform would be a painful adjustment process, which would incur high switching costs (Zhang Jie 2005b).

In Zhang's model, the critical factor is the position (slope) of the social cooperation path curve. The slope of *SCP* lines represents the various combinations of systems and, therefore, economic structures. The question to ask is how the slope of *SCP* is determined. Zhang thinks that the slope is determined by the cultural difference between different economic entities. Therefore, the slope is stable and cannot be simply replicated. Different effective institution combinations represent different market economies. There is no sufficient evidence to support the notion that one type of effective institution combination is better than the other. Institutional arrangements and market portfolios have proven to be effective in one of the effective institution combinations may not be so in another combination. Therefore, a country must establish its own market economic system in regard to its own conditions. An accurate determination of the starting point of economic reform and the social cooperation path are crucial to the performance of economic reform and the cost of creating the market portfolio.

Zhang's model was originally designed to analyze the financial systems of different countries using endogenous government factors. The model is also applicable to China's rural financial system. Both government and market factors are essential to the establishment of the financial system. The weighting of the two types of factors is determined by the cultural heritage of society.

Even though Zhang did not define "cultural heritage" in his article, the term implies individual behavioral pattern and risk preference. We mentioned in Chapter 2 that China's rural households have a small relationship circle and are rather reluctant and unable to extend social trust, which shows that they have little incentive and ability to cooperate in society. Under such conditions, the social cooperation path for China's rural households has a flat slope. In other words, theoretically, the current China's rural society calls for more government intervention in order to attain the optimal conditions for the rural financial system.

In Zhang's model, it should be noted that while the *SCP* line can be different with respect to different economic entities, the social cooperation line based on specific economic entities is highly stable. Regardless of the twists and turns in the path of economic reform, the path revolves around a specific *SCP* line and would eventually end in one of the equilibrium points on the line. The *SCP* line is stable and remains constant all the time.[6]

We disagree with Zhang. The choice and development of institution are dynamic. The *SCP* line is relatively stable only in a specific historical period or under special social conditions. A constant *SCP* line does not exist in long-term social and historical development. In other words, we think that social conditions and individual social cooperation ability can change, and the system can develop accordingly, which is manifested as the change in the slope of the *SCP* curve in terms of effective institution combinations. We agree that intervention of the government and market factors should be constrained. There is no unlimited government intervention (the slope of the *SCP* curve equals zero) or market monopoly (the slope of the *SCP* curve equals infinity). Assume minimum government intervention (maximum market intervention) as SCP_{min}, and maximum government intervention (minimum market intervention) as SCP_{max}, there is a "tension space" between SCP_{min} and SCP_{max}, which represents the possible choices of institution combinations across time (see Fig. 4.3).

Fig. 4.3. Tension space and the development of institutions

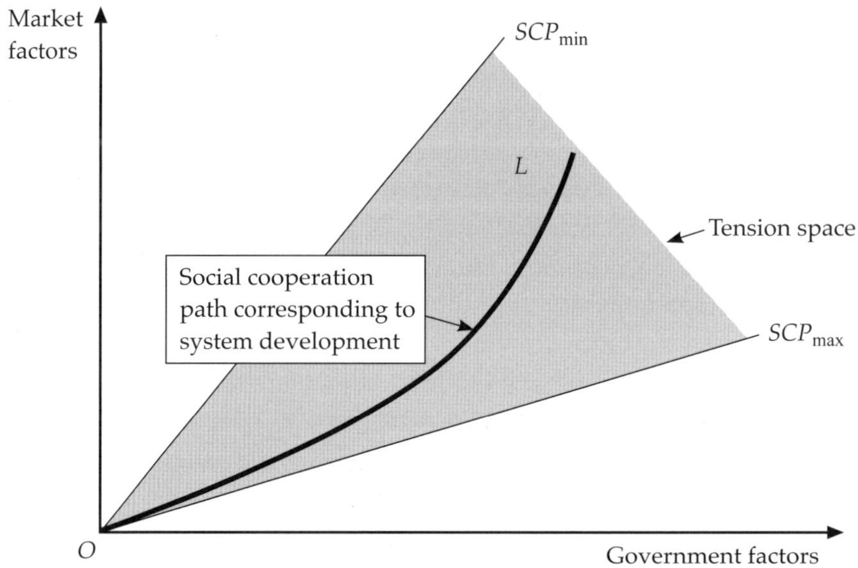

China's rural financial system should be studied from a continuous and dynamic perspective: As marketization progresses, contract credibility which can be more easily expanded and represents stronger social cooperation ability of the households would gradually substitute kinship credibility. One this transition occurs, the *SPC* curve will become steeper, and the optimal social cooperation path will move upward. Furthermore, if the transition sustains, the social cooperation path curve would form a *SCP* line which curves upward (*L* in Fig. 4.3).

The status of the government in rural finance: Functions and effects

According to Stiglitz and Weiss's theory (1981) of credit rationing, to avoid adverse selection and moral hazard under information asymmetry, the sole supplier of capital would not achieve market equilibrium by merely raising the interest rate.

Rather, the supplier would impose an interest rate at which return would be maximized based on the expected risk and his own experience, which implies that credit rationing is inevitable. In Fig. 4.4, assume that the agricultural loan market has a relatively stable credit demand curve D and a supply curve of financial institutions is S_1, under credit rationing, the interest rate is set at R_1. The excess demand for credit represented by CA cannot be satisfied.

Fig. 4.4. The effect of government intervention in alleviating credit rationing

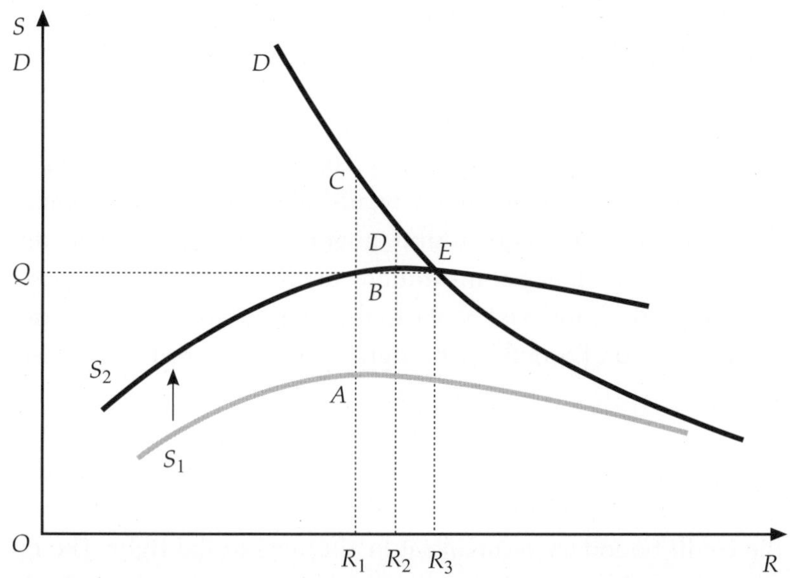

When there is a lack of agricultural development, increasing the supply in rural finance can bring about positive externalities. Not only can it raise the income level of Rural households, but it can also support the transformation of rural households' production to individual businesses, specialized breeding farms, and forming rural cooperatives, through encouraging specialization, economies of scale, and innovation. This kind of externality is public and long-term. Therefore, in theory, it is essential and practical for the government to intervene as the third party to compensate for the risk and to maximize social benefits.

Generally speaking, there are two ways to increase the financial supply in the agricultural loan market: (1) the government set up policy financial institutions to offer low-interest or subsidized credit; (2) to expand the scope of credit offered by commercial financial institutions thought introducing third-party compensation. The former would work in the area where commercial financial institutions cannot enter; the latter can increase the total supply which the supply from commercial financial institutions is already part of. Regardless of the method, the economic function is to provide abundant credit to agricultural items which have a rate of return lower than the market's required rate of return, or have positive externalities but are facing the financing constraints.

The government should be the main supplier of policy-based finance and third-party compensation in the agricultural loan market. As it is not desirable for the government to be the direct supplier, it can consider setting up policy financial institutions to provide non-profit-making policy credit. Or the government can use commercial financial institutions as agents and to direct their credit input through the leverage of subsidies. Considering the current situation of marketization of agriculture and the sustainable development of rural finance, it is expected that providing third-party compensation to compensate commercial financial institutions for their service expansion should be the dominant form of government intervention. The form of intervention would allow financial leverage to refine agricultural insurance and agricultural guarantee fund; offer an agricultural discount to commercial financial institutions to encourage them to increase input into agriculture; lead commercial banks to invest a certain proportion of capital in agriculture and the rural economy through tax policy in order to boost the rural financial supply.

As shown in Fig. 4.4, government intervention can raise the supply curve in the agricultural loan market from S_1 to S_2 and reduce the shortage of credit from *CA* to *DB*. Third-party compensation (risk compensation or price compensation) can expand the credit boundary of financial institutions to the right. The quantity of supply moves from *B* to *E*. At *E*, The supply and demand in the agricultural loan market is in equilibrium. Credit rationing dies out.

To accurately define function of government intervention requires in-depth research into the endogenous features of the rural financial market. As the rural financial market is special, the time, format, and degree of government intervention in rural finance are different from those in equilibrium under general market conditions. In the next section, we refer to the characteristics of China's rural financial market in the discussion about the status of the government.

The double imbalance of the internal market structure

The double imbalance is manifested at two levels: (1) In the macro view, some of the rural areas are so well-developed that they almost catch up with the urban areas. Their production structure is no longer dominated by small-farm production.

Improved productive forces and economic benefits can attract more financial resources. Some of the rural areas lag behind in development. As traditional production is inefficient and brings few benefits, these areas cannot attract financial resources or prevent capital outflows. (2) In the micro view, even in rural areas that are less developed, there are differences between the rich and the poor, advanced and traditional productions, which differentiate two groups of financial demand.

Without a doubt, different groups have different financial demand, which is satisfied by financial supply of different nature and forms. The internal imbalance of China's rural financial market has defined two financial contracts of different nature: commercial and non-commercial. The former can effectively allocate financial resources under self-initiated market adjustment because of better economic development and self-sustainability. The latter cannot form a contract relationship on its own because it cannot satisfy the risk-return ratio as commercial contracts do. In other words, targeting more developed rural areas and the richer households, commercial financial institutions would volunteer to offer financial contracts; regarding less developed rural areas and the poorer households, there is a need for government directed DFIs to provide non-commercial contracts to alleviate poverty.

Form a macro perspective, non-commercial contract is a form of policy-based finance which bears some features of public goods. Considering that one of the risks in the long-term development of China's economy is the issue of unsustainability under the dual structure during economic transaction, to preserve the control of the state over the risk of transition, how the government tackles the Matthew effect[7]—the rich get richer and the poor get poorer—brought about by the imbalance in rural finance has become an important and urgent economic and political issue. Therefore, government intervention in less advanced areas and the non-commercial financial aspect of the poor is justified. The revenue of government intervention in the supply of non-commercial contract cannot be evaluated using simple marketization logic. Apart from economic cost, factors such as the control over the risk of transition, the promotion of balanced growth, and maintenance of social stability should be included in the government's utility function, and they may take up a larger proportion than economic benefits under certain conditions. Furthermore, with the catch-up effect, the long-term economic effect of government intervention may not be low. To rural households which for a long time receive little income and have a lack of capital, the inflows of financial resources may allow them to accumulate enough resources in a short time to transform or expand production. Their income may increase multiple times. When the growth rate of rural income is higher than that of urban income, the urban-rural gap closes up.

Insufficient demand and supply

There is a blind spot in China's rural financial studies. They focus on the insufficient financial supply (especially the supply of informal finance) but neglect the lack of demand. The prevalent explanation for the insufficient supply of China's rural financial resources is that rural finance is being heavily suppressed. Whether it is the coverage of financial institution outlets, support from credit capital, or the business and variety of financial services, none of them can satisfy the rural financial demand. However, this is only one side of the problem. From many field studies, we discovered that as the state's microcredit policies begins to take form, the coverage of microcredit in some areas has risen to over 90%, but the deposit ratio at the local RCCs is less than 60%. The interviews with rural households reveal that due to the lack of investment items and opportunities, and the households are rather conservative, their credit demand cannot effectively be expanded or released. This shows that not only the supply side but also the demand side are responsible for the ineffective allocation of rural financial resources. Therefore, in the long run, to promote the coordinated and sustainable development of financial institutions and rural households, the suppression of the households' financial demand should be taken seriously. The self-development ability of rural households should be improved so that their potential effective demand will be released.

While guiding rural households toward improving viability can bring positive viability, but the commercial suppliers would not be responsible for the expenditure. Therefore, when market mechanism cannot fully function, government intervention is necessary and inevitable. As previously mentioned, due to the lack of material capital, the conservative mind, old habits, and limited awareness of the world strongly influence the rural households' behavior. They have little motivation and are unwilling to employ new technology: When they are guaranteed to obtain more revenue by using new technology, they generally wait and observe rather than taking risk. Under such circumstances, rural households need a demonstration for technological reform and production transformation. China's economy has long been directed by the government, and rural households have immense respect for, and faith in, the government. Under such conditions, if the government sets up a corresponding "demonstration-diffusion" system, it is possible and incurs a lower cost to guide and motivate rural households to transform production and improve their self-development ability.

The lack of market development and institutional norms

The World Bank (1989) pointed out in their study that the rural financial market in developing countries cannot function properly and market failure is common. The lack of market development is obvious in China. Low population density, market segmentation, difficulties in risk control, and income fluctuation and high transaction cost caused by seasonal factors render it difficult for the rural financial market to disperse risk without conventional collaterals. Under such conditions, profit-making financial institutions would not enter the market. Because of the inherent shortcomings of China's rural financial market, if the constraints on rural finance relax, credit allocation of financial institutions would be out of control and rent-seeking behavior would appear. Many financial institutions may eventually lose the ability to repay and go bankrupt.

Without a doubt, when there is a lack of market development and institutional norms, the government should actively nurture the market by providing an appropriate policy environment and law and regulations, as well as reinforcing property rights and market constraints. Currently, hampered by the problems such as the lack of regulatory rules and supervision mechanism, and a weak regulatory basis, the supervision of rural finance is inefficient, if not ineffective. As the entry policy relaxes, a new form of rural financial institutions such as rural banks, credit enterprises, rural RCC funds emerge. Law and regulations on these institutions such as *Rural Cooperative Financial Law* and *Community Banking Law* are vague. The vacuum of supervision has become a potential problem in the accelerated development of rural finance. It is worth noting that the development of policy-oriented rural finance would give rise to the issue of political economics of finance: In resources allocation which is strongly directed by the government, the distribution of political authority may affect the process of and results of credit issuance. Much "power rent" would be generated, which would challenge the already loose supervision on rural finance.

To a certain extent, China's rural financial supervision is a paradox of form and substance: the formality of the administration and the system of approval to some extent can help control financial risk at the expense of efficiency. Rent-seeking behavior and corruption arise as the government devises preferential policies for the Three Rural Issues. Undoubtedly, if the goal is to open and expand the market in a short period of time, and the supervision system cannot catch up with the development, the potential risk in the rural financial system is much higher than imagination. Therefore, policy support and encouragement for rural finance should be able to encourage competition and reinforce supervision: Apart from regulating the entry, operation, and exit of financial institutions through law and regulations, the government should consider including informal finance, which is very prevalent, in their scope of supervision. Opportunistic behavior should be minimized through tighter supervision under relatively loose policies in order to promote stable development.

Is China's National Agricultural Loan Mechanism Efficient?[8]

Under resources allocation by the market forces, capital flows toward the most efficient sector. As China's rural households in transformation are naturally fragile, they are not entirely rational toward credit capital. In recent years, the government has been promoting the credit for Three Rural Issues, hoping that credit capital would improve the production ability and hence the income of rural households, as well as agricultural production. Normally, credit issued to rural households by licensed financial institutions is referred to as national agricultural loans.

There are two distinctive views on the efficiency of national agricultural loans. One of the views is that national agricultural loans can effectively improve the benefits of rural households despite the high cost. The World Bank (1995, 1998, and 2001) mentioned three types of national agricultural loans which are efficient: Thailand's Bank for Agriculture and Agricultural Cooperatives, Indonesia's Unit Desas of Bank Rakyat Indonesia, and Grameen Bank in Bangladesh. It believes that these three institutions significantly improved the benefits of local households. Some Chinese economists hold a similar view. Lin Yifu (2006) analyzed the rural credit situation in three counties (cities). He discovered that national agricultural loans can affect the fixed assets for production of rural households, private loans cannot substitute national agricultural loans, but the issuance rate of national agricultural loans is low, and general credit constraints exist. Li Rui (2004) analyzed the influence of borrowing on the benefits which rural households enjoy. The results show that every RMB100 borrowed can increase the net income of rural households by RMB93.05 and non-land assets by RMB15.24. The rate of return of rural loans is 108.29%.

Others are more cautious toward the efficiency toward national agricultural loans. Besley (1985) analyzed the effect the credit market has on agricultural production and believed that national agricultural loans are in reality an intervention in the administration of the rural credit market, which causes moral hazard and market monopoly. The efficiency of credit capital allocation is severely reduced and, therefore, national agricultural loans cannot promote agricultural production. Kochar (1997a, 1997b) analyzed the 1981–1982 data of land lease in

India and examined the performance of national agricultural loans: Even though rural households can obtain national agricultural loans, credit capital brings no effect to the benefits of rural households. As a whole, national agricultural loans are ineffective. There are studies of the motivations for the national agricultural loans in China which cast doubts on the efficiency of the loans. For example, Zhang Jie (2004) thinks that the national agricultural loans are the products of the division of the little residual balance of agriculture between the state and rural households. In the absence of a rational market, the efficiency of national agricultural loans would not be high.

The domestic quantitative analyses are not in-depth. Zhang Jie's study (2004) focused on the institutional level without the use of econometrics; Lin Yifu (2000) provided a descriptive analysis of rural loans but not a systemic empirical analysis; Li Rui (2004) used combined data of national agricultural loans and informal loans for analysis, which are not suitable for estimating the efficiency of national agricultural loans.

With the above considerations in mind, this section attempts to provide a quantitative analysis of the national agricultural loans with reference to the characteristics of rural households.

Sampling and the model design

Sluggish production of rural households is an institutional motivation for the implementation of national agricultural loans. To fully understand China's national agricultural loans, we must first analyze China's rural households. To understand the situation of the use of national agricultural loans and obtain empirical data, we conducted survey sampling. Data were collected in several phases with the help of RCCs. The structure of agricultural industry in different regions varies to a large extent. If we make the 31 provinces (districts, cities) the sampling units, the difference in samples may lead to deviation in the results of the quantitative analysis. In the first phase, we conducted a preliminary sampling survey in seven regions: eastern, southern, northern, central, northeastern, southwestern, and northwestern China. We chose northern China as our research area. In the second phase, we conducted systematic sampling in five counties (districts, cities) in northern China. The per capita GDPs of Hebei Province and Tianjin ranked second and fourth respectively among the five provinces (districts, cities). The two locations were chosen as research subjects. We randomly chose three to four districts, counties, or cities at the county level, which were Jinghai County, Ji County, Dagang District, and Xiqing District in Tianjin, and Huanghua, Wuqiao County, and Funing County in Heibei Province. In the third phase, we ranked all sample administrative villages chosen in the second phase in terms of wealth. Then, we employed cluster sampling through judgment sampling,[9] choosing two administrative villages in the middle of the list. We filtered out villages in county seats and administrative towns. In the fourth phase, we conducted a census of the sample rural households in administrative villages who possessed RMB500,000 or less assets. The census was conducted in the form of household survey and centralized questionnaire sessions. Some answers did not match the business situation or living conditions of the households. Filtering out the suspicious data, we obtained data of the business situation of 1,918 households, which describes the use of national agricultural loans in 2006.

Table 4.2. The strata of rural households in the sample areas

Household strata	Xiqing District (Tianjin) N=87	Dagang District (Tianjin) N=156	Ji County (Tianjin) N=380	Jinghai County (Tianjin) N=160	Huanghua (Hebei Province) N=284	Wuqiao County (Heibei Province) N=473	Funing County (Heibei Province) N=378	Average of samples N=1918
(a) RMB100,00 or more household assets (%)	6.97	5.12	1.31	1.89	1.41	0.63	0.80	1.67
(b) RMB50,000–100,000 or more household assets (%)	37.20	30.76	7.91	14.55	7.77	6.72	5.92	10.94
(c) RMB50,00 or less household assets (%)	55.81	64.10	90.76	83.54	90.89	92.64	93.26	87.37

Notes: 1. Due to issues with fluidity, property rights, etc., the value of the properties which the households were living in could not be estimated and therefore not included in the calculation of the household assets: household assets = deposit + securities + fixed assets for production + durable consumption goods. Fixed assets for production and family electrical appliances were calculated using their current value.

2. Percentage of rural households = Number of sample households in the stratum / Total number of sample households in that area x 100%

3. Percentage of agricultural income = Σ households' agricultural income / Σ households' total income x 100%

4. Agricultural income = income from land and planting + income from small-scale farming + income from farming and planting + income from agricultural by-products and primary processing

5. Percentage of means of production in total assets per household = Σ households' means of production / Σ household assets x 100%
6. a + b + c = 100%. Any deviations are rounding errors.

Households with RMB50,000 or less assets account for 87.37% of the samples. The net accumulation of these households ranged normally from RMB2,000 to RMB5,000. Scott (1976) thinks that traditional rural households are living on the brink of bankruptcy. They need to choose between labor hardships or to meet the subsistence needs. Toni (1966) described rural households in south-east Asia as such: "A person who stands in the middle of a river whose water level is neck-high, he will drown when small waves hit." Both Scott and Toni think that survival is the primary goal of poor households. In order to survive, serious self-exploitation leaves no room for the households to care about profit. Assume that survival is the motivation behind poor households' production (Only the concept of means of subsistence extends to include modern factors such as a change in the social strata and self-financed elderly population), according to Scott and Toni's theories, households with RMB50,000 or less assets are defined as "surviving small farmers." They borrow loans to satisfy subsistence needs. Households with more than RMB50,000 in assets account for 12.61% of the total number of households, of which those with more than RMB100,000 assets account for 1.67%. It is found in the study that these households have a net accumulation of over RMB5,000 a year. Households with more than RMB50,000 assets are regarded as rich in the sample areas. Schultz (1950) proposed that rural households can also be entrepreneurs and merchants at the same time, and their required efficiency for resources allocation is higher than farm owners. Similarly, their business goal is to maximize profit. They would stop bringing inputs when marginal benefit equals marginal cost. Based on Schultz's theory, we defined households with more than RMB50,000 in assets as "rational small farmers." Their behavior is guided by the principle of profit maximization. While drawing the line at RMB50,000 seems subjective, but this corresponds with the actual situation as shown in Table 4.2. We also discovered that the demand for national agricultural loans concentrated on "rational small farmers." 92.3% rational small farmers hope to obtain national agricultural loans. Their use of loans is closely driven by production, which accounted for 77.24% of national agricultural loans. Comparatively, only 31.27% of surviving small farmers hope to obtain national agricultural loans for building houses, education, and savings. Only 22.76% of national agricultural loans were allocated to "surviving small farmers."

It should be noted that even though we can directly observe the production situation of rural households, we cannot presume the production behavior of households after they obtain national agricultural loans. Production behavior is a latent variance, which makes the random disturbance term. When the random disturbance term does not equal zero, the estimated results would be inaccurate. Heckman (1974, 1979) proposed a two-stage estimation model to rectify sample bias through inverse mill ratio (IMR). We employ Heckman's two-stage estimation model to measure the execution efficiency of national agricultural loans.

The production functions for rural households' production are as follows:

$$UB_i = r_0 + r_1 B_i + r_2 X_i + u_{1i}$$

$$W_i = \beta_0 + \beta_1 X_i + u_{2i} \quad (4\text{–}1)$$

UB_i represents the total social output of rural households.[10] As the situation of rural households after obtaining national agricultural loans cannot be observed, UB_i is a latent variance. B represents the volume of national agricultural loans. Rural households would adjust B based on their marginal product and cost of funds. W_i represents the total social output of rural households after they have obtained national agricultural loans, and X represents other factors of production, where $X = (x_1, x_2, \cdots, x_n)$. Based on Heckman's conclusion, we assume the ith rural household chooses national agricultural loans, $UB_i = W_i$ must be satisfied.

$$B_i = (\beta_0 + \beta_1 X_i - r_0 - r_2 X_i) \,/\, r_1 + (u_{2i} - u_{1i}) \,/\, r_{1i} \quad (4\text{–}2)$$

When $B > 0$, households can obtain national agricultural loans; when $B \leq 0$, they cannot. From 4–2, we can obtain the following:

$$(u_{2i} - u_{1i}) \leq r_0 - \beta_0 + r_2 X - \beta_1 X \quad (4\text{–}3)$$

In terms of statistics, if u_{1i} and u_{2i} distribute independently, then they accord with the joint normal distribution with mean value being zero. Var $(u_{2i} - u_{1i}) = \sigma^2$, $u\,(u_{2i} - u_{1i}) = \sigma$, $\sigma_{1u} = \text{Cov}\,(u_{1i}, u)$, $\sigma_{2u} = \text{Cov}\,(u_{2i}, u)$. The probability of rural households not choosing national agricultural loans is as follows:

$$\Pr\,(B \leq 0\,) = \phi\,(r_0 - \beta_0 + r_2 Z - \beta_1 X \,/\, \sigma) = \phi\,(\Delta) \quad (4\text{–}4)$$

In (4–4), $\phi\,(\bullet)$ is a function with normal distribution, and $\Delta = (r_0 - \beta_0 + r_2 Z - \beta_1 X \,/\, \sigma)$. Therefore, the maximum likelihood function is as follows:

$$L = \prod_{B>0} f\,(W, B) \prod_{B\leq 0} \phi\,(\Delta) \quad (4\text{–}5)$$

f is a joint normal distribution function. In (4–5), truncation errors are not rectified. Heckman later proved the following:

$$E\,(u_2 / B > 0) = E\,(u_2 / u > \Delta) = \frac{\sigma_2^2\,\sigma_1^2}{\sigma} \times \frac{\phi\,(\Delta)}{1 - \phi\,(\Delta)} \qquad (4\text{–}6)$$

From (4–6),

$$u_{2i} = u \times \frac{\phi\,(\Delta)}{1 - \phi\,(\Delta)} + v_2 \qquad (4\text{–}7)$$

u_{2i} represents IMR in Heckman's two-stage model. v_2 is a random disturbance term which has a mean of zero, and hence truncation errors are eliminated. Put (4–7) into (4–1),

$$W_i = \beta_0 + \beta_1 X_i + \frac{u_{2i} - u_{1i}}{\sigma} \times \frac{\phi\,(\Delta)}{1 - \phi\,(\Delta)} + v_2 \qquad (4\text{–}8)$$

In the first stage, assume A as the increase in productive fixed assets:

$A_i = 0$, if $A_i = 0$
$A_i = 1$, if $A_i = (0, +\infty)$

The formula is as follows:

$$Pr\,(A) = \xi_0 + X'_{1i}\,\xi_1 + \xi_2 \log\,(B) + u_{1i} \qquad (4\text{–}9)$$

Apply Probit regression to (4–9), we get u_{2i}, i.e., $\frac{u_{2i} - u_{1i}}{\sigma} \times \frac{\phi\,(\Delta)}{1 - \phi\,(\Delta)} + v_2$, which will be represented by λ_1.

In the second stage, (4–8) can be represented as follows:

$$E\,(A_i / B_i^* > 0,\, A_i^* > 0) = \beta_0 + \beta_1 X + \beta_2 B + \beta_3 \lambda_1 + v \qquad (4\text{–}10)$$

In (4–10), $E\,(A_i / B_i^* > 0, A_i^* > 0)$ represents that rural households have obtained national agricultural loans and there is positive output. λ_1 is IMR, v is a random disturbance term, and other parameters are the same as in (4–1). (4–10) eliminates truncation errors. Based on the observable *UB*, *W* can be estimated. The influence of national agricultural loans on the survival of rural households can be examined.

Other vectors apart from national agricultural loans can also affect the fixed assets of rural households. Summarizing former research, we identify the vectors which affect the fixed assets of rural households[11]: (1) Informal loans affect the means of production. (2) Ravallion (1999) investigated the reasons behind the income-gap in China. He thinks that the Educational level is one of the major factors in determining the income level. We set the Educational level of households labor force as one of the vectors in our study. (3) Kochar, in his study, used arable land, power of machinery, local level of wages as factors affecting the efficiency of the use of loans of rural households. Following Kochar, we use arable land per household, power of machinery, and local level of wages as vectors affecting the fixed assets of rural households. (4) With reference to the actual current situation of China's rural areas, we set assets for non-production and labor force as vectors which affect the production of rural households.

Empirical analysis and examination

From the analysis above, it can be seen that the production performance of surviving small farmers and rational small farmers are very different. If they are regarded as a whole, the research conclusion may be inaccurate. Therefore, we estimated the efficiency of the use of national agricultural loans of the two types of households separately. In the first stage, we employed Probit estimation formula (4-9) and confirmed IMR. The results are shown in Table 4.3. The coefficient of Probit model itself is meaningless. Only when it is considered with the sign of correlation coefficients can it help reflect the case-and-effect relationship among variables. If rural households are considered as a whole, the national agricultural loans at 10% confidence level cannot pass the z-test and therefore does not significantly affect the production of rural households. Other variables including educational level, Quantity of household labor force, value of agricultural machinery, and salary can encourage households to purchase fixed assets. From the results of separate estimation for the two types of households, at 5% confidence level, national agricultural loans affects "rational small farmers." At 1% confidence level, it affects "surviving small farmers." However, the correlation coefficient is negative. The national agricultural loans significantly lower the probability for surviving small farmers to purchase fixed assets. This agrees with the results of the survey. "Surviving small farmers" lack capital. Their credit capital is mostly allocated to aspects other than production. Therefore, the probability for them to purchase fixed assets is even smaller. The estimated results using formula (4-9) may be affected by sample selection bias so that we cannot be sure of the conclusion. Nonetheless, we obtained IMR (λ_1).

Table 4.3. Results of the estimation of agricultural loans using the Probit model

Variables	Probit—all small farmers			Probit—rational small farmers			Probit—surviving small farmers		
	Correlation coefficient	z-value	Probability	Correlation coefficient	z-value	Probability	Correlation coefficient	z-value	Probability
Constant	−4.7115***	−4.4250	0.00	−7.9502	−1.2016	0.23	−4.0669**	−3.0988	0.01
Assets for non-production	0.0560	0.3415	0.73	0.4595	0.3574	0.72	−0.2217	−0.9605	0.34
National agricultural loans	−0.0420	−0.6917	0.48	0.2810**	2.1817	0.03	−0.288***	−3.0822	0.00
Informal loans	0.0919	1.4432	0.14	−0.1404	−0.9203	0.35	0.2223**	2.4121	0.02
Educational level	0.4123*	1.7351	0.08	0.0574	0.1007	0.92	0.4118	1.3821	0.17
Quantity of household labor force	0.4053**	2.2163	0.02	1.4002**	2.1288	0.03	0.3758	1.5258	0.13
Arable land per household	0.0365	1.2670	0.20	0.1328*	1.7008	0.09	0.0002	0.0036	0.99
Value of agricultural machinery	0.3043**	2.4396	0.01	−0.1759	−0.4636	0.64	0.5228**	3.0707	0.01
Salary	0.3720***	4.3657	0.00	0.7278**	2.5266	0.01	0.3871***	3.3373	0.00
	MACD=0.4927			MACD=0.6667			MACD=0.4086		

Notes: 1.*at 10% confidence level, **at 5% confidence level, ***at 1% confidence level.

2. To smooth data, the logarithm value of national agricultural loans, informal loans, assets for non-production, value of agricultural machinery, and salary are used. The goods in assets for non-production and the agricultural machinery are calculated using the present value.

3. Assets for non-production include savings, durable consumption goods, etc., which represent accumulation of rural households. The value of agricultural machinery can reflect the production status and ability of the households. Years of education refers to the sum of that of the most educated member of the households and that of follow-up education. It is to reflect the educational level. The Quantity of household labor force counts only the labor force of household members who can continuously work eight hours a day, but it does not include students. Arable land includes both private land and rented land.

Formula (4–10) eliminates sample selection bias and captures the non-zero disturbance. Mean correction standardizes the estimation results. Same as above, we applied second-stage examination to three categories: all small farmers, "rational small farmers," and "surviving small farmers." Results are shown in Table 4.4. Considering all farmers, R^2 in formula (4–10) is 0.698. At 10% confidence level, national agricultural loans do not pass the t-test or significantly affect the production of "surviving small farmers." R^2 in the regression equation for rational small farmers equals 0.7528. At 5% confidence level, national agricultural loans pass the t-test. Results show that national agricultural loans affect the production of "rational small farmers." Assets for non-production are another factor which affects the purchase of fixed assets, but its influence coefficient is smaller than that of national agricultural loans. Among all sources of capital, rational small farmers first opt for national agricultural loans and then household accumulation. Informal loans are insignificant to them. They are more likely to invest in production. Informal loans cannot satisfy their demand for capital. At the same time, household accumulation suffices to pay for the large sum of expenditure, mainly in the form of investment in production. However, the empirical results show that household accumulation of rational small farmers cannot satisfy their own demand for investment. They need to rely on national agricultural loans.

Table 4.4. Estimation of the efficiency of national agricultural loans

Variables	Second-stage— all small farmers		Second-stage— rational small farmers		Second-stage — surviving small farmers	
	Correlation coefficient	T-value	Correlation coefficient	T-value	Correlation coefficient	T-value
Constant	–13.6659***	–4.9224	–4.7362**	–2.1641	–12.0131***	–3.5507
Assets for non-production	0.2007	1.3581	0.6784*	1.8716	0.5066**	–2.9624
National agricultural loans	0.8273	1.2826	1.1149**	2.6177	–0.1768	–0.2565
Informal loans	0.3306***	4.1521	–0.0398	–0.6536	0.7514***	7.0376
Educational level	1.1990***	4.4963	–0.0020	–0.0130	1.4700***	4.4526
Quantity of household labor force	0.7404***	3.4057	0.1396	0.4438	0.8217***	3.1618

(Cont'd)

Variables	Second-stage—all small farmers		Second-stage—rational small farmers		Second-stage —surviving small farmers	
	Correlation coefficient	T-value	Correlation coefficient	T-value	Correlation coefficient	T-value
Arable land per household	–0.0805	–1.6616	0.0312	0.9731	–0.0877	–1.5512
Value of agricultural machinery	0.9339***	5.8927	0.0318	0.3850	1.3792***	5.9462
Salary	0.8612***	7.2387	0.1292	0.8544	0.9854***	5.5338
λ_1	1.8803	6.2719	0.2072	0.8771	1.9607	4.3474
	$R^2 = 0.698$		$R^2 = 0.7528$		$R^2 = 0.7788$	

Notes: *at 10% confidence level, **at 5% confidence level, ***at 1% confidence level.

The R^2 of surviving small farmers is 0.7788. At 10% confidence level, national agricultural loans do not pass the test and therefore do not significantly affect "surviving small farmers." The order of the factors affecting fixed assets of surviving small farmers in terms of the influence coefficient is as follows: educational level, value of agricultural machinery, salary, quantity of household labor force, and informal loans. Same as Ravallion's study (1999), we determine that educational level is the factor which affects the production of surviving small farmers most. The value of agricultural machinery represents the present production ability, and assets for non-production represent the current household accumulation. While informal loans and assets for non-production affect the purchase of fixed assets for production, their combined influence is not on par with that of the value of agricultural machinery. As confirmed by the survey, the two factors correlate with the level of non-productive consumption. For example, building houses is weakly related to fixed assets for production. Surviving small farmers mainly invest in animal husbandry, which has relatively high natural and market risk. Once business fails, it is difficult to recover. Both surviving small farmers and financial institutions bear these types of risk. It is therefore not surprising that national agricultural loans do not affect the production of surviving small farmers.

Conclusions

Based on survey data, we apply Heckman's two-stage method to estimate the efficiency of national agricultural loans in China and reach the following conclusions:

(1) Rational small farmers are the main clients of national agricultural loans: while they only make up 12.61% of total rural households, they account for the use of 77.24% national agricultural loans. They tend to borrow national agricultural loans to invest in production. Conversely, surviving small farmers which make up 87.37% of total rural households only obtain 22.76% of national agricultural loans and they use the loans to pay consumption expenditure.

(2) We agree with the World Bank (1995, 1998, 2001) that national agricultural loans significantly affect rational small farmers' production as it is the main source of capital for purchasing fixed assets. Household accumulation also affects the purchase but to a smaller extent than the national agricultural loans.

(3) We agree with Besley (1985) and Kochar (1997a, 1997b) that national agricultural loans do not significantly affect surviving small farmers' production. The most important factor which affects their purchase of fixed assets for production is educational level. The more educated the households are, the more fixed assets for production they buy. When it comes to the sources of capital, the order of the factors affecting the purchase of fixed assets in terms of the influence coefficient is as follows: educational level, value of agricultural machinery, salary, quantity of household labor force, and informal loans. The last two factors have little influence.

Based on the above conclusions, we believe that, on the one hand, national agricultural loans can support the production of households who have certain production ability and financial basis. This reflects that licensed financial institutions can explore the market related to supporting rural households and agricultural development. On the other hand, to surviving small farmers who have little production ability, credit capital is seldom used to invest in technology which would improve production or bring capital accumulation. Their credit input is inefficient. It reflects that pure credit input can hardly encourage the transformation of rural households who have little production ability and capital deposit.

Intervention of Local Government and Misallocation of Credit Resources of RCCs

In recent years, under a series of preferential policies, the credit support for agriculture of RCCs has been enhanced and set up an optimal business management system through measures such as expanding the ownership structure, improving the governance of legal personality, and replacing bad debts with central bank bills. However, the reforms of RCCs have not concentrated on providing financial support to the Three Rural Issues as expected. On the contrary, RCCs have gradually weakened the financial support, diverting capital which should be used to boost agriculture to various extents. Microcredit which has formerly satisfied the capital demand of rural households is going downhill. Many studies have claimed that RCCs are not motivated enough to provide loans for rural economic activities (Zhang Qi et al. 2004). Loans which are used in supporting rural areas, agricultural production, and business are very limited. Whether in areas that are economically well-developed or highly urbanized, or the vast mid-western area and agricultural provinces in the east, RCCs show the features of non-agricultural and urbanized, which are manifested in the trend of urban institutionalization in the branches of RCCs, cash flow to urban areas, and that the employees are predominantly urban residents (Sheng Yongwei 2001). Apparently, under the cloak of commercialization, RCCs are going down the path of de-agriculturalization, deviating from the state's original financial policies to boost agriculture.

Corresponding to RCCs' weakened financial support for the Three Rural Issues, the target clients of RCCs have shifted to urban residents in recent years. Especially after the authority of RCCs was handed over to the local governments, the tendency toward de-agriculturalization has become more obvious.[12] From the form and official positioning, RCCs are cooperative organizations. Their property rights are well-defined and the RCCs are owned by the members. However, the property rights of investors are not comprehensive as they have no management authority (management authority is given to local governments). Recently, in some provinces, the local government attempts to merge RCCs within its jurisdiction to form large-scale commercial banks (or financial holding groups) in order to issue large project loans. RCCs themselves can hardly finish the task. A transformation of RCCs directed by the local governments would cause a large-scale diversion of agricultural credit capital and the absence of financial services. Upon government intervention, the capital drawn from rural areas will flow to large projects which can boost the local GDP. This will promote economic overheating, causing issues with macroeconomic regulation and control. The potential problems caused by the local governments' reckless transformation of RCCs and administrative intervention should not be neglected.

This section attempts to examine de-agriculturaliztion of RCCs' credit resources under intervention of the local government, which would help us take precautions against the potential problems with the local governments' control over RCCs. First, we establish our model regarding RCCs' decision-making on the allocation of credit resources. Then, through several expansions of the models, we investigate the misallocation of credit resources caused by local protectionism. Lastly, we offer conclusive comments.

RCCs' decision-making on the allocation of credit resources: A basic model

There are some basic assumptions in our model. According to the basic principles of political economics, the government and RCCs are rational and selfish. Under constraints, they want to maximize their own utility (economic benefits). As the target utility functions of the two parties are different, the government prefers large-scale projects which can directly boost the GDP, and RCCs hope to maximize economic benefits under certain government constraints. In order to examine the decision-making of the RCCs on the allocation of credit resources, we first distinguish between two kinds of investment projects: projects related to the Three Rural Issues and projects directed by the local government. The former reflects a tendency toward supporting the macroeconomic policies of the state, and the latter toward improving the benefits of the local government (directly propel the growth of the local GDP). In order to examine the effect of the uncertainty of the projects and local protectionism of the local government have on the decision-making of RCCs on agricultural credit, we included the probability of stochastic return and bankruptcy and liquidation as factors in our model. During the decision-making process, RCCs target to maximize their own expected utility. Their utility function includes project investment return as well as fixed cost and the cost of risk.

To simplify the analysis, we standardize the total amount of loanable funds (i.e., the total volume of project loans in RCCs) as 1, of which those allocated to support projects related to the Three Rural Issues is represented as l_p and those allocated to projects directed by the local government as l_g. Therefore, $l_p + l_g = 1$. If $\pi\ (l_p, l_g)$ represents the revenue of RCCs, and $C\ (l_p, l_g)$ the costs of loans, the RCCs' decision-making should be aiming at maximizing its target utility function[13]:

$$U\ (l_p, l_g) = \pi\ (l_p, l_g) - C\ (l_p, l_g)$$

Below we examine the structure of $\pi\ (l_p, l_g)$ and $C\ (l_p, l_g)$.

In order to focus on the study of the influence of capital and neglect production factors such as labor force for now, the production functions for the two kinds of projects can be represented as follows:

Projects directed by the local government: $Y_g = (g + \varepsilon)\ K_g$

Projects related to the Three Rural Issues: $Y_p = (p + \varepsilon)\, K_p$

In the formulae, Y_i represents output; K_i represents capital deposit; ε and represents a random variable such as uncertainties (risk) in production, which include weather, market situation, etc. To preserve generality, assume $E(\varepsilon) = 0$ and ε follows the uniform distribution of $[-h, h]$ $(0 < p, g < h)$, its density function is as follows:

When $\varepsilon \in [-h, h], f(\varepsilon) = \frac{1}{2h}$; when $\varepsilon \notin [-h, h], f(\varepsilon) = 0$

The corresponding return on capital for projects related to the Three Rural Issues is $R_p = p + \varepsilon$, that for projects directed by the local government is $R_g = g + \varepsilon$. Let the loan rate of RCCs be r, and $r > 0$. With reference to the general debt contract, when the return on capital of the project $R_i \geq 1 + r$, RCCs receive the total amount of payment as agreed in the contract: $1 + r$. When $R_i \leq 0$, the projects close, and RCCs receive no payment. When $R_i \in (0, 1 + r)$, the payment RCCs receive equals R_i. Based on the formulae above, the expected value of the operating revenue of RCCs can be represented by the sum of the revenues of the two kinds of projects: $E\pi = E\pi_g\,(l_g) + E\pi_p\,(l_p)$, of which:

$$E\pi_g(l_g) = \int_{1+r-g}^{h} l_g(1+r)\, f(\varepsilon)\, d\varepsilon + \int_{-g}^{1+r-g} l_g(g+\varepsilon)\, f(\varepsilon)\, d\varepsilon = \frac{h + g - 1 - r}{2h}\, l_g(1+r) + \frac{(1+r)^2}{4h}\, l_g$$

$$E\pi_p(l_p) = \int_{1+r-p}^{h} l_p(1+r)\, f(\varepsilon)\, d\varepsilon + \int_{-p}^{1+r-p} l_p(p+\varepsilon)\, f(\varepsilon)\, d\varepsilon = \frac{h + p - 1 - r}{2h}\, l_p(1+r) + \frac{(1+r)^2}{4h}\, l_p$$

In terms of the cost of loans, RCCs face fixed costs:

$$C_1(l_i) = c_i\, l_i \text{ and } i = p, g$$

c_i represents the coefficient of the cost of loans. As the fixed costs of RCCs include loan approval, loan issuance, and post-loan management which are related to a fixed work flow, these costs mainly depend on the number of issuances of loans. If the total amount of loan is constant, the greater number of issuance incur higher costs; on the contrary, the smaller number of issuance (implies that the amount of each issuance is larger) incur lower costs. As credit issued to projects related to the Three Rural Issues are usually small in amount but done multiple times (especially the microcredit which targets dispersed rural households), it is difficult to achieve economies of scale. Therefore, the coefficients of the cost of loans satisfy $c_g < c_p$.

Apart from fixed costs, RCCs also face the costs of risk of project failures. We assume that when the return on capital for projects related to the Three Rural Issues

$R_p \le 0$, the actual probability of liquidity is γ_p $(0 \le \gamma_p \le 1)$. When the return on capital for projects directed by the local government $R_g \le 0$, the actual probability of liquidity is γ_g $(0 \le \gamma_g \le 1)$. Once the project is liquidated, RCCs cannot receive payments for the loans, which would become bad debts. As the number of bad debts increases, RCCs faces stronger cost pressures and tougher conditions to survive. The cost of RCCs rises as projects are liquidated and bad debts start to build up. Based on some general cost functions, we can assume that in such a situation the features of the cost function of RCCs matches that of a quadratic function: $C_2(l_i) = \gamma_i \frac{1}{2} l_i^2$, and $i = p, g$. As a result, the total cost for RCCs to issue credit is $C = C_1 + C_2$. Therefore,

$$EC = EC_1 + EC_2 = c_g l_g + c_p l_p + \gamma_p \frac{1}{2} l_p^2 \int_{-h}^{-p} f(\varepsilon)\, d\varepsilon + \gamma_g \frac{1}{2} l_g^2 \int_{-h}^{-g} f(\varepsilon)\, d\varepsilon$$

$$= c_g l_g + c_p (1 - l_g) + \frac{\gamma_g (h-g)\, l_g^2}{4h} + \frac{\gamma_p (h-p)(1-l_g)^2}{4h}$$

With the above hypotheses, we know that the goal of RCCs is to maximize their expected utility through the allocation of l_p and l_g:

$$\text{Max } EU(l_p, l_g)$$
$$s.\ t.\ l_p + l_g = 1$$

According to aforementioned hypotheses, $U(l_p, l_g) = \pi(l_p, l_g) - C(l_p, l_g)$, therefore $EU(l_p, l_g) = E\pi - EC$.

Put $E\pi = E\pi_g(l_g) + E\pi_p(l_p)$ and the value of EC into the equation above:

$$EU(l_p, l_g) = \frac{(1+r)^2}{4h} + \frac{(1+r)(g-p)}{2h} l_g + \frac{(1+r)(h+p-1-r)}{2h}$$
$$- c_g l_g - c_p (1 - l_g) - \frac{\gamma_g (h-g)}{4h} l_g^2 - \frac{\gamma_p (h-p)}{4h} (1 - l_g)^2$$

The first derivative of l_g is

$$\frac{\partial (EU)}{\partial l_g} = \frac{(1+r)(g-p)}{2h} - c_g + c_p - \frac{\gamma_g (h-g)}{2h} l_g + \frac{\gamma_p (h-p)}{2h} (1 - l_g)$$

and the second derivative is

$$\frac{\partial^2 (EU)}{\partial l_g^2} = -\frac{\gamma_g (h-g)}{2h} - \frac{\gamma_p (h-p)}{2h}$$

With reference to the settings of parameters, we know that $0 \le \gamma_p \le 1$, $0 \le \gamma_g \le 1$, $p, g < h$, $h > 0$, and can derive $\dfrac{\partial^2 (\mathrm{E}U)}{\partial l_g^2} = -\dfrac{\gamma_g (h-g)}{2h} - \dfrac{\gamma_p (h-p)}{2h} < 0.$

From the first-order conditions, the optimal l_p and l_g of EU (l_p, l_g) are as follows:

$$l_p = \frac{(1+r)(p-g) + 2h\,(c_g - c_p) + \gamma_g (h-p)}{\gamma_g (h-g) + \gamma_p (h-p)} \tag{4–11}$$

$$l_g = 1 - l_p = \frac{(1+r)(g-p) + 2h\,(c_p - c_g) + \gamma_p (h-p)}{\gamma_g (h-g) + \gamma_p (h-p)} \tag{4–12}$$

As $c_g < c_p$, $0 \le \gamma_p \le 1$, $0 \le \gamma_g \le 1$, $h > 0$, $p, g < h$ and $1 + r > 0$, from (4–11) and (4–12), we arrive at the following proposition:

Proposition 1: The amount of credit RCCs allocate to projects related to the Three Rural Issues l_p decreases as the probability of liquidation γ_p increases, and increases as γ_g increases; the amount of credit RCCs allocate to projects directed by the local government l_g increases as the probability of liquidation γ_p increases, and decreases as γ_g increases.

Because $\dfrac{\partial l_p}{\partial (c_g - c_p)} = \dfrac{2h}{\gamma_g (h-g) + \gamma_p (h-p)}$ and $\dfrac{\partial l_g}{\partial (c_g - c_p)} = \dfrac{-2h}{\gamma_g (h-g) + \gamma_p (h-p)}$, based on the conditions of parameters, $\dfrac{\partial l_p}{\partial (c_g - c_p)} > 0$ and $\dfrac{\partial l_g}{\partial (c_g - c_p)} < 0$, and gives the following proposition:

Proposition 2: As the difference between the fixed costs of projects related to the Three Rural Issues and those of projects directed by the local government $(c_g - c_p)$ increases, the amount of credit capital RCCs allocate to projects related to the Three Rural Issues l_p increases, and that allocated projects directed by the local government l_g decreases.

Expansion of the basic model

Analysis I: Introduction of local protectionism

First, we introduce local protectionism into our model. Local protectionism refers to the government's rescue behavior to prevent liquidation of the projects it directs, but the government does not provide assistance to projects related to the Three

Rural Issues. Under local protectionism, the probability for liquidation is much higher for projects related to the Three Rural Issues than for projects directed by the local government, i.e., $\gamma_p > \gamma_g$.

In order to investigate the effect of local protectionism on the RCCs' strategy of allocation of credit resources, a comparison between the amounts of credit capital allocated to the two types of projects is made. From (4–11) and (4–12), we can derive the following:

$$l_g - l_p = \frac{2g\,(1+r) + 4h\,(c_p - c_g) + \gamma_p\,(h-p) - \gamma_g\,(h-g)}{\gamma_g\,(h-g) + \gamma_p\,(h-p)} \tag{4–13}$$

When $p = g,\ Z = l_g - l_p = \dfrac{2g\,(1+r) + 4h\,(c_p - c_g) + (\gamma_p - \gamma_g)(h-p)}{\gamma_g\,(h-g) + \gamma_p\,(h-p)}$

Based on the setting of the model, $0 < p,\ g < h,\ c_g < c_p,\ r > 0,\ 0 \le \gamma_p \le 1$, and $0 \le \gamma_g \le 1$. When $\gamma_p > \gamma_g,\ Z = l_g - l_p > 0$.

When $p < g,\ g = p + \Delta$ and $\Delta > 0$. By the same principle, the following can be derived:

$$l_g' - l_p' = \frac{2g\,(1+r) + 4h\,(c_p - c_g) + (\gamma_p - \gamma_g)(h-p) + \gamma_p\Delta}{\gamma_g\,(h-g) + \gamma_p\,(h-p)} = Z + \frac{\gamma_g\Delta}{\gamma_g\,(h-g) + \gamma_p\,(h-p)}$$

Based on parameter settings, $\dfrac{\gamma_g\Delta}{\gamma_g\,(h-g) + \gamma_p\,(h-p)} > 0$ and $Z > 0$. The following can be derived: $l_g' - l_p' > Z = l_g - l_p > 0$.

Proposition 3: Even if the rates of return for projects related to the Three Rural Issues and projects directed by the local government are equal, i.e., $p = g$, under local protectionism, the amount of credit capital RCCs allocate to the Three Rural Issues l_p is smaller than that to projects directed by the local government l_g. If the rate of return of projects related to the Three Rural Issues is smaller than that of projects directed by the local government, i.e., $p < g$, RCC's allocation of credit capital would be more biased toward projects directed by the local government.

Analysis II: Introduction of the change in the scale of the total amount of loanable funds

Previously we standardized the total amount of loanable funds ($l_p + l_g$) as 1. Below we study how the change in the scale of the total amount of loanable funds affects RCC's allocation of credit resources. Let $l_p + l_g = L$, repeating the previous steps, the following is derived:

$$EU(l_p, l_g) = \frac{(1+r)^2}{4h} L + \frac{(1+r)(g-p)}{2h} l_g + \frac{(1+r)(h+p-1-r)}{2h}$$
$$- c_g l_g - c_p (L - l_g) - \gamma_g \frac{(h-g)}{4h} l_g^2 - \gamma_p \frac{(h-p)}{4h} (L - l_g)^2$$

From the first-order conditions, the optimal l_g and l_p to maximize $EU(l_p, l_g)$ are as follows:

$$l_g = \frac{(1+r)(g-p) + 2h(c_p - c_g) + \gamma_p (h-p)L}{\gamma_g (h-g) + \gamma_p (h-p)}$$

$$l_p = \frac{(1+r)(p-g) + 2h(c_g - c_p) + \gamma_g (h-g)L}{\gamma_g (h-g) + \gamma_p (h-p)}$$

Therefore,

$$\frac{l_g}{l_p} = \frac{(1+r)(g-p) + 2h(c_p - c_g) + \gamma_p (h-p)L}{(1+r)(p-g) - 2h(c_p - c_g) + \gamma_g (h-g)L} \quad (4\text{–}14)$$

From (4–14), it can be derived that $\lim\limits_{L\to\infty} \frac{l_g}{l_p} = \frac{\gamma_p (h-p)}{\gamma_g (h-g)}$ (4–15)

In (4–15), as the difference between $(h-p)$ and $(h-g)$ is small, when L is large and there is local protectionism, i.e., when $\gamma_p > \gamma_g$, $\frac{l_g}{l_p} \approx \frac{\gamma_p}{\gamma_g} > 1 \Rightarrow l_p < l_g$.

Compared to Proposition 3,when the amount of loanable funds is huge, the decision-making of RCCs on the allocation of credit resources is mainly affected by γ_p and γ_g. Apparently, under local protectionism, even though projects related to the Three Rural Issues have a higher rate of return, they would be crowded out by the projects directed by the local government, which implies that there is a misallocation of RCC's credit resources. In the end, it is the projects protected by the local government which receive credit support, not those with a high return rate. For instance, in the most extreme situation, when the probability of liquidity of projects related to the Three Rural Issues $\gamma_p = 1$ (utterly unprotected), that of projects directed by the local government $\gamma_p = 0$ (under total protection):

$$l_p \to 0, \; l_p \to +\infty$$

This is to say that all credit resources are allocated to projects directed by the local government, and projects related to the Three Rural Issues are entirely crowded out. It is obvious that extreme local protectionism leads to extreme misallocation of credit resources of RCCs.

From the analysis above, we arrive at an enhanced proposition: Proposition 4: When the amount of loanable funds is huge, even though projects related to the Three Rural Issues have a higher rate of return, under local protectionism, RCCs' allocation of credit resources is biased toward projects directed by the local government. The stronger local protectionism is, the more serious the misallocation is.

Analysis III: Introduction of the constraints of financial regulation on local protectionism

Generally speaking, meticulous financial regulation would suppress the financial intervention of the local government and local protectionism. At the same time, if the central government regards providing financial support to the Three Rural Issues as major issues on its political agenda and attempts to suppress the intervention of the local governments by reinforcing financial regulation, after the financial regulation is implemented, local protectionism would be suppressed: The local government can hardly keep "rescuing" the projects they preferred. The probability of liquidity of projects directed by the local government γ_g would increase.

Based on the logic above, γ_g is an increasing function in the degree of financial regulation $\phi: f = \gamma_g(\phi)$, and $f'_\phi > 0$. Substituted with ϕ, the costs of risk is represented as $C_2(l_g, \phi) = \gamma_g(\phi)\frac{1}{2}l_g^2$. Combined with the function of optimization,

$$l_g(\phi) = \frac{(1+r)(g-p) + 2h(c_p - c_g) + \gamma_p(h-p)}{\gamma_p(\phi)(h-g) + \gamma_p(h-p)} \tag{4–16}$$

$$l_p(\phi) = \frac{(1+r)(p-g) + 2h(c_g - c_p) + \gamma_g(\phi)(h-g)}{\gamma_p(\phi)(h-g) + \gamma_p(h-p)} \tag{4–17}$$

It can be seen from (4–16) and (4–17) that $\gamma_g(\phi)$ increases as ϕ grows. Therefore, $l_g(\phi)$ decreases and $l_p(\phi)$ increases as ϕ increases.

Proposition 5: Suppressing the intervention of the local governments by reinforcing financial regulation can reduce the bias toward projects directed by the government in the allocation of credit resources caused by local protectionism, as well as increasing the credit supply to the Three Rural Issues following the intention of the state.

Conclusions

We have established a basic model for the allocation of credit resources of RCCs.

By expanding the model, we explained effect of the intervention of the local government in the decision-making of RCCs, and the opposite constraints financial regulation has on local protectionism. Although the local governments favor large-scale projects, credit issued to projects related to the Three Rural Issues are usually small in amount but done in multiple times (especially the microcredit which targets dispersed rural households), it is difficult to achieve economies of scale. Diseconomies of scale suppress the credit supply to a certain extent. We discovered in our model that even if diseconomies of scale are eliminated, there is still misallocation of RCCs' credit resources under local protectionism. We obtained the following conclusions:

(1) Under local protectionism, there is misallocation of RCCs' credit resources which favors projects directed by the local government.
(2) When the amount of loanable funds is huge, under local protectionism, the misallocation is more serious even though projects related to the Three Rural Issues have a higher rate of return.
(3) The stronger local protectionism is, the more serious the misallocation is.
(4) External financial regulation is effective in suppressing local protectionism. It can reduce the bias toward projects directed by the government in the allocation of credit resources caused by local protectionism, as well as increasing the credit supply to the Three Rural Issues following the intention of the state.

The above conclusions have profound political implications. As RCCs are monopolistic in the financial system, RCCs' credit capital drawn from projects related to the Three Rural Issues to projects favored by the local governments has caused a vacuum of supply in rural finance. Worse still, some RCCs take advantage of the preferential policies of the state towards the Three Rural Issues to obtain more credit capital and utilize the capital in projects favored by the local government. RCCs have abandoned rural households, agriculture, and rural areas. Their financial support is under transformation, which casts shadows on the economic reform that is trying to resolve the Three Rural Issues: The long-term lack of support in rural finance has been a bottle-neck in the development of agriculture and rural economy. Once the monopolistic RCCs retreat from rural finance, and other financial institutions cannot fill in the role left of RCCs, there is a larger vacuum of financial services. By that time, it would be difficult to obtain enough credit support and services needed for production transformation and the rearrangement of the rural property structure on time.

Much literature (e.g., Zhang Jie 1996, and Zhang Jun 2005) has pointed out that propelled by the urge to attain a higher GDP, local governments are eager to centralize the control of financial resources. RCCs' capital for projects related to the Three Rural Issues is requisitioned to support projects the local government favors, which are usually large in scale. These projects are usually the direct cause of economic overheating. Judging from this, when the authority over RCCs is handed over to local governments, external financial regulation should be tightened in order to prevent the misallocation of credit resources and risk externalization.[14]

Conflict of Interest, Expectation of Capital Injection, and Business Difficulties of RCCs

Reforms and development of RCCs is an essential topic in the study of China's rural finance, not only because of the importance of RCCs in rural finance, but also of its complicated relations with China's own politics, economy, and culture. RCCs have deep roots in rural areas, but they are migrating to urban areas; they were originally cooperative, but cooperation is breaking down; shareholders were expected to manage the RCCs, but now the government has taken up the responsibility. Especially after the State Council of the People's Republic of China had announced the reforms of RCCs in *Document No. 15*[15] in 2003, the reforms and development of RCCs instigated by capital injection became a red-hot topic in academia.

The reforms agenda announced in 2003 stipulated the regulatory system of RCCs: "the state shall exercise macroeconomic regulation and control and reinforce supervision; provincial governments shall obey the law in its governance and execute the assignment; RCCs should exercise self-constraint and be risk-bearing." Also, the provincial governments were assigned the responsibilities to regulate RCCs and manage the risk of RCCs. It is obvious that the reforms agenda was proposed under the difficult circumstances of the development of RCCs such as vague property rights, unclear responsibilities, internal control, low efficiency, and poor management. Given that self-help is a dead end for RCCs, society has had high hopes on the costly establishment of a regulatory system.

But, can money buy a system? Before the reforms, by the end of 2002, the national balance of non-performing loans of RCCs was RMB514.7 billion, actual insolvency RMB330 billion, and accumulated losses RMB130 billion. After reforms had begun, by the end of 2006, the central bank had issued special bills amounting to RMB165.6 billion.[16] By the end of 2008, the national balance of non-performing loans in RCCs reached RMB600 billion, and accumulated losses RMB60 billion. Over 900 counties (or cities) suffered insolvency, which amount to RMB230 billion. Furthermore, many issues regarding the regulation of RCCs were sustained. The reforms of property rights were not thorough and the management was not smooth. The measure of dispersing equity not only failed to prevent or alleviate the problem of internal control of RCCs, rather, it aggravated the problem.

Looking back to the reforms of RCCs, RCCs have been running at low efficiency. Non-performing loans have repetitively occurred, and there have been repetitive rearrangements, write-offs, and capital injections. There are historical reasons for such circumstances, but the critical cause is rooted in the complicated interest relationships among the state, RCCs, and local governments.[17] Under special social and historical context, conflict of interest, expected / expectation on capital injection, and the plight of RCCs entangled with one another, which is why reforms of RCCs has failed many times.

There are many domestic studies about the reforms and development of RCCs in China, such as those conducted by Xie Ping (2001, 2005), Cao Yuanzheng (2004), Zhang Jie (2006), and Wang Shuguang (2008), etc. In early representative research, Xie Ping (2001) summarized the basic ideas of the reforms in eight aspects: cooperative system, rural financial system, the organization of RCCs, industry management system, conflicts of multiple business targets, history, failure of bankruptcy constraints and moral hazards, and government behavior.[18] Zhang Jie and Gao Xiaohong (2006) discussed the issue from a financial perspective. They thought that capital injection from the central government starts a financial game among government bodies. Every move in the reforms is destined to become part of the game of the financial interest groups to seize benefits.

While studies are abundant, from an economic perspective, most of them are descriptive and focus on explicating the authors' view. There is a lack of a formal economic model. Therefore, we attempt to establish a basic model framework to answer the following related questions: (1) For a long time, why have the RCCs been operating at low efficiency? (2) Why are the shareholders not motivated to inject long-term capital into RCCs? (3) How does the capital aid of the state further bring down the efficiency of the RCCs?

In the following parts, we will first introduce the framework and the basic settings of the model; Second, we answer the three questions through analyses using our model. Lastly, we offer a conclusion.

Model framework and basic settings

We based our model on Hong Zheng's model framework (2006). While Hong focused on corporate management of commercial banks, we turn our attention to RCCs. Special features of RCCs need to be included as major parameters in our analysis. Overall, our model differs from Hong's model in the following aspects: (1) The objective function of the three interest entities (operators of RCCs, local governments, and depositors) is determined by the special shareholding structure of RCCs and the status of the competition for interest which stems from that structure. The objective function for management is different. (2) The risk preference and bias toward self-interest of operators of RCCs are the focuses in our study, which differs from Hong who placed the level of risk management as the core of the research. (3) In this study, the monitoring cost of operators is regarded as private cost. The cost varies with respect to the effort of the "behavioral man." Greater effort implies a greater cost. (4) Capital injection is an important topic in the study of China's reforms of RCCs. Our study analyzes the moral hazard caused by the reforms based on the effect of capital injection on the probability of liquidation as well as self-interest of internal parties.

First, the amount of financing is standardized as 1 and assume that the ratio of own capital of RCCs is α ($0 < \alpha < 1$). Therefore, to form the portfolio, RCCs have to obtain the remaining capital ($1-\alpha$) from external investors. It is also assumed that the risk market players have to bear is of medium level, and the required rate of return of internal parties (operators of RCCs and shareholders) and external depositors are r_1 and r_2, respectively.

The model contains two phases. In the first phase, internal parties and external depositors sign a financing contract. Operators of RCCs decide to make effort of level e and choose the portfolio he prefers. The incentive scheme of the owner is $w = w_0 + u(e)$, where u is the function which reflects the level of effort made. $u' > 0$ represents a favorable scheme. The private cost of RCCs operators for monitoring the portfolio is $c(e)$. As the level of effort increases, operators need to bear more material cost and time cost. Therefore, $c_e' > 0$. Private monitoring costs rise as more effort is made.

In the second phase, the portfolio generated benefits $\tilde{R}$. It is assumed that the benefits of portfolio is related to the level of effort made by operators of RCCs, risk propensity, and risk management level, it can be represented as $R = ae + bs$, where $a > 0$ represents a positive effect of the level of effort on the benefits of portfolio, and s represents the risk management level. The success rate and fail rate of portfolio are represented by p and q, respectively. In a favorable situation with p, $R_1 = ae + bs_1$; in a unfavorable situation with q ($q = 1-p$), $R_2 = ae - bs_2$ and $s_1, s_2 > 0$. The major factor which affects p is the risk propensity of operators of RCCs. The higher the risk propensity, the smaller p is.

Based on the above settings, the expected benefits of portfolio can be represented as $E\tilde{R} = \bar{R} = pR_1 + (1-p)R_2 = ae + b\,[ps_1 + (1-p)(-S_2)] = ae + b\bar{s}$, where $\bar{s} = ps_1 + (1-p)(-s_2)$, which represents the expected risk level of portfolio and reflects the risk propensity and risk management level of operators of RCCs. When p is constant, a higher $\bar{s}$ represents a higher risk management level.

For simplicity, we assume the incentive scheme of operators of RCCs is based on the average performance of RCCs:

$$w = w_0 + t\bar{R} = w_0 + tae + tb\bar{s}, \text{ where } 0 < t < 1.$$

Assume that benefits can be verified, external depositors rank higher than shareholders in terms of liquidation order, and the remaining benefits would be allocated to internal parties. At the same time, assume regardless of the business of RCCs, operators can obtain private benefits B through related lending, asset transfer, and on-the-job consumption. In reality, private benefits are normally related to the size of related lending. As related lending is usually obtained because the operators intend to seek rent, a portfolio which contains a higher proportion of related lending would have a lower success rate than that of a portfolio which is composed of general loans. Therefore, when the operators obtain related lending to seek rent, the private benefits they receive would be an increasing function of the fail rate of the portfolio q ($q = 1 - p$): $B'_q > 0$ (or $B'_p < 0$). In other words, operators can choose a portfolio with a lower success rate in return for more private benefits.

Analysis of the model

Long-term unsatisfactory operation

Level of effort of operators

Factors that affect the performance of RCCs include both internal management, and external business environment. From the perspective of the operators of RCCs, performance is mostly determined by the level of effort of the operators: greater effort brings better performance. On the contrary, if operators do not have incentive to work hard, the management will be slack and the performance will be dragged down.

In order to investigate whether operators take the initiative to maximize their effort, and whether their effort meets the demands of shareholders and depositors, we perform the following comparative analysis.

(1) The level of effort demanded by shareholders

The benefits of shareholders of RCCs are based on the equity contract: When the status of the portfolio is good, the benefits shareholders would receive are the remains after taking into account the claim of external depositors and the incentive scheme of the operators. When the status of this is poor, the benefits of shareholders equals 0 as the benefits of the portfolio is smaller than the investment of external investors (i.e. $R_1 > 1 - \alpha > R_2$). When shareholders and operators do not conspire, shareholders would minimize the private benefits of operators (B). Following the settings in the previous section, the required rate of return of shareholders is r_1 and their own capital is α. Therefore, the representative objective function of shareholders is $F_1 = p\,[R_1 - (1-\alpha)\,r_2 - w] - B - \alpha r_1 = p\,[R_1 - (1-\alpha)\,r_2 - w_0 - tae - tb\bar{s}] - B - \alpha r_1$ The first derivative of F_1 is as follows:

$$\frac{\partial F_1}{\partial e} = p\,(a - ta)$$

$p > 0, a > 0, 0 < t < 1$. Therefore, $\frac{\partial F_1}{\partial e} > 0$, which means that the value of the objective function of shareholders increases as the level of effort increases.

The results above show that in order to maximize the objective function, shareholders of RCCs would require operators to work hard and maximize their level of effort.

(2) The level of effort demanded by external depositors

Because the contract between external depositors and RCCs is a debt contract, if RCCs do not go bankrupt, depositors receive fixed benefits (principal and interest). Therefore, depositors expect minimum benefits which can cover the interest of the principal at maturity.

The participation condition for depositors is as follows:

$$\bar{R} - w - B \geq (1-\alpha)\,r_2$$

Putting in relevant formulae,

$$ae + b\bar{s} - w_0 - tae - tb\bar{s} - B \geq (1-\alpha)\,r_2$$

Which can be represented as

$$a\,(1-t)\,e - w_0 + (1-t)\,bs - B \geq (1-\alpha)\,r_2$$

In the above formula, as $a > 0$ and $0 < t < 1$, and under the conditions that capital ratio α and the required rate of return of depositors r_2 remain unchanged, the greater e is, the easier to satisfy the participation constraint. This implies that in order to ensure the safety of capital, depositors would demand operators to maximize their level of effort.

(3) The actual level of effort of RCCs operators

According to the basic model setting, the benefits of the RCCs operators include two parts: benefits from the incentive scheme based on the performance of RCCs (w) and private benefits (B). The net benefits of the operators is the sum of the two parts minus private cost $c(e)$. Therefore, the representative objective function of the operators is as follows:

$$F_2 = B + w - c(e) = B + w_o + tae + tb\bar{s} - c(e)$$

From the first-order conditions of the objective function, we obtain

$$\frac{\partial F_2}{\partial F} = ta - c'(e) = 0 \Rightarrow c'(e^*) = ta$$

The formula above shows that in order to maximize the objective function, a rational RCC operator would choose a level of effort e^* at equilibrium where the product of the conversion coefficient of marginal revenue (t) and incentive coefficient (a) equals marginal cost (c'). The economic implication is clear, RCC operators would not indefinitely improve their level of effort but strike a balance between private benefits and cost to ensure that the level of effort is within the range in which there is positive marginal revenue.

Summarizing the analyses (1), (2), and (3), by comparing the level of effort of RCC operator demanded by shareholders and external depositors with the level of effort the operators opt for, it can be easily seen that the corresponding expectations and demands are different, as the three parties all have different objective functions: Shareholders and external depositors demand the operators to maximize the level of effort, but the operators do not have the motivation to maximize it. Rather, they would choose to operate at a level of effort which their own benefits are maximized. Apparently, as the objective function of operators is to maximize their own benefits rather than those of shareholders, when they do not operate at the maximum level of effort, the performance of RCCs would be negatively affected.

Proposition 1: Due to the difference in objective functions, the level of effort of RCC operators is usually lower than the expectation of shareholders and external depositors.

Project preference of operators

The performance of RCCs is not only related to the subjective level of effort of the operators, but also the project preference of them: When the operators face two options of project, the key question is how to make sure the operator choose the project with higher expected benefits and success rate.

It should be noted that when the chosen project may generate private benefits of different amounts, RCC operators are motivated to choose an "unfavorable project portfolio" (high risk and low return). A typical situation is where they include more relationship loans in the loan portfolio. While the expected return is low, the operators can obtain more private benefits. In particular, when the risk of the projects included in the loan portfolio can hardly be accurately estimated, few constraints can be formed beforehand, which implies that the operators have the motivation and opportunities to choose a high-risk portfolio.

We assume the operators have two options for project portfolio A1 and A2. A1 represents favorable project portfolio. The probability for it to attain a favorable status is represented as p_1, the incentive scheme of operators as w_1, and private benefits as B_1; A2 represents unfavorable portfolio. The probability for it to attain a favorable status is represented as p_2, the incentive scheme of operators as w_2, and private benefits as B_2. According to previous settings, favorable and unfavorable project portfolios should satisfy the following: $p_1 > p_2$, $B_1 > B_2$. The private cost of RCC operators for monitoring various project portfolios is c, which gives the following:

The expected net benefits of A1: $R_1 = B_1 + w_1 - c$

The expected net benefits of A1: $R_2 = B_2 + w_2 - c$

Only when $R_1 > R_2$ can the operators choose A1 to improve the performance of RCCs. The next question to ask is whether $R_1 > R_2$ can be easily satisfied.

Following the model settings and putting in the corresponding expressions:

$$R_1 - R_2 = (B_1 - B_2) + tb\,(\overline{s_A} - \overline{s_B}) = (B_1 - B_2) + tb\,(p_1 - p_2)\,(s_1 + s_2)$$

As B_1 and B_2 are benefits transfer brought about by related lending. In normal circumstances, a smaller change in $(p_1 - p_2)$ can cause a greater increase in private benefits. In addition, the conversion coefficient of marginal revenue of the level of effort (t) is usually small.[19] Therefore, the drop in $(B_1 - B_2)$ is greater than the growth in $tb\,(p_1 - p_2)(s_1 + s_2)$, and $(R_1 - R_2)$ is usually smaller than 0. In other words, it is difficult to satisfy $R_1 > R_2$, which is the incentive condition for A1. Normally, RCC operators would opt for an unfavorable portfolio in order to maximize private benefits.

Proposition 2: As prior constraints weaken, RCC operators would choose an unfavorable portfolio in order to maximize private benefits.

Drawing from propositions 1 and 2, it can be seen from the perspective of internal management that the "incentive paradox" is the reason behind the long-term

Unsatisfactory operation of RCCs: Operators have not the incentive to maximize the subjective level of effort or preference for favorable portfolios. It implies that shirking and careless (or deliberate) mistakes in choosing investment portfolio commonly exist. These behaviors which deviate from the course of maximizing the value of shareholders have a serious adverse effect on the performance of RCCs. As a result, the performance deteriorates.

Why capital injection is short-lived?

RCCs ask for capital injections to cover their loss and maintain their operation. However, in the reforms of RCCs, apart from the fact that the state has repeatedly injected capital, write-offs, and reissued loans in the name of their "policy mission," there is little incentive for real market entities to inject capital in RCCs. From the reforms in 2003, abiding by regulations, the central government had taken care of 50% of the insolvency of RCCs by 2002. The other 50% was to be borne by local governments. Nevertheless, few local governments were willing to pay. They tended to increase their investment and let the new investors bear the 50% loss. In order to increase their capital stock to meet the state's requirements for capital injection, the activities of RCCs or the local governments are short-lived. They attract farmers' investment by promoting national credit. Under such circumstances, the investors of RCCs either seek loans or a year-end bonus. They are not real shareholders and they do not care about the management of RCCs (Zhang Jie and Gao Xiaohong 2006).

It is obvious that short-lived capital injections reflect the lack of incentive for market entities to inject capital in RCCs. Then, why do market entities lack the incentive to inject long-term capital into RCCs?

Benefits of shareholders

Whether shareholders have the incentive to input more capital is manifested as whether marginal revenue increases as the ratio of capital input α increases.

Shareholders need an objective function of maximization:

$$F_1 = p\,[R_1 - (1-\alpha)\, r_2 - w] - B - \alpha r_1 = p\,[R_1 - (1-\alpha)\, r_2 - w_0 - tae - tb\bar{s}] - B - \alpha r_1$$

By obtaining the first derivative of α, we have $\dfrac{\partial F_1}{\partial \alpha} = pr_2 - r_1$.

According to basic economic principles, the risk of equity contracts is higher than that of debt contracts. Therefore, following the principle of risk-return ratio, the required rate of return of external depositors r_2 should be smaller than that of shareholders r_1 in general, i.e. $r_2 < r_1$. Meanwhile, as $0 < p < 1$, we have $\dfrac{\partial F_1}{\partial \alpha} < 0$.

This shows that raising the capital input ratio cannot increase the return of shareholders. Shareholders do not have the incentive to input more capital. Rather, on the contrary, they have the incentive to input less.

Proposition 3: Shareholders have the incentive to input less capital from the perspective of return maximization.

Risk propensity

Obviously, as typical highly leveraged enterprises, the own capital ratio α of financial institutions is normally lower than that of general enterprises. Therefore, a lower p can satisfy the participation condition of shareholders:

$$p\,[R_1 - (1-\alpha)\,r_2 - w] - B \geq \alpha r_1$$

Like any financial institution, shareholders of RCCs have higher risk propensity. However, it is not the whole picture. Under information asymmetry, both RCCs operators and shareholders are internal parties, and it is possible that they conspire.

A typical conspiracy is a series of hidden contracts of transfers of benefits between operators and shareholders. For example, operators may transfer some of their benefits to shareholders in exchange for connivance of their pursuit of private benefits. In the end, the performance of RCCs deteriorates because of conspiracy, and operators and shareholders obtain more private benefits as the total private benefits increases. As a result, benefits are transferred from external depositors to internal parties.

In the situation in which operators and shareholders conspire, assumed that γ is the proportion of private benefits operators would transfer to shareholders, $0 < \gamma < 1$. The objective function of shareholders is

$$F_c = p\,[R_1 - (1-\alpha)\,r_2 - w] + \gamma B - \alpha r_1$$

The corresponding participation condition becomes

$$p\,[R_1 - (1-\alpha)\,r_2 - w] + \gamma B \geq \alpha r_1$$

As γ and B are larger than 0, the participation is easier to satisfy in comparison to that when there is no conspiracy $p\,[R_1 - (1-\alpha)\,r_2 - w] - B \geq \alpha r_1$. It implies that RCCs have a higher risk propensity in the presence of conspiracy.

As internal parties of RCCs, operators and shareholders know clearly that high risk propensity has a negative effect on the long-term performance of RCCs. As the expected long-term risk is high, there is no incentive for shareholders to input more capital. When external supervision and internal management are loose, they may conspire with operators to obtain more benefits through transfer.

Proposition 4: Internal conspiracy increases the risk propensity of RCCs. When the expected long-term risk is high, shareholders lack incentive to increase their capital, and their behavior would be short-lived.

Why the state cannot continue to issue bills?

As mentioned before, replacing the non-performing loans of RCCs with central bank bills was regarded as "paying money for mechanism." The results fall short of the expectation. When the state's capital has been paid, there has been no significant improvement in the RCCs' mechanism, administration, external constraints, performance, etc. By the end of 2001, non-performing loans of RCCs in China amounted to RMB529 billion and accumulated losses RMB125 billion. By the end of 2008, the balance of non-performing loans of RCCs was RMB600 billion, accumulated losses RMB60 billion, and the provision gap was RMB190 billion. So, why does capital injection not achieve the expected results?

When RCCs encounter business difficulties and the threat of bankruptcy, if there is always free capital injection to compensate for their loss, the liquidation probability is significantly brought down. However, once the expectation of free assistance takes shape, it would aggravate moral hazard among internal parties (shareholders and operators), forming soft budget constraints.

Under our basic model, we assume that any free capital injection M lowers the liquidation probability of RCCs θ, and when M increases, θ decreases, i.e., $\theta(M) < \theta(0)$ and $\theta'(M) < 0$. Also, we assume the liquidation value of RCCs is E. As loans take a longer time to generate revenue, advanced liquidation would lead to depreciation of loan items. Therefore, the liquidation value of RCCs is usually small, which cannot compensate the external depositors for their retained revenue, i.e. $E < (1-\alpha) r_2$.

With bankruptcy aid included, the target function for external depositors is

$$\theta E + (1-\theta)[\overline{R} - w - B] \geq (1-\alpha) r_2$$

Putting in relevant expressions, it gives

$$e \geq \frac{(1-\alpha) r_2 - \theta E}{(1-\theta)(a-ta)} + \frac{B + w_0 - (b-tb)\,\overline{s}}{a-ta}$$

Therefore,

$$\frac{\partial e_{min}}{\partial \theta} = \frac{(1-\alpha)\, r_2 - E}{(1-\theta)^2}$$

Because $E < (1-\alpha)\, r_2$ and $\frac{\partial e_{min}}{\partial \theta} > 0$, the level of effort of RCC operators and liquidation probability change in the same direction. The drop of liquidation probability would lead to "double moral hazard" of internal parties of RCCs and external supervising parties: On the one hand the moral hazard of operators aggravates; on the other hand, the participation constraint of external depositors relaxes, lowering their intention to monitor the RCCs.

In addition, when there is external capital injection, there is an opportunity for internal parties to gain private benefits. The more the aid funds, the more private benefits internal parties can gain, i.e. $B'(M) > 0$. Our numerous studies of Western China demonstrate that when many RCCs obtained cash through central bank bills, the first thing they did was not improve asset quality or business administration, but increase dividends, bonus, and salary and improve benefits.[20]

The objective function of operators of RCCs is $F_2 = B + w - c(e)$. As $B'(M) > 0$ and F_2 is an increasing function of M, there is the incentive for operators to seek maximum external aid funds. If shareholders conspire with operators, the objective function of shareholders is $F_c = p\,[R_1 - (1-\alpha)\, r_2 - w] - \gamma B - \alpha r_1$, which is also the increasing function of M as $\gamma > 0$. This signifies that shareholders also have the incentive to seek as much external aid funds as possible. In addition, the participation constraint is $p\,[R_1 - (1-\alpha)\, r_2 - w] + \gamma B \geq \alpha r_1$. When there is external capital injection, B increases. The participation constraint becomes easier to satisfy, which implies that external aid funds would raise the risk propensity of RCCs.

The conclusions above offer a clear picture of the issue of capital injection of the state: To RCCs, capital injection of the state is "free lunch." They use the free aid funds to compensate for their inefficient operation. The presence of bankruptcy aid eliminates any threats of bankruptcy and repeatedly aggravates moral hazard so that RCCs continue to have high risk propensity and low efficiency in operation, and keep waiting for external aid.[21]

Proposition 5: When RCCs encounter business difficulties and the threat of bankruptcy, capital injection of the state leads to serious problems with moral hazard, bringing down the level of effort of operators, the external depositors' incentive to monitor business, and enhancing the risk propensity of RCCs.

Conclusions

We have established a basic model framework and begun to understand the high risk propensity and level of effort of RCC operators and the increasingly high degree of moral hazard brought about by capital injection in the presence of conflict of interest. The analysis shows that the conflict of objectives constitutes a situation in which RCC operators, shareholders, and external depositors are entangled and compete with one another, resulting in the long-term inefficiency of RCCs.

During the reforms of RCCs which are filled with conflicts and paradoxes, there are three logical puzzles which form the whole picture: (1) the fall in the level of effort and the change in risk propensity of RCC operators cause a drop in the operating efficiency of RCCs. (2) Local governments as an internal party as well as an administrative body can hardly act according to the preference and interest of the state. Rather, there is a chance that they conspire with RCC operators in benefit transfers. (3) The Three Rural Issues have become political. Moral hazard brought about by capital injection of the state and the problem with the expectation of aid have allowed RCCs to develop dependence on them when the operation of RCCs is inefficient and have high risk propensity. It deviates from the idea of reform through marketization.

(1) The business difficulties of RCCs. The business situation of RCCs has never been favorable since they were first established. Before the reforms in 2003, by the end of 2002, the loss of RCCs across the state amounted to 55%. After reforms started in 2003, in order to cash the central bank bills, the asset quality of RCCs improved for a short period of time.[22] However, after they cashed the bills, their operating efficiency deteriorated: By the end of 2008, the balance of non-performing loans of RCCS amounted to RMB600 billion. The research in this book illustrates that the "incentive paradox" is why RCCs have been inefficient for a long time. In the absence of owner and the weakening of external constraint mechanism, not only would RCC operators not maximize their level of effort, but they would also show a preference for risk in their choice of project. The objective function and behavior of RCC operators change, the business of RCCs obviously deviates from the maximization of the value of the company. The inevitable result is the long-term poor performance of RCCs.

(2) The administration difficulties of local governments. Among RCCs, the state (central government), and local governments, the state has the least information. It cannot closely supervise the actual operation of numerous RCCs. Before the reforms of RCCs, due to serious issues of soft budget constraints, the capital of RCCs, as capital of the central government, has

become the rent RCC operators and local governments seek. After reforms have begun, the responsibilities of local governments in the administration of RCC and risk handling are clear. But as the Three Rural Issues have become political, local governments still expect the state to clear all problems. Therefore, even though local governments, as the manager, know that the administration of RCC is loose and the business risk is too high, they lack the incentive to improve administration, let alone spending money to do so.[23] To local governments, RCCs are like a sick child adopted from the central government. Their top priority after adoption is not to cure the child, but to squeeze more "medical subsidies" and "support payments" from the central government. When the central government cannot monitor the operation and has to bear the risk of RCCs because of the importance of the Three Rural Issues, it can be expected that difficulties in administration for local governments would continue to exist.

(3) Capital injection of the state in the form of central bank bills. As discussed earlier, if there is capital injection whenever RCCs face business difficulties or the threat of bankruptcy to compensate for their loss,

The bankruptcy constraints of RCCs vanish. Once RCCs expect the state to come to their aid, it would aggravate moral hazard of the internal parties, resulting in the fall of the level of effort of operators and the loosening of supervision of external depositors, which further raise the risk propensity of RCCs. To RCCs, central bank bills are negative incentives. This lowers the subjective level of effort of internal parties, and some RCCs deliberately incur greater business loss so as to obtain maximum aid. Once the first set of bills is cashed, they ask for compensation for non-performing assets again. What is intriguing is that the first set of bills compensated for RMB160 billion non-performing assets, the new request shot up to RMB300 billion.[24] As long as the expectation of aid is fulfilled, moral hazard is exacerbated. RCCs would continue to have high risk propensity and low efficiency in operation, and keep waiting for external aid.

The policy recommendations drawn from the conclusions above are clear:

(1) As the shareholder structure is loose, there is the absence of owners, and, therefore, RCCs are controlled by internal parties. The government should reform the government-dominant administration, revise their policies, and encourage RCCs to converge shareholders, who would be given the administrative and decision-making authority. This is core to the refinement of corporate governance of RCCs.

(2) Classification reform of RCCs should aim at clear positioning and definition of responsibilities. The boundary between policy-based finance and commercial

finance should be clearly drawn. Specialized policy-based financial institutions should be responsible for business related to policies. RCCs which are to be transformed to commercial financial institutions should be self-financing on the basis of commercial sustainability. They should not use the Three Rural Issues as an excuse for being a burden of the government.

(3) Distorted authority structure and interest structure are the main reasons for the long-term poor performance of RCCs. Therefore, the system of provincial credit associations, in which ownership and actual control power are reversed, should be reformed. The administration of RCCs by the provincial government conflict with the market-oriented operation and the function transformation of governments. Administrative responsibility should be transferred to the RCCs themselves as legal persons.

(4) Based on classification reform, a regulated exit mechanism should be established in the rural financial market as soon as possible so as to eradicate moral hazard caused by RCCs' expectation of national assistance.

New-Style Institutions in Rural Finance

Background

Large commercial banks gradually retreat from rural areas, and RCCs are in the process of transformation. How to manage with the vacuum of rural financial services has become a popular concern. Theorists hold that rural credit demand has the features of "small quantity and high frequency." Large commercial banks providing corresponding services would place themselves in diseconomies of scale. According to the theory of comparative advantage, the retreat of large commercial banks is inevitable. Under such circumstances, the objective of the system of rural financial services has changed from stock adjustment to increasing the quantity of entities inside the system, such as the new rural financial institutions in recent years.

When traditional financial institutions are reluctant or unable to enter the rural financial market, it is only natural to have high hopes for the new grassroots financial institutions. According to the original policy plan, new-style financial institutions would be located in rural areas so as to shorten the distance between them and rural areas, and to utilize "acquaintance information" to reduce transaction cost, ensure that capital is circulated within rural areas, develop more financing channels for rural households and rural areas, and increase the supply of rural credit. Further, the best result is that, through policies, an endogenous and sustainable system of financial institutions (organizations) which can meet the rural market demands can emerge from the rural financial market.

With this plan in mind, China Banking Regulatory Commission (CBRC) announced the *Adjusting and Relaxing the Access Policies for Banking Financial Institutions in Rural Areas and Better Supporting the Construction of New Socialist Country Side* on December 21, 2006. Pilot new-style financial institutions which included village and township banks, lending companies, rural mutual cooperatives were selected in Sichuan, Inner Mongolia, Gansu, Qinghai, Jilin, and Hubei Provinces. Later, CBRC announced *Document No. 23: Guiding Opinions of China Banking Regulatory Commission and the People's Bank of China on the Pilot Operation of Small-Sum Loan Companies* to include microcredit companies as pilot institutions.

We summarize the definitions, requirements for establishment, scope of service, interest rate control, etc., of village and township banks, lending companies, rural mutual cooperatives, and microcredit companies in Table 4.5.

It seems that new rural financial institutions such as village and township banks, lending companies, rural mutual cooperatives, and microcredit companies has filled in the vacuum of financial services to a certain extent and expanded the financial coverage in the pilot areas. At the same time, they have explored and experimented with the development of the rural financial market. As it is still in the early stages of the pilot period, the performance of new-style financial institutions awaits further observation before evaluation can be done.

There are several standards to judge whether new-style financial institutions can activate the rural financial market: (1) The institutions have comparative advantage in serving the Three Rural Issues. They can increase the effective supply of rural credit and improve rural financial services, which is manifested as the relaxation of credit constraint and the increase in the availability of financial services. (2) The development model of the institutions can be reduplicated and is generally applicable, which can be applied to rural financial markets that bear the same features. Clues can be found when success of these (or a type of) institutions is general, not a special case. (3) The institutions are commercially sustainable. Their revenue can cover their cost, and have a lower rate of non-performing loans and better risk-control ability.

We will provide a summary of the situations of village and township banks, microcredit companies, and rural mutual cooperatives, and the issues with the development process.

Table 4.5. Introduction of new rural financial institutions

Institution	Definition	Requirements for establishment	Scope of service	Loan and deposit rates
Village and township banks	Funded by domestic and foreign financial institutions, domestic non-financial enterprise legal persons, and domestic natural persons. Banking institutions established in rural areas which provide financial services to local households and for agricultural and rural economic development.	Sponsors or investors should own at least one banking institution, and the maximum stake should be 20% or lower. To register the bank in counties or cities, its registered capital should not be less than RMB3 million. To register the bank in towns or villages, its registered capital should not be less than RMB1 million. Registered capital is paid-in capital. One-time full payment is made by sponsors or investors.	To absorb public deposits; issue short-term, medium-term, and long-term loans; manage domestic settlement, bill, acceptance and note discounting; perform interbank-lending; act as an agent for issuing, chasing, and underwriting government bonds, for receipts and payments, and insurances; and run other businesses approved by the CBRC.	Maximum deposit rate imposed, which is the benchmark deposit rate of the same grade. Minimum loan rate imposed, which is 0.9 times the benchmark loan rate of the same grade.
Lending companies	Rural non-banking institutions set up by domestic commercial banks or rural cooperative banks specialized in providing financial services to rural households, for agricultural and economic development in the county.	Investors must be domestic commercial banks or rural cooperative banks, and the asset size should not be smaller than RMB5 billion. Registered capital should not be less than RMB0.5 million and is paid-in capital. One-time full payment is made by investors. Branches can be set up in the county after gaining approval from the CBRC.	To manage loans, note discounting, asset transfers, and settlement of loan items. Can run other asset-related business approved by the CBRC. Companies cannot absorb public deposits.	Minimum loan rate imposed, which is 0.9 times the benchmark loan rate of the same grade.
Rural mutual cooperatives	Community and benefit banking institutions set up by voluntary shareholders: villages (counties), households in administrative villages, and rural small enterprises to provide deposit, loan, settlement services, etc. to members.	There should be more than 10 sponsors who are qualified members. Cooperatives set up in villages (towns) should have at least RMB0.3 million registered capital. Those set up in administrative villages should have at least RMB0.1 million. Registered capital should be paid-in capital. Members who want to become shareholders must pay with money. They cannot pay with any other objects or loans.	Members' deposits, donations, and capital from other banking financial institutions are their major financing channels. Their capital is used as loans to members. Surplus capital is deposited in banking financial institutions or used to purchase national bonds and financial bonds. They are not allowed to absorb deposit of non-members, issue loans, operate other business, or provide external guarantee.	Maximum deposit rate imposed, which is the benchmark deposit rate of the same grade. Minimum loan rate imposed, which is 0.9 times the benchmark loan rate of the same grade.
Microcredit companies	Limited liability companies or limited companies set up and invested by natural persons, enterprise legal persons, and other social organizations. They do not absorb public deposits and issue microcredit.	Limited liability companies should be funded by fewer than 50 shareholders. Its registered capital should be at least RMB5 million. Limited companies should have 2–200 sponsors. Its registered capital should be at least RMB10 million. The total amount of shares held by a single natural man, enterprise legal men, other social organization, and other related personnel should not be more than 10% of the registered capital. Registered capital is paid-in capital.	The capital of shareholders, donated funds, and capital from two or fewer banking financial institutions are the major financing channels. They should be serving the Three Rural Issues by issuing small quantity and high frequency loans. They are not allowed to participate in any illegal fund-raising activities.	Minimum loan rate imposed, which is 0.9 times the benchmark loan rate of the same grade.

Village and township banks

CBRC issued the *Adjusting and Relaxing the Access Policies for Banking Financial Institutions in Rural Areas and Better Supporting the Construction of New Socialist Countryside* and other documents in December 2006. Village and township banks, as the front-runner of new-style financial institutions, have never left the public eye. On January22, 2007, CBRC announced the *Interim Provisions on the Administration of Village and township banks*, which stipulated the provisions on the nature, legal status, organizational form, establishment method, qualification of shareholders, institutional framework, business operation, supervision, market withdrawal of village and township banks in accordance with their principle of "low threshold and tight supervision." In order to fully implement tight supervision, guard the village and township banks against risk, and protect the legal right of depositors and other clients, CBRC issued the *Opinions on Strengthening the Supervision over Village and Township Banks* on May 22, 2007. On October 12, 2007, CBRC announced that the pilot area for the relaxation of the access policies on rural banking financial institutions would be expanded. The area expanded from six provinces (districts) to twenty-five provinces (districts, cities). By December 2008, there were 91 village and township banks in business, which were set up by China-funded financial institutions such as China Development Bank, City Commercial Banks, and RCCs, as well as foreign-funded ones such as the Hong Kong and Shanghai Banking Corporation.[25]

In the times of rural financial reforms and development, the intention of CBRC's top-down policy on the setting up of village and township banks is very clear: When commercial banks shy away from tackling the Three Rural Issues, RCCs tend to transform, and policy banks cannot extend their services to rural households. Through establishing village and township banks which favor agriculture and the rural areas at the suitable time, small financial institutions, which have the comparative advantage, can provide effective financial services to households, agriculture, and the rural economy to boost rural income and agricultural development. According to the original policy design, new village and township banks have a more simple and convenient flow in credit issuance. They target rural households and village small enterprises, respond more quickly, and have a shorter decision-making chain. Therefore, they create new and specific financial products and tailor their services to the present situations of agriculture and rural economic development. Further, village and township banks bring competition to the market to dissolve monopoly, propel the reform of formal financial system, and encourage the formal financial institutions to provide better services.

On March 1, 2007, the first township and village bank of the state Sichuan Yilong Huimin Village or Township Bank opened business. Its registered capital amounted to RMB2 million. Nanchong City Commercial Bank, as the major investor, invested RMB1 million, accounting for 50% of the total investment. As of June 2009, Sichuan Yilong Huimin Village or Township Bank attained a deposit balance of RMB152 million, loan balance RMB69 million, and business profit RMB3.31 million. Collateral loan constituted the major part of loans, taking up to 60.6% of the total loans. Most loans were shot-term loans. 82.28% of loans had a loan period of one year or shorter. The loan rate ranged between 4.05% and 12.05% and had a weighted average of 8.61%.

In Table 4.6 and 4.7, we present the status of major village and township banks (VTBs) in Sichuan Province. The following conclusions can be drawn from the information in the two tables: (1) The difference of deposit to loan ratio among banks was large. Some banks had a huge deposit gap, and some had a greater loan balance than deposit balance.[26] (2) Collateral loans still accounted for most of the loans. Credit constituted very little. (3) The loan period was usually within one year. Some banks did not issue medium- or long-term loans which have a loan period of over one year. (4) The loan rate ranged between 3.36% and 18%. The minimum weighted average rate was 5.63% and maximum 10.48%. (5) The business situations of the banks were mixed. Of the eleven banks on the list, four attained negative profit.

For a while, VTBs were regarded as the solution to the problems of little coverage, insufficient financial supply and competition of rural banking. However, pilot VTBs have encountered various degrees of difficulties. The following problems are encountered during development:

(1) Difficult to absorb savings. VTBs have been set up for a short time and their network is small. Even though they position themselves as "banks for the poor," rural households think they have lower credibility in comparison to large-scale financial institutions which have quasi–state credit and many branches (e.g. state-owned commercial banks, the Postal Savings Bank of China, and RCCs). In addition, the rural credit foundations were banned several years ago. Rural households are speculative toward the credibility of VTBs. They wait and observe. According to the random interview of 100 households, about 80% of them thought that VTBs could not guarantee the safety of their savings, and about 60% preferred depositing their money in state-owned banks or RCCs. The 10% who were willing to deposit money in VTBs were mainly attracted by the preferential loans of the banks.[27]

Table 4.6. Business performance of major village and township banks in Sichuan Province (RMB10,000)

Village and township banks	Deposit balance	Loan balance	Types of loans				Business performance		
			Credit	Collateral	Co-guarantee	Others	Operating revenue	Operating expenses	Operating profit
Yilong Huimin Village or Township Bank	15,242	6,942	102	4,209	0	2,631	331	237	94
Mianyang Beichuan Fumin Village and Township Bank	5,355	3,099	522	1,420	51	1,106	113	14	93
Guangyuanbaoshangguimin Village or Township Bank	7,820	7,047	2	4,117	0	2,928	103	157	–54
Dujiangyan Jindu Village or Township Bank	35,962	39,010	800	5,390	0	32,820	926	572	354
Qionglai Guomin Village or Township Bank	6,392	8,211	123	4041	0	4,047	428	258	170
Shuangliu Chengmin Village or Township Bank	17,028	18,194	0	8,005	2,284	7,905	340	390	–50
Dayi Bocom Xingmin Rural Bank	2,331	9,166	0	426	8	8,732	187	218	–31
Pengzhou Minsheng Village or Township Bank, Co., Ltd.	12,324	6,570	0	1,005	686	4,879	185	165	20
Xuanyi Chengmin Village or Township Bank	5,890	3,888	0	1,190	0	2,268	90	107	-17
Shifang Siyuan Village or Township Bank	8,911	6,484	31	1,536	80	4,837	126	109	18
Mianzhu Pufa Village or Township Bank	41,991	2,940	0	710	0	2,230	259	110	149

Table 4.7. The loan period and loan rate of major village and township banks in Sichuan Province (up to the end of June 2009)

Village and township banks	Loan distribution at different length of maturity (RMB10,000)		Loan rate (%)		
	Within one year	Above one year	Weighted average	Maximum	Minimum
Yilong Huimin Village or Township Bank	5,712	1,230	8.61	12.04	4.05
Mianyang Beichuan Fumin Village and Township Bank	2,887	212	7.09	9.83	4.78
Guangyuanbaoshangguimin Village or Township Bank	3,394	3,652	9.94	18.00	6.00
Dujiangyan Jindu Village or Township Bank	12,183	26,827	5.63	6.75	4.50
Qionglai Guomin Village or Township Bank	8,211	0	7.39	9.56	3.36
Shuangliu Chengmin Village or Township Bank	14,094	4100	6.37	6.90	5.76
Dayi Bocom Xingmin Rural Bank	9,066	100	6.00	7.00	6.00
Pengzhou Minsheng Village or Township Bank, Co., Ltd.	6,570	0	10.48	15.03	4.86
Xuanyi Chengmin Village or Township Bank	3,885	3	8.47	8.50	6.37
Shifang Siyuan Village or Township Bank	5,487	997	8.08	11.21	5.31
Mianzhu Pufa Village or Township Bank	2,940	0	6.84	8.50	5.31

(2) Business administration is not independent. Many of the staff at VTBs are delegated from commercial banks, and their salaries are paid by the commercial banks. Therefore, they may internalize the ideologies of business administration of commercial banks, who are the major shareholders of the VTBs. In fact, in the beginning when commercial banks decided to set up VTBs, they treated it as expansion of their own business. Therefore, they

expected the operation of VTBs to be in sync with them. VTBs cannot isolate themselves from commercial banks. They depend heavily on the latter for credit techniques, business administration, and capital. As a result, they are "shadow institutions" of commercial banks and do not have the advantages of providing personal services.[28]

(3) Product homogeneity and comparative disadvantage. Product homogeneity is evident in the types of services VTBs provide, i.e. saving and lending. Whether it is loan type (e.g. microcredit, specialized household loans, and microenterprise loans) or loan administration and the risk-sharing method (e.g. co-guarantee, collateral, etc.), VTBs follow the RCCs. VTBs and RCCs have the same target group of clients and are, therefore, in direct competition. The clients of VTBs are those filtered out by RCCs. Some clients have acquired loans over the line of credit of RCCs. Some have a poor record of credibility at RCCs. In such a market situation which VTBs can only take on board the clients rejected by RCCs, the comparative disadvantage of VTBs is obvious.[29]

(4) Poor understanding of the public hinders business development. As the state-owned banks offer national credit and RCCs have served rural areas for a long time, rural households respect these large-scale financial institutions which represent the state and the government. The public considers the institutions trustworthy. On the contrary, there is little understanding but many fallacies of the grassroots VTBs. The Research Group of Mianyang Society for Finance and Banking (2005) interviewed 100 random farmers and found that 92% of them did not know that a VTB is founded by a banking institution which is also the major shareholder, and they thought that one could set up a bank as long as one had enough money; 17% regarded VTBs as poverty-relief organizations and thought that loans from VTBs were policy funds of the state which needed not be repaid; 96% were reluctant to deposit money in VTBs fearing scams.

Microcredit companies

In May 2008, CBRC and People's Bank of China together issued the *Guidance on Pilot Microcredit Companies* (hereinafter as the *Guidance*), which defines the nature, requirements for establishment, and sources of capital of microcredit companies. Microcredit companies are limited liability companies or limited companies which do not absorb public savings. They adopt marketized operation and are independent in terms of business, finances, self-constraints, and risk-bearing. They are invested by natural persons, enterprise legal persons, and other social organizations. They accept funds from shareholders, donations, and two or fewer banking financial institutions.[30] The loan rate is not strictly controlled[31] except for a minimum of 0.9 times of the benchmark rate of the central bank. The range of fluctuation allowed is determined by the companies following the principle of marketization. The loan period and terms are determined by the lender and borrower in accordance with the law. According to the *Guidance*, qualified microcredit companies can upgrade to become VTBs on a voluntary basis.

In terms of the definition of microcredit companies, privatization and a lending-only system are new creations in the rural financial market. Although microcredit companies do not absorb public savings and are non-banking institutions, based on their business and developmental direction, they can be categorized as an intermediate between banks and company and private finance. Such ambiguous positioning of microcredit companies implies the multiple considerations of the policy-making body while it tries to excite and reform the rural financial market: (1) As private finance has yet to be legalized, its development cannot be regulated. The emergence of microcredit companies is a manifestation of the policy-making body's approval of private finance. (2) Because the property rights relationships in the private sector is very clear, microcredit companies do a better job in exciting and directing private capital than other financial institutions. The flexibility of private capital and property rights relationships are two prerequisites for promoting endogenous growth. (3) The risk of microcredit companies is shared by shareholders. If business fails, the company will go bankrupt and close down following the market principle. Not only does it shatter the rural financial institutions' expectation of aid, but it also creates a new exit mechanism for the institutions. (4) Microcredit companies mainly provide financial services. When they meet certain requirements, they can transform to VTBs, which is a bridge between private finance and formal finance.

Around 2006, People's Bank of China set up seven pilot microcredit companies in provinces (districts) including Shanxi, Sichuan, and Guizhou (See Table 4.8). Of the seven companies, Rongfeng Microcredit Co., Ltd. in Inner Mongolia had the most registered capital, amounting to RMB50 million, and Jinyuantai Microcredit Co., Ltd. in Pingyao County, Shanxi Province had the smallest, amounting to RMB16 million. All companies were limited liability companies except Jiangkou Huadi Microcredit Ltd., which is a limited company.

Table 4.8. The status of the seven pilot microcredit companies

Company	Company location	Date of establishment	Registered capital (RMB million)	Organizational form
Shanxi Pingyao Jinyuantai Microcredit Co., Ltd.	Pingyao County, Shanxi Province	Dec. 27, 2005	16	Limited liability company
Shanxi Pingyao Rishenglong Microcredit Co., Ltd.	Pingyao County, Shanxi Province	Dec. 27, 2005	17	Limited liability company
Sichuan Guangyuan Quan Li Microcredit Company	Guangyuan City, Sichuan Province	Apr. 10, 2006	20	Limited liability company
Guizhou Jiangkou Huadi Microcredit Co., Ltd	Jiangkou County, Guizhou	Aug. 19, 2006	30	Limited company
Xi'an Xinchang Microcredit Co., Ltd.	Hu County, Shaanxi Province	Sep. 18, 2006	22	Limited liability company
Xi'an Dayanghuixin Microcredit Co., Ltd.	Hu County, Shaanxi Province	Sep. 18, 2006	21	Limited liability company
Neimenggu E'erduosi Rongfeng Microcredit Co., Ltd.	Ordos City, Inner Mongolia	Oct. 12, 2006	50	Limited liability company

The actual operation of microcredit companies vary with respect to time and location. The variations are found in the following aspects:

(1) Composition of clients. The companies' clients are mainly microenterprises, private individuals, and rural households. As of August 2006, Wanlitong Microcredit Company issued 96% of its loans to rural enterprises and individual industrial and commercial households; Shanxi Pingyao Rishenglong Microcredit Co., Ltd. issued almost all its loans to rural households (animal husbandry loans accounted for 52%); Guizhou Jiangkou Huadi Microcredit Co., Ltd. issued 72% of its loans to rural individual business households; 14%

of the loans issued by Sichuan Guangyuan Quan Li Microcredit Company were animal husbandry loans. In order to achieve the goal of serving the rural financial market, some microcredit companies set up restrictions on the proportion of agricultural loans when they were established. For example, in the tender documents of Neimenggu E'erduosi Rongfeng Microcredit Co., Ltd., it is stated that loans to the Three Rural Issues cannot be less than 10% in the first few years, and it cannot be lower than 25% at the sixth year of establishment; Jiangkou County in Guizhou Province requires a minimum of 30%; and Pingyao County in Shanxi Province a minimum of 70%.[32]

(2) Composition of loan types and loan limits. There are mainly three types of loans: credit, guaranteed loans, and collateral loans. The small loan limit is to break loans into several smaller loans. For example, the proportion of credit takes up 61% of the total loans of Sichuan Guangyuan Quan Li Microcredit Company; collateral loans account for more than 71% of the total loans of Shanxi Pingyao Rishenglong Microcredit Co., Ltd., and Guizhou Jiangkou Huadi Microcredit Co., Ltd. In terms of loan limit of a single loan, Sichuan Guangyuan Quan Li Microcredit Company and Guizhou Jiangkou Huadi Microcredit Co., Ltd. set a loan limit at 2% of the total capital; Neimenggu E'erduosi Rongfeng Microcredit Co., Ltd. at 5% of the total capital; the two companies in Pingyao County in Shanxi Province at RMB100,000, and they require that rural loans which are smaller than RMB50,000 should constitute 70% of the total loans.

(3) The loan rate reflects marketization. There is no fixed maximum loan rate. The interest rate can vary within four times the benchmark determined by the microcredit company and the borrower. The company has a larger role in setting the loan rate and can vary the rate according to situations. As a whole, the loan rates of microcredit companies distribute in a wide range. The average loan rate is higher than that of financial institutions over the same period, almost as high as that of private loans. Some companies offer preferential loans towards the Three Rural Issues under certain policies. The loan rates for agricultural loans and animal husbandry loans are significantly lower than those for industrial and commercial loans, transportation loans, and loans to the services sector.

(4) Preference for short loan period. For example, all loans of Shanxi Pingyao Rishenglong Microcredit Co., Ltd. have a loan period of one year or shorter, of which three-month loans account for 12%, half-year loans for 66%, one-year loans for 22%; Guizhou Jiangkou Huadi Microcredit Co., Ltd. offers short-term loans, taking up 78% of total loans. It specializes in three-month and half-year loans; Sichuan Guangyuan Quan Li Microcredit Company offers

one-month, two-month, three-month, five-month, half-year, and one-year loans, of which one-year loans constitute 38%; Shanxi Pingyao Jinyuantai Microcredit Company mainly issue six-month loans, which account for 54% of the total loans.

From the perspective of innovation, microcredit companies are a new channel for private capital to enter the scope of finance, so that capital operation[33] of private capital can be legally used under certain policies. It will become more difficult to practice "underground finance," easier to divert and absorb private capital, and regulate private lending. Further, microcredit companies can absorb private capital from traditional industries and pave the way for the transformation of private finance into formal finance. In reality, microcredit companies contribute to the diversity of financial supply, alleviate the insufficient rural financial supply, and propel the improvement of financial services by bringing competition to the market.

It should be pointed out that pilot microcredit companies have clearly defined property rights, are financially independent and risk-bearing. Whether they will contribute to a sustainable financial supply mechanism and become a market-stabilizing force in the rural financial market requires further observation. At least, the current situation reveals the following problems with the development of the companies:[34]

(1) The lack of credit techniques. The rural financial market is difficult to activate. One of the obstacles is that there is a lack of deposit capital and acceptable collaterals. The credit techniques of traditional commercial banks cannot effectively deal with the rural financial demand. Drawing from international experience, the policy-making body set up new-style financial institutions as they intend to utilize microcredit as a solution to the problem of the lack of guarantee or collateral for loans which is suitable to China's own rural financial market. However, the actual operation of microcredit companies shows that they simply copied the commercial banks credit products and market development, and mainly offer guaranteed loans and collateral loans. There has been no development in rural credit. In terms of credit techniques, many microcredit companies in China are falling behind their international counterparts and large-scale financial institutions such as commercial banks and RCCs.

(2) Little awareness and ability of risk-control. In the beginning when microcredits were first established, the policy-making body required microcredit companies to "strengthen internal control, establish well-regulated asset categorization and provision systems, accurately categorize assets, counting and drawing allowance for doubtful accounts, and ensure the asset loss reserve ratio is

higher than 100%" in order to cover all risk. However, in reality, few companies have a decent management structure. The decision-making procedures, loan administration, and internal audit systems are poor. Some pilot companies' investments are too concentrated and deviate from the principle of "small amount" and "diverse" as stated in the *Guidance*. As they cannot obtain capital from banks through financing, some of them start to issue entrusted loans. Not only does this deviate from the developmental pathway, but it is also very risky. Some hold the view that as microcredit companies are not financial institutions, the credit risk is directly borne by the investors of the companies, and it will not incur systematic risk. Therefore, the risk of microcredit companies is not worrisome. We believe that this is a view that has not considered the whole picture of China's rural financial development. Rural society is in a critical transition period, and rural households' credibility and transactions are in rapid marketization.[35] To the companies themselves, shutting down is a minor problem, but it brings a lot of problems to rural finance. The credibility environment would worsen and the market basis for rural finance would be demolished.[36]

(3) Crowding-out effect and unsustainability caused by a high interest rate. Some microcredit companies directly set the interest rate at the maximum, which is four times the benchmark.[37] Individuals or enterprises engaged in agriculture, which is a weak industry, cannot bear such a high interest rate. As a result, the high interest crowds out the loans regarding the Three Rural Issues which have a lower loan rate.[38] Reality also shows that many microcredit companies target clients such as local microenterprises, individual industrial and commercial households, and paid workers including civil servants, but not rural households.[39] Apart from the crowding-out effect, a high interest rate has a negative effect on the sustainability of microcredit companies. A high interest rate inevitably causes adverse selection and moral hazard. The clients of microcredit companies are filtered out by formal financial institutions. Those clients have no choice but to bear a high interest rate. The result is that there is over-concentration of high-risk investors in the pool of clients of the companies, which implies that the law of large numbers, which is the basis for risk-management, will not be effective. The credit market is at risk of collapse.[40]

(4) The lack of supervision and constant violation. According to the *Guidance*, microcredit companies, which only issue loans but do not accept deposits, are not under strict supervision of the CBRC. Provincial governments can appoint the finance office or relevant organizations to supervise microcredit companies and bear the loss incurred by risk-handling in case the pilot companies fail.

At present, local governments pay all their attention to establishing large-scale financial institutions, and they have none to spare for the microcredit companies which cannot manage themselves. The branches of People's Bank of China and affiliated organizations of CBRC at most ask the companies to report on their financial status. There is no actual supervision. In other words, microcredit companies are unsupervised at this moment. As external supervision is slack, many microcredit companies violate the regulations and even the law in their actual operation. Some of the companies were set up not to serve the Three Rural Issues but as a legal way to issue loans at a high interest rate. It is not uncommon to find virtual capital, acceptance of deposits against regulations, chaotic capital flows, and usury.

(5) A dispersed shareholding structure and the lack of motivation for change. In order to disperse risk, the *Guidance* pointed out: "The total amount of shares held by a single natural man, enterprise legal men, other social organization, and other related personnel should not be more than 10% of the registered capital." In fact, based on the reform of the shareholding structure of RCCs, this kind of measure to enhance the shareholding structure does not help corporate management. Worse still, it discourages foreign microcredit companies which have experience and intention to invest from entering the market. In addition, while the *Guidance* states that microcredit companies can transform into VTBs,[41] in reality, the companies face a dilemma in terms of transformation: Almost all the current pilot microcredit companies are privately owned. However, according to *Interim Provisions on the Administration of Village and township banks*, a VTB must have a banking financial institution as its holding company, or be wholly-owned by a banking financial institution. So, if microcredit companies transform to VTBs, shareholders have to give up equity. On the one hand, they are motivated by the upgrade of qualification. On the other hand, they lose control of the company. Either way, it is a tough choice to make for those private entrepreneurs who hope to transform from industrial capitalism to financial capitalism.

Table 4.9. The influence on corporate management of different shareholding structures

Management mechanism	High concentration, with an absolute holding stockholder	Low concentration, no substantial shareholder	Average concentration, with holding stockholders
Incentive mechanism	Strong	Weak	Average

(Cont'd)

Management mechanism	High concentration, with an absolute holding stockholder	Low concentration, no substantial shareholder	Average concentration, with holding stockholders
Supervision mechanism	Average	Weak	Strong
The takeover market	Weak	Strong	Average
Competition for right of agency	Weak	Strong	Strong

Source: OECD.

Rural mutual aid organizations

At present, there are two types of rural mutual aid organizations: the pilots of the poverty aid system and the pilots of financial regulation department (CBRC). The former are community foundations and mutual aid funds developed using fiscal capital or capital of international financial organizations. They include pilot mutual aid funds for the development of poor villages, pilot of the operation of rolling development capital in rural communities supported by the World Bank (TCC5 project[42]), etc. The pilots of financial regulation departments mainly refer to rural mutual aid funds which aim at improving rural financial services.

Regardless of the types of pilots, they share the following features: (1) Their main types of business are loans and other financial services. (2) They are based in the location (villages) of the target groups of community service. (3) They are cooperative. The two types of pilots are different in the following aspects: (1) The pilot of the poverty aid system is targeted at alleviating poverty. Their business is more than issuing loans. They stress cooperation among poor households in terms of production and sales. They hope to build a platform for mutual aid. Rural mutual cooperatives (RMCs) set up by CBRC aim at improving rural financial services through establishing new-style financial institutions which are suitable for the rural market. They search for a better system which can satisfy the rural financial demand. Poverty alleviation is not their goal. (2) Pilot poverty alleviation organizations are mostly established using government fiscal poverty alleviation fund. They are non-profit-making private organizations with government support. The requirements for establishment are less strict and they are not included in the formal financial supervision system. The operation mechanism of rural mutual aid funds is more commercial. The requirements for establishment and being a shareholder, paid-in capital, internal administration structure, allocation of profits, and the standard of supervision required are similar to those of commercial financial institutions. In summary, the pilots of poverty alleviation systems aim at alleviating poverty and encouraging mutual aid. Those of RMCs are after mutual aid though capital among private parties (Lin Wanlong et al. 2008).

Since 2006, during the pilot period of rural mutual aid funds, some better or possibly sustainable modes of operation have emerged. The two representatives are Yilong County in Sichuan Province and Huoshan County in Anhui Province (Wu Zhong, Cao Hongmin, and Lin Wanlong et al. 2008). The former is directed by the public while the latter is directed by the government. The mutual cooperative in Wangcang County, Sichuan Province (pilot of TCC5 project) is between the two modes.

Table 4.10. A summary of the differences among the modes of mutual aid funds

Pilots		Sichuan Yilong County Poverty Alleviation Mutual Cooperative	Anhui Huoshan County Fund for the Development of Poor Villages	Sichuan Wangcang County Community Mutual Cooperative
Status	Main organizers	Poverty alleviation unit in the County government, Yilong County Village Development Association (NGO)	Poverty alleviation unit and the finance department in the County government	Poverty alleviation unit in the County government
	Registered unit	Ministry of Civil Affairs	Unregistered	Ministry of Civil Affairs
	Sources of capital	Fiscal poverty alleviation fund, shares bought by rural households	Fiscal poverty alleviation fund at various level, capital for supporting farmers	Fiscal poverty alleviation fund, mutual aid funds collected from members
	Service area	The administrative village in which it is located	The villager group which it belongs	The administrative village in which it is located
	Number of pilots	27	154	10
	Total number of members (household)	4,441	3,863	1,724

(Cont'd)

Pilots		Sichuan Yilong County Poverty Alleviation Mutual Cooperative	Anhui Huoshan County Fund for the Development of Poor Villages	Sichuan Wangcang County Community Mutual Cooperative
Status	Total amount of capital	480.95	312.9	156.98
	(RMB10,000)	270.15	210.8	140.00
	Of which: Fiscal capital Capital of members	210.80	31.1	16.98
Fund-raising mechanism	Format	Shares: Poor households are given shares for free, general households are allocated shares, rich households can buy shares.	Agricultural supporting fund. There is no stock equity.	Agricultural supporting fund, with equity.
	Limit	RMB1,000 per share. A household may be allocated two shares, or given for free one share at most.	RMB100–200 per household	RMB50–100 per household
	Input of fiscal capital	Poor households are given shares for free. Allocated shares to general households should be on an individual basis.	Fiscal capital is used by the community. There is no stock equity	There is collective equity (community shares)
Situation of loans and deposits	Deposit absorption	Yes	No	No
	Loan limit	5% of total assets	RMB5,000	RMB4,000
	Nominal rate of annual occupancy expense	8%	7.2%	7.2%
	Repayment method	By installment (10–15 days), with principal and interest	One-time, with principal and interest	By monthly installment, with principal and interest

(Cont'd)

Pilots		Sichuan Yilong County Poverty Alleviation Mutual Cooperative	Anhui Huoshan County Fund for the Development of Poor Villages	Sichuan Wangcang County Community Mutual Cooperative
Profits allocation, poverty targeting, and economic activities	Profits allocation	Salaries for managers Administrative cost Welfare reserves Provident fund Bonus allocated to shareholders	Administrative cost. Transferred to principal, no bonus.	Administrative cost Transferred to principal Provident fund Bonus allocated to shareholders who are rural households. Holders of community shares are not allocated any bonus.
	Poverty targeting	Give free shares to poor households	Not specific policy	Give special status and issue loans at special terms to poor households.
	Economic activities	Loan services, cooperative production.	Loan services	Loan services

Note: 1. The data of the pilots in Yilong County and Huoshan County are up to May 2007.
2. The data of the pilots in Wangcang County are up to July 2008.

Source: Lin Wanlong et al., "The modes and performance of poverty alleviation mutual cooperatives" (2008).

In Table 4.11, we illustrate the status of some of the RMCs in Sichuan Province. It shows the following: (1) Most of the RMCs are set up by the government. Few are initiated by rural households. (2) The rural mutual aid funds' annual rate is calculated based on the loan rate collar within 10%, which is lower than that of VTBs, lending companies, and other new rural financial institutions over the same period. (3) The loan limit of RMCs ranges from RMB5,000 to RMB30,000. Most of them set the limit at RMB5,000. (4) They generally have capital amounting to less than RMB200,000. The value of shares bought per household is within RMB500.

Table 4.11. The status of some of the rural mutual cooperatives in Sichuan Province

Region	Number of mutual aid organizations	How it was initiated		Range of loan rate (annual rate, %)			Highest loan limit (RMB)	Average capital (RMB 10,000)	Average number of shareholding households	Average value of shares per household (RMB)
		By the government	By rural households	Maximum	Minimum	Average				
Deyang	2	X		8.00	8.00	8.00	10,000	31	257	298
Mianyang	48	X		8.64	7.20	7.80	5,000	18	105	250
Guangyuan	1		X	10.44	10.44	10.44	30,000	31	1767	175
Nanchong	26	X		8.00	6.00	7.90	10,000	87	111	931
Luzhou	30	X		9.60	7.00	7.70	8,000	18	132	210
Meishan	23	X		9.60	7.20	8.13	5,000	15	129	333
Ziyang	20	X		9.00	7.00	7.61	5,000	22	996	325
Neijiang	23	X		14.40	6.00	9.00	5,000	18	465	375
Dazhou	43		X	12.00	8.00	9.00	5,000	16	114	296
Suining	23	X		8.00	8.00	8.00	5,000	13	97	356

Note: Information as of March 2009.

Rural mutual aid funds in different regions have different goals and environment. Therefore, there are some variations in the operation mechanism. Based on the definition of rural mutual aid funds stated in CBRS's *Document No. 7*, a typical operation mechanism is as shown in Fig. 4.5.[43]

Fig. 4.5. Operation mechanism of rural mutual cooperatives

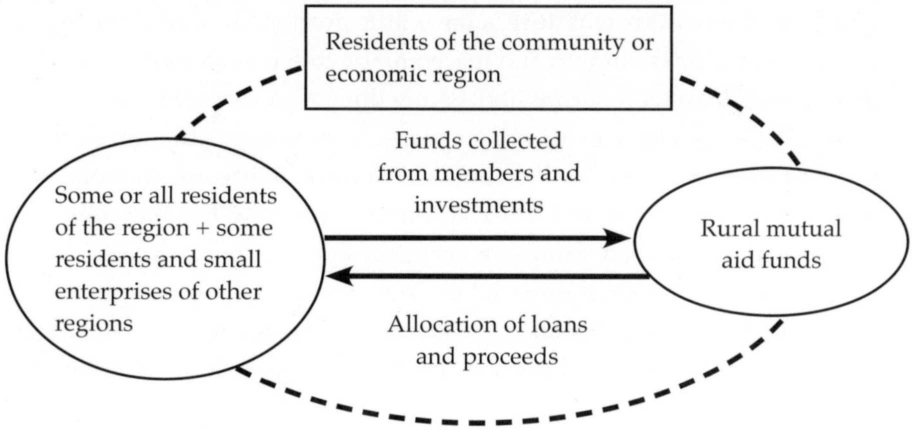

Looking at the current situation, the following problems can be identified in the development process of rural mutual funds:

(1) The participation of rural households in the rural mutual funds is usually short-term. Mutual aid is not fully achieved. Research has found that rural households have little initiative in participation. They need someone to be the leader. Most of them do not join the mutual aid funds for long-term economic partnership, and they do not borrow money for developing production. They join because they want to enjoy the benefits of the poverty aid fund. Once they have private capital, they are unwilling to borrow from the mutual aid funds. The long-term cooperative function of mutual aid funds is suppressed.[44] Under such circumstances, whether in terms of capital operation or the actual functions, it is difficult for rural mutual aid funds to operate in the long run.

(2) Development directed by the government deviates from the target of "endogenous finance." By logic, as cooperatives, RMCs should be set up by rural households voluntarily and bear the features of endogenous finance. As China's rural households are not keen on cooperating with external parties (See chapter 2), self-development cannot be achieved in a short period of time, and they rely on the government. Research has found that most of the RMCs were set up under the direction of the government. Few emerged among rural households. As external forces have substituted for endogenous self-development, it is not strange to see that many RMCs are not actually cooperative.[45]

(3) Self-management ability is low and incentive mechanism fails. The risk-prevention system of the pilot RMCs is based on the assumption that managers are responsible. There are no regulations on risk-management or corresponding disciplinary measures, and external supervision is slack, which are the reasons why RMCs have little awareness of risk-management. Capital operation is random and it is common to see violations and alteration of the use of loan with permission. Safety threats are everywhere.

(4) Some RMCs are eager to absorb deposits. The current situation shows that the management, capital ability, and risk-control ability are far from what is required for managing and utilizing public savings. Once they fail in their use of deposits, it may trigger a series of events, cause chaos in finance, and damage the regional financial ecology. Some RMCs are eager to absorb deposits and are ready to do so. Under the circumstances in which there is little self-development of RMCs and external supervision, attention should be paid to the eagerness. RMCs should be stopped from using a high interest rate to attract deposits.

To sum up, as one of the manifestations of new rural finance, the nature of RMCs has determined that they target the low-income group in rural areas. They aim at helping rural households to improve production and business, and continuously raise rural income though cooperation among members. RMCs should serve its geopolitical community and cooperative members through mutual aid funds.

Needless to say, as financial institutions based on mutual aid and cooperation, RMCs face the constraint of low willingness of rural households to cooperate with other parties. It is unrealistic to hope that rural households would initiate a mutual cooperative in the recent future. Thus, how to capitalize on the comparative advantages of the government, community organizations, and rural households to establish an interactive mechanism, which is directed by the government, supported by the community, and rural households cooperate with, is the key question.

New-style financial institutions as "marginal increment"

As a trial in the reform and development of rural finance, these new types of financial institutions act as deposit-type financial institutions (RCCs, commercial banks, the Postal Savings Bank of China, policy banks) in the form of "marginal increment" in the rural financial system. So, how can these institutions be a new market force? What "marginal effects" will they have on the whole rural financial market? We will dissect the questions from three perspectives: (1) Under the relaxed market access policy, what effects will the rapidly increasing number of new types of financial institutions have on the rural financial market? (2) With a liberalized loan rate, is the strategy of setting a high loan rate sustainable for the institutions? (3) In terms of the long-term development of the rural financial market, what is the goal of the institutions?

The market structure: Does an open rural financial market equal the new institutions better?

In order to alleviate the insufficient demand in the rural financial market and explore the development of rural financial institutions, policy and supervision departments have lowered the entry threshold to the market. Policies are devised to encourage and support the institutions in the hope of accelerating the opening up and activation of the market.

Form a closed market in which there is continuous capital outflow to a more open one in which capital remains or flows back, the transformation and development of rural finance has come a long way. As policies relaxed, new rural financial institutions mushroomed in a short period of time. The new institutions are valuable pilots of the reform. However, we should be taking one step at a time in the reform of rural finance. More and more new institutions rush, or even swarm into the market under government's encouragement. In some cities, there is a licensed new-style financial institution every few hundred meters on the street. Does an open market mean the more the better?

Theoretically, a lower entry threshold has helped to create a "free market." The question is: Does free competition bring about the optimal number of financial institutions? According to Salop's circle model (1979), the answer is negative.

Consider there are n ($n = 1, 2, 3 \ldots, N$) banks distributed on a circle. The banks absorb public deposits and invest them in risk-free assets with a rate of return r.

Each depositor owns one unit of cash endowment, and the depositors are jointly distributed on the circle. They cannot make direct investment like the banks do. They have to deposit their money into the banks. The transportation cost of making deposit αx is a ratio of the distance between the depositors and the banks x. The circumference of the circle is assigned to be one unit, and depositors are represented as D.

As depositors are concentrated in one location, the optimal distribution of banks is that n banks are symmetrically located. The distance between any two banks is $1/n$. When a consumer comes between two banks, the shortest distance is $\frac{1}{2n}$. Therefore, the total transportation cost of all depositors is

$$2n \int_{0}^{\frac{1}{2n}} \alpha x D dx = \frac{\alpha D}{4n}$$

Assume the cost of establishing banks per unit is F. From the perspective of maximizing social benefits, minimizing establishment cost and transportation cost would give the optimal number of banks:

$$\min nF + \frac{\alpha D}{4n}$$

From the first order condition $F - \frac{\alpha D}{4n^2} = 0$, the optimal number of banks n^* can be obtained:

$$n^* = \frac{1}{2}\sqrt{\frac{\alpha D}{F}}$$

With no (or few) entry constraints, banks seem to be in free competition. When n banks enter the market, they are evenly distributed on the circle and set the deposit rates at $r_D^1, r_D^2 \ldots, r_D^n$. When the difference between the return of deposit and the transportation cost is the same for making deposits in both banks (As in Fig. 4.6), both banks will maintain a stable deposit.

Fig. 4.6. Market distribution in Salop's circle model

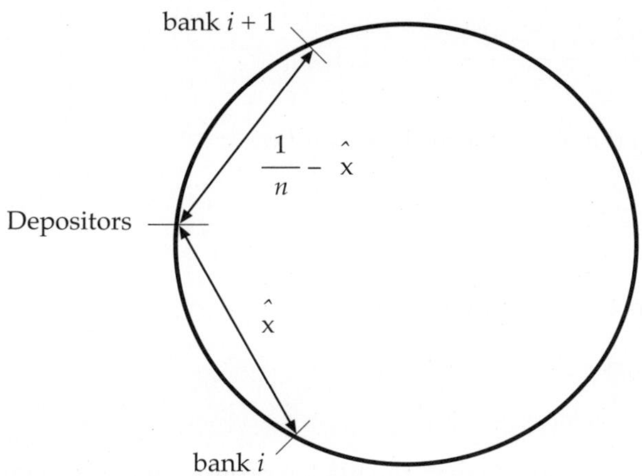

The distance between marginal depositor and the bank $\hat{x}$ is expressed as follows:

$$r_D^i - \alpha\hat{x}_i = r_D^{i+1} - \alpha\left(\frac{1}{n} - \hat{x}\right),$$

And,

$$\hat{x}_i = \frac{1}{2n} + \frac{r_D^i - r_D^{i+1}}{2\alpha},$$

$$\hat{x}_{i-1} = \frac{1}{2n} + \frac{r_D^{i-1} - r_D^i}{2\alpha},$$

Correspondingly, the total amount of deposits bank i absorbs is

$$D_i = \left|\hat{x}_i - \hat{x}_{i-1}\right| D = \left(\frac{1}{n} + \frac{2r_D^i - r_D^{i+1} - r_D^{i-1}}{2\alpha}\right) D$$

As the model is built upon the circumference of a circle, therefore

$$r_D^{n+1} = r_D^1,$$

$$r_D^n = r_D^0$$

The profits of bank i is

$$\pi_i = D\,(r - r_D^i)\left(\frac{1}{n} + \frac{2r_D^i - r_D^{i+1} - r_D^{i-1}}{2\alpha}\right)$$

For all i, at r_D^i, π_i is maximized and at equilibrium,

$$r - r_D^i = \frac{\alpha}{n} + \frac{2r_D^i - r_D^{i+1} - r_D^{i-1}}{2},\ i = 1,2,3...,n.$$

The only solution to the above formula is as follows:

$$r_D^i = ... = r_D^n = r - \frac{\alpha}{n}$$

And all the banks receive the same profits:

$$\pi_1 = ... = \pi_n = \frac{\alpha D}{n^2}$$

As there is no entry constraint, when the banks' profits equal the establishment cost F, the number of banks at equilibrium is n^{**} :

$$n^{**} = \frac{1}{2}\sqrt{\frac{\alpha D}{F}}$$

Comparing n^{**} and n^*, it can be seen that without entry constraints, free competition would give rise to too many banks. The distribution of banks is not compatible with the market structure which maximizes social benefits.

Without a doubt, Salop's circle model (1979) has strong implications on the rapid development of the new rural financial institutions. In general, as financial intermediaries, financial institutions must have a certain number of clients to survive. When there are too many institutions competing for clients, it becomes difficult for them to gain enough revenue to continue their business. When the entry threshold lowers, the franchise value of banks drops significantly. This increases the banks' risk propensity and lowers their incentive to run business carefully. In fact, much research (e.g. Keeley 1990) has found that the increase in competition, the drop in the franchise value, and the bankruptcy rate of banks are all directly related.

Therefore, the phenomenon of streets overcrowded with new-style financial institutions will eventually disappear. A prevalent view is that the risk of bankruptcy of those institutions is borne by the shareholders. The bankruptcy of many of those institutions would not affect the entire financial system and this is, therefore, not very worrying. This carefree attitude has allowed people to vastly underestimate the adverse effect over-competition has on the market. In an overcrowded market, feeling the pressure of survival, financial institutions would inevitably go into disorderly competition. When many undeserving borrowers obtain loans because of the over-competition and they become common-place in the market, many financial institutions would be on the brink of bankruptcy and the credibility order and credit environment would be in chaos. As a result, not only would the financial institutions collapse, so too would the credit basis on which market transactions are built. If shareholders bear the loss of financial institutions which go bankrupt, who or which party will bear the long-term damage of the credit basis of the rural financial market?

Price-setting mechanism: Is a free and high loan rate the key to sustainability?

To new rural financial institutions, the interest rate ceiling is high. The interest rate is basically free to vary. According to the law, the price set at an interest rate within four times of the benchmark is under legal protection. The intention to raise the interest rate ceiling is clear: On the one hand, the costs for agricultural loans and agricultural microcredit are high; the loan rate needs to be able to generate enough interest to cover the cost so that business can sustain. On the other hand, more importantly, loosening the control on the interest rate gives new-style financial institutions greater freedom to set their loan rates. Loosening control encourages them to explore which price-setting mechanism can be applied to the rural financial market and vary the price to suit different situations.

However, the efforts of the policy-making unit of using the market mechanism to guide new-style financial institutions in setting the price are offset by the market strategies of financial institutions as they are hungry for profits. Many of them directly set the loan rate at the maximum (four times the benchmark). The overall loan rate of all kinds of new-style financial institutions is as high as three times the benchmark over the same period. So, is a free and high loan rate the key to sustainable development of new-style financial institutions?

Many new-style financial institutions do not emerge from local private finance. A lot more are transplanted top-down and from other areas. Therefore, they face the problem of high information cost and information asymmetry in the early stages of development. In such a situation, simply raising the loan rate to compensate for the risk may backfire. The following model will illustrate.

Assume an enterprise with medium risk needs to borrow capital L to finance a project. Following Stiglitz and Weiss (1981), the probability of success of the project[46] is P_i and the corresponding rate of return is R_i; the probability of failure is

$(1 - P_i)$ and the corresponding return is 0. All projects have the same expected rate of return, i.e. $p_i R_i = p_j \bar{R}_j = R$, $i \neq j$. The density function of the probability of success of the project is $f(p_i)$ and the corresponding distribution function is $F(p_i)$. The loan rate for the enterprise to borrow from the bank is r. If the investment project succeeds, the enterprise has to pay the bank $L(1+r)$; if the investment project fails, the enterprise has to pay the bank a proportion γ of the principal, where $0 < \gamma \leq 1$. If the bank, with medium risk, is in a competitive credit market, the supply of credit capital is an increasing function of return on loan per unit, i.e. $S = S(\rho)$, $S' > 0$, of which ρ is the return on loan per unit.

The expected profit of the enterprise is

$$E\pi = pL(R - 1 - r) - \gamma(1 - p)L$$

Only when the expected profit is larger than 0 will the enterprise apply for loans. Assume $\hat{p}$ to be the critical success rate of the project at every interest rate, which means $\hat{p}$ is the success rate when $E\pi = 0$ is satisfied. From the above equation, the following can be obtained:

$$\hat{p} = \frac{\bar{R} - \gamma}{(1 + r) - \gamma}$$

Because $dE\pi / dp = -L(1 + r - \gamma) < 0$, only when $p < \hat{p}$, will the enterprise apply for loans. As $\hat{p} \geq 0$,

$$\frac{\partial \hat{p}}{\partial r} = \frac{\gamma - \bar{R}}{(1 + r - \gamma)^2} < 0$$

The above formula shows that when the loan rate rises, the critical success rate of the investment project will fall. Because the overall average success rate of the projects is $\bar{P} = \int_0^{\hat{p}} pf(p)\,dp \,/\, F(\hat{p})$, we can obtain $\frac{\partial \bar{p}}{\partial r} < 0$. Therefore, as the loan rate rises, the quality of projects which will be financed by the loan will drop.

The model illustrates that simply raising the loan rate or raising it to a level which is too high could change the risk status of the entire market. As more and more high-risk borrowers enter the market, the accumulated risk may trigger the collapse of the credit market. What is interesting is that the design of new-style financial institutions gives marketization and risk-management high priority. But, at a high loan rate, the risk distribution of the clients has a systemic change. The law of large numbers based on normal distribution becomes inapplicable (see Fig. 4.7).

Fig. 4.7. Concentration of risks in the market triggered by the high loan rate

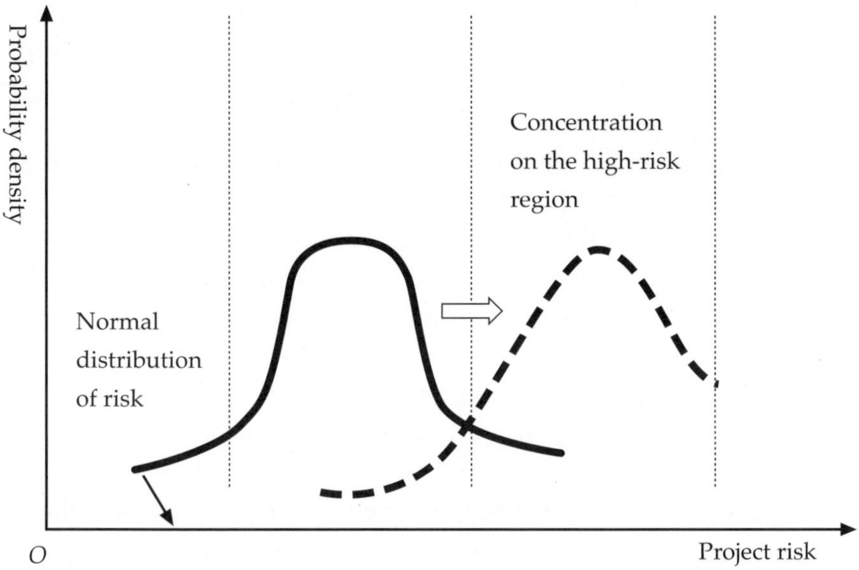

As "transplantations," new-style financial institutions have inherited the laziness to innovate from traditional formal financial institutions, which is reflected in their interest rate setting. Different types of new-style financial institutions have coincidentally opted for the "lazy strategy" of raising the interest rate. This undifferentiated price-setting strategy is a reflection of the typical want of the institutions to marketize in a short period of time, as well as the lack of an incentive to innovate (perhaps they lack price-setting techniques).

When many new-style financial institutions rush into the rural financial market and employ the high interest rate strategy, the following will happen: On the first level, the high interest rate will crowd out the investments in the Three Rural Issues as the investors cannot bear the high loan rate.[47] And the institutions do not help increase the supply of loans to the Three Rural Issues. On the second level, the high interest rate will crowd out the general investors, leading to a concentration of high-risk investors in the market and the probability for financial institutions to go bankrupt will increase. This is especially true in regions with an overcrowded market. The high interest rate could also trigger more serious adverse selection and moral hazard, causing the collapse of the credit market.

What is the goal of reform?

Past experience has demonstrated that merely depending on policy loans or promoting the development of the branches of commercial banks in villages cannot resolve the chronic problems with the rural financial market. It means that new rural financial institutions, as "marginal increment," should not aim at simply raising capital input. They should breakaway from the old system which is not compatible with the market and explore a new mechanism which suits the market in terms of financial demand and sustainable self-development. Yi Gang, deputy governor of the People's Bank of China once said, "The goal of developing new rural financial institutions is to find a new "order" in the market, rather than a growth in scale like going from '$X + Y = Z$' to '$2X + 2Y = 2Z$.'"

Will the entry of new rural financial institutions bring about a new order in the market? In terms of the competitive relationships among market entities, if the new deposit financial institutions are complementary to those already present in the market, the answer is yes. However, if the new institutions and those already there have the same competitive relationships based on the same market and same business, the entry of the new institutions is merely a change in the number of participants in the market.

Once the goal of the reform sets up the new order in the market, there is no need to fix the old rural financial system. The reform should motivate the nurture and growth of the new financial factors from inside the market and promote the formation of an endogenous rural financial system. With the new system, rural finance no longer needs to depend on growth by replication.

The pilot period of the new institutions has been motivated by external forces. The new institutions or organizations have an inherent lack of endogeneity. The twisted interest relationship between government intervention and passive participation of financial institutions and rural households caused the distortion of the incentive mechanism. The exogenous transplantation of financial institutions cannot internalize the rural households. It is under such conditions that we can see the paradoxes and difficulties in the rural financial market. For example, the government has devised policies and provided financial support to promote the OECD, but rural households do not show a strong willingness to cooperate. They join the specialized farmers cooperative (SFC) only to obtain the state's fiscal capital. While regulations on substantial shareholder are stipulated in the *Law of the People's Republic of China on Specialized Farmers Cooperatives*, democracy in administration and decision-making in the form of "one vote per household" is only talk. Authority is generally held in higher regard than cooperation.[48]

On a deeper level, the bottle-neck of the rural financial reforms is the failings of the mutual aid financial organizations and systems of which rural households are a major part. The decentralized management in rural areas has hindered the development of mutual aid cooperatives as well as diminishing the bargaining power of rural households as an entity in market economy.[49] The dilemma is constituted by government dominance and submissiveness of rural households. On the one hand, "horizontal finance" which is based on the cooperation among rural households is what suits rural areas. However, with a decentralized management structure, rural households have little intention to cooperate. It is difficult for a rural financial institution or system which has endogenous features to evolve from rural households and society. On the other hand, the government undoubtedly has the intention and capability to build a rural financial system which satisfies the demands of the development of rural society and economy. Nevertheless, for a long time, the financial system has been urban-biased and absent in the lives of rural households and rural society. As a result, any financial system which is based on the old system or horizontally "transplanted" to the rural financial market falls short of expectations. Therefore, there is no market force great enough to give rise to a horizontal financial organization which is endogenous and self-sustainable in the rural society and economy. The vertical financial force external to the society and economy cannot penetrate the economy and internalize into an eligible financial institution. The rural economic structure is like having an outer shield. Endogenous elements do not emerge and exogenous ones cannot enter. Difficult endogenous growth and internalization is a typical depiction of China's rural finance.

The dispersed small farmer's production is a fundamental constraint on rural financial reforms and development, as well as a crucial breakthrough in nurturing the ability of self-development of rural finance. Under the current structure, VTBs and (micro)credit companies have little effect in nurturing production factors in rural finance. They cannot resolve the conflicts between small-scale production and the market. In this respect, the direction for the long-term development of new rural financial institutions should depend on the rural OECD. Through nurturing them, the dispersed market entities would be consolidated, the bargaining power and status in transaction of rural households would be reinforced.[50] These provide the foundation for the new rural financial system.

Major Conclusions and Policy Implications

(1) The relationship between the government and the market gradually moves from opposing to cooperative. The core of the issue has changed to the role of the two entities under different conditions. Government intervention should take into consideration the three basic characteristics of the rural financial market: "double imbalance" of the endogenous market structure, insufficient demand and supply, and the problems with market development and institutional norms.

(2) As local governments are granted the authority over RCCs again, credit allocated to the agricultural industry has dropped. The potential problems of the local governments' in the intervention in, and remodeling of, RCCs should not go unnoticed.

(3) Inappropriate government intervention would cause misallocation of RCCs' credit resources, which would be aggravated under local protectionism. By introducing an external and independent financial regulatory mechanism, misallocation of credit resources caused by local protectionism of the local governments would be rectified.

(4) During the reforms of RCCs which are filled with conflicts and paradoxes, there are three logical puzzles which form the whole picture: (a) the fall in the level of effort and the change in risk propensity of RCC operators causes a drop in the operating efficiency of RCCs. (b) Local governments as an internal party as well as an administrative body can hardly act according to the preference and interest of the state. Rather, there is a chance that they conspire with RCC operators in benefit transfers. (c) The Three Rural Issues have become political. Moral hazard brought about by capital injection of the state and the problem with the expectation of aid have allowed RCCs to develop dependence on them when the operation of RCCs is inefficient and have high risk propensity. It deviates from the idea of reform through marketization.

(5) Four core issues of the reforms of RCCs:

   (a) As the shareholder structure is loose, there is the absence of owners, and, therefore, RCCs are controlled by internal parties. The government should reform the government-dominant administration, revise their policies, and encourage RCCs to have a smaller number of shareholders, who would be given the administrative and decision-making authority. This is core to the refinement of corporate governance of RCCs.

   (b) Classification reform should aim at better positioning and clearer definition of responsibilities of RCCs. The boundary between policy-based finance and commercial finance should be clearly drawn. Specialized policy-based financial institutions should be responsible for business related to policy. RCCs which are to be transformed to commercial financial institutions should be self-financing on the basis of commercial sustainability. They should not use the Three Rural Issues as an excuse for being a burden of the government.

   (c) Distorted authority structure and interest structure are the main reasons for the long-term poor performance of RCCs. Therefore, the system of provincial credit associations in which ownership and actual control power are reversed should be reformed. The administration of RCCs by the provincial governments conflicts with market-oriented operation and the functional transformation of governments. Administrative responsibility should be transferred to the RCCs themselves as legal persons.

(d) Based on classification reform, a regulated exit mechanism should be established in the rural financial market as soon as possible so as to eradicate moral hazard caused by RCCs' expectation of national assistance.

(6) There are several standards to judge whether new-style financial institutions can activate the rural financial market: (a) The institutions have a comparative advantage in serving the Three Rural Issues. They can increase the effective supply of rural credit and improve rural financial services, which is manifested as the relaxation of credit constraint and the increase in the availability of financial services. (b) The development model of the institutions can be reduplicated and is generally applicable, which can be applied to rural financial markets that bear the same features. Clues can be found when success of (a type of) these institutions is general, not a special case. (c) The institutions are commercially sustainable. Their revenue can cover their cost, and have a lower rate of non-performing loans and better risk-control ability.

(7) The rural financial market is complex and multi-layered. Having a free loan rate is beneficial for refining the differential pricing mechanism and the sustainable development of rural financial institutions. This is not an encouragement for setting a high loan rate. Relaxing the constraints on the loan rate is a measure to refine market mechanisms but not a goal.

(8) When many new-style financial institutions rush into the rural financial market and employ the high interest rate strategy, the following will happen: On the first level, the high interest rate will crowd out the investments in the Three Rural Issues as the investors cannot bear the high loan rate. And the institutions do not help increase the supply of loans to the Three Rural Issues. On the second level, the high interest rate will crowd out the general investors, leading to a concentration of high-risk investors in the market and the probability for financial institutions to go bankrupt will increase. Therefore, the interest rate cannot stay too high for a long time.

(9) The dispersed small farmer's production is a fundamental constraint on rural financial reforms and development, as well as a crucial breakthrough in nurturing the ability of self-development of rural finance. Under the current structure, VTBs and (micro) credit companies have little effect in nurturing production factors in rural finance. They cannot resolve the conflicts between small-scale production and the market. In this respect, the direction for the long-term development of new rural financial institutions should depend on the rural OECD.

Feature 4–1
The Imbalanced Chain of Interest and the Disadvantaged Status of Rural Households in the Market: Case Study of the Hog Industry[51]

The chain of interest in the hog industry

The flow of hogs (pork) in the local market

In City B which we conducted our study on, about 25% of the hogs are purchased by meat-processing enterprises, 75% circulate in the local market. There are three stages before the hogs reach the urban market from the farm: (1) The intermediary (hog traders) buy hogs from rural households and the hogs are slaughtered; (2) the intermediaries sell the pork to retailers (butchers); (3) retailers sell the pork to consumers.

The gain of hog farmers in the chain of interest

Of the 50 households of hog farmers surveyed, 47 suffered loss and three could break even. Calculated with the market price of RMB5 per catty,[52] a piglet which weighs 40 catties costs RMB200. It takes four and a half months to feed the piglet to 200 catties. During that period, 550 catties of feeds are consumed, which costs RMB605. RMB10 is added for epidemic prevention. Therefore the cost of raising a hog for sale is RMB815. At present, the market price per catty of hogs has dropped to RMB4. A hog which weights 200 catties can be sold at RMB800. Before the price drop, using cheaper feeds can yield the net income of RMB200–400. At present, the revenue cannot cover the cost, even without taking into consideration the risk of epidemic, price of feed, and the risk of fluctuation of the market price.

The gain of hog traders in the chain of interest

Hog traders are usually in a group of two to three people. Their business is very flexible. They can alter the number of hogs they purchase or demand a lower price from the hog farmers depending on the market situations of hog farmers and retailers. The number of hogs they purchase every day greatly varies. They may purchase from three to more than 10 hogs every day. Sometimes, they even do not purchase any. If the traders purchase one hog at RMB4 per catty and sell the slaughtered hog at RMB5.5 per catty to butchers, they can gain RMB290 per hog. When sales are good, traders can earn RMB700–1200 a day. Even on the worst days, they can still earn RMB500–700.

The gain of hog retailers in the chain of interest

Usually, butchers are in a group of two. We studied the business performance of 12 butchers who had five years of experience in the business in four counties in City B. The business of retailers varies on a daily basis. On better days, they can sell three to five hogs. Yet, the sales have dropped to two to three hogs per day in recent months. They buy pork from butchers at RMB5.5 per catty and sell it at RMB6–7 to consumers. When business is good, retailers can earn RMB400 or more. Even though business is not as good recently, they can still earn around RMB300 a day.

The effect of the imbalanced chain of interest on the stability of the hog industry

To make hog farmers lose confidence in the market

Not taking into account the risk of the market price, with reference to the production mode of the hog industry in the inland mountain area, each household can nurture 20 hogs for sale in five months without bringing in extra labor. If each hog yields a net income of RMB200, 20 hogs can bring a net income of RMB4,000. Assuming that every household has three units of labor force, the per capita income of a hog farming household per month is RMB267, that of hog traders is RMB4,000, and that of hog retailers is RMB3,100. This estimation is confirmed by the three parties. It can be seen that even when the industry is stable, rural households do not benefit most. Consumers can choose not to buy pork at a high price, but hog farming households would suffer a loss when the price is low. Hog farming households are oversensitive to the market and have few expectations on the return. The imbalanced chain of interest is a major factor which affects the stability of the hog industry.

To concentrate risk of hog industry on hog farming households

The direct risks hog farmers have to bear include the following: (1) Epidemic. Once an epidemic happens, all the inputs into the production cycle are losses, which are difficult to compensate for. (2) While the state provides subsidies for rural households for buying sows, the insurance coverage, amount, and mechanism offer very limited protection. (3) When the market price fluctuates, intermediaries would push down the market price. If the hogs are not sold in time, it seriously affects the gain of hog farmers. The risk is high. (4) There is also the risk of the market price, the cost of feeds, and many other risk factors which need to be taken into consideration. The risks mentioned above all concentrate in the first stage of the chain of interest of the hog industry: the hog farming households. The study shows that they receive the lowest returns, but bear almost all the risk.

The imbalance of risk and interest in the hog industry

The study found that as hog farming households have little ability to bear market risk and respond to market signals, they are usually passive in transactions. Traders and retailers are flexible in their businesses and are more active. They can push down the price or stop making purchase according to the changes in the market. The seven traders and 12 retailers we interviewed thought that they bore little risk, or even no risk at all. If epidemic happens and the sale of pork plummeted, they would stop making purchases or push down the market price, or go into other business.

The economic impact of the imbalanced chain of interest

The imbalanced chain of interest leads to the vicious circle of the demand and supply

In recent years, the hog industry has not been flourishing. The fundamental reason is the issue with interest of different parties. At present, when the price of pork rises, hog farmers benefit the least; when the price falls, hog farmers suffer the most. Theoretically, the market price of pork is determined by the demand and supply, which are represented by the hog farmers and consumers respectively. However, hog farmers lose confidence in the market as the chain of interest has been imbalanced for a long time. The excessive fluctuations of the market price of pork caused by the fluctuations in the quantity of hogs at farms are usually short-term. Therefore, the reason behind the fluctuations of the market price is not the interaction between production and demand and supply. It is the vicious circle of demand and supply caused by the imbalance of the chain of interest of the hog industry.

The loose production chain gives rise to too many entities in the chain of interest

In the inland of the Western region, dispersed small-farm businesses in animal husbandry has led to a loose production chain in the hog industry. There are several stages in the circulation of hogs (pork), and parties involved in each stage would retain some profit. The total profit of the process is divided into several parts. Although there are several channels for hogs to enter the market for sale, indirect sale remains the major one. More entities are attracted to be involved in the circulation. This is due to the commoditization of rural areas, the immature market, and the little organizational structure among rural households. Originally, the hog farmers sell hogs to the state directly. Now, they sell more to the traders. Even many state-owned hog-processing enterprises enlist the help of traders. As a result, the market price of pork is pushed up, and the farmers are deprived of their profit.

The lack of bargaining power of hog farming households widens the gaps in the chain of interest

The dispersed production chain of the hog industry and too many stages of circulation only scratch the surface of the problem. The real problems are the small scale of production, dispersed business, and the disadvantaged status of hog farming households in the production chain. Especially in the inland of the western region, rural households and hog forming households are a weak power in the market. They lack bargaining power in the circulation stages. Many middlemen have been involved in the agricultural industry. In the circulation of agricultural commodities, they seize a large part of profit. When the market situation is poor, they transfer risk to rural households by pushing down the price so that they would not suffer a loss. Even when the market situation is promising, rural households fail to gain as much as the middlemen. Furthermore, some monopolistic small and medium-sized food-processing enterprises exploit the rural households by seizing their benefits, which further widen the gap between rural households and the middlemen.

5 Chapter

Understanding China's Rural Finance: The Transformation of Rural Households and the Financial Layout

The only constant is change.

—Heraclitus

The lives of famers in China have greatly improved in recent years. Of course, this is inadequate. If their lives do not become better off, nothing will. We should by all means maintain the rate of improvement, mainly by helping famers to make their living...

—Steven N. S. Cheung

Reinterpreting Rural Households' Credibility and the Agricultural Loan Market

As the Three Rural Issues have garnered more and more attention from the ranks of managers and the general public, more financial research has been conducted into rural households' credibility and the agricultural loan system. In academia, when research touches on the system, the focus is on whether farmers' behavior conforms to the classical economic assumption of rationality (to maximize profits): Some scholars stress the rationality of small farmers, upholding the assumption; others incorporate elements of sociology and history into their analyses, proposing the "survival logic" of small farmers. This kind of debate not only directly touches on the explanation of rural economic behavior but has affected the arrangements of the systems (including the financial systems) in both past and future.

In this section, we try to interpret rural households' credibility and the agricultural market from another perspective. In order to avoid the categorization of rural households[1] made by other research, we consider it possible for rural households to transform from one type to another type under specific constraints. We will try to explain the transformation. Other major issues such as private financing (including usury), national financial support, the accumulation of social capital, etc., will be addressed under this new framework.

Literature review

There are two schools of thoughts in the study of rural households' production and investment behavior. Schultz (1964) and Popkin (1979) advocated the theory of "rational small farmers" based on classical economic analysis. They think that rural households are the same in nature as enterprises in the capitalist market economy. They follow the principles of rational investing to pursue benefit maximization which would transform into entrepreneurial spirit when conditions permit and promote a suitable allocation of resources (including credit resources). Chayanov

(1925), Polanyi (1957), and others support the theory of "surviving small farmers." They incorporate elements of sociology and history in their analyses and think that small farmers' behavior tends to deviate from the economic calculation. They explain the reason that some economic behavior stemmed from specific social relationships and traditions, not simply a calculation of cost and benefit. This view is similar to Scott's "moral economy" (1976).

In terms of the economic functions of the rural households, Nobel laureate Gary Becker (1981) believed that although the socio-economic environment changes, the family system is largely inherited. The internal structure of a family is similar to that of an enterprise, and output maximization is still a major pursuit of a family as an economic unit. Huang Zongzhi (1985, 1990) holds a different view following the crutch logic. He thinks that non-agricultural income is supplementary to agricultural income. The expansion of the market economy does not weaken but reinforce the family production of small farmers.[2] Becker's theory of the family confirms rationality in family production, but Huang's crutch theory casts doubt on that.

Studies prior to the 1990s have touched on the issues of rural households' credibility and the agricultural loan market in China's rural financial system, but they were rather sporadic and unsystematic. In the past decade, as financial reform accelerated and the Three Rural Issues became more urgent, research on rural finance became more prominent. In the beginning, research was all about the commercialization of rural financial institutions. Gradually, research touched on rural households' credibility and the system of the agricultural loan market. Representative studies include works of Lin Yifu, Feder, Lau Juen-yee, and Luo Xiaopeng (1989), Xie Ping (2001), Zhang Jun (1999), Wen Tiejun (2004), Zhang Jie (2004, 2005), etc.

Early research can be considered to be in the realm of classical economics, while recent research on the rural financial system has taken into accounts factors of sociology and history. The theories of "rational small farmers" and "surviving small farmers" have touched on the basis of economics: the assumption of rationality. "Surviving small farmers" do not produce to pursue maximization of benefits (even the pursuit for higher marginal profit is not motivated by the need to accumulate fortune). Instead, their production principle is a passive choice since the rigid and inefficient traditional agricultural production process cannot sustain their lives.

From the economic perspective, the conclusion of the theory of "surviving small farmers" seems incredible. It is hard to imagine that most rural households would give up on the way to fortune but choose to stay on the land which keeps them in poverty out of psychological dependence and sentiment inertia. If this is the situation in China, 800 million famers, accounting for 70% of the total population, is the major obstacle for marketization because their behavior does not conform to the market principles of benefit maximization.

The theory of "surviving small farmers" is too pessimistic. In fact, the behavior of "surviving small farmers" is only a superficial phenomenon. There are economic reasons behind what the theory claims. If so, what are the reasons? Apparently, if culture, habits, and sentiments cannot fully explain the behavior of rural households which is considered irrational in economics, the possible explanation is not that they do not want to maximize benefits but the conditions do not allow them to do so.

The segmented economy and indivisible investments: Inefficient equilibrium in the poverty trap

The economy in developing countries is usually segmented. Many economic entities (enterprises, residents, and government institutions) are isolated from one another. They face different factors of production and prices of products. They have different levels of technology and a return of assets ratio. And there is no effective market mechanism to eliminate the difference (McKinnon 1973). In fact, this incompleteness exists not only in the real economy but also in the financial sectors. When financial sectors face a segmented market, the information and transaction costs per unit of capital are different. Therefore, the interest rates, as the prices of financial products, will vary.

Investments are indivisible. In a segmented economy, simple production at an inefficient equilibrium can hardly receive external financing. Furthermore, if internal accumulation cannot support large-scale investments in new technologies, the economy would be in an inefficient equilibrium. McKinnon (2006) explains:

> *Typically, investments associated with the adoption of markedly improved technologies bulk large in the eyes of small-scale entrepreneurs. Investing in an improved breed of dairy cattle, buying a simple lathe or sewing machine, or assembling a new combination of seeds, fertilizers, and pesticides necessarily require quantum changes in cash outlays from a net income that may be barely sustaining the entrepreneur and his family. Poverty and the inability to borrow to finance discrete increases in expenditures can be formidable barriers to the adoption of even the simplest and most productive innovations...With indivisibilities so important on practice, however, financially isolated entrepreneurs can easily be caught in a low-level equilibrium trap, where innovation is completely blocked except for a small handful of the very wealthy, who get wealthier...Without [the access to external financial resources], the constraint of self-finance sharply biases investment strategy toward marginal variations within the traditional technology.*

In order to apply the above model to explaining rural households' credibility and the agricultural loan market, we assume that rural households face various investment opportunities: (1) simple agricultural production (I1); (2) expanded agricultural production (I2); (3) large-scale or specialized production (I3).

Simple agricultural production refers to the idea that production remains the same as in the old days in terms of scale, quality, and methods. People are familiar with, and generally adopt, this type of agricultural production. Therefore, production can be repeatedly carried out by using initial capital and technology without extra capital (including human capital). Of course, there is no comparative advantage and hence the rate of return would never be higher than the average.

Expanded agricultural production refers to agricultural production whose scale has expanded or technology has improved. The expected rate of return of this type is higher than that of simple agricultural production. It needs to be supported by more capital (including human capital).

Large-scale or specialized production denotes that traditional rural households can adjust production according to the marginal return on capital (including human capital), increase investment under the conditions that the marginal cost is smaller than the marginal revenue to produce in large scale. Therefore, this type of production has a higher rate of marginal return and average return, but also requires a huge initial capital input.

The three types of investment opportunities I1, I2, and I3 have an increasing order of average rate of return on investment $R_1 < R_2 < R_3$ as well as capital input. As shown in Fig. 5.1, the amount of capital needed for I1 is not more than *OA*, for I2 is larger than *OA*, and for I3 is larger than *OB*. Given that investments are indivisible, rural households who possess capital smaller than *OA* can only carry out simple production I1. Those with capital between *OA* to *OB* can carry out expanded agricultural production I2, but not large-scale or specialized production I3. As the amount of capital of rural households increases, the marginal return on capital first diminishes before rising, and it breaks at *B* and diminishes again. In Fig. 5.1, with capital within *OA*, a small increase in capital does not bring about the opportunities to invest in I2. Rural households can only repeat I1 production. Marginal returns would inevitably diminish. When rural households possess capital larger than *OA* but smaller than *OB*, in *AB*, they can carry out I2 production. As I2 production is assumed to be preferable to I1 in terms of return on investment, marginal return on capital would rise (technology is repeatedly employed due to the stimulation caused by the higher profit, the expansion of production continues as long as marginal return increases). *B* marks the real point of change. Once rural households have more capital than *OB*, they would utilize this sum of indivisible capital to invest in large-scale or specialized production I3. I3 represents investment opportunities of modern production which is not hampered by traditional constraints and brings expected returns. Therefore, rural households with capital larger than *OB* face an abrupt rise in the marginal return on capital curve *MR*. As seen in Fig. 5.1, *MR* is divided into MR_1 and MR_2 at *B*. MR_2 represents a more advanced form of production than MR_1 and hence has an average level of return much higher than MR_1 ($R_3 > R_2 > R_1$). Marginal returns diminish at a higher level as capital increases.

Fig. 5.1. Indivisible investments and the fractured curve of return on capital

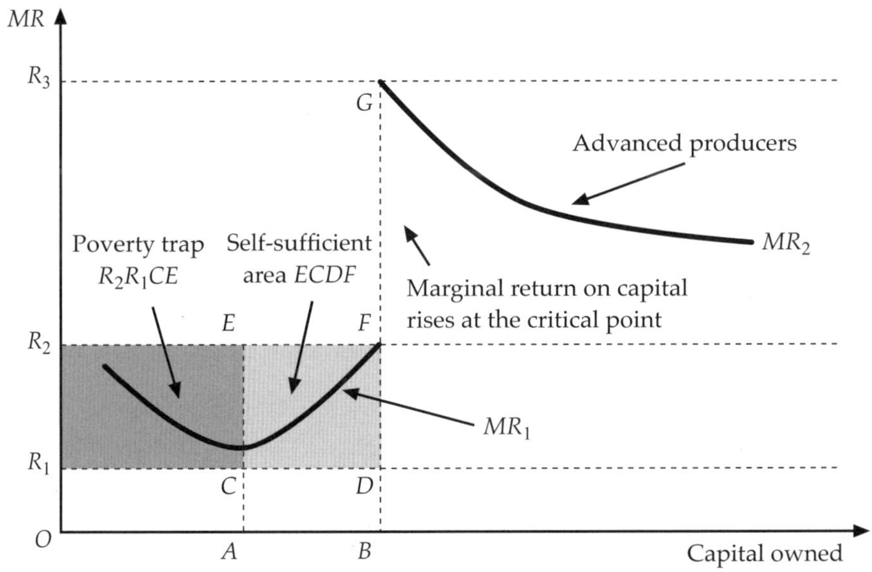

With the knowledge of the segmented marginal return on capital curve, we can analyze how the poverty trap is formed, persists, and can be broken through from. We assume R_2 to be the lowest average rate of return on capital in the regular commercial credit market. Any investment project with a rate of return on capital lower than R_2 would not be able to obtain regular commercial credit in the market. In Fig. 5.1, the entire MR_1 is below R_2. Rural households who have capital smaller than *OB* (lying in area OR_2FB) cannot obtain external and regular commercial financing. For those who have capital smaller than *OA*, i.e. when MR_1 is diminishing, as a small increase in capital deposit can only bring repeated simple production but not marginal returns, R_2R_1CE represents the poverty trap: As capital deposit and the increments of obtainable capital are very insufficient, rural households are confined to simple and repetitive production. Facing diminishing marginal returns, even if they obtain some production surplus, they would invest it in inefficient and repetitive simple production. Rather, they would spent it on non-production, such as consumption, or keep it as savings. As long as obtainable capital increment is smaller than *OA*, this type of inefficient equilibrium would persist.

The situation was different in the part where marginal returns increase. The increase in capital deposit makes raising production efficiency by employing new technology a possibility. Facing a rising marginal return curve, rural households who have a certain amount of capital deposits can invest in I2 production by borrowing loans and utilizing the surplus they have accumulated, gradually extricating themselves from the poverty trap. However, even though the simultaneous increase in capital deposit and return is possible in area *ECDF*, the marginal return is still lower than R_2. Rural households remain unable to obtain financing from the regular commercial credit market. Their financing channels are mainly accumulated surplus, private lending (loans from family and friends, and usury), and non-commercial loans (e.g. policy loans). Therefore, this area is termed "self-sufficient area." When capital deposit is larger than *OA*, increasing marginal returns encourage rural households to break through from the poverty trap to realize self-sustainability (self-development). Through capital accumulation, some may break through at *B* and develop into advanced producers. Their production I3 abides by the law of return on capital. In addition, once they become I3 producers, the marginal and average return would always be higher than R_2. In other words, in the area where MR_2 lies, rural households would be able to obtain regular commercial credit. There is no low-level equilibrium and rural households have extricated themselves from the poverty trap.

Borrowing behavior in the self-sufficient area: The logic of usury

As mentioned in the previous section that rural households who have capital deposit larger than *OA* would possess the ability to be self-sustainable and would obtain various types of loans to compensate for the capital shortage in order to achieve higher marginal and average returns. A logical deduction is that rural households with capital deposit between *AB* would frequently borrow loans. As the amount of capital deposit approaching *B*, the demand for loans is stimulated by the expected profit as marginal return increases. It is logical for usury to emerge as the marginal and average returns R_3 of investment in I3 are much larger than the interest paid for usury, especially when a small amount of usury would make the originally impossible investment in I3 possible. With more capital deposit, investments are no longer limited to projects with a level of return between R_1 to R_2. With reference to the face value of usury, the interest rate may be extremely high. However, considering the driving effects of it which brings very high marginal utility (bringing the drastic increase of the rate of return on capital from R_2 to R_3), the weighted average interest rate of usury with respect to the total capital input may be much lower than R_2.

To explain the above logic, we employ the following mathematical deduction. Assume rural households carry out I2 production, which has an average rate of return R_2, and the total capital deposit is C_1. Now, the households face an investment opportunity to transform their production into I3 production, which pushes up the rate of return on investment from R_2 to R_3, but an indivisible initial capital input C ($C > C_1$) is required. The households consider borrowing loans at an interest rate R.

The amount of capital needs to be borrowed: $L = C - C_1$

Interest paid on maturity: $I = LR = (C - C_1)R$

The total income by investing in I3: $T = CR_3$

The final rate of return on investment: $\dfrac{T-I}{C_1} = \dfrac{CR_3 - (C - C_1)R}{C_1} = \dfrac{C}{C_1}R_3 - \dfrac{C}{C_1}R + R$

The condition for rational borrowing: $\dfrac{C}{C_1}R_3 - \dfrac{C}{C_1}R + R \geq R_2$

If $\dfrac{C}{C_1} = m$ (as $C > C_1$, $m > 1$), the condition for borrowing is $R \leq R_3 + \dfrac{R_3 - R_2}{m-1}$. Obviously, when is R_3 increases and m decreases, the loan rate which the households can bear would increase. In other words, they may be able to tolerate usury. Also, a small m implies a large C_1. When C_1 approaches the capital deposit needed for investment in I3, a small capital increment ($L = C - C_1$) would be able to satisfy the indivisible initial capital input C. Usury is economically rational.

From the above deduction, it can be further deduced that, due to the fact that investment is indivisible and the sudden rise in the marginal return on capital, as capital deposit approaches the critical point of investment B, the occurrence of usury is more frequent.

The government and the agricultural loan market: Corner solution or interior solution?

The coexistence of formal and informal financial institutions is common in developing countries. The theories of financial repression represented by McKinnon (1973) claim too much government intervention causes inefficiency and financial repression, which gives rise to the dual financial structure. New structuralism represented by Stiglitz and Weiss (1981) stresses that the dual structure can be explained by information asymmetry, the difference in selection, supervision, and contract costs. Further research has found that informal finance is still common in countries or regions where there is financial liberation. Lin Yifu and Sun Xifang (2005) set up a model of both the formal and informal financial markets, which has several information structures. It confirms that the existence of informal finance can improve the efficiency of capital allocation in the credit market.

Regarding borrowing in China's rural agricultural loan market, Zhang Jie (2005a, b) believed that there is a special corner solution. It is either interest-free borrowing or usury. Zhang Jun (1997) studied the informal financial sector in Wenzhou. He proposed that the interest rate is a filter in the private loan market. The high interest rate of informal institutions reflects the information asymmetry of the risk of repayment in the market.

In our model, rural households in the poverty trap have a marginal return and an average return smaller than those required by formal finance institutions (e.g. commercial banks). Therefore, profit-making formal and commercial finance has no reason to enter the market. If rural households must borrow to sustain their lives, the emergence of usury as a monopoly in the credit market is natural. Rural households have to borrow in spite of their unwillingness. Usury is "evil finance," because the debts and interest would worsen the situation of the already extremely low marginal return of rural households. As Zhang Jie (2005a, b) said, when people need to choose between death and usury, many would choose the latter.

The situation may be different for rural households who have certain capital deposit, i.e. self-sustainable deposits. Facing a segmented marginal return curve, potential I3 production lets rural households achieve a significant rise in the marginal return and average return, higher than the lowest rate of return required for formal finance. This provides the basis for the entry of formal finance. The question is: why is formal credit still insufficient for rural households? The author thinks that the answer lies in the constraints of information identification and diseconomies of scale on formal finance.[3] Together, they cause the diseconomies of credit, which target small and scattered households.[4] It should be noted that the logic of the emergence of usury cannot be fully explained by Zhang Jun's proposal (1997) of the interest rate being a filter and the reflection of the information asymmetry of the risk of repayment in the market. In fact, many studies have found that the lenders and borrowers of usury usually know each other well and there is no information asymmetry.[5] We believe that the high interest rate reflects two facts. First, as there is an agreement with the use of loans in investment, the high interest rate reflects the expected high return of the project. The usurer is not only a lender but similar to a shareholder. Second, as it is difficult to obtain external regular commercial credit, rural households who have the opportunity to carry out high-return production face limited credit supply. In the situation where the demand for credit is greater than the supply, a high interest rate reflects the shortage of credit. Especially when investment is sensitive to time, a short-term demand for capital may intensify the shortage. In other words, the emergence of usury is encouraged by the demand and supply situation in the market, not an information premium under information asymmetry. This is why we think that such a kind of usury is different from the usury of "evil finance" in the poverty trap. It is economically natural and proper, as well as an agreement between those who lack capital and those who have a surplus.

Of course, as rural households accumulate more capital and break away from the poverty trap, and successfully transform to advanced producers, their marginal return and average return are above the lower threshold for formal finance. Their production and investment behavior would not be shut out of the formal finance. Financial institutions such as commercial banks would issue loans accordingly and determine the interest rate following the risk-return trade-off principle.

The corner solution in rural loan system proposed by Zhang Jie (2005a, b) is applicable to explaining the borrowing behavior of rural households who are still in the poverty trap. To those who are out of the poverty trap, commercial loans, equity financing, relationship loans, etc. are potential channels of capital for investment in production. They, as advanced producers, face an interior solution.

Out of the poverty trap: Collective cooperation, financial support, and rural social capital

The indivisible initial capital input which cannot be smaller than *OB* is the obstacle for rural households who want to break through from the poverty trap and become advanced producers. To some, accumulation of capital may bring them out of the poverty trap, but the process is long, painful, or even insufferable. So, to households who cannot free themselves by capital accumulation, what other options are available for them to gather enough capital?

One of the options is to initiate organizations so that there will be collective cooperation among rural households. One household may be lacking in capital, if many households gather their capital to become one production unit, the amount of capital and potential capital would be more than *OB*. If this is realized, the households may invest in high-return I3 production as a cooperative organization. Yet, organizations like this may have to bear huge operating costs (relevant co-production costs such as organizing, communication, coordination costs), which increase as the number of members grows. Therefore, if the capital deposit of each household is so low that it requires many individual households to gather more capital than *OB*, cooperative organizations are difficult to form because of the high operating cost. This may explain why such organizations may develop rapidly in some regions but fail in some other. The difference in operating cost may be huge, as it is influenced by the average capital deposit per household, their intention to cooperate, and their sense of cooperation.[6] It should be noted that these organizations are self-organized. They were unlike the communes formed before reform and opening up. Those communes were set up and operated like political units. They cannot salvage the imbalanced incentive mechanism or internalize the return.

Another option is government intervention, which has been widely discussed in recent years. We believe that it is most important to define what the government should and should not do, and under what conditions it can intervene. First, rural households who are deep in the poverty trap cannot raise the marginal output of agricultural production within a short period of time. Agricultural production is unlikely to generate a positive rate of return on social capital. Rural households are fragile. The cost incurred by fluctuations (utility, health, chances of survival, etc.) at a low level of consumption is very high. Therefore, the more impoverished the household is, the greater the incentive to stabilize the fluctuations by credit (Bardhan and Udry 1999). Under the circumstances that external credit resources are unavailable, rural households either abandon themselves or resort to usury. This presents an opportunity for usury to enter the market in the form of "evil finance." Usury would give rise to the relations of personal dependence, which represent feudalism, and social instability. To those rural households, national poverty alleviation loans and interest-free loans are not only important, but also necessary.[7]

To those who have a certain amount of capital deposit and lie in the "self-sustainable area," small, half-policy and half-commercial credit resources (e.g. discount loans of RCCs) are effective. Such capital should be treated as a means to help rural households improve their self-development ability rather than to make profits.

Those who have broken through from the poverty trap to become advanced producers should not be allowed to obtain national credit resources. The market should be allowed to serve its function of resources allocation and let nature take its course.

In our discussion about the credibility of the rural households and the agricultural loan market, we mentioned the owned capital of rural households, which would help us understand the capital formation mechanism better. Here, we borrow the concept of social capital.[8] Social capital includes all capital which can raise the availability of resources (including credit) for rural households, both tangible and intangible. It also includes human capital which can be transformed into production force, as well as various relation resources. The "deepening" of social capital refers to the sources of capital expanding from inside the concentric zone to the outside, and eventually formal finance becomes one of them. This process helps to break through from the differentiated mode of association in traditional rural society so that rural households' sources of capital would not be confined to kinship and relationships in the social network.[9] Self-organized cooperative organizations and government financial support are intended to expand the availability of the sources of capital so that rural households would be able to accumulate more capital and develop better.

As can be seen, policy loans are important and necessary to aid and guide rural households out of the poverty trap. Private loans, policy loans, and commercial loans can work together to help those households who are in the self-sustainable area. When households are out of the poverty trap and become advanced producers, with their marginal return on capital (i.e. MR_2 curve), formal finance (e.g. commercial banks and capital market) would become available.

Conclusions

The theoretical separation of "surviving small farmers" and "rational small farmers" is flawed. It establishes the unnecessary mutual exclusivity and denies the possibility of dynamic transformation between the two.[10] Supporters of the theory of "rational small farmers" analyze the issues from the traditional economic perspective. They lack understanding of the characteristics of the behavior and situation of rural households, i.e. the constraints are not clearly defined. Their conclusions of providing financial support for the development of rural households tend to be too optimistic. Supporters of the theory of "surviving small farmers" focus too much on the specificity and path-dependency of rural households' behavior. They establish the logic of self-evolution which is outside the realm of economics. Their conclusions tend to be too pessimistic. Obviously, the two different interpretations of rural credit and the agricultural loan market stem from the separation of "surviving small farmers" and "rational small farmers" in the first place. We believe that the separation should be abandoned. Instead, the connection and dynamic transformation between the two should be considered, and the focus of study should be on the mechanism of such transformation. It would give us a more objective basis for the study, which would have stronger explanatory power over the formation, current status, and development of rural credit and the agricultural loan market.

We do not deny the value of the theories of "surviving small farmers" and "rational small farmers." On the contrary, we believe in understanding their logic and the suitable use of these entities. What we do is establish another economic framework for the understanding of rural credit and the agricultural loan market. In this framework, "surviving small farmers" and "rational small farmers" are not mutually exclusive. They can co-exist, develop, or transform into one another. There are several major issues in the transformation. First, how capital deposit influences the rural households' ability to obtain further capital? Second, rural households with little capital face the issue of repressed agricultural production and technological innovation caused by the indivisibility of investment. Third, which type of capital is needed to compensate the capital gap of a different nature in different situations?

Our model states that rural households in different situations face different capital constraints. Those in the poverty trap do not have enough owned capital to satisfy the basic needs and their ability to obtain external capital is very low. Their capital gap is motivated by maintenance demand which has a low elasticity. Those who are in the self-sustainable area have a higher ability to obtain capital through capital accumulation. However, their ability and speed to obtain capital cannot satisfy the demands for production development. The capital gap here is more of a reflection of the production demand which has a higher elasticity. Only when rural households become advanced producers can they carry out production in a larger market which includes formal commercial finance. The availability of capital is much greater. Rural households would depend less on informal finance and their demand for capital would be very elastic.

Because of the different nature and degree of capital gap, we suggest that there should be a different financial supplier of a different nature in different situations. In the poverty trap, the policy poverty alleviation fund is the most important. In the self-sustainable area, private loans, national poverty alleviation loans, and formal commercial finance are effective. In advanced production, the supply of capital should come from formal finance.

Based on the indivisibility of investments, through the study of the interest rate mechanism in the agricultural loan market, it is found that there are two types of usury. "Evil usury" in the poverty trap preys on little marginal return of rural households. "Rational usury" in the self-sustainable area is more of a reflection of the credit shortage in rural areas.

From crutch logic to poverty trap, we believe that rural households are not economically irrational or confined by traditions and culture. The difficulties and feeble financial system originate from the unsynchronization of traditional agricultural production, capital accumulation, and the financial system. As production and capital accumulation improves, rural households would encounter opportunities to transform. Suitable financial support from the government and marker forces should and will play a role in the process.

The Capital Mechanism in the Transformation of Rural Households

The theory of "surviving small farmers" includes some social and historical factors in their analysis to explain the behavior of rural households who are in disadvantaged economic situations. It should be pointed out that there are few places in the logic that require further discussion before the conclusions of those analyses can be directly applied to the situation of China's rural finance. First, if it is said that rural households have not discarded the survival logic, is it due to the social and historical factors proposed by the analyses?[11] Second, many studies categorized households into "rational small farmers" and "surviving small farmers." However, in a longitudinal study, the categorization causes "horizontal problems." This is because the possibility of the transformation from "rational small farmers" to "surviving small farmers" or the other way round cannot be eliminated with any basis. If the transformation does happen, the conclusions will change. Lastly, from the economic point of view, the claim that the survival logic has remained unchanged for the past few thousand years in terms of culture and history lacks convincing evidence.

In this section, we attempt to dissect the issues of rural credit and the agricultural loan market in modern market economy, taking continuity into account. The dissection is based on the effects of the capital and financial mechanisms. The structure of this section is as follows: First, we offer a literature review and propose the hypotheses about the transformation mechanism of small farmers. Second, we examine the hypotheses by empirical analysis. Third, we conclude the section.

A hypothesis

The issue of "surviving small farmers" and "rational small farmers" is also present in the studies of rural credit and the agricultural loan market, which is illustrated in the model below.

Fig. 5.2. Loan boundaries, loan preference, and the transformation of rural households

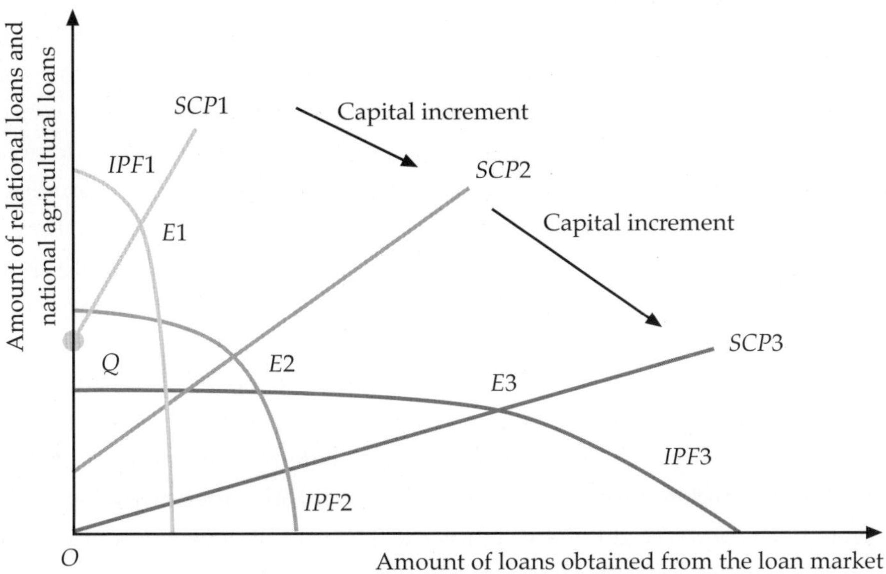

As shown in Fig. 5.2, *IPF*1 is the efficient frontier of borrowing of "surviving small farmers." Along *IPF*1, rural households rely on borrowing from friends and family or national agricultural loans. *SCP*1 represents the loan preference of "surviving small farmers." According to the theory, rural households who cannot obtain loans from inside the concentric circles are unlikely to obtain loans from the credit market. Therefore, *SCP*1 does not begin from the origin *O*. The credit equilibrium is at *E*1, at which the amount of relational loans and national agricultural loans is much higher than the amount of loans obtained from the credit market.

The theory of "rational small farmers" hypothesizes the efficient frontier for borrowing behavior to be *IPF*3. A relatively flat *IPF*3 shows that rural households mainly obtain capital from the credit market. *IPF*3 and the loan preference curve *SCP*3 intersect at *E*3, the credit equilibrium. At *E*3, the amount of relational loans and national agricultural loans is much lower than the amount of loans obtained from the credit market.

It should be noted that Zhang Jie (2005a, b) thinks that the rural households' demand for credit has the typical characteristics for the application of the corner solution. Either rural households borrow relational loans or interest-free national agricultural loans. In this case, the credit equilibrium is at *Q* but not *E*1.

As illustrated, the two theories are opposing. We believe both of them have neglected the dynamic transformation between "surviving small farmers" and "rational small farmers." Instead, we address the issue from a continuous perspective. Considering the operating mechanism of the credit market and the principles of risk control, formal financial institutions require borrowers to offer sufficient guarantee and collaterals. From the perspective of the institutions, rural households obtaining loans is a form of capital production, which requires stable and sufficient cash flow so that repayments are made on time. Given that concern, the institutions would not issue loans to rural households who have little owned capital. As a result, rural households are confined to "survival small farmers" as represented by *IPF*1. However, as rural households acquire more capital, they can utilize the capital as guarantee or collaterals to improve the problem of information asymmetry in the credit market by signaling. As a result, they have a greater chance of obtaining formal loans. Their efficient frontier for borrowing behavior becomes *IPF*3, which intersects with the new loan preference curve *SCP*2 at equilibrium *E*2. At *E*2, rural households rely less on relational loans and national agricultural loans. They impact the credit market and obtain more loans from it. As rural households accumulate more capital, the efficient frontier for borrowing and the loan preference curve would move rightward. The households eventually become "rational small farmers" – they are basically economic entrepreneurs.

Based on the above logic, we propose the following hypothesis of two-way strengthening of the capital mechanism and financial mechanism: Capital shortage is the reason why rural households are confined to low-level production and cannot obtain formal credit. As they accumulate more capital their ability to obtain financial resources (credit) would improve. The capital accumulated and the newly obtained financial resources would further increase the economic income of rural households. They have the chance to transform from "surviving small farmers" to "rational small farmers" as represented by the process of *SCP*1→*SCP*2→*SCP*3 in Fig. 5.2.

Empirical analysis

The model design and variables

In order to analyze the relationships between rural credit and the types of rural households, we have designed the following models:

Model 1: $Y_1 = C_1 + \alpha X_i + \varepsilon_i$, in which $i = 1, 2, 3\ldots, 13, 14, 15$.

Model 2: $Y_2 = C_2 + \alpha X_j + \varepsilon_j$, in which $j = 1, 2, 3\ldots, 12, 13, 14$.

Model 3: $Y_3 = C_3 + \alpha X_k + \varepsilon_k$, in which $k = 1, 2, 3\ldots, 11, 12, 13$.

There are three explained variables: Rural households' demand for loans (Y_1), the line of credit RCCs offer to rural households (Y_2), and rural households' annual income level (Y_3). Y_1 reflects the demand in the agricultural loan market and Y_2 the supply. Changes in Y_3 would show whether the income level of rural households is related to the explanatory variables.

The indexes we have chosen as explanatory variables are related to the level of capital of rural households. The actual and potential capital levels are classified into four types: (1) Capital deposit represents the amount of owned capital, as measured by the total assets of rural households and per capita area of farmland. (2) Capital flow represents the sources of regular income which can be converted to capital, as measured by the income of agricultural production and the income from non-rural jobs. (3) Human capital represents human technology which is involved in the formation and transformation of capital, as measured by the labor force to household member ratio, educational level, level of agricultural technology and knowledge, and other technology and techniques. (4) Social relationship capital represents social relationship resources which can be converted into capital, as measured by whether any family member is a village cadre, a member of the Communist Party, or there is a relative living in the urban area.

Control variables including the regional classified index, rural households' loan preference, their consumption and investment preference, and their understanding of policies of agricultural loans which are considered in this analysis.

The above explanatory and explained variables are based on the indexes assigned and data from 1,100 questionnaires on information of rural households. Table 5.1 shows the label and illustrates the assignment of the value of each variable.

Table 5.1. The explanation of the explanatory variables

Variables	The label and the assignment of the value of the variable, and its implication
Regional economic situation	Regional classified index (X_1): With respect to the actual situation of the sample regions in the studies, rural residential areas are divided into dam area and mountain area. In general, the economic conditions of dam area (such as economic development, commercial trade, transportation, etc.) are better than those of mountain area. A higher assigned value represents a more developed economy in that area.

(Cont'd)

Variables	The label and the assignment of the value of the variable, and its implication
Rural households' capital deposit	Total assets index (X_2): Calculated with the total assets of rural households, which include savings, properties, livestock, economic fruit, agricultural machines, etc.
	Area of arable land per capita index (X_3): Based on the area of arable land per capita. Farmland is a long-term stable capital of rural households which allows continuous production and income.
Rural households' income level	Income of agricultural production (X_4): Calculated with the income of agricultural production of the entire household, which includes the incomes of grain crop, cash crop, and animal husbandry.
	Income from non-rural jobs (X_5): Calculated with the total income of the entire household earned through working outside.
Human capital	Labor force to household member ratio (X_6): In rural areas, every household is a production unit. The labor force of each household is the basic human resources for agricultural production, which is at the same time the one for generating non-agricultural income.
	Educational level (X_7): Educational level is recognized by many studies as the foundation of the accumulation of human capital. We assign the value according to the highest educational level in the household. A higher value represents more human capital.
	Level of agricultural technology and knowledge (X_8): It is the dominant factor in raising agricultural productivity. The introduction of agricultural production technology (especially advanced technology) can significantly increase the ability to produce and develop of the rural households. We assign the value according to whether the household is willing to participate in agricultural technological training (include self-learning). A higher value represents a higher level of agricultural knowledge and technology.
	Other technology and techniques (X_9): It is a supplement to agricultural technology. Non-agricultural technology can increase the sources of income of rural households as well as become the main source of income of those who transform to commercialists. We assign the value according to whether the rural households know other technology (which can increase income). A higher value represents more advanced non-agricultural production technology.

(Cont'd)

Variables	The label and the assignment of the value of the variable, and its implication
Social relationship capital	A village cadre in the family(X_{10}): In rural areas, village cadres, whether elected or recommended, generally have better connections. Their social scope and communication network are significantly larger than general households. A higher value represents a higher level of social relationship capital.
	A member of the Communist Party in the family (X_{11}): In rural areas, most households are non-members of the Party. A member serves the function of signal transmission. Only those who are privileged in life can be a member of the Party. A higher value represents a higher level of social relationship capital.
	A relative living in the urban area. (X_{12}): To those who live in less advanced rural area, having a relative in the urban area (implies higher income level and broader horizon) means more potential sources of capital and, possibly, information, technology, and developmental opportunities. A higher value represents a higher level of social relationship capital.
Control variables	Rural households' loan preference (X_{13}): The borrowing records of the past three years are considered. A high value represents that the household has a stronger tendency to borrow and it prefers banks to private lending.
	Rural households' consumption and investment preference (X_{14}): The valued is assigned according to how capital is used. A higher value is assigned if the household uses the capital to invest and expand production rather than putting it in the bank or using it for consumption.
	Understanding of policies of agricultural loans (X_{15}): The value is assigned according to the rural households' understanding of the nation's policies of agricultural loans. A higher value represents a better understanding of the agricultural loan policies of the nation (RCCs).

Note: Information is based on the questionnaire survey conducted in 11 counties in City A.

Results of empirical analysis

We first study the demand (rural households' actual situation of borrowing) in the agricultural loan market. We apply OLS regression to the factors which affect the demand of loans and the results are shown in Table. 5.2.

Table 5.2. The results of regression analysis of model 1

	Demand for loans Y_1	Demand for loans Y_1	Demand for loans Y_1	Demand for loans Y_1
Constant (C)	0.288627*** (3.590784)	0.287482*** (3.551964)	0.282291*** (3.496421)	0.278712*** (3.464101)
Regional classified index (X_1)	0.075480*** (3.367754)	−0.075420*** (-3.362772)	−0.075212*** (−3.355030)	−0.077785*** (−3.469489)
Total assets index (X_2)	−0.002858 (−0.250831)	−0.002923 (−0.256183)	−0.002842 (−0.249351)	−0.001403 (−0.123016)
Area of arable land per capita index (X_3)	0.011534 (1.357117)	0.011659 (1.361806)	0.012451 (1.453107)	0.011726 (1.381187)
Income of agricultural production (X_4)	0.012929** (2.006122)	0.012946** (2.007452)	0.012927** (2.005604)	0.012741** (1.979119)
Income from non-rural jobs (X_5)	0.009636 (0.866748)	0.009644 (0.867086)	0.009923 (0.892102)	0.011012 (0.989569)
Labor force to household member ratio (X_6)	0.051079 (0.938809)	0.051140 (0.939479)	0.047896 (0.878108)	0.053245 (0.979557)
Educational level (X_7)	−0.044306*** (−4.901244)	−0.044219*** (−4.874947)	−0.042430*** (−4.558632)	−0.040688*** (−4.408037)
Level of agricultural technology and knowledge (X_8)	−0.035645** (−2.514240)	−0.035248** (−2.425039)	−0.034010** (−2.376707)	−0.032949** (−2.315059)
Other technology and techniques (X_9)	0.015195 (0.869015)	0.015193 (0.868496)	0.015655 (0.894802)	0.019950 (1.130596)
Rural households' loan preference (X_{13})	0.175009*** (14.46521)	0.175035*** (14.45869)	0.175209*** (14.47712)	0.175190*** (14.49679)
Rural households' consumption and investment preference (X_{14})	0.045989*** (5.926542)	0.046050*** (5.920213)	0.045957*** (5.921521)	0.046580*** (6.004820)
Understanding of policies of agricultural loans (X_{15})	0.033609** (2.098070)	0.033807** (2.099255)	0.034622** (2.155042)	0.032021** (1.998545)
A village cadre in the family(X_{10})	—	−0.002165 (−0.124941)	—	—
A member of the Communist Party in the family (X_{11})	—	—	−0.019282 (−0.847672)	—
A relative living in the urban area. (X_{12})	—	—	—	−0.025859* (−1.886444)
Adjusted R^2	0.239126	0.238436	0.238929	0.240915

Notes: 1. The bracketed value is the t-value.

2. *at 10% confidence level, **at 5% confidence level, ***at 1% confidence level.

From the above analysis, we can see that rural households' demand of loans is statistically related to some of the factors. With reference to the sign of the coefficients, it can be found that the amount of actual loan increases due to the following factors: (1) a better regional economic situation; (2) higher income of agricultural production; (3) a stronger sense of investment; (4) formal finance ranks higher in rural households' preferred financing order (i.e. they tend to borrow from banks or RCCs rather than private lenders); (5) a better understanding of policies of agricultural loans; (6) a lower educational level and level of agricultural technology and knowledge; and (7) fewer relatives who live in the urban area.

Below we study the supply (factors which affect the line of credit RCCs offer to rural households) in the agricultural loan market. We apply OLS regression to the line of credit and the results are shown in Table. 5.3.

Table 5.3. The results of regression analysis of model 2

	Actual line of credit Y_2	Actual line of credit Y_2	Actual line of credit Y_2	Actual line of credit Y_2
Constant (C)	0.442634 (1.509213)	0.476398* (1.664209)	0.464210 (1.623993)	0.535265* (1.878670)
Regional classified index (X_1)	0.354269*** (4.139116)	–0.357475*** (–4.191548)	–0.357036*** (–4.186686)	–0.345145*** (–4.057043)
Total assets index (X_2)	0.324647*** (7.535643)	0.327742*** (7.707540)	0.327678*** (7.708076)	0.320059*** (7.543039)
Area of arable land per capita index (X_3)	0.104033*** (3.206518)	0.106131*** (3.335092)	0.108512*** (3.407944)	0.107243*** (3.417581)
Income of agricultural production (X_4)	0.056632** (2.303596)	0.056722** (2.307040)	0.056876** (2.314045)	0.057989** (2.367656)
Income from non-rural jobs (X_5)	0.159065*** (3.753422)	0.158800*** (3.747309)	0.159180*** (3.754844)	0.150941*** (3.567170)
Labor force to household member ratio (X_6)	–0.217382 (–1.048359)	–0.219331 (–1.057853)	–0.223059 (–1.073330)	–0.232193 (–1.123747)
Educational level (X_7)	0.164476*** (4.765424)	0.165306*** (4.799615)	0.168487*** (4.760403)	0.145882*** (4.178459)
Level of agricultural technology and knowledge (X_8)	0.090133* (1.666125)	0.091580* (1.678306)	0.096892* (1.808156)	0.080824 (1.525095)
Other technology and techniques (X_9)	0.219538*** (3.289349)	0.222386*** (3.352824)	0.223313*** (3.364323)	0.196426*** (2.943980)

(Cont'd)

	Actual line of credit Y_2	Actual line of credit Y_2	Actual line of credit Y_2	Actual line of credit Y_2
Rural households' consumption and investment preference (X_{14})	0.047308* (1.615634)	0.047110* (1.605532)	0.047554* (1.624347)	0.044171 (1.513021)
Understanding of policies of agricultural loans (X_{15})	0.024561 (0.401587)	—	—	—
A village cadre in the family(X_{10})	—	0.014942 (0.226987)	—	—
A member of the Communist Party in the family (X_{11})	—	—	–0.024895 (–0.287469)	—
A relative living in the urban area. (X_{12})	—	—	—	0.147815*** (2.834538)
Adjusted R^2	0.203432	0.203351	0.203374	0.209159

Notes: 1. The bracketed value is the t-value.

2. *at 10% confidence level, **at 5% confidence level, ***at 1% confidence level.

The above analysis shows the statistical relationship between the line of credit RCCs offer to rural households and various factors. With reference to the sign of the coefficients, it can be found that the line of credit increases due to the following factors: (1) a better regional economic situation; (2) a greater amount of total assets; (3) higher income of agricultural production and non-rural jobs; (4) greater area of arable land per capita; (5) a higher educational level; (6) greater knowledge of other technology and techniques; and (7) and more relatives who live in the urban area. It should be noted that the significance of the coefficient of other technology and techniques is greater than that of agricultural technology and knowledge. It suggests that RCCs tend to favor issuing non–agricultural production loans to rural households.

We have gained basic understanding of the factors which influence rural credit from the analyses of the demand and supply in the agricultural loan market. We move on to investigating whether the demand for and supply of loans, and also the ability to obtain loans, can affect the income level of rural households. We use the explained variables Y_1 and Y_2 as explanatory variables in model 3 and apply OLS regression analysis to the annual income of households. Results are shown Table 5.4.

Table 5.4. Results of regression analysis of model 3

	Annual income of households Y_3	Annual income of households Y_3	Annual income of households Y_3	Annual income of households Y_3
Constant (C)	0.189043 (1.024988)	0.183000 (0.986055)	0.222047 (1.202028)	0.238894 (1.295585)
Regional classified index (X_1)	0.160097*** (3.020656)	–0.159709*** (–3.011180)	–0.160959*** (–3.042127)	–0.153375*** (–2.901301)
Total assets index (X_2)	0.393839*** (14.66949)	0.393572*** (14.64545)	0.393361*** (14.67679)	0.389533*** (14.54665)
Area of arable land per capita index (X_3)	0.061520*** (3.073473)	0.062236*** (3.086488)	0.055740*** (2.765590)	0.056245*** (2.797449)
Labor force to household member ratio (X_6)	0.178011 (1.390434)	0.178455 (1.393230)	0.196248 (1.532318)	0.183083 (1.431875)
Educational level (X_7)	0.087638*** (4.052786)	0.088111*** (4.062373)	0.076138*** (3.427367)	0.067605*** (3.016010)
Level of agricultural technology and knowledge (X_8)	0.027202 (0.814432)	0.029534 (0.861286)	0.017252 (0.512714)	0.010622 (0.315504)
Other technology and techniques (X_9)	0.106722*** (2.583256)	0.106725*** (2.582241)	0.103460** (2.507036)	0.088975** (2.140746)
Understanding of policies of agricultural loans (X_{15})	0.099109*** (2.615278)	0.100244*** (2.631282)	0.092836** (2.447026)	0.098855*** (2.606978)
Demand for loans (Y_1)	0.190554*** (2.986256)	0.190925*** (2.990268)	0.192674*** (3.024394)	0.198961*** (3.128430)
Actual line of credit (Y_2)	0.203531*** (10.96833)	0.203592*** (10.96639)	0.203762*** (10.99978)	0.199211*** (10.72999)
A village cadre in the family(X_{10})	—	–0.012358 (–0.302673)	—	—
A member of the Communist Party in the family (X_{11})	—	—	0.117465** (2.192031)	0.096874* (1.791589)
A relative living in the urban area. (X_{12})	—	—	—	0.082710** (2.528345)
Adjusted R^2	0.428402	0.427924	0.430394	0.433206

Notes: 1. The bracketed value is the t-value.
2. *at 10% confidence level, **at 5% confidence level, ***at 1% confidence level.

The results show that the factors which affect the annual income of rural households include the type of regional economy, total assets of the households, area of arable land per capita, educational level, the level of other technology and techniques, understanding of the policies of agricultural loans, demand for loans, actual line of credit, whether a family member is a village cadre, and whether a relative lives in the urban area. Also, the answer to the question of whether rural households' ability to obtain financial resources affects their income is clear; both the demand for loans and the line of credit RCCs offer have a positive effect on the income level. The same goes for the two substitution variables, whether a family member is a village cadre and whether a relative lives in the urban area. It suggests that social capital which rural households own can be converted to an increase in income.

Conclusions

In this section, we examine the influence of rural households' capital level, including both owned capital and the ability to obtain social capital, on rural credit and rural income. Rural households' actual capital levels and potential capital levels are categorized into four types: capital deposit, capital flow, human capital, and social relationship capital. The following conclusions are drawn from empirical analyses:

(1) The factors which affect the rural households' demand for credit are the levels of capital flow, human capital, and social relationship capital. The demand rises when the capital flow or human capital increases, and when social relationship capital decreases.

(2) The factors which affect the supply of credit include the levels of capital deposit, capital flow, human capital, and social relationship capital. The rise of the four factors stimulates RCCs to supply more credit to rural households. As rural households have a higher level of total capital, they have stronger ability to obtain financial resources. It should be noted that RCCs tend to favor non–agricultural production loans. This is a proof for the claim that RCCs look for high commercial return from issuing loans.

(3) The ability to obtain financial resources has a significant effect on the income level of rural households. Those who borrow loans have a higher income level than those who do not. Also, those who obtain a greater line of credit from RCCs have a higher income level. In addition, it is found that rural households who have more social relationship resources (capital) have a higher income level. This signifies that social relationship capital can be converted to an actual increase in income.

(4) The regional economic situation, rural households' loan preference, their consumption and investment preference, and their understanding of the policies of agricultural loans all affect rural credit, the demand and supply in the agricultural loan market, and the income level of rural households.

Drawing from the conclusions above, if we look at the transformation of rural households from the lower-income group to higher-income group as a continuous process, the effect of the capital mechanism is prominent. The amount of owned capital and potential capital determine not only the rural households' demand for credit but also their ability to obtain certain amounts of credit resources. And rural households' demand for credit and the actual amount of credit they obtain determine their income level. There is a progressive capital formation cycle:

Actual capital level→credit demand and supply→increase in potential capital level→ increase in credit demand and supply

It is in this self-actualizing and self-strengthening mechanism that rural households transform from one type to another.

The mechanism can also explain the hypothesis we proposed that the transformation from "surviving small farmers" to "rational small farmers" is possible. The two are not segmented or mutually exclusive. There is an economic mechanism and motivation for the transformation. Capital formation is important to the transformation because only when rural households attain a certain capital level can they gradually improve their ability to acquire and utilize financial resources, especially formal ones. Once they enter into the virtuous circle of capital formation and the utilization of financial capital, transformation based on the increase in income would become possible.

From another perspective, many rural households remain as "surviving small farmers" with a low income and low production level because they were constrained by the capital level. They probably face a low initial capital level and therefore lack the opportunity to increase capital or use financial resources. As a result, their capital, income, and production are all at low levels, and they are trapped.

Removal of Credit Constraints

The core question of the research on China's rural finance are the credit constraints the rural households face and how to remove the constraints. There are a few related questions to ask: (1) How are credit constraints formed? (2) What factors affect the degree of credit constraints (the size of credit gap)? (3) What policies or measures are helpful to remove the credit constraints?

In past research on the mechanism of the formation of credit constraints, the focus had been on the insufficient financial supply. The issue was seldom discussed from the perspective of rural households' demand. Literature which discusses the interactions of demand and supply is scarcer. In fact, both the rural households' demand for credit and the financial institutions' supply of credit are dynamic. Only when the demand is not satisfied would there be a credit gap. For example, if the demand for credit is small and the aggregate supply is larger than the demand, there would be no credit gap even if the aggregate supply is small. Therefore, credit gap and suppressed demand (the lack of effective demand) should be distinguished. It is inappropriate to define credit gap using aggregate and scale. To consider the dynamic interaction between the credit demand of rural households and the credit supply of financial institutions, the two should be studied under the same framework.

In this section, we provide an extended analysis of credit freeriding and the effect of cross-subsidization. Based on the two ideas that rural households' actual credit demand is driven by return maximization, and the incentive compatibility constraint is introduced in the decision-making of financial institutions on credit input, the credit gap is defined or observed within the real demand and the range of credit input. By extending the model, we analyze the decision-making of financial institutions on credit input under information asymmetry. We obtain a few inferences of theoretical, as well as policy, implications by conducting comparative and static analysis of the model. The inferences are related to the influence of the interest rate on the demand and supply, the issues of credit expansion under information asymmetry and regional economic development, and the multiple driving effects of the rise in the rate of return of agriculture.

Basic model: Credit constraints on rural households

Following the general settings of economic models, we assume that there are two types of rural households I and II in the rural financial market. Type I households have a higher capita level and ability to produce and invest than type II households. Therefore, they have a higher marginal product of capital. Assume that proportion of the financial market the two types of households take up are α and $1 - \alpha$ $(0 < \alpha < 1)$ respectively. Their corresponding functions of return on product are $F_1(L)$ and $F_2(L)$, of which L is the amount of credit households receive. According to the law of diminishing marginal returns, The first and second order conditions of the functions should satisfy $F_i'(L) \geq 0$ and $F_i''(L) \leq 0$ $(i = 1,2)$. Based on the assumption of the marginal product, $F_1'(L) > F_2'(L)$. Assume that r is the market loan rate, the cost for rural households to borrow loans for production would be $(1 + r) L$. Considering the return function and cost function of rural households, the profit function should be $\prod_i = F_i(L) - (1 + r) L$, of which $i = 1, 2$.

Profit function of type I rural households: $\prod_1 = F_1 (L) - (1 + r) L$

Profit function of type II rural households: $\prod_2 = F_2 (L) - (1 + r) L$

Based on the above functions, the optimal quantity demanded for credit L_i^* is determined by the following first order condition:

$$F_i' (L) = (1 + r), \text{ where } i = 1, 2. \tag{5–1}$$

In order to consider the cost for rural households to breach the contract, we take into account the gaming between them and financial institutions. In contractual relationships, once rural households do not abide by the contract (refuse to repay debts), financial institutions would not issue loans to them in future. The opportunity cost for the breach of contract $C(L)$can be represented as the discount of profit incurred by the credit demand at a certain time in future:

$$C_i (L) = \sum_{t=1}^{\infty} \gamma^t [F_i (L) - (1 + r) L], \text{ where } i = 1, 2.$$

In the formula, γ $(0 < \gamma < 1)$ is the factor of the discount on expected income, which is generally regarded as the required rate of return of agricultural investment. rural households, as rational economic men, only choose to repay debts when $C_i (L) \geq (1 + r) L$. Therefore, the credit constraints can be simplified as follows:

$$F_i (L) \geq \frac{1 + r}{\gamma} L, \text{ where } i = 1, 2. \tag{5–2}$$

It determines the credit boundary and maximum line of credit for rural households.

Let L_i^* be the upper limit of the credit range. From (5–1) and (5–2), it can be obtained that when $L_i^* > \bar{L}_i$, rural households face financing constraints. Financial institutions implement credit rationing. When $L_i^* < \bar{L}_i$, the optimal quantity demanded for financing lies inside the credit range. Financing constraints are removed. Rural households can determine the actual line of credit they prefer. Fig. 5.3 and Fig. 5.4 show the situation with and without financing constraints respectively.

Fig. 5.3. Credit boundary with financing constraints

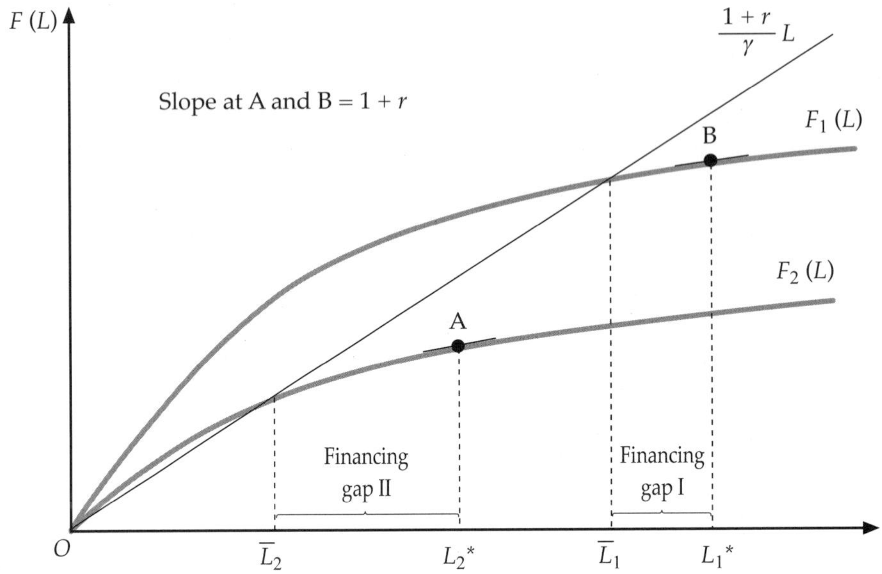

Fig. 5.4. Credit boundary without financing constraints

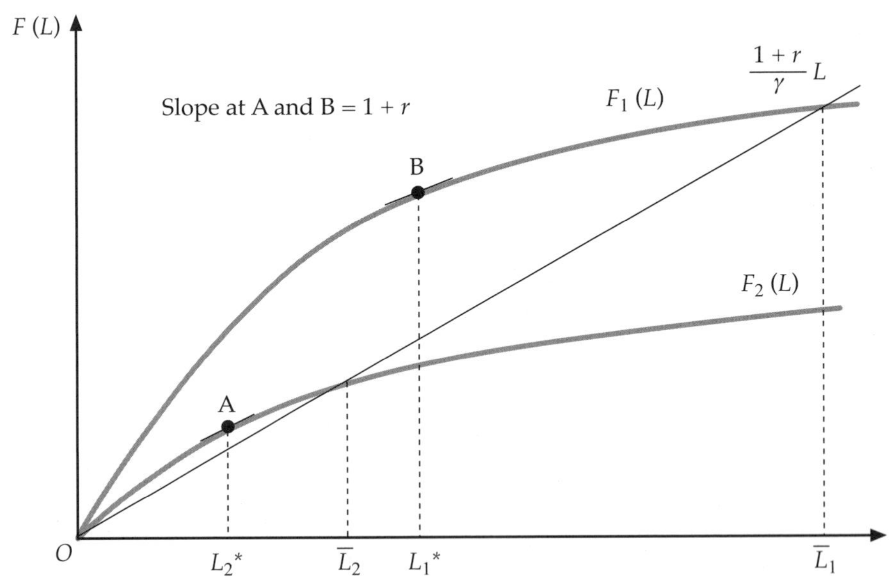

As shown in Fig. 5.3, the credit limit of rural households is determined by the intersection of $F_i(L)$ and $\frac{1+r}{\gamma}L$, of which those of type I and type II rural households are $\overline{L}_1$ and $\overline{L}_2$, respectively. The demands $L_1{}^*$ and $L_2{}^*$ for credit of type I and II rural households equal to the slope of the tangent point of their own return of product functions $(1 + r)$. As both $L_1{}^*$ and $L_2{}^*$ are larger than their corresponding credit limit $\overline{L}_1$ and $\overline{L}_2$, both types of rural households face credit constraints. The financing gap for type I rural households is $L_1{}^* - \overline{L}_1$ and for type II is $L_2{}^* - \overline{L}_2$. Of course, changes in the parameters of the model would change the positions of the curves and the slopes. Once the optimal quantity demanded for credit falls below the credit limit, financing constraints would be removed (see Fig. 5.4).

Model extension: Information asymmetry and credit differentiation

If there is no information asymmetry in the rural financial market, information of type I and II rural households are public. Any financial institutions in the market can obtain that information. They would be able to determine the line of credit for each household. When the type of household can be distinguished, financial institutions would offer $\overline{L}_1$ and $\overline{L}_2$ as the upper limit of credit ranges. Credit demand which does not fall in the ranges would lead to credit rationing. In other words, when there is sufficient and symmetrical information, any financial institutions can employ credit differentiation, i.e. offering more credit support to rural households who have more assets and a higher return. Credit differentiation is similar to the microeconomic concept of price discrimination. Under perfect information, financial institutions can devise the strategy to issue different amount of credit to different parties so as to achieve optimization of the credit structure and return maximization.

Under information asymmetry, what credit allocation strategy do financial institutions adopt? According to general game theory, when financial institutions cannot distinguish between two types of rural households, they estimate the distribution probability of the two types of households from experience and first thoughts. They employ the strategy of mixed equilibrium in credit issuance. Based on our model, the cost of breach of contract for type I rural households is $C_1(L)$ and that for type II is $C_2(L)$. The proportions for type I and type II rural households are α and $1-\alpha$, respectively. Therefore, the cost of breach of contract of rural households expected by financial institutions is $EC(L) = \alpha C_1(L) + (1 - \alpha) C_2(L)$

For rural households to repay their debts, the condition that $EC(L) \geq (1 + r) L$ must be satisfied. As a result, the incentive compatibility constraint is represented as

$$F(L) = \alpha F_1(L) + (1 - \alpha) F_2(L) \geq \frac{1 + r}{\gamma} L$$

The marginal rate of output of the type I households is larger than that of type II, i.e. $F_1{}'(L) > F_2{}'(L)$. Therefore,

$$F_1'(L) > F'(L) > F_2'(L)$$

The mixed equilibrium lies between $F_1(L)$ and $F_2(L)$. The corresponding credit limit $\overline{L}$ lies between $\overline{L}_1$ and $\overline{L}_2$, i.e. $\overline{L}_2 < \overline{L} < \overline{L}_1$ (see Fig. 5.5).

Fig. 5.5. Information asymmetry, credit differentiation, and mixed equilibrium

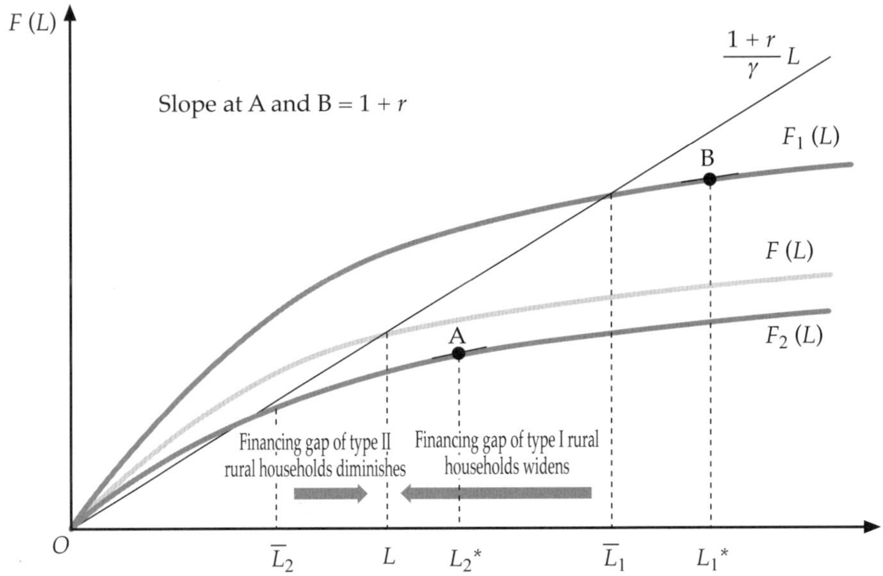

The above analysis illustrates that, to financial institutions, credit differentiation under symmetric information is preferred to mixed equilibrium strategy under asymmetric information. The reason is that with mixed equilibrium strategy, type II rural households which incur higher risk and a lower rate of return on investment take up part of the line of credit of type I rural households. It equals to substituting low-risk high-return investment for high-risk low-return investment. Moreover, type I rural households incur lower risk and a higher rate of return on investment. However, under information asymmetry and with mixed equilibrium strategy, the line of credit type I rural households diminishes because of standardization. They now face tighter financing constraints, which is not favorable for developing agricultural production or investment as type I rural households have better conditions to transform or provide demonstration.[12]

Obviously, information asymmetry in the rural financial market has economic significance to both rural households and financial institutions. To rural households, those who have higher production and investment ability (type I) face a widened credit gap, but those who have lower ability (type II) face a reduced one. Efficiency is sacrificed in this type of credit allocation using low marginal production ability to substitute low marginal production ability, which is favorable to agricultural development.[13] To financial institutions, they cannot employ credit differentiation to offer a reasonable line of credit to different types of rural households. Credit allocation using the mixed equilibrium strategy is biased toward type II rural households who have low efficiency. Financial institutions face higher risk and a lower rate of return on portfolio. When the expected rate of return is smaller than their total cost, they have no choice but to exit the market.

Inference 1: Under information asymmetry, financial institutions can only estimate the distribution of risk and return in the market from experience and first thoughts. They employ the strategy of mixed equilibrium in credit issuance. Under such strategy, rural households who have higher production and investment ability (type I) face a widened credit gap. Efficiency is sacrificed in this type of credit allocation using low marginal production ability to substitute low marginal production ability, and financial institutions face higher risk.

Inferences from comparative static analysis

The effect of the loan rate on demand and supply

In our model, when the loan rate r decreases, the slope of tangent point $1 + r$ and the constraint line $l = \frac{1+r}{\gamma} L$ move to the right, causing the equilibrium quantity demanded for credit L_i^* and the credit limit $\overline{L}_i$ to move rightward. When r increases, the slope of tangent point $1 + r$ and the constraint line $l = \frac{1+r}{\gamma} L$ move to the left, causing the equilibrium quantity demanded for credit L_i^* and the credit limit $\overline{L}_i$ to move leftward. This is to say that when the loan rate drops, rural households' credit demand increases, and financial institutions offer a higher credit limit to rural households; vice versa.

Although the change in the loan rate causes changes in the same direction in the tangent point and the credit limit, the extent of the change is different. Due to the parameter γ ($0 < \gamma < 1$, the discount factor of expected income), the change in r exerts an effect on the optimal quantity demanded for credit and the credit limit to different extents. When r drops by one unit, the slope of the tangent point $1 + r$ drops by one unit, but the slope of the constraint $l = \frac{1+r}{\gamma} L$ line drops by $\frac{1}{\gamma}$ times of one unit. In other words, the constraint line moves rightward faster than the tangent point does. When the loan rate falls continuously, credit constraints follow suit. Take type I rural households as an example, as seen in Fig. 5.6, when r

drops to r', the tangent point moves from A to B and the constraint line from $l = \frac{1+r}{\gamma} L$ to $\frac{1+r'}{\gamma} L$. Correspondingly, when the equilibrium quantity demanded for credit increases from L_i^* to L_i^{**}, the credit limit moves from $\overline{L}_i$ to $\overline{L'}_1$. As the credit limit rises faster than the quantity demanded for credit, the credit gap diminishes. In the figure, the new credit limit $\overline{L'}_1$ is larger than the new quantity demanded for credit L_i^{**}, which means that there is no more credit gap. It is worth mentioning that, under information asymmetry, even when financial institutions offer an undifferentiated line of credit to rural households (using the mixed equilibrium strategy), the credit would increase as the loan rate falls.

Fig. 5.6. The effect of the loan rate variation on rural households' credit demand

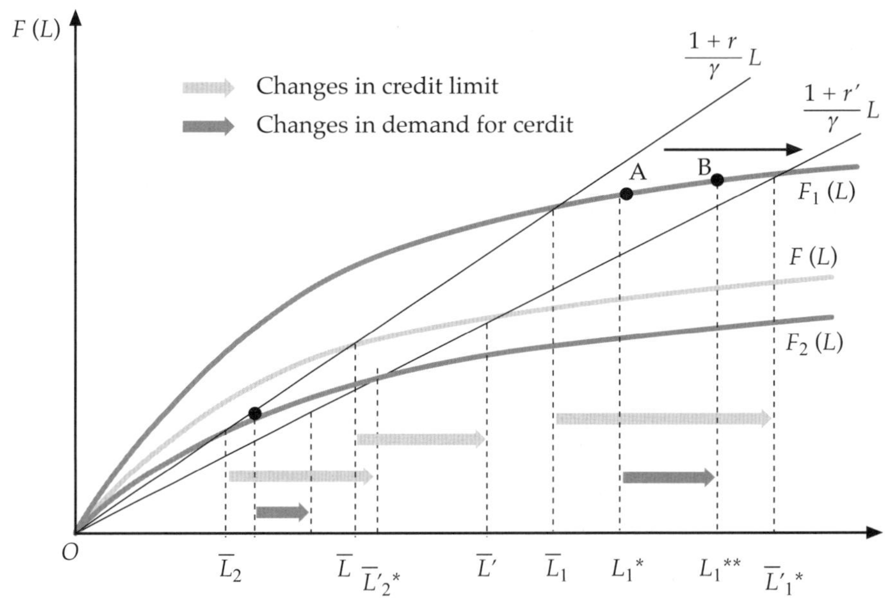

Based on the comparative static analysis, when the loan rate falls, credit constrains loosen; vice versa. This is to say that the continuous rise in the loan rate implies the continuous tightening of credit constraints. This is because when rural households face an increasingly high loan rate, the profit margins of return on investment would diminish. Smaller profitability implies higher credit risk, which suppresses the credit issuance of financial institutions. In extreme situations, even if the loan rate rises higher than the rate of return on agricultural investment, the profitability of rural households is negative. Financial institutions would not issue loans to rural households and the credit demand is entirely suppressed.

Inference 2: When the loan rate falls, rural households' demand for credit increases, and financial institutions issue more credit. When the loan rate rises, the profit margins of the rate of return on investment diminish. Rural households' demand for credit drops, and financial institutions issue less credit. When the loan rate rises higher than the rate of return on agricultural investment, the profitability of rural households is negative. Financial institutions would not issue loans to rural households and the credit demand is entirely suppressed.

Credit expansion in the development of regional economy under information asymmetry

In the extensive model, we obtained the incentive compatibility constraint and hence determined the mixed equilibrium as $F(L) = \alpha F_1(L) + (1-\alpha) F_2(L) \geq \frac{1+r}{\gamma} L$. As $F_1'(L) > F'(L) > F_2'(L)$, the mixed equilibrium lies between $F_1(L)$ and $F_2(L)$ curves, and the corresponding credit limit $\overline{L}$ lies between $\overline{L}_1$ and $\overline{L}_2$. In Fig. 5.7, the shaded area between $F_1(L)$ and $F_2(L)$ defines the positions of $F(L)$ curves with all possible values of α. Assume the initial position of $F(L)$ is at l_1 and that for the credit limit is at $\overline{L}$ corresponding to A. As α increases, $F(L)$ moves up to l_2. The new credit limit is at $\overline{L}'$ corresponding to B. Given that $\overline{L}' > \overline{L}$, as α increases, credit issuance increases.

We assumed in our model that type I rural households account for a proportion α and type II for $1-\alpha$ of total households, and type I have a better capital foundation and marginal productivity. Therefore, the higher α is, the larger the proportion type I rural households takes up, which implies a better foundation and potential for market development. From the above analysis, it can be seen that the value of α reflects the developmental level of a region. A higher value of α implies a higher developmental level of the region, and vice versa. The economic implication of the change in α is clear. Under information asymmetry, the more developed the regional economy is, the greater the credit issuance is with the strategy of mixed equilibrium, and rural households face smaller financing constraints.

Fig. 5.7. Credit expansion in the development of regional economy under information asymmetry

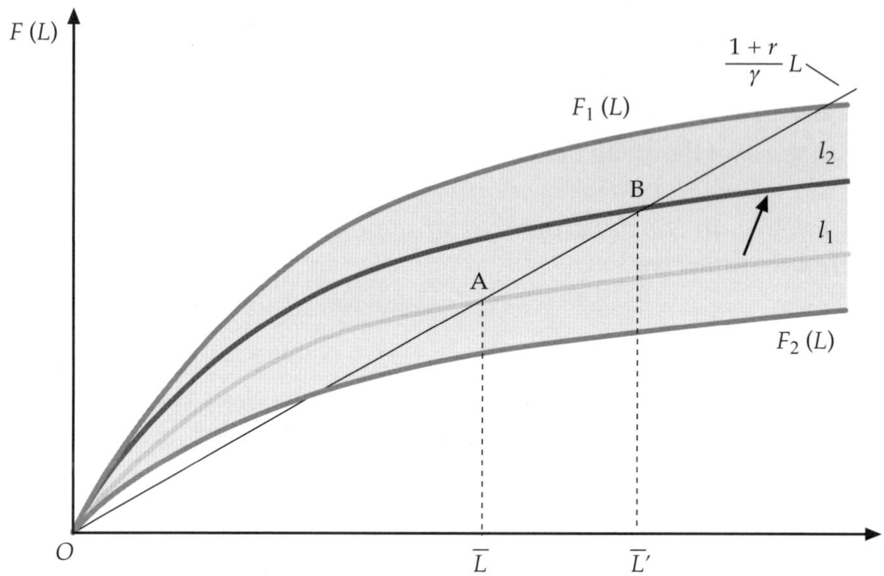

Inference 3: Developing the entire regional economy is the fundamental way to loosen credit constraints caused by information asymmetry. The more developed the regional economy is, the greater the credit issuance is with the strategy of mixed equilibrium, and rural households face smaller financing constraints.

The multiple driving effect of the rise in the rate of return on agriculture

In our model, the line of credit financial institutions offer to rural households is determined by $\frac{1+r}{\gamma}L$ and $F_i(L)$. When $F_i(L)$ remains unchanged, the credit limit $\overline{L}_i$ is mainly determined by the loan rate r and the discount factor γ.

In Fig. 5.8, when the discount factor increases from γ to γ', the curve $l=\frac{1+r}{\gamma}L$ moves rightward to $l'=\frac{1+r}{\gamma'}L$; ceteris paribus. There is a new credit boundary. The credit limits of type I and type II rural households increase from $\overline{L}_1$ and $\overline{L}_2$ to $\overline{L}'_1$ and $\overline{L}'_2$ respectively. The credit limit per household also increases from $\overline{L}$ to $\overline{L}'$. It is obvious that the rise in the discount factor γ brings systematic improvement to the financing constraints.

Fig. 5.8. The effect of the rise in the rate of return of agriculture on rural credit

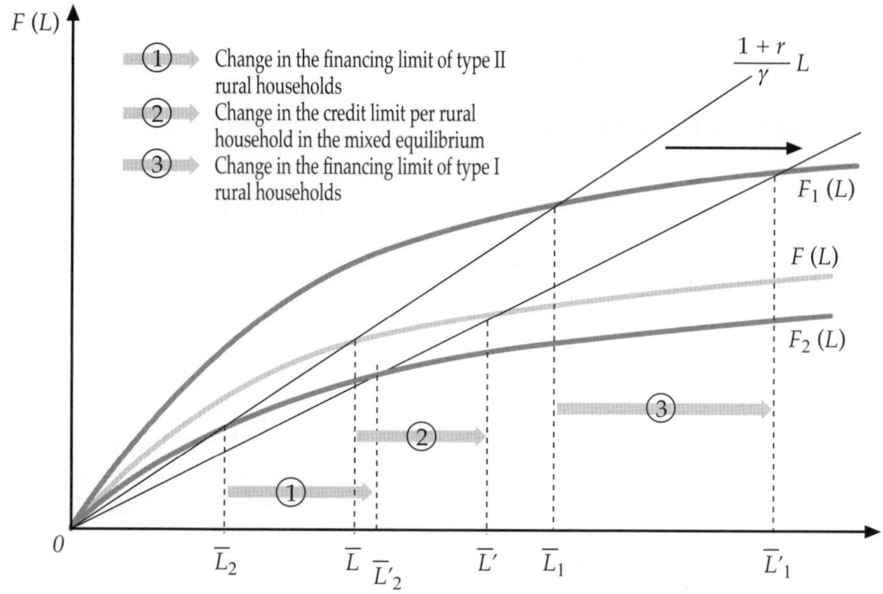

It is worth noting that the increase in γ has a multiplier effect on the expansion of the credit boundary. Through increasing the multiplier factor of index $f(x) = x^{-(1+r)} = \frac{1+r}{x}$, a small change in γ can cause a large change in the feasible region of credit. We have pointed out that γ can be regarded as the required rate of return on agricultural investment. The rise in the rate of return on agriculture would loosen credit constraints and attract more input of credit resources, which is the primary effect of the change in γ. Furthermore, the rise in γ implies the lowering of risk of the entire agricultural industry and the increase of returns. These certainly will attract more financial resources. As competition in the rural financial market becomes keener, the competition between creditors would push the loan rate r down. The effect of the lowering of r is multiplied by γ, leading to the double–multiplier effect in which γ and γ interact. As it can be seen that a rise in the rate of return on agriculture can loosen financing constraints on rural households, increase agricultural credit input, and enhance competition in the market through the multiplier effect. This effect can promote the simultaneous long-term development of the agricultural industry and rural finance, leading to a virtuous cycle and a self-sustainable mechanism.

Inference 4: The rise in the rate of return on agriculture can loosen the credit constraints on rural households, as well as lower the financing cost by increasing credit issuance and promoting rural financial competition. The lowering of the financing cost has a multiplier effect, leading to the formation of the long-term virtuous circle of mutual stimulation and development of agriculture and rural finance.

Further analysis and evaluation

We developed several inferences of information in the agricultural market, interest rate, regional development, and the level of return on agriculture from the extension of the model and comparative static analysis. The systematic analyses of credit constraints and the credit behavior of financial institutions offer some policy implications.

Information asymmetry in the rural financial market

Our first inference is that, under symmetric information, financial institutions can apply credit differentiation to offer a different line of credit to different clients. Under information asymmetry, financial institutions can only employ the strategy of mixed equilibrium in credit issuance based on experience and first thoughts. This strategy is not preferred even if the distribution of households in the market is accurately estimated. Efficiency is sacrificed in this type of credit allocation favoring households with low marginal production ability and financial institutions face higher risk.

The key questions are: Is there information asymmetry in the market? If yes, how does it come into existence?

Undoubtedly, financial institutions which have been serving rural areas for a long time or are established in rural areas have better information of rural areas and rural households (level of assets, production and investment ability, credit level) than bankers at large-scale financial institutions. While bankers try to find the value of α to determine the line of credit for rural households, front-line officers of rural financial institutions (organizations) know clearly the details and situation of each household. The "grassroots" rural financial institutions have an information advantage over urban-based formal financial institutions. These "grassroots" institutions can apply credit differentiation as they have close to perfect information. The allocation of credit resources follows more closely the risk-return trade-off principle. In contrast, formal financial institutions not only face the cost of setting up the financial network in rural areas and obtaining market information, but they are also at a disadvantaged position in terms of the method and channels for information collection. Therefore, they have little economic motivation to enter the rural financial market, especially the microcredit market.

It should be noted that although RCCs are seen as having a nature of formal finance, they possess an information advantage of the wide coverage of their network and front-line credit officers. Regardless of the nature of RCCs, they are grassroots organizations in terms of their operating methods, which is the reason why they have an edge over formal financial institutions.

Interest rate policy in the rural financial market

Our second inference is that when the loan rate rises, the quantity of rural households' demand for credit decreases, the profit margins of the rate of return on investment diminishes, and financial institutions issue more credit. When the loan rate rises higher than the rate of return on agricultural investment, financial institutions exit the market. Rural households' credit demand is entirely suppressed. An implication is clear: A loan rate which is too high is unfavorable to both rural households and financial institutions.

In recent years, in order to encourage financial institutions to increase credit input given the condition that the return can cover risk, the state has raised the upper limit on the interest rate to four times the benchmark. Not only does this policy encourage financial institutions such as RCCs to issue more loans to rural households, but it also promotes the establishment of new-style financial institutions such as village and township banks (VTBs) and credit companies, which often adopt a higher loan rate. According to our sentinel surveillance of 13 new rural financial institutions (10 VTBs and three credit companies) in Sichuan Province, the highest loan rate of VTBs Is 18% with an average of 8.34%, that of credit companies is 13.61% with an average of 11.22%. The data of April 2009 shows that there were seven VTBs and one credit company which suffered losses, accounting for 70% and 33% of their respective category. In terms of loan allocation, 90% were issued to rural small and medium-sized enterprises and less than 10% to rural households. Whether a high loan rate can ensure financial institutions to obtain return high enough to cover their risk and rural households to receive more credit support is uncertain. In the situation in which the rate of return on agriculture is generally low, simply raising the loan rate to cover the cost of financial institutions can hardly expand the loans issued to rural households. It would even discourage rural households from obtaining loans. According to our survey on the field staff (each member was responsible for 2,700 rural households on average) of seven RCCs in two provinces in Western China, if the loan rate rises to higher than 12%, the rural households' quantity demanded for credit drops significantly. If the loan rate rises to higher than 15%, rural households dare not obtain loans. We gave our questionnaire to 70 households in four towns in the two counties. The answer to the question "Can you bear a loan rate of 15% for production or consumption?" was 100% negative. The study of the research group of *The Chinese Banker* (2007) gave a similar conclusion: while rural households can bear a wide range of interest rates, they have little intention to bear high ones. Of the 330 qualified samples, 70% households answered that they could only bear a loan rate lower than 10% and only 30% could bear a loan rate higher than 15% (see Table 5.5).

Table 5.5. The affordability of rural households towards loan rates

The highest loan rate which rural households can bear (X)	Number of households	Proportion (%)
$X \leq 5\%$	84	25.5
$5\% < X \leq 7\%$	62	18.8
$7\% < X \leq 10\%$	110	33.3
$10\% < X \leq 15\%$	62	18.8
$X > 15\%$	12	3.6

Source: Research group of Research Institute of The Chinese Banker, "Financial demand in traditional rural areas and the distribution of institutions," *The Chinese Banker* 7 (2007).

The long-term sustainable development of rural areas and the rural financial market

Our fourth inference is that an increase in the rate of return on agriculture can loosen the credit constraints on rural households, as well as lowering the financing cost by increasing credit issuance and promoting rural financial competition, leading to the formation of the long-term virtuous circle of mutual stimulation and development of agriculture and rural finance. Finance is an intermediary industry. If the return on the input into the market cannot compensate for the risk or cannot reach the required level, commercial financial institutions lack the incentive to enter the rural financial market. On the contrary, if the risk-adjusted rate of return on agricultural loans is higher than the average profitability of financial institutions, their profit-making motives would lead them into entering the market and expanding their business in credit. Therefore, the rise in the rate of return on agriculture causes not only an increase in the inflow of financial resources, it also improves the sustainability of existing financial resources. Only a continuous rise in the rate of return can lead to a win-win situation of long-term development of agriculture and rural areas. A further inference is that the allocation of financial resources should target an improvement in the rate of return on agriculture. Any financial supply which cannot do so is ineffective (or even predatory). Therefore, being efficiency-oriented is the basis for the long-term development of agriculture and rural finance.

Other factors also play a role in loosening the credit constraints. In our framework, credit constraints on rural households are closely related to the rate of return on agriculture as well as the regional economy. Our third inference is that developing the entire regional economy is the fundamental way to loosen credit constraints caused by information asymmetry. In regions with a better economy, even under information asymmetry, financial institutions tend to issue more credit to rural households. When financial institutions cannot identify the types of rural households, they refer mainly to the developmental level of the regional economy to determine the line of credit. In other words, the developmental level of the regional economy has a signaling effect. It should be noted that urban-based large-scale commercial banks are the main financial institutions troubled by information asymmetry. They are reluctant to enter the market as they face higher information costs. When the regional economy sends out encouraging signals, these financial institutions can expand credit issuance as more type II rural households transform to type I. The implication is that promoting the development of the regional economy is a major channel for attracting external financial resources. As the rural economy develops, it is possible that urban-based financial institutions would naturally re-enter the rural financial market or increase credit issuance.

In conclusion, the rate of return on agriculture should be continuously stimulated and development of the rural economy should be promoted in order to attract the inflow of external financial resources into the rural financial market based on efficiency. In the end, the mutual development of agriculture and rural finance will be achieved.

Modernization of China's Rural Finance

The present layout and future of China's rural financial market

The layout of China's current rural financial market can be divided into three layers: (1) The high-end market, which is represented by competitive enterprises involved in agricultural industrialization, is seized by large-scale commercial banks, such as the Agricultural Development Bank. But only a few enterprises involved in agricultural industrialization are qualified to obtain loans. The market awaits expansion. (2) The middle-end market, in which there are mainly small and medium-sized enterprises and marketized rural households, is dominated by RCCs. At the same time, RCCs are trying to enter the high-end market. New-style financial institutions such as VTBs and (micro) credit companies, and the reformed Postal Savings Bank of China are competing with RCCs for the existing quality customers. There is over-competition for quality clients but too little financial supply provided for general rural households. (3) In the low-end market taken up by general and impoverished rural households, commercial financial institutions are reluctant to enter this market except some mutual aid cooperatives. However, the financial demand of rural household groups cannot be satisfied by the small number of mutual aid cooperatives. Remote areas without any branch of financial institutions are "forgotten corners of finance" (see Fig. 5.9).

Fig. 5.9. The coverage of financial institutions in rural finance

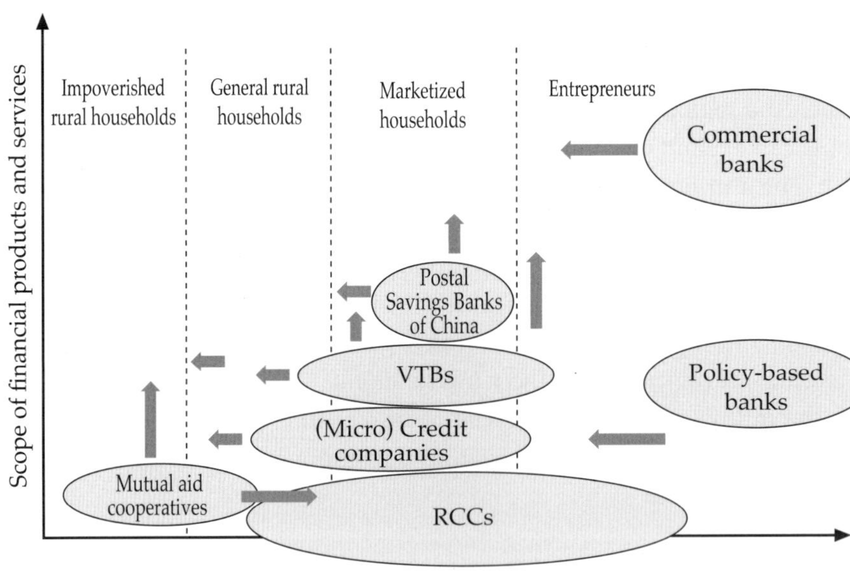

Based on the above layout, we predict that there are three basic pathways and directions for the development of the market: (1) As agricultural industrialization progresses, more quality enterprises will emerge in the high-end market. Large-scale commercial banks will compete for providing financial support to them. At the same time, the banks will go down the chain of industry to explore the middle-end market. (2) As the reform of RCCs deepens and new-style financial institutions develop, the over-competition for quality clients in the middle-end market will evolve into orderly competition and differentiated services will be offered. This transformation will give play to natural selection in the market. (3) As the major participant in the low-end market, mutual aid cooperatives should develop into composite and open poverty-aid organizations with the support of the state. As credit techniques mature, new-style financial institutions are expected to expand their services to the low-end market. The arrows in Fig. 5.9 represent the potential expansion directions of financial institutions in the rural financial market.

The future system of rural financial services

Judging from the current situation and the trends of development, China's future rural financial services will be cooperative, commercial, and policy-based.

Cooperative finance stimulates endogeneity of rural finance. It will resolve the conflict between small-scale production and the huge market, and promote the development of social credit during the transformation of rural households.

Commercial finance will expand the market space under the irreversible marketization progress, as the transformation of rural households, agricultural industrialization, and urbanization of rural areas. The credit techniques and services of the institutions will be refined.

Policy-based finance will cover the disadvantaged rural areas neglected by commercial finance. These areas are positive externalities.

The combination of cooperative, commercial, and policy-based finance will be able to fully cover the market, giving rise to a mutual complementary market structure. Advantageous resources of rural households, financial institutions, and the state will be combined and rearranged so that the market will be in the optimal condition.

Cooperative finance: Simulation of endogeneity in rural finance

For a long time, the scattered business put rural households in a disadvantaged position in the market and, eventually, the economy. Therefore, to resolve the conflict between small-scale production and the huge market, it is fundamental to enhance rural households' cooperation ability and the self-developmental ability of RCCs in order to raise the income of rural households. Regarding the endogenous development of rural finance, cooperative finance assumes a clear comparative advantage. To disadvantaged rural households, financial cooperation can improve their self- and external financing ability, bargaining power, and market negotiation ability. Of course, at the moment, rural households have little intention and ability to be cooperative, and thus the promotion of cooperative finance still faces the constraints of the initial conditions. It is impractical to expect the emergence of many cooperative financial organizations in the market within the short period of time. It is more feasible to capitalize on the advantage of the government, community, enterprises, and rural households. To establish an effective multi-cooperation mechanism in which the government provides guidance, the community offers support, enterprises interact with each other, and the rural households cooperate with the other parties is more suitable for traditional rural areas. Once the market breakthough from the constraints of initial conditions occurs, cooperative finance may have unexpectedly ample room for economic development. For example, research has found that, in Jiang Su and Zhe Jiang provinces, the scale of financing through cooperative finance is larger than that through RCCs and the Agricultural Bank of China, accounting for 55% (Hu Yijing 2003, Lou Yuan 2003).

It should be noticed that rural households' intention and ability to cooperate is the basis for cooperative finance to exist and develop. During the crucial period of transiting from relationship credibility to contract credibility and marketization, it is important to establish a "market carrier" which can enhance personal credibility and is beneficial for the development of horizontal credibility through institutional arrangements. The market carrier can be either new cooperative financial institutions or new financial entities created by current institutions. The latter are very practical in operation. In fact, the current new financial products (see Table 5.6) which are popular have the nature of being cooperative. And cooperation is crucial to the development of cooperative financial institutions. In terms of long-term development, the design of financial products should focus on the cooperation among rural households, between rural households and enterprises, community, the government, and social organizations. It can also be horizontal cooperation among entities or vertical cooperation along the chain of industry.

Table 5.6. Examples of popular new financial products in the rural financial market

Business	Description	Nature	Service area
Mutual-aid credit	Set up mutual aid cooperative, jointly guaranteed by the members. It provides balance control, turnover of capital, and issuance of co-guarantee loans.	Microcredit	Henan Province, Hubei Province, Shandong Province, etc.

(Cont'd)

Business	Description	Nature	Service area
Company + rural households; company + associations + rural households	Organizations involved in agricultural industrialization (companies, professional associations, and economic cooperatives) develop composite financial services.	Credit guarantee	Across the country
Insurance + RCCs + credit	Supported by policy-based insurance, RCCs and professional associations provide credit services.	Innovative composite financial services	Anhui Province, Henan Province, Chongqing Province, etc.

Source: Li Jiayan and Tao Changgao, "Thoughts on the Development of China's Village and Township Banks," *The Chinese Banker* 11 (2008).

Commercial finance: Natural selection in the market

In irreversible marketization, with the transformation of rural households, agricultural industrialization, and urbanization of rural areas, commercial finance is essential and has ample room for development. The rural financial market is undeveloped but has a lot of potential.

There are two types of financial institutions in the rural financial market: "stock" and "incremental" financial institutions. The former refers to mainly the four state-owned banks (Bank of China, Agricultural Bank of China, Industrial and Commercial Bank of China, and China Construction Bank), RCCs, joint-stock banks, and local banks. The latter refers to policy-motivated new-style financial institutions such as VTBs, credit companies, and mutual aid cooperatives. On the one hand, RCCs and the Agricultural Bank of China continue to provide financial services in the market. On the other hand, other urban-based commercial banks may extend their network and services or cooperate with small-scale institutions in wholesale lending to extend services to traditional rural areas.

The positioning of new-style financial institutions is clearer. They target "micro" clients such as rural households and rural microenterprises in the low-end market. They specialize in developing microcredit techniques and financial services as they have a comparative advantage in providing flexible, quick, and immediate services.

In terms of the relationship between stock and incremental financial institutions, during initial development and the pioneering process, many stock financial institutions except RCCs and Agricultural Bank of China are unwilling to enter the rural financial market. Also, as the development of new-style financial institutions is immature, they do not possess a comparative advantage with their microcredit techniques. As a result, most new-style financial institutions are in homogenous competition with stock financial institutions (mainly RCCs). Especially when they face limited quality clients, over-competition is not unexpected in the market. However, as the transformation of rural households and agricultural industrialization progress, the pioneering process in the rural financial market ends. Traditional small-scale peasant economy is substituted with intensified agricultural economy. The gradual upgrade of industrial structure would bring huge financial surplus. At this time, stimulated by profit, more commercial financial institutions would enter the rural financial market spontaneously under the effect of the market forces. At the same time, as the specialized credit techniques of new-style financial institutions become mature, the relationship between stock and incremental financial institutions is no longer competitive but complementary. In an idealistic situation, different types and scales of commercial financial institutions would cover different levels and clients in the market. They would develop specialized credit techniques and financial services based on their comparative advantage. In the end, they would be in differentiated competition and complement each other in the market.

Apart from commercial financial institutions, other types of financial institutions will emerge in the market as marketization is underway. According to the theory of comparative advantage, large-scale commercial banks should devise strategies revolving around the chain of industry. They should provide credit supply and financial services tailored to middle- or high-end clients. Micro-financial institutions should aim at providing composite financial services and developing microcredit techniques targeted at the low-end market. Our field study of western China shows that, for rural households under transformation, the value of financial services such as information, market, financial, and technical consultations is not smaller than credit supply, because the shortage of the former is more evident.

Policy-based finance: The importance of a clear boundary

The global trends of policy-based finance exhibit three basic features: (1) Policy-based finance relying on fiscal subsidies is unsustainable. (2) As marketization deepens and the financial system develops, the scale of policy-based finance diminishes. (3) As market forces strengthen, the scope and functions of policy-based finance would change correspondingly (Cheng Yulu and Ma Yong 2006).[14]

In developing countries, the rural financial market is typically underdeveloped and waiting for pioneer institutions to develop. This causes the market under the dual economic structure to lag behind the urban market. Market failure is aggravated. At the same time, unlike those in developed countries which are confined to areas without market forces, market failures in developing countries soften concerns of the entire market. This extreme status restricts the speed and scope of the workings of market forces. When commercial finance is unwilling and unable to serve the rural financial market, policy-based finance directed by the government becomes essential in tackling external problems. As a representation of social benefits, policy-based finance emphasizes the long-term efficiency of resource allocation and social rationality, unlike commercial financial institutions which avoid the market because of business considerations.

Using policy-based finance to promote agricultural development has been a practical choice of many countries. America's Commodity Credit Corporation, Japan's Norinchukin Bank, and France's Crédit Agricole are policy-based financial institutions. This type of finance commonly exists across the world for several reasons: (1) To tackle the problem of insufficient agricultural investment during industrialization and to prevent the imbalanced development economic structure from dragging down the national economy. (2) Agricultural development is dependent on natural conditions (e.g. geography, weather, availability of resources). In the initial stages, investment in infrastructure and technology brings little profit. Profit-maximizing institutions would not invest capital in agriculture. At the time, policy-based finance should intervene as they maximize social benefits. (3) The elasticity of demand for agricultural products is small. In order to stabilize the expectations on production and consumption, under the cobweb model, price fluctuations call for the intervention of policy-based finance to prevent disequilibrium in the demand and supply in the market and lower the systematic risk. (4) Not only does unstable supply of agricultural products cause sway in the economy, but it also gives rise to problems related to social well-being. Therefore, the stabilization of the market price is economical as well as political.

As a major developing economy, it is difficult to imagine that the government of China has no effect in the agricultural sector. Also, the government has a history of directing economic development. It is expected that there is a higher degree of government intervention in agriculture, one of the weaker sectors. Given these initial conditions, the key question is not whether policy-based finance should exist, but how to capitalize on it.

It is important to clearly define the boundary between policy-based and commercial finance. The entry of policy-based financial institutions which enjoy a low financing cost to the market will bring chaos to orderly competition. Stiglitz (1996) pointed out that effective policy-based finance (providing low-cost financing to specific sectors) should not exploit the profit of banks. Much research illustrates that efficiency is often sacrificed in the administration of policy-based financial institutions. Therefore, the positioning of the institutions in the market should target the aspects which commercial finance cannot serve and which offer positive externalities. The institutions should be complementary rather than substitutional, or else fair competition is disrupted and efficiency is sacrificed.[15]

Table 5.7. Market constraints and policy-based finance

Market constraints	Countermeasures	Implications
Due to monopoly, the financial sector enjoys supernormal profit.	Confine monopoly, relax market entry, and improve the competitiveness of the market structure.	Develop functions which can counteract monopoly.
The capital demand for enterprises with externalities is insufficient.	Coordinate individual and social interests through subsidies and tax.	Reduce the cost for collecting information of subsidized subjects through financial transactions.
Because of information asymmetry, the capital supplied to small and medium-sized enterprises is insufficient	Subsidize the sunk cost for accumulating information of clients.	Government financial institutions bear the information cost instead of private institutions.
Lack of a long-term capital market.	Subsidize the cost for infrastructure and information collection.	Government financial institutions bear the information cost and the cost of building infrastructure.

Source: Hidenobu Okuda, "Policy-based finance and market mechanism," *Economic Lectures* 1 (1996).

The operating format of policy-based finance should be reformed. As mentioned earlier, the issues with information and costs make it difficult for the state to monitor the microscopic operation of commercial financial institutions. At present, commercial financial institutions are also responsible for policy-based finance, which encourages rent-seeking behavior from the institutions on the national capital. Such behavior counteracts the effort in risk management and instigates serious moral hazard. Commercial financial institutions tend to blame their loss on policy loans. The state is obliged to take care of the risky and careless actions of the institutions. The difficulties RCCs are experiencing are related to this to a certain extent.

In terms of long-term development, under the condition that policy-based finance is completely separated from commercial financial institutions, the resources of financial institutions can be combined and rearranged. On the one hand, the status of the Agricultural Development Bank as a policy-based financial institution should be strengthened. On the other hand, RCCs in areas with a less advanced economy can be transformed into poverty-aid institutions or branches of other policy-based financial institutions and terminate their business in commercial finance. This can be done if the RCCs cannot be transformed into commercial or cooperative financial institutions. When conditions are ripe, new and specialized policy-based financial institutions can be established. In the near future, the network coverage of the Agricultural Development Bank may still be insufficient and the establishment of new institutions may run into difficulties. Commercial financial institutions could be allowed to carry on with their business in policy-based finance. However, the government should impose tight supervision and adopt an independent account system. This system refers to the fact that business in policy-based finance should have an independent account, and any loss is borne by fiscal capital. On the other hand, the other commercial business is autonomously managed and has separate finance. Tax discounts may be given when necessary. To strengthen the use of independent accounts, the business of policy-finance can be taken up by specialized subsidiary company.[16] Regardless of the format, there should be an incentive scheme and an evaluation system. The performance of the institutions is evaluated to ensure sustainability and the quality of services. We introduce the evaluation system The World Bank (2002) recommends in the last section.

Agricultural insurance: A catalyst in the financial mechanism

China's agriculture suffers relative serious natural disasters. During 2001–2005, on average of 50 million hectares of crops were affected and 27.3 million hectares were destroyed, accounting for 18.8% of the sown area. Agricultural production and rural lives were threatened (Chan Yulu and Zhao Wei 2007). China's agricultural insurance coverage has been very insufficient. In recent years, the insurance penetration and insurance density have decreased.[17] Agricultural insurance provides little economic security. In addition, the agricultural insurance industry is commercialized but not policy-based. As a result, agriculture continues to suffer loss.[18] With little insurance, the efforts of rural households are all destroyed when disaster strikes. And natural disasters are frequent in China. In order to avoid risk, financial institutions cut down on their credit issuance to agriculture and rural households.

The risk of natural disaster is not within the scope of risk management of financial institutions,[19] which also lacks the required techniques. Therefore, it is important to have an insurance company or institution to be responsible for managing such risk. In terms of financial support, agricultural insurance isolated the risk of natural disasters, providing a buffer zone for institutions. The institution will be able to concentrate on credit administration and financial services which they specialize in. A well-established insurance system is a catalyst in the financial system, which helps channel more financial resources into agriculture.

Much research illustrates that credit insurance increases the credit supply of financial institutions (Hatch et al. 1980, Hogan 1983). Many institutions minimize credit risk through insurance. Agricultural insurance becomes a prerequisite for obtaining credit services (ALIDE and FAO 1996). Binswanger (1980) thought that insurance serves a similar function as collateral. It lowers the chance of breach of contract, which encourages banks to increase credit supply.[20] Misha's research (1994) illustrates that with crop insurance, the coverage of agricultural credit and the amount of credit per household have increased, as well as the rate of debt repayment. It confirms the proposition that insurance is a substitution of collaterals.

Many countries have developed agricultural insurance or agricultural credit insurance. Generally speaking, the agricultural credit insurance covers the credit issued to rural households, and compulsory insurance is required for official credit. Indemnity refers to the harvest paid to the creditor by the debtor when he or she cannot make full payment by money. In the U.S., the Agricultural Credit Insurance Fund specializes in the operating of agricultural credit; in Brazil, ProAgro provides insurance to rural households so that they can resume production quickly when disasters strike. Similar credit insurance schemes are established in Indonesia, Thailand, the Philippines, Mexico, Panama, Mauritius, Sri Lanka, Bangladesh, etc (Ma Jiujie 2004).

The system of agricultural insurance is different across countries. The U.S. adopts a multi-layer system directed by the government; Japan adopts a cooperative system supported by the government; Spain adopts a public subsidy system; the Philippines adopts a system of selective national support; Mexico adopts a system in which state-owned insurance companies dominate and commercial ones are supplementary. Judging international experience and the current situation, China should follow three principles in developing agricultural insurance: (1) The mode of development should be chosen with reference to the situation of the state. (2) Agricultural insurance should be regulated by the law. (3) The design of the risk dispersion mechanism should be scientific (Chen Yulu and Zhao Wei 2007). See Feature 5–2 for further discussion.

The design of the insurance system should revolve around the combination of policy-based and commercial agricultural insurance. A subsidy mechanism should be designed, and insurance and reinsurance should be encouraged to combine (see Fig. 5.10). In the near future, agricultural insurance industry is still frail, and commercial agricultural insurance can hardly serve its function. It can be considered that development should be centered on policy-based agricultural insurance and help should be required from local governments. Factors such as the level of economic development and agricultural production, the characteristics of agricultural production and natural disasters, and the market demand should be taken into consideration. When it comes to long-term development, considering the transformation of rural households and agricultural industrialization, the operating of agricultural insurance should be based on the market principles. The state should offer policy support (fiscal, taxation, and monitoring). A diverse system should be established.[21] As the agricultural insurance is difficult and the loss ratio is high, in order to disperse risk over a large area, an all-round reinsurance system should be set up to ensure the business stability of the insurer. Further, a special catastrophe risk fund should be set up for agricultural disasters for large-sum insurance payment.[22]

Fig. 5.10. China's insurance system

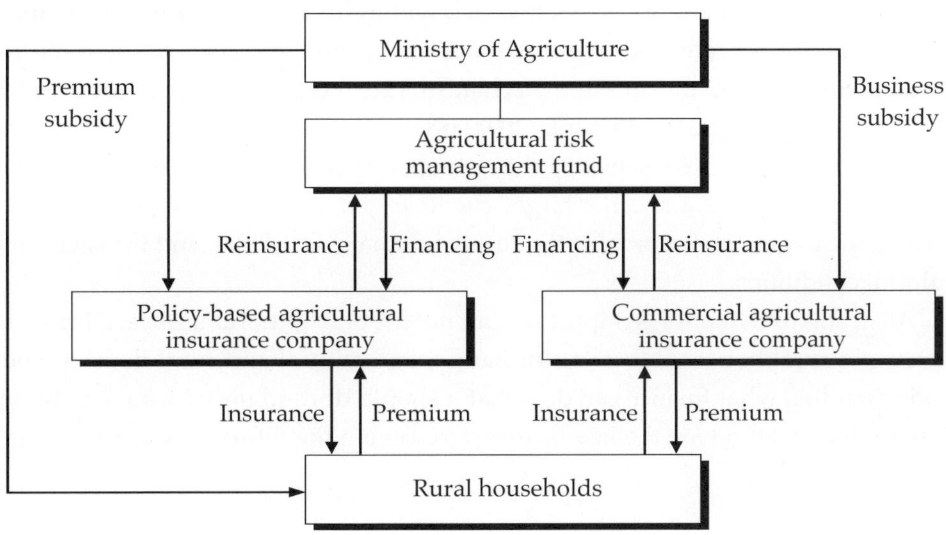

Is finance the only important issue?

We have taken a continuous and dynamic perspective on the present and future development of China's rural finance. While there will be endless debate on certain details, the importance of finance in rural households' transformation, agriculture, and rural areas cannot be denied. An unhealthy rural financial system would obstruct the development of the three rural entities; a well-designed one can provide leverage and bring about the increase in social resources and services for raising the income of rural households, agricultural development, and rural construction.

As Chaves and Sanchez (1995) pointed out, nothing is more complicated than agriculture. Because of the complexity of the industry, no single financial instrument can thoroughly resolve the problem. Even a well-designed financial institution and system require a basic environment and external conditions for operation. For example, continuous chaos in macroeconomy will disturb and harm the rural financial market, uncoordinated industry policies will cause resources misallocation, and agricultural and rural development will constrain the sustainability of rural finance. The financial mechanism never works in isolation. Only when it is installed in the network system of socioeconomic development can it serve its functions to the fullest. Every aspect of rural society needs to be taken into consideration. For instance, in most cases, poverty is related to the limited contact with the market, network, and techniques rural households have. This implies that non-financial services such as technical training can improve the rate of return on investment of the poor, which will in turn improve the environment of rural finance. Moreover, the culture is also crucial to the success of some specific systems. Some credit transmission mechanisms are more successful in society with certain culture. As The World Bank (2002) points out:

"Explore strategies for selecting the appropriate institutional design and modes of operation to serve a specific target clientele given the political and economic setting, the degree of maturity of the rural and financial sectors, and the social and cultural conditions."

All in all, rural finance is important, but not the only important issue. During the process of rural households' transformation, agricultural and rural development, understanding what finance can do, what it should do, and under what conditions to use which method are the key factors to resolving the difficulties facing China's rural finance.

Major Conclusions and Policy Implications

(1) Rural households are not irrational. They, however, face special external conditions. The interaction of their low ability to accumulate capital and indivisible investment leads to low-level equilibrium—the poverty trap.

(2) As capital accumulates and agricultural production progresses, rural households gradually encounter the opportunity to transform. A suitable

amount of government support and market forces are necessary for the process.

(3) The clear-cut distinction between "surviving small farmers" and "rational small farmers" neglects the dynamic transformation between the two. A continuous perspective should be adopted to explain rural households' economic behavior under modern market conditions.

(4) An increase in the rate of return on agriculture can loosen the credit constraints on rural households, as well as lower the financing cost by increasing credit issuance and promoting rural financial competition. This would lead to the formation of the long-term virtuous circle of mutual stimulation and development of agriculture and rural finance. Therefore, an efficiency-oriented principle is the foundation of long-term agricultural and rural financial development.

(5) China's future rural financial services will be cooperative, commercial, and policy-based. Cooperative finance stimulates endogeneity of rural finance. Commercial finance will expand the market space as the transformation of rural households, agricultural industrialization, and urbanization of rural areas. The credit techniques and services of the institutions will be refined. Policy-based finance will cover the disadvantaged rural areas where there are positive externalities but which commercial finance neglects. It will support the weaker regions and manifest the strategies of the state.

(6) A well-established insurance system is a catalyst in the financial system, which helps channel more financial resources into agriculture. When it comes to long-term development, the operating of agricultural insurance should be based on the market principles, corresponding to the transformation of rural households and agricultural industrialization,. The state should offer policy support (fiscal, taxation, and regulatory policies). A diverse system should be established.

(7) Because of the complexity of the agricultural industry, no single financial instrument can thoroughly resolve the problem. Even a well-designed financial institution and system requires a basic environment and external conditions for operation. During the process of rural households' transformation, agricultural and rural development, as well as an understanding of what finance can do and the methods used, are the keys to resolving the difficulties China's rural finance faces.

Feature 5–1
Evaluation of the Performance of Rural Financial Institutions[23]

For many years, there has not been a standard set of indexes of the performance of rural financial institutions. The Financial Ratio Analysis is generally adopted. The analysis does not take into account various subsidies the institutions receive or special goals assigned to the institutions. The evaluation framework Yaron (1992) proposed in 1992 has been accepted by academia and practitioners (The World Bank 2002).[24] There are two basic indexes: the coverage of target clients and the sustainability of rural financial institutions (see Fig. 5.11). Although these indexes cannot offer an all-round evaluation on the economic influence of the institutions, they can measure the degree of success institutions have in pursuing their goals using quantitative analysis and shed light on the social cost of support institutions.

Fig. 5.11. The evaluation standard of rural financial institutions

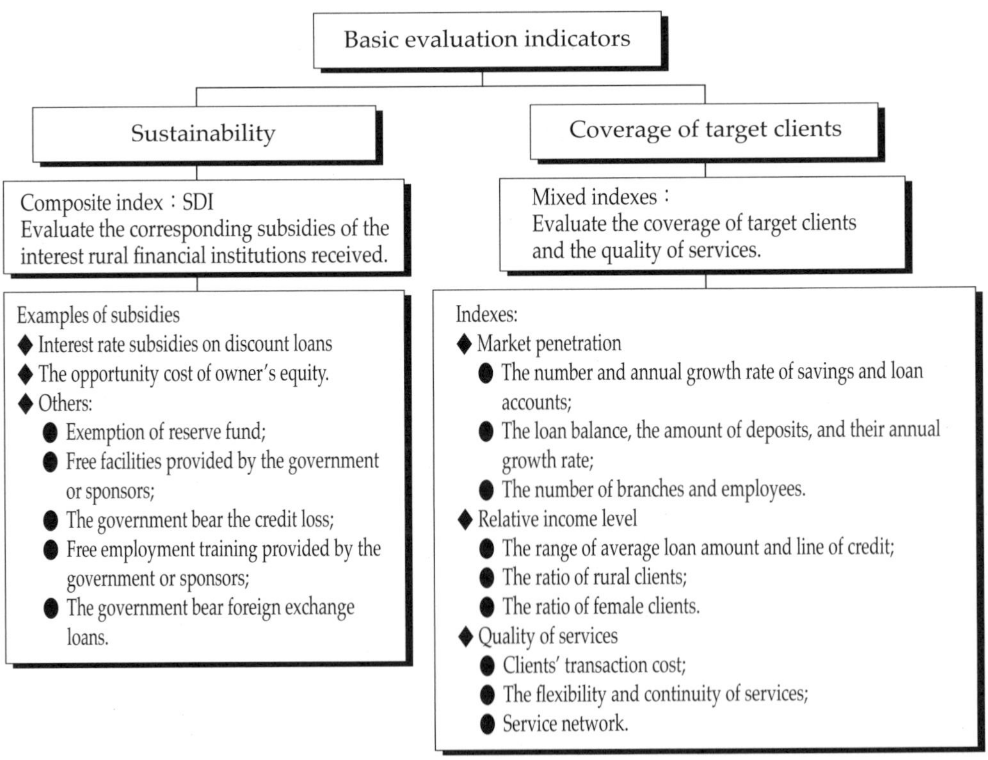

The evaluation standard

Coverage

Coverage are mixed indexes which measure the success institutions have on serving target clients and satisfying the clients' demand for financial services. The index is both qualitative and quantitative. It can measure the depth (the type and degree of poverty of the clients) and the scope (the number of clients served using different methods). The weighted average of the indexes and their quantification can be calculated according to their relations with a specific society. For example, if there is no gender constraint on credit, the weighting of female clients drops to below 1, or 0. Evaluation can be conducted only when information of that institution and information related to that institution exists. During the evaluation of business performance, accounting principles should be followed, and an external audit should be done regularly.

Sustainability

Previous intervention policies have not taken the sustainability of rural financial institutions seriously. Standard profitability (e.g. the rate of return on owner's equity, and on assets) can be used in evaluating the financial performance of profit-maximizing institutions, but not state-owned rural financial institutions. State-owned institutions are not profit-maximizing and hence they receive benefits from subsidies. Such subsidies incur social cost. The calculation of profitability of rural financial institutions using standard financial ratios does not take subsidies into account. Profitability may increase with the injection of discount capital or other forms of subsidy even though the business performance of the institution is poor. By the same principle, a fall in profitability does not necessarily reflect a drop in operating efficiency of the institution but a drop in subsidies received.

Subsidies given to state-owned rural financial institutions are usually in the form of the opportunity cost of owners' equity (which the institutions consider no cost) and discount loans. Under most circumstances, owners' equity is not determined by the institution's ability to borrow or its cost of borrowing. The interest rate of discount loans state-owned institutions enjoy is determined by the central bank and relevant departments, not the market. There are political and economic concerns involved. Therefore, the difference between owners' equity and external financial debts of state-owned institutions and profit-maximizing institutions has no explanatory power. Although discount loans have a great influence on the rate of return on owners' equity and on assets of the institutions, as financial profitability is externally determined, the influence of administration is very small, if there is any.

The basic indexes can be represented by two axes (see Fig. 5.12). Some scholars believe there is conflict between coverage and sustainability. In fact, many policies adopted by institutions to expand coverage also benefit sustainability. Improvement in performance requires improvement in at least one index, and performance should be measurable.

Fig. 5.12. Optimization of business performance of rural financial institutions

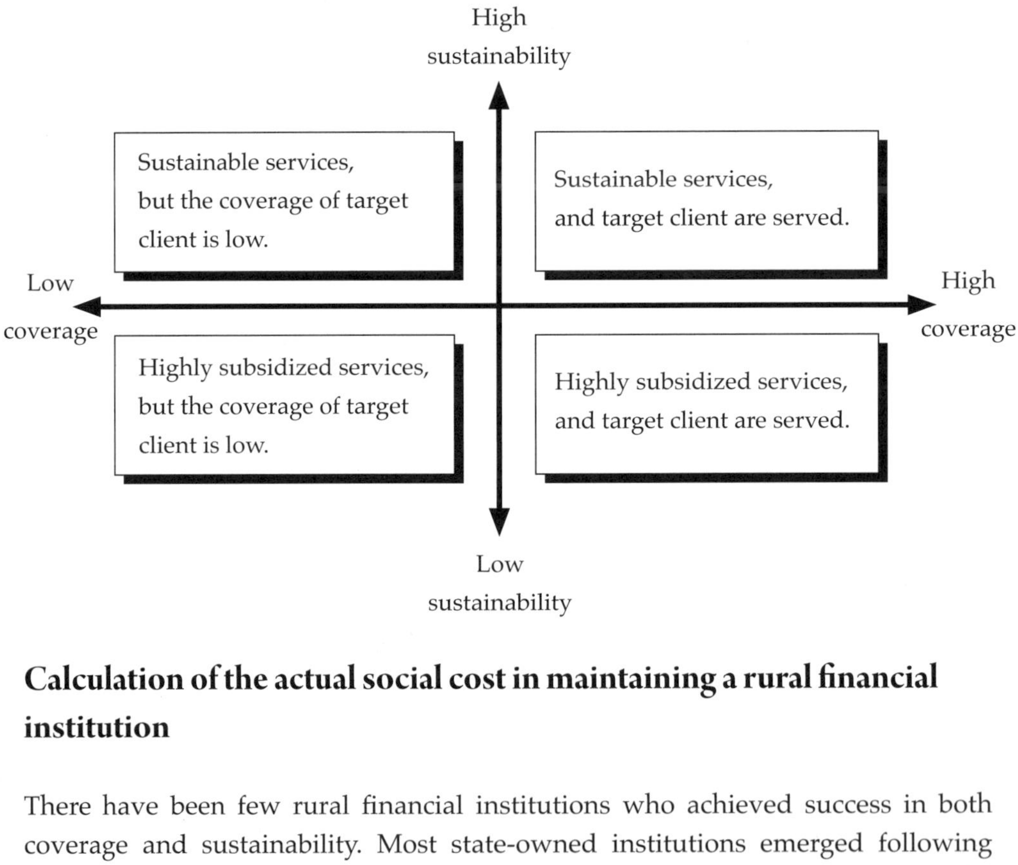

Calculation of the actual social cost in maintaining a rural financial institution

There have been few rural financial institutions who achieved success in both coverage and sustainability. Most state-owned institutions emerged following traditional government intervention. They focus on the issuance, but not the quality, of loans. They are concerned about offering a low loan rate but not offering loans to a larger scope of clients. They worry about the diversity of agricultural production but not the market-oriented rural economy. Their poor performance makes them dependent on subsidies, which takes a heavy toll on the government finances and seizes capital from other departments. The soft budget constraints on state-owned institutions disturb the discipline of finance and their clients, as well as the established institutions and people's incentive to improve the institutions.

To calculate the actual social cost in maintaining a rural financial institution, the subsidies they receive should be considered while evaluating their business performance. Subsidy dependence index (SDI) is a composite index for the evaluation of financial performance. It takes subsidies into account and does not focus on profitability. Therefore, it is more suitable than standard financial indexes. SDI is the percentage increase in the loan rate in a given year if all subsidies are taken away. It can be used in the calculation of the amount of subsidy an institution needs to maintain operation and the relationship between the amount of subsidy and the interest institutions receive from the market. The minimum SDI is –100%, and there is no maximum. When SDI equals 0%, the institution has achieved total sustainability. When SDI equals 100%, it represents that the average loan rate must double before subsidies can be taken away. A negative SDI represents that the institution that is completely sustainable and whose profit is larger than the amount of any subsidies they receive in that year. Such institutions can lower their average loan rate and receive no subsidy but are still sustainable. In some situations, SDI can be viewed as the minimum requirement for raising the loan rate. Under the current interest rate for savings, if the business performance of an institution is very poor, it is very difficult for it to obtain full-funding for any activities.

All subsidies should be taken into account in the calculation of the SDI. The total amount of subsidies is divided by the product of the average loan rate and the annual average loan balance (i.e. the interest income in the profit and loss account). The value represents the percentage increase in interest income required for the institution to cut off all subsidies. According to Yaron (1992), SDI can be calculated as follows:

$$SDI = \frac{S}{LP \times i} = \frac{A(m - c) + [(E \times m) - P] + K}{LP \times i}$$

S = The total amount of subsidies received

$LP \times i$ = Annual average interest income

A = Annual average balance of discount capital borrowed

m = Interest rate the institution needs to bear if there is no discount loans[25]

c = The weighted average interest rate which the institution pays for discount loans

E = Annual average owners' equity

P = Annual profit before tax (Adjusted for the loss of reserve for loans and inflation, etc.)

K = Annual total subsidies received[26]

LP = Annual average loan balance

i = Weighted average loan rate = Annual interest income / Annual average loan balance

Through calculating the extra cost of using subsidies, SDI predicts the actual financial cost of market intervention and sheds light on the survival ability and life expectancy of institutions. SDI helps the government, sponsors, and managers of the institutions to better allocate and utilize resources. First, by externalizing subsidies the institutions receive, SDI calculates the total cost of an institution. This does not imply that the institution has achieved its socioeconomic target or provides a complete cost-benefit analysis. However, it does offer a starting point for the comparison of cost with other public intervention policies (The World Bank 2002).[27] Second, SDI can be used by institutions which provide services to similar clients as a reference for their financial performance and dependence on subsidy. Third, SDI is a tool for the government, sponsors, and managers to plan and monitor the long-term sustainability of institutions. An analysis of the channels and the use of subsidy of institutions can further confirm the value of subsidies (Yaron 1992).

Four factors which help eliminate dependence on subsidies are a suitable loan rate, high rate of repayment, the use of reserve, and the control over administrative cost.

Feature 5–2
International Experience of Agricultural Insurance Development[28]

Establishing the agricultural insurance system is a complicated system of engineering. Experiences of the U.S., Japan, France, India, South Africa, etc., are used as reference.

Choosing the development model based on national conditions

In the U.S., the scale of agricultural production is large and the level of intensive farming is high. The country's export of agricultural products ranks high in the international market. Such advantage is inseparable from the security its agricultural insurance system provides. Since 1922, the government has been exploring a system suitable for the U.S. The federal government chartered the Federal Crop Insurance Corporation (FCIC), which specializes in policy-based insurance of agricultural products. At the same time, the government also devises preferential policies to support private insurance companies as well as mutual insurance companies across states to provide agricultural insurance. In recent years, the FCIC no longer directly provides insurance. It has recruited private insurance companies and agencies for the selling of insurance policies. In the beginning, agricultural insurance was voluntary. The policyholder could choose between FCIC and private insurance companies and also select the policy they preferred. Later, mandatory insurance was introduced.

Agriculture in Japan has the characteristics of decentralization and individual business is of a small scale. The institutions responsible for agricultural insurance are neither the government nor commercial insurance companies. It is the non-profit-making agricultural cooperatives. There is a three-tier system. On the lowest tier are local cooperatives which are responsible for all kinds of agricultural insurance. On the middle tiers are prefectural federations, which support the services of local cooperatives. On the highest tier is the National Mutual Insurance Federation of Agricultural Cooperatives at the Ministry of Agricultural, Forestry, and Fisheries. Mandatory agricultural insurance is required for major crops and livestock which have a strong influence on agricultural income and the public's livelihood. Insurance on other cash crops and pets is voluntary.

France is the second largest agricultural country in the world. It has a well-established agricultural insurance system. Insurance is taken up by self-organized agricultural insurance mutual aid associations. Insurance is totally voluntary. Farmers are policyholders as well as insurers. In 1984, the Assurances Mutuelles Agricoles (AMA) was founded. Agricultural insurance was further developed.

As a developing country, the development of India's agricultural insurance is more difficult. The Crop Insurance Scheme on H-4 cotton and Comprehensive Crop Insurance scheme were abandoned in 1972 and 1985 because the loss ratio was too high. In 1999, the government commenced a new national agricultural insurance scheme. All rural households are covered. The central government subsidizes the development of agricultural insurance schemes and all states organize non-subsidized and state-specific insurance schemes. Judging from the current situation, the new scheme is very promising. Agricultural development is promoted and it becomes an example for developing countries.

In South Africa, there is a high degree of marketization in agricultural insurance. As the economic scale there is relatively large, marketized commercial insurance is affordable. Also, the insurance industry is well-developed and the variety of products is wide, the government seldom intervenes. Instead, it encourages farm owners to purchase commercial insurance to reduce loss.

Guiding and protecting the development of agricultural insurance by the law

All-round legislation is a prerequisite for the development of agricultural insurance. Agricultural insurance is a kind of policy-based and non-profit-making insurance. It is most concerned about the safety of the national agricultural strategies and the stability of the entire economy and society. Therefore, general insurance law concerning commercial insurance is not suitable for the development of agricultural insurance. Agricultural insurance law should echo the goals of the state's macroeconomic policies. Representative examples are found in the U.S., Japan, and South Africa.

During the late 19th century and the early 20th century, some private insurance companies in the U.S. were once engaged in agricultural insurance. However, they all failed because of the small scale, lack of a risk dispersion mechanism, insufficient underlying data of insurance, poor insurance policies, etc. In 1922, the Treasury Department established the department of agricultural disaster insurance and a special commission for research on agricultural disaster insurance. In 1933, Roosevelt's government enacted the *Agricultural Adjustment Act* in an attempt to raise the price which had plunged during the Great Depression. Yet, the droughts in 1934 and 1936 incurred gigantic losses on agricultural products. The *Act* failed to serve its purpose. Later, the executive committee of crop insurance studied the security problems with crop failures. It proposed that the expected cost of the natural risk of agricultural production should be treated as a premium to establish a reserve insurance fund of common property, which could be used to compensate the loss incurred by natural disasters. Rural households would not confine their investment in land and would stop worrying about natural risk. Land resources would be fully and reasonably used. On this basis, in 1939, the *Federal Crop Insurance Act* was introduced and the FCIC was established. The trial of growth-period crop insurance commenced. The *Act* was enacted nationwide in 1980 and it has been amended 12 times. In 1994, the United States Congress amended the *Act*, especially regarding the high loss ratio of successive years. In the end, the *Federal Crop Insurance Reform Act of 1994* was announced.

Japan enacted the *Livestock Insurance Act* in 1929, the *Crop Insurance Act* in 1938, and the *Agricultural Disaster Compensation Law* in 1947. It shows the adjustment of the goal of national macroeconomic policies. The *Livestock Insurance Act* intended to provide insurance compensation for farmers who suffered natural disasters and to resolve the conflict between the landlords and tenant farmers. The *Agricultural Disaster Compensation Law* introduced after the Second World War was intended to encourage agricultural production, reduce the losses in an era of war-time disasters, and guarantee the production and supply of agricultural products. At that time, there was a dire shortage of food. The government cannot import food. In order to stabilize society, it imposed strict price-control, suppressing food production and supply. As Japan quickly finished its post-war reconstruction, the goal of agricultural insurance is no longer to protect the supply of agricultural products. Rather, it is becoming a benefit farmers can enjoy.

The strong marketization of agricultural insurance in South Africa is a result of the policy-making of the government. After the 1990s, the international community started to lift the economic sanctions on South Africa. The pressure of self-sufficiency of agricultural products is relieved. The economic scale is large and the insurance market is mature. Instead of continuing its direct intervention in agricultural insurance, the government encourages farm owners to purchase commercial insurance to reduce the loss they suffer when natural disasters hit. It has announced the *Consumer Protection Act* and the *Financial Advisory and Intermediary Services Act* to reinforce supervision over insurance market entities and to protect the benefits of policyholders.

Scientific design of a risk dispersion mechanism

Choosing the right development mode and legislation are measures to disperse risk. Agricultural production is constrained by natural conditions. Any natural disasters or plague would incur huge loss. Farmers have little awareness of insurance and can hardly afford insurance. They usually do not purchase insurance voluntarily. During the underwriting process, the eligibility of clients of agricultural insurance can hardly be evaluated, and the coverage can hardly expand. The lack of development ability of agricultural insurance directly confines the amount of payouts. In terms of claims, when catastrophe hits, insurance companies have to pay a huge sum of payouts. Their premium income usually cannot cover the payouts. Therefore, an effective risk dispersion mechanism is essential to the long-term development of agricultural insurance. In the international community, risk dispersion is mainly in the form of tax exemption, reinsurance systems, and national fiscal subsidies.

Reinsurance is insurance which is purchased by insurers to disperse the risk of paying compensation. It is especially important for companies providing agricultural insurance. France is one of the representative countries which have set up an agricultural reinsurance system. As the scale of the French Agricultural Insurance Mutual Aid Association is small, it can only bear low risk. The government established an agricultural reinsurance company so that there is one agricultural reinsurance institution in every region. Some of these are reinsured by the Union of Central Funds for Agricultural Mutual Insurance. The Mutual Fund was founded in 1964 and managed by the French Reinsurance Fund. Half the fund comes from the extra premium farmers paid in mutual insurance associations. The other half comes from the national budget. When catastrophe strikes, the Union of Central Funds for Agricultural Mutual Insurance will make appropriations to agricultural reinsurance institutions and the French Agricultural Insurance Mutual Aid Association in order to increase the compensation of farmers. If the amount of loss reaches 60% or more of the insured agricultural products or assets, the Union of Central Funds for Agricultural Mutual Insurance will pay part of the interest (less than 50%) of agricultural loans for the first two years of the Mutual Aid Association.

In recent years, as financial techniques and industrial techniques work more closely together, the variety of financial products widens. Indexation and securitization of agricultural insurance in the capitalist market have become part of the trend. Weather index insurance is an example of such products. This type of insurance connects the volume of agricultural products to the weather conditions in terms of indexes. The insurance contract is based on the indexes. When the indexes reach a certain level, the policyholder (not necessarily farmers) can obtain a corresponding payout. During 1998–2003, the total purchase of weather index insurance in the international market amounted to more than USD16 billion. Relevant products developed by The World Bank are promising in Canada,

Mexico, India, Argentina, South Africa, etc. Moreover, reinsurance companies can use the reinsurance premium as solvency margin and issue weather index bonds. The nominal interest rate of bonds is usually fixed and higher than the average return on investment. The fund raised by reinsurance companies is mainly used in investment in high-grade bonds with fixed returns. During the term of a contract, if no claims are made, the investor can obtain the total principal and interest. The difference between the actual return of bonds and fixed return is subsidized by reinsurance companies. If claims are made, reinsurance companies should extend the contract, or retain a certain amount of, or all, the principal and interest. Funds raised by issuing bonds are used as insurance payouts.

The state should provide essential fiscal subsidies

While tax exemption for agricultural insurance business is possible, even with all-round policies and a reinsurance system, the agricultural insurance industry does not normally earn profit and therefore needs national subsidies. Across the world, the last resort for agricultural insurance is national fiscal subsidies.

The U.S. federal government has the most extensive measures regarding subsidies on agricultural insurance. It provides a different amount of subsidy for all farm owners who purchase insurance. In 2000, the amount of subsidy was 53% of the net premium (on average USD6.6 per acre of land). Those who purchased agricultural catastrophe insurance had all premiums subsidized. In other words, farm owners need not pay premiums and only need to pay USD60 registration fee (impoverished rural households are exempted from this fee). Once their loss of crops rendered their output value lower than the average of those of the past four to 10 years, they would be covered by insurance. When the loss is confirmed and verified, farm owners would be subsidized with 55% of the highest market price in that year announced by the Risk Management Agency. Crop insurance of various risks and income insurance have a subsidy rate of 40%.

The federal government also subsidizes private insurance companies. Companies which offer crop insurance receive government subsidies at 20–25% of their operating cost. The government also subsidizes various costs of crop insurance companies and also the costs of promotion and education.

In France, the government subsidizes 50–80% of the premium rural households have to pay. That means that they only have to pay 20–50%. Agricultural insurance is a kind of government measure. Its administrative cost, deficit of the agricultural insurance fund, etc., are directly subsidized by the government. The total amount of subsidy is within the range of 20–50% of the premium.

The Japanese government subsidizes agricultural insurance in four aspects. First, apart from voluntary insurance, rural households who purchase agricultural insurance receive subsidy on their premium. Second, the expenditure of local cooperatives and prefectural federations is born by policyholders who are rural households. In order to relieve the burden of rural households, the government subsidizes the cooperatives and federations. Third, local cooperatives can purchase reinsurance from prefectural federations, which can purchase reinsurance from the state. The state has a special financial project responsible for agricultural reinsurance. Risk is widely dispersed. At the same time, the government injects fiscal capital to ensure that payouts are made. The ratio of reinsurance and the ratio of payouts born by the government vary according to the policy holders (i.e. the severity of disasters).

It is worth noting that fiscal subsidies cannot replace tax exemption or the reinsurance system. The well-established latter two can greatly relieve the pressure on fiscal expenditure.

Notes

Chapter 1

1. Fei and Ranis (1964) believe that the transfer of labor can be divided into three stages: First, when the marginal productivity of the agricultural sector equal zero, there is obvious surplus labor in rural areas, and its supply is perfectly elastic. Second, when the marginal productivity of the agriculture sector is between zero and the constant wage, there is disguised unemployment. Third, when the productivity in agricultural sector is higher than the constant wage, the surplus labor will disappear, the balance between agricultural and industrial development is achieved, and labor transfer enters a period of commercialization. This states that the root of dual economy is the unlimited supply of labor of the traditional sector (especially the agricultural sector). The key to transformation is the continuous promotion of the transfer of surplus labor from the agricultural sector to the non-agricultural sector.
2. Joint Research Group of Development Research Center of the State Council and Society of Research on the Labor Force in China's Rural Areas 2005.
3. Zhang Jie (2003) believes that the allocation of financial resources in an endogenous financial system is a manifestation of the government's preference and intention in financial control.
4. The World Bank 2002 (see Feature 1–1).
5. Other major channels of capital outflow include the branches or affiliated institutions of the four state-owned commercial banks at or below county level.
6. Although many economists reckon that the dual-sector model has simplified the industrialization process of developing countries in the real world, it cannot be denied that the division of sectors (the economy of a country is divided into modern and traditional, or industrial and agricultural sectors) captures the characteristics of the economy and society of developing countries. It helps us to understand the influence agriculture has on economic development.

Chapter 2

1. It includes rural household loans, rural microcredits, rural household joint-guarantee loans, loans to economic organizations of agriculture, and rural industrial and commercial loans.
2. Of course, the periodicity of the overall financing demand may possess other qualities and character in regard to the actual economic activities the rural households engage in.
3. The assets used as guarantee can be easily transferred from the borrower to the lender.
4. It can be easily turned into cash.
5. The more valuable an asset is to the borrower, the better collateral it is.
6. During the contract period, the collateral cannot depreciate or be damaged.
7. The borrower has to bear certain transaction cost.
8. Mainly rural credit cooperatives. Village and township banks, and lending companies are also involved.
9. At present, if the administration of rural credit cooperatives is fine, the rate of non-performing loans of rural microcredit is extremely low.

Notes

10. City A is a typical agricultural prefectural city in western China. There are 113 townships and 11 counties in City A. The total area is 29,459 kilometer square, of which 187,672 hectares are farmland. The total population is 3.46 million, of which 3 million are engaged in the agricultural industry.
11. Of the sample households, during 2004–2006, 289 households obtained loans or borrowed money. The total number of borrowing amounted to 488, of which 304 were loans from RCCs. The tendency to borrow from RCCs is 62.3%. 171 loans were borrowed from friends or families, and 13 from other channels.
12. See the previous section.
13. When there is lending/borrowing behavior, people are concerned about the execution of contract.
14. Nanchong MicroCred is one of the eight pilot microcredit companies of the People's Bank of China. See Feature 2–1 for further details.
15. Up to the end of 2008, Nanchong Microcred has issued loans amounting to RMB34.16 million. Its loan balance is RMB18 million. It has served 1,908 households. Each households on average obtained RMB23,000 loans. The rate of non-performing loans is 0.9%. It has a profit of RMB0.92 million.
16. Actually here refers to the entire low-end financial market where there is no collateral, guarantee, or credit accumulation.
17. McKinnon (1973) pointed out: "Even the most innovative person has to narrow the space span and selectively study and discuss the policy issues." We think that it is not having doubts about the capability of economists. The definition of constraints is the basis and prerequisite for any economic research, and the definition may become vague. Once the constraints change, the conclusions would be different. We also think that the theory of moral small farmers causes the confusion of the motivation for and the constraints on the behavior of rural households. History, culture, and traditions, regardless of how deeply ingrained they are, can only alter the "feasible choice set" of the economic behavior of rural households. Their basic economic behavior remains unchanged.
18. Surviving small farmers and rational small farmers will be further discussed in later sections.
19. It is estimated that capital outflow from rural areas in China amounts to at least RMB300 billion (Tang Min 2006).
20. This section is co-authored by Prof. Yang Dong of the China Financial Policy Research Center, Renmin University of China.
21. Price (market), authority (the state), and trust (interpersonal network) are three entities which ensure the running of society and economic development. Classical economics has relevant research on the three entities. Neoclassical economics analyze a market with the assumptions of perfect competition, perfect information, and no transaction cost. Authority and trust are neglected, which echoes Hayek's words: "... in the social sciences often that is treated as important which happens to be accessible to measurement." (Ye Chusheng and Sun Yongping 2005).
22. According to Émile Durkheim, the culture of a group is created by a group of people who share the same set of values and style of living. The culture of a community has its own form and structure. Members have the same preference and are encouraged to act within the boundaries of the institutional framework (i.e. collective consciousness).

23. The concept of "social capital" was first proposed by the French sociologist P. Bourdieu. Bourdieu believes that "social capital" is highly productive which brings economic resources to its user, and it is also a form of relationship in the social network. Robert Putnam looks at "social capital" on the collective level. He thinks that "social capital" is constituted by attitudes and the set of values which are relevant to the trust among people, cooperation and mutual benefits. "Social capital" makes people become more cooperative, trusting, understanding, and considerate. There are several definitions of "social capital" in economics. Routledge and Vou Amnsberg define "social capital" as the existence of cooperative equilibrium in the prisoner's dilemma game. Dasgupta thinks it refers to interpersonal network. Fafchamps and Minten defines it as the social network.
24. His study of Longshuitou village in Shanxi Province shows an extremely low rate of non-performing loans.
25. Slater found that the size of the group influences the distribution of interaction. He proposed the index of inhibition. The index increases as the size of the group decreases.
26. We repeatedly asked rural households and RCCs why they did not favor co-guarantee loans. They gave answers such as "troublesome" and "redundant." In fact, much domestic research has shown that rural households encounter difficulties in forming co-guarantee group. For example, Zheng Guiyang (2007) analyzed the gradual fall in the co-guarantee loans issued in Ningde. It is found that rural households seldom participate in co-guarantee group. They participate in groups which would bring them economic benefits. Households that do not share the same type of assets or economic benefits can hardly form a co-guarantee group. The state requires members of the co-guarantee group to not be immediate family members. However, in reality, unrelated people are not willing to guarantee for one another. This regulation does not help promote the loans. It even hampers the promotion.
27. Ancient China implemented the mandatory system of dividing the legacy among sons. This explains why ancient China had more domination over the people than Western countries did during feudalism.
28. Hao Fang (2007) and others have found that rural households misunderstand the credit issued by RCCs as poverty alleviation fund or aid fund due to the influence of the past and the government. They spend the loans on maintenance of lives but not agricultural production. The loans cannot generate income and therefore the rural households cannot repay the loans. Some rural households even refuse to repay or evade repayment.
29. After all, although the state intends to develop policy loans, if the plan does not work, it opts for stability. As a result, rural households expect the state to buy bills in exchange for their support.
30. "Fractured society" refers to the separation of society into two worlds—rich and poor, urban and rural, and upper- and lower-stratum. The fracture is spatial as well as temporal. It is a fracture of the economy as well as society. A fractured society is the co-existence of elements of different times. There is not a mechanism to connect and organize them. Please see details in Sun Liping. 2003. *Fracture: The Chinese Society Since the 1990s*; ibid. 2004. *Disequilibrium: The Operation Logic of Fractured Society*; ibid. 2006. *Gaming: Conflicts of Interest and Harmony in Fractured Society*. The three books are termed the "Trilogy of Fractured Society."

31. Georg Simmel pointed out in *The Philosophy of Money* that value is measured by cash in modern society. Our complex life skills compel us to build measures upon measures until the real objectives which the measures are supposed to serve draw back to the horizon of the consciousness, and eventually below the horizon. In this process, money plays the most significant role.
32. Microcred Group is an investment company whose headquarters are in Paris. It has much experience and a good reputation in managing microcredit. "Microcred" is under its administration. Its mission is to provide financial services to micro-entrepreneurs unserved or underserve the traditional financial sector. By the end of 2011, it has set up microcredit companies in 15 countries, including Mexico, Madagascar, Senegal, and China.
33. "Microcred" would adjust the repayment method according to the business situation of clients who face dire conditions or suffer serious accidents. The loan period may be lengthened or the repayment amount may be reduced or waived.

Chapter 3

1. Marx and Engels think that a small farm economy should have four basic characteristics: (1) Rural households own small pieces of land, which are part of their businesses. (2) Rural households use backward production tools and traditional techniques. (3) Production should be self-subsistent. It depends on natural exchange, not social relations. (4) Low living standards.
2. The theories of social agricultural study include the definition, nature and function of farmers, and small-scale peasant economy, both micro- and macroscopic.
3. Zhang Jie (2007) describes that to rural households and farmers the land is not the only source of income. While they can find a substitute for economic benefits, they cannot find one for traditions, culture, dignity, and sentiments which are deeply ingrained in the land and agriculture.
4. Zhang Jie (2005) thinks that, in China, there has been little balance in the division of limited rural surplus ... Therefore, merely changing the agricultural loan system (such as commercialization) would not help ... In the long run, it would be the increase in income of rural households and the progress of agricultural economy which determine the performance of the reform of the agricultural loan system, not the determination and effort of policymakers.
5. In the first period, people always forgo consumption and make investment in order to expand the output which can be used in consumption in period 2. The x-axis represents the income or initial capital Y and consumption C in the first period. Increasing investment in the first cycle would raise the income in the second period, as represented by the y-axis. Opportunities for internal investment, original capital of the enterprise, and the possibility for the enterprise to obtain external loans are also shown in the diagram.
6. For the explanation on the concentric zones, see Fei Xiaotong (1985).
7. We think that the efficiency of this type of national aid fund should be evaluated in the long run. The fund requires subsidies and fiscal input of the state. Therefore, its return is not realized in the short run. It should be noted that the fund is intended to help rural households out of the dilemma. Once they are not in the dilemma, they would form a virtuous circle by increasing their capital (income) and commercial loans. The potential return is huge. Based on that, we believe that fiscal assistance and policy loans targeting impoverished households are essential and worthwhile. There are a lot

of successful examples in our studies. For instance, Ma, a disabled teenager in County A in City A set up his business of selling duck eggs using policy agricultural loans. He had an annual income of RMB20,000. According to statistics, during 2006 to August 2007, County A input RMB97.23 million of fiscal agricultural capital to support manufacturing flue-cured tobacco, planting of walnuts, mining, and animal husbandry. Some impoverished farmers have made a good fortune thanks to the development of a suitable land system.

8. Of course, in a small farm economy, financial institutions pursuing economies of scale face problems of scattered rural households and small villages and towns, which cause diseconomies of scale. At present, all RCCs are commercialized. Many of them have retreated from remote villages and towns mainly because of the small number of rural households and the economy. The business cannot support the basic operation of a branch. According to our study on one of the counties of City A, a RCC branch needs to issue more than RMB2.5 million in loans to maintain operation. However, some branches cannot achieve the target as they suffer loss and do not receive subsidies. The only rational choice for RCCs which are trying to maximize profit is to retreat from those areas.

9. Quoted in The World Bank (Yaron, J., Benjamin, M. P., and Piprek, G.) (2002).

10. We think that as farmers have accumulated little knowledge, they cannot acquire the techniques or ability to disperse risk or connect with the market. Relevant enterprises should help them develop new technologies through experiments and demonstrations so as to improve their production capability. Research has shown that, whether it is a group or an individual, the development of techniques is constrained by the level of knowledge accumulated. The wider scope of knowledge and deeper understanding of a specific area help improve the ability to learn and the development of techniques. (Kneller, 2005) As the development is influenced by past experience, it is path-dependent and locking. To switch from one area of expertise to another is very difficult. One needs to learn many techniques and accumulate much knowledge. (Winter, 1982; Teece et al., 1997) And one may fail. (Kim, 1999) That means if a farmer who has been growing rice needs to switch to growing wheat, it may be disastrous to his production and life. Quoted in The World Bank (Yaron, J., Benjamin, M. P., and Piprek, G.) (2002).

11. Our field study shows that government participation has significant influence on the rural financial ecology. The rural market is underdeveloped and the level of informatization is low. Rural households and agricultural enterprises make wrong decisions because they do not receive enough market signals. Therefore, there are a lot of constraints solely relying on the market mechanism to promote projects. Effective government participation is important for the promotion of projects as well as a healthy financial ecology in rural areas.

12. There are cases where government participation fails. In our research, in one of the counties in City A, the project of flax growing failed. Due to the poor soil quality, weather, and techniques, the flax fiber produced did not meet the international standard. Another example is the raising of dairy cattle. The project failed because of the government's enforcement of the project against the will of rural households, who lacked the capability. Therefore, the author thinks that financial institutions, rural households, the government, enterprises and other entities in the financial ecology should be supplementary. The government should pay attention to the following regarding its participation: (1) It should oversee everything and transmit market information to rural households. (2) It should

restrict its participation to the ineffective aspects of the market. (3) It should act as a link between financial institutions, and rural households and enterprises.

13. As the reform of the circulation of grain, cotton, and oil deepens, the business of the Agricultural Development Bank diminishes. Even its existence is in question.
14. Adverse selection is resolved by credit rationing in Stiglitz and Weiss's model. Credit rationing means that when commercial banks face an excessive demand for loans, they do not raise the interest rate and increase the supply of deposit. Rather, they reject some loan applications and keep the interest rate low to achieve equilibrium. Although to a certain extent the allocation of capital is inefficient, the credit risk is lowered. Stiglitz and Weiss analyze adverse selection and moral hazard in the credit market to demonstrate that equilibrium can exist in the credit market by credit rationing, which may cause a concave credit supply curve. Raising the interest rate cannot increase the supply of deposit.
15. According to our research, the lender and borrower of this type of super-short-term usury usually know each other and the investment project well. The risk of investment is low and the credibility of both parties is reliable. In our research, there is almost no incident of breach of contract.
16. Unlike the high interest rate of super-short-term loans, the widening of the gap between interest rates under such circumstances is not due to the shortage of credit resources but typical interest rate risk premium. If rural households can obtain loans with a loan period longer than one year with their credibility (including using "rolling loans" to achieve mid- to long-term turnover of capital), they would not go to usurers.
17. It should be noted that in areas where there is little coverage of formal finance (implying that it is less probable and more inconvenient to obtain loans, even those with a loan period of less than a year), the term structure of interest rate of private loans may not be a U-shape, but an inverted U–shape. This is because when formal financial institutions cannot serve their function of financing at a particular time or in a specific region, there would be a change in the mechanism to obtain capital. As the preferred loan or turnover period ranges from six months to one year, if there is not enough supply of loans from formal financial institutions at a certain interest rate, excessive demand would push up the interest rate for that type of loans.
18. This is similar to options mortgage. When rural households cannot repay the principal and interest, the lender can handle (sell) the crops of the borrower. The money gained would be counted as repayment. In some situations, when the revenue of selling the crops cannot repay all the debt this year, the lender has the right to handle the harvest next year.
19. When rural households cannot repay their loans, they provide labor for the lender as repayment.
20. In some sense, using human resources as collateral may give rise to relations of personal dependence. However, our study shows that it is more a manifestation of an economic relationship. Under most circumstances, lenders only demand borrowers to provide labor as a form of repayment in substitution for money. They are not trying to control personal relationships of the borrowers. Of course, the value of labor borrowers provide may be greater than the value of the principal and interest.
21 Quoted from The World Bank (Yaron, J., Benjamin, M. P., and Piprek, G.) (2002).

22. In this type of arbitrage, the loan period is a little bit shorter than that of RCCs', but the interest rate is multiples. As the lenders know the situation of the borrowers very well, there are few problems in terms of repayment.
23. There are international studies which show that usury is common in the rural financial market, and the interest rate is very high. People think the usurers can only cover the operational cost (Bottomlet, 1963). However, the usurers monopolize the market as they possess an information advantage (Virmani, 1982). In an unhealthy market, the price of the loans is higher than the marginal cost of lenders. In terms of the whole economy (relative to the maximization of personal benefits), credit supply is insufficient.
24. In the current state of the agricultural loan market, informal finance cannot be eradicated. Instead of banning it, it is better to disperse it.
25. Institute of Finance and Banking, Chinese Academy of Social Sciences, 2008.
26. There are many thoughts on financial ecology stemming from various schools of thoughts of ecological economics: First, the "environmental view," which comes from early ecological economics. Second, the "combination view," which claims that financial ecology is the combination of finance and ecology. It comes from the view that ecological economics is a marginal school of thought of economics and ecology. Third, the "view of quasi-ecology," which comes from the view that ecological economics is an economic version of ecology. Fourth, the "economic ecology view." This view holds that finance itself is a kind of ecology. It is based on economic ecology or the theory of economic evolution.
27. Here, financial entities refer to the producers of financial products and services. The financial institutions and the financial market directly provide products and services. The decision-making and regulatory financial institutions directly control and regulate the market operation and the supply of services through implementing policies. The financial ecological environment includes two parts. The consumer group consists of residents, enterprises, the government, and relevant foreign bodies. The institutional environment constituted by the economy, society, legal system, culture, and traditions, which influence the formation, operation, and development of financial entities.
28. In its report, the Institute of Finance and Banking, Chinese Academy of Social Sciences stated for the first time the nine factors in evaluating the financial ecological environment of a region. The contribution of factors to elasticity making up 50 medium or large cities (the influence of each factor has on the composite index of financial ecological environment) was analyzed. The influence of each factor on the urban financial ecological environment in the descending order is as follows: legal system (0.19), economic basis (0.18), development of regional finance (0.14), independence of the financial sector (0.12), culture of integrity (0.12), social intermediary services (0.09), social intermediary services (0.07), credibility of enterprises (0.06), and social security level (0.03). The value bracketed is the contribution to elasticity.
29. Some data for Tibet cannot be obtained. Hong Kong, Macau, and Taiwan are excluded due to unavailable data.
30. *China Statistical Yearbook 2008;* China Economic Information Network Database.
31. The level of social credibility is adopted from Zhang Weiying and Ke Yongzhu, 2002.

32. Rural population to total population ratio (P) is calculated using the basic data from the database of China Economic Information Network. P = Rural population/Total population.
33. Institute of Finance and Banking, Chinese Academy of Social Sciences, 2008.
34. County K1 is typical agricultural county. There are nine townships, 23 races, amounting to a total population of 277,000, of which 257,000 accounts for agricultural population. The total area is 2,533 kilometers square, of which 183.33 kilometers square is farmland.
35. Many farmers in County K1 realize that having good credibility would help the village to be graded as a credit village and enter the virtuous circle of "credit development–being credible–benefit the whole village." In some villages, there are a number of villagers who owed RCCs money, which lead to the fact that the village was not graded as a credit village. When they know that they could not enjoy benefits when they apply for loans, villagers and village officials raise money to repay the debts. A leader of a village group said that being graded as a credit village is not immunity because the village is reviewed every month. But it cultivates the habit of making repayments on time in villagers. In the end, the villagers gain.
36. The indexes are assigned with reference to the data collected from questionnaires distributed to RCCs front-line loan officers in 11 counties under the jurisdiction of City A. The progress of setting up credit villages and towns is used as reference. If the process has started, it is assigned the value 3; if only part of the process has started, it is assigned the value 3; if the process has not started, it is assigned the value 0. The final value assigned is a weighted average calculated according to the answers of the loan officer. As a whole, the value reflects the different state of development of financial ecology in various counties.
37. The assignment of indexes is the same as the previous one.
38. In July 2001 County K1 implemented the Rural Credit Cooperatives Microcredit Administration Procedure and started to follow the principle: "voluntary application, targeting microcredit, single approval, no restriction on the use or limit of credit, balance control, unlimited borrowing, quarterly interest settlement, offering revolving credit, repayment at the end of loan period." Since 2002, there have been several reforms, symbolizing the gradual development of financial ecology which relies on the setting up of "credit villages and towns." After that, County K1 put forward the "four cards," assessed the credit villages, expanded the services of RCC from microcredit to more types of credit to satisfy different clients. The assessment of credit villages are "easy to conduct, covers many aspects, with grading and actual benefits."
39. Quoted in The World Bank (Yaron, J., Benjamin, M. P., and Piprek, G.) (2002).

Chapter 4

1. The concept of "effective government" is explained in *World Development Report 1997: The state in a Changing World* (The World Bank 1997).
2. Regarding the use of subsidies in rural finance, The World Bank (2002) stressed that "For private institutions, subsidies should be limited to providing start-up capital, lowering initial transaction cost, and offering training in order to promote the institution's capability and achieve economies of scale and opportunities. Once the rural financial institutions become profitable, they could be partially or wholly privatized."

3. Simeon Djanbov, Edward Glaeser, Rafael La Porta, Florencio Lopez-de-Silanes, Andrei Shleifer (2003) proposed the institutional possibility frontier (IPF): In a two-dimensional space where there is no order and is autocratic. DGLLS outlined how an institution is compromised by disorder and autocracy, which are predominantly caused by the private sector and the government sector, respectively.
4. Area COD represents the effective combinations of institutions dominated by the private sector.
5. Area AOB represents the effective combinations of institutions dominated by the government sector.
6. Zhang Jie (2005b) pointed out that "If we decide that the social cooperation path reflects the long-time and stable accumulation of a particular institution. The intersections of two optimal combinations of institutions E_1 and E_2 should line on SCP_1 and SCP_2, respectively. Any effective combination points deviating from the SCP lines are unstable. In other words, even when the combination points deviate from the SCP lines, it would be temporary. The effective combination of institution would eventually go back to lying on the SCP line.
7. "Matthew effect" was first used in sociology: When any individual, group, or region achieves success or improves, he/it will accumulate advantage and, therefore, have a greater chance to succeed and further improve. Economics borrowed the term to refer to the phenomenon of the rich get richer, and the poor get poorer. In neoclassical economics, the convergence hypothesis in the growth model describes that when there are diminishing returns to capital in developed regions, capital would flow to developing regions in which returns have not started to diminish. As a result, the growth rate of developed regions would fall and that of developing regions would rise, until the growth rates equalize. In reality, however, this is not the case when factors such as institution and human resources are taken into account. Matthew effect is commonly found. Resources in developing regions flow toward developed regions. And the institution in developing regions is less advanced than that of developed regions. They enter into a vicious circle, and the gap between regions increasingly widens.
8. Yang Dong, Professor at The China Financial Policy Research Center (FRC) of Renmin University of China, co-authored this section.
9. Judgment sampling refers to the survey method of first understanding the whole picture before choosing representative subjects as samples.
10. To accurately calculate the total social output, rural households should be audited. Even an in-house survey may not be able to assess the actual amount of capital rural households possess. It is more difficult to assess their income in terms of physical goods. In many representative studies (e.g. Kochar, 1997b; Besley, 1985; Khandler, 2001), an indicator which is more strongly related to credit capital is chosen as substitution variable. Jaynes (1984) and Eswaran (1989) have shown that producers would adjust their plan for purchasing fixed assets with reference to the capital flow. Based on that, we use the change in fixed assets as a substitution variable for the total social output.
11. We discovered in our research that there is a diversity of goods which rural households sell. As there is no suitable price index, we do not include the price of agricultural goods as a vector affecting the fixed assets of rural households. As cross-sectional data are used in the empirical study, the omission of price would not affect the validity of the conclusions.

12. It should be noted that, in China, RCCs are not ordinary cooperative organizations, but established top-down by the government as part of its financial institutional arrangements. They are official institutions, not financial organizations endogenous to the rural agricultural market. On this basis, it is natural for the government (including local governments) to intervene in RCCs. Xie Ping (2001) also pointed out that RCCs have had little cooperative nature since they were administered by the Agricultural Bank of China. They deviated from their mission of serving agriculture and rural households.
13. In this section, subscript p marks the loans to the projects related to the Three Rural Issues, and subscript g marks the loans to the projects favored by the local governments.
14. To local governments who fervently pursue a high growth rate, having more direct or indirect control over financial resources can provide continuous financial support to large-scale projects in order to stimulate the rapid growth of the demand for investment. The local governments think that the cost of doing so can be externalized. For example, when some of the projects fail, the local governments do not always need to pay for the bad debts. They expect the central government to come to their aid. This is because the financial sector is important to the national economy. When projects fail, financial institutions may go bankrupt. To avoid system risk and to stabilize society, the central government would help the local governments by capital injection or by being the lender of last resort. As a result, the local governments expect that financial risk can be externalized.
15. A new wave of reform of RCCs started in 2003. In June, the Stat Council announced the *Notice Regarding Pilot Program for Deepening Rural Credit Cooperatives Reform*. It stipulated that the reform on the administration of RCCs and the property rights system should be accelerated. Property rights relationship should be clear, constraint mechanism should be strengthened, the service functions should be enhanced, the state should provide suitable support, and the government should be responsible. In August, pilot RCCs opened in eight provinces (districts, cities) including Jiejiang and Shangdong Provinces. On August 10, 2007, the last provincial rural credit union opened in Hainan Province, signifying the completion of the new administration framework. The first phase of reform of the pilot program was completed.
16. RCCs receive extra RMB18.7 billion in the form of interest rate subsidy and tax reduction.
17. In the gaming of the state, RCCs, and the local governments, the government has strong control and the strengthening of internal control of RCCs have made it almost impossible for rural households (the shareholders) to influence the development and reform of RCCs.
18. The conclusion is that the reform of property rights is crucial. RCCs should set their primary target as pursuing economies of scale. The establishment of rural finance should be diversified and combined with the reform of systems to solve the problem of historical issues.
19. The incentive scheme is based on the average performance of RCCs, i.e. $w = w_0 + t\bar{R}, 0 < t < 1$. Obviously, under normal circumstances, after taking out the constant w_0, extra bonus given to individuals may be an extremely small proportion of the total expected return, which implies that the value of t is very small.
20. In our study of RCCs in the western regions, we noticed a strange phenomenon. Many managers at struggling RCCs complained to us about how RCCs urgently need more capital and policy support, but they themselves were enjoying luxury, such as fancy cars, expensive tobacco, and high-

end fashion. In many places, the staff of RCCs have a higher income than those at commercial banks at the same rank.

21. On October 15, 2003, in the conference on the reform of RCCs in Jilin Province, the Vice Governor Wang Rulin said that it was a valuable opportunity as the state was using money to "repair" the RCCs.
22. At that time, in order to cash the central bank bills, RCCs across the country all frantically started to issue more shares to raise capital. Through attracting deposits by issuing shares and issuing more loans, the capital adequacy ratio and the non-performing loans ratio improved in a short period of time. By the end of 2005, the value of the total net assets, average capital adequacy ratio, and total profit of RCCs across the country had changed from negative to positive. In addition, the balance of non-performing loans (including RCCs, rural commercial banks, and rural cooperative banks) had dropped to RMB325.5 billion.
23. According to Zhang Jie and Gao Xiaohong (2006), throughout the years, the transformation of village and township enterprises under the direction of local governments caused more than RMB86 billion of non-performing loans in RCCs. Local governments at county and village levels borrowed more than RMB40 billion. Together, they added up to more than RMB126 billion. At the same time, loss and loss brought forward amounted to more than RMB125 billion.
24. Data adopted from *Caijing* (Finance), April 30, 2007, No.184, 40–42.
25. Foreign banks see VTBs as a stepping stone for entering China's financial market. They take it as a long-term strategic move and do not mind the loss in the short run. On December 13, 2007, the first foreign VTB, Cengdu HSBC Rural Bank, was established in Suizhou in Hubei province. It is entirely owned by Hong Kong and Shanghai Banking Corporation (HSBC). It had a registered capital of RMB10 million, which expanded to RMB40 million in March 2008. In March 2008, HSBC established the Chongqing Dazu HSBC Rural Bank, which is similar to that of the Chengdu bank. Australia & New Zealand Banking and the Bank of East Asia have also started their move.
26. Some VTBs issue loans using their own capital so that the loan balance is larger than the deposit balance.
27. In some especially underdeveloped regions, due to the constraints of geography, society, and the degree of openness, farmers have little income and hence very limited idle capital. To a certain extent, it limits the growth of deposits in VTBs.
28. The administration of loans in VTBs and RCCs are the same in nature as it depends on the experience and judgment of loan officers. VTBs have inherited the loan approval system and techniques from commercial banks. Their risk management is not significantly better than other institutions in the rural financial market.
29. VTBs have not been set up for a long time. Compared to RCCs which have been in operation for a long time and have a broader network, VTBs have no advantage in terms of information of rural areas. They may even be in a disadvantaged position. In addition, they have little capital and information. They can hardly compete with RCCs for better clients. Furthermore, as postal savings institutions, the Agricultural Bank of China and Agricultural Development Bank of China change their business concept and expand their services, VTBs face fiercer competition.

30. The balance of capital financed from banking financial institutions cannot be greater than 50% of net capital.
31. But it cannot be exceed the upper limit imposed by the legal department (four times the benchmark). According to *Recommendations on the Handling of Cases Related to Lending of the People's Court* announced by the Supreme People's Court of the People's Republic of China in 1991, as long as the interest rate of private lending is not more than four times the benchmark, it is under legal protection.
32. See *Plan for the Establishment of Pilot Microcredit Companies in Pingyao County.*
33. Capital operation is a concept emerged in China. It refers to pursuing profit maximization and capital appreciation though managing the value. Various types of capital of the enterprise are rearranged with capital from other enterprises or sectors to achieve a dynamic reorganization of optimal allocation of production factors and property structure. The ultimate goal is to achieve a continuous increase in the enterprise's own capital. (Retrieved from http://www.asianbusinessschool.net/zkcmk/bgfx/zbyy.html).
34. The problems here are specific to most microcredit companies across the country. "Meixin" (see Chapter 2) has overcome these problems, which is why it deserves attention and analysis.
35. See "Rural credibility in a transforming society: Changes may be brewing" in Chapter 2.
36. Credit risk may trigger social problems such as repayment with violence.
37. For example, the interest rates of one-month, three-month, half-year, and one-year loans of Sichuan Guangyuan Quan Li Microcredit Company were four times those of the central bank. Calculated with the interest rate at the end of 2008, the interest rate for half-year and one-year loans is as high as 22%.
38. According to *21st Century Business Herald,* while the loan rate is too high for farmers, many microcredit companies have no intention to lower it. On the one hand, there are people who can accept the high loan rate. On the other hand, the cost of loans makes the companies worried of lowering the rate. Zhao Qiong, manager of Sichuan Guangyuan Quan Li Microcredit Company, expressed the idea that the little interest that they earn was not enough to cover the cost of travelling to the doorstep of borrowers who live in remote areas to demand repayment.
39. For example, since opening on July 21, 2008, Sichuan Guangyuan Rong Li Microcredit Company has issued loans amounting to RMB14 million by December 2008, but has not issued any to farmers. The company's data also shows that during April 2006 to December 2008, it issued 51% of loans to microenterprises, 19% to individual commercial households, and 30% to rural households.
40. In Diamond's delegated monitoring model (1984), the law of large numbers should stand in order for risk management to work. When financial institutions build their portfolios according to principles of distribution, under normal circumstances (e.g. the risk distribution of investors is in normal distribution), the probability for a portfolio to fail is usually small, which guarantees that the expected return of financial institutions will be positive. In other words, if financial institutions do not have a portfolio which has normal distribution of market risk but one which has an over-concentration of high-risk investors, the law of large numbers would not be applicable.
41. The *Guidance* stipulated that microcredit companies which abide by the law and have no bad credit record can be transformed into VTBs based on the regulations stated in the *Guidelines for*

Examination and Approval of the Establishment of Village and Township Banks and the *Interim Provisions on the Administration of Village and Township banks.* The transformation should be initiated by shareholders.

42. The pilots of TCC5 project is a sub-project of "Reinforcement of the Administration of China's Fiscal Alleviation Fund" co-developed by the State Council Leading Group Office of Poverty Alleviation and Development, Agricultural Department of the Ministry of Finance, and the World Bank. The project opened on December 4, 2006 in Beijing. Wangcang County in Sichuan province and Ye County in Henan Province are pilot counties. Pilots were selected based on the aims and features of TCC5: (1) The villages have a low average per capita income and a large proportion of poor households. (2) The number of natural villages, distribution of residents, and the number of households are representative. (3) Rural households have potential (natural resources and labor force) in developing agricultural production. (4) The villages are not credit villages approved by RCCs for microcredit. (5) Village Party Branch and Village Committee have good organizational ability. (6) There has been no industrialization project.
43. CBRC's *Document No. 7* stipulates that rural credit union funds are mutual aid banking financial institutions approved by banking regulatory institutions and formed by shareholders including the village (township), residents of administrative villages, and small rural enterprises. They provide deposit, loans, and settlement services for members.
44. A study found that, in the early stages, rural credit union funds with less than RMB200,000 can barely cover their operational cost by the returns of the occupation fee of capital. However, as business expands, the operational cost increases. Returns generated would gradually fail to cover the cost. Therefore, if the capital relationship between rural households and the union funds is unstable, the volume of capital of the union funds would shrink when rural households withdraw. In the end, the development of union funds cannot be sustained.
45. The study shows that under government domination, the rural credit union funds are strongly influenced by the government. Many chiefs of the union funds are taken up by the village leader or the Secretary of the Village Party Branch, and auditors are those who also work in Village Committee. Management is troublesome. Using the method of administration to manage the capital of union funds may cause confusion of responsibilities. As it is almost the same group of people who possess the authority of administration and capital management, they may utilize the capital of union funds as the fiscal capital of the village. The development of the union funds cannot be sustained. Some union funds target professionals or enterprises. They deviate from their aim of providing mutual aid.
46. The success rate of a project is private information of enterprises.
47. Many new rural financial institutions set their annual interest rate at higher than 20%, which is too high for households to bear with their income from agricultural production. Wu Xiaobei (2009) conducted a questionnaire survey on rural farming households in Junlian County, Yibin, Sichuan Province. They asked the subjects about their level of income and the level of loan rate they can bear. Taking into account the market risk and appreciation of agricultural capital, the County Peasant and Workers Department estimated that the yield of input of farming households is around 11.7%, those who are engaged in logistics, industry, or commerce 14.5%. If natural disasters or plague strike, the loss rural households suffer is gigantic. It is hard to imagine how farmers bear an interest

rate of 15%. Wu conducted random sampling on the field staff of seven RCCs in Gong and Junlian Counties. Each field staff member had to face 2,730 households on average. It was found that if the annual loan rate is higher than 12%, the households' demand for loans would fall significantly. If it is higher than 15%, the households do not apply for loans.

48. In the newly prevalent farmers' professional cooperatives (FPCs), the issues with substantial shareholders commonly exist. In some extreme cases, the substantial shareholders control the FPCs. Under the current institutional arrangements, rural households without capital and business and management skills can hardly set up their own cooperatives without the help of the local governments and grassroots organizations. Since the *Farmers' Professional Cooperatives Law* was implemented, those who have taken the lead to set up FPCs are the rich households, businessmen, or agents in the village. They hold most of the shares of the FPCs. Sometimes, one party dominates. Naturally, they are the main members of the institution which administer the FPCs, as well as the heads of the FPC Council. As they are responsible for the daily management of FPCs, they are also responsible for fund-raising for any business activities. Rural households can only rely on them. As a result, there is little democracy in administration and decision-making. The paradox cannot be resolved. If there had not been these substantial shareholders, FPCs could not have been set up. But the domination of the substantial shareholders and subordination of rural households were established in the beginning. Democracy would eventually subside under authority in terms of decision-making.
49. The disadvantages of decentralized management are as follows: (1) The business scale of rural households is too small, the production and transaction costs are too high. The lack of specialization, mechanicalization, and technicalization are hurdles to achieving economies of scale. (2) The industry chain for agricultural products is short. Selling primary agricultural products yields little profit. (3) There is little organization and market information. Farmers continue to produce without considering other factors.
50. See Feature 4–1 for a case study of the hog industry.
51. Adopted from Wu Xiaobei (2009), "Analysis on the Trend of the Short-term Fluctuations of the Market Price of Pork: The Effect of an Imbalanced Chain of Interest on the Stability of the Hog Industry."
52. 1 catty = 0.6 kg approximately.

Chapter 5

1. Rural households are categorized into "surviving small farmers" and "rational small farmers."
2. Huang's conclusions are based on the study of 600 years of historical materials from 1350 to 1850.
3. For further explanation, see Stiglitz and Weiss, 1981 and Diamond, 1984.
4. For example, commercial banks cannot issue credit following the law of large numbers.
5. Even if the lender and borrower are not familiar with each other, there is a middleman who knows both parties well (friends or family members) to help form an agreement between them.
6. It is worth mentioning that some top-down management methods have formed large-scale cooperative organizations. Through reorganizing the internal structure, including division labor

and specialization, a production mode similar to modern production can be achieved. To a large extent, it can reduce the operating cost incurred by the large number of members. At present, there are successful cases of collective production and transformation. The reasons behind the successes are worth studying (i.e. whether they are specific or generally applicable).

7. It should be noted that the government has been issuing discount loans to rural areas. However, due to poor administration and credit rationing, many discount loans were allocated to richer households or used in consumption. The policy could not achieve the expected results and even distorted the allocation of financial resources (Wu Guobao 1997). The low-income group still had to satisfy their credit demand through informal finance.
8. The definition socioeconomic concept of "social capital," regretfully, has been vague in many sociological and economic studies. Here, we give a definition of the concept specific to our area of study.
9. As for the differentiated mode of association, please see Fei Xiaotong (1985).
10. Supporters of "rational small farmers" believe that the basic production behavior of rural households can be explained by the modern theory of entrepreneurship and the formal commercialized financial system can flourish. Supporters of "surviving small farmers" think that the production behavior of rural households does not follow the maximization of return. Taking the historical and cultural factors into account, survival has become natural and inevitable. Any attempt to reform the financial system or administration would be to no avail.
11. In other words, how other factors can be eliminated.
12. Taking the demonstration effect into account (see the section on rural credit and loan preference in Chapter 2), the logic of "let some people get rich first" in China's reform may have specific significance for rural development.
13. In economic literature, cross-subsidization effect refers to the phenomenon in which rural households who have low production ability take a free-ride over those who have high production ability.
14. For the global trends and dynamics of the development of poly-based finance, please refer to Chapter 4 in Joint Research Group, Renmin University of China and China Development Bank, *Kaifaxing jinrong lungang* 開發性金融論綱 (Development Financing) (Bejing: Renmin University Press, 2006).
15. Li Yang (2006) advocated that the reform of policy-based finance and the institutions in the market economy should be in the following directions: (1) It should be a national goal. Policy-based finance should not revolve around the interest of shareholders or be profit-maximizing like commercial finance does. It should focus on the adjustment of the social structure, economic development, social stability, and financial safety in the hope of maximizing social interest, (2) The credibility of policy finance stems from the government. The institutions should not only obtain capital through market competition like commercial financial ones do. They should be allowed public funds, or obtain low-cost commercial capital capitalizing on the government's credit. (3) The administration of policy-based finance should not be the same as that of the government. There should be an internal administration system similar to that of commercial financial institutions. Their business should develop according to the principles of the market economy.

16. Examples are policy-based banks in Germany.
17. China's agricultural insurance showed a typical inverted U-shape from 1982 to 2002. During 1982–1992, the premium increased. In 1992, agricultural premium peaked at RMB817 million, accounting for 2.16% of the total premium. Insurance penetration and insurance density were 0.14% and RMB0.96, respectively. After that, the volume of insurance plunged. In 2002, agricultural premium dropped to RMB500 million, accounting for 0.16% of the total premium. Insurance penetration and insurance density fell to 0.03% and RMB0.64 respectively. At the peak in 1992, the underwriting of grain crop was 4.8%, cash crop 11.1%, cattle for ploughing 3.66%, dairy cows 1.87%, hogs 1.18%, poultry 1.3%, aquaculture 2.5%, and forests 4.59%. The coverage of cash crop is over 10%, and that for other items is below 5%.
18. The natural disasters the plantation industry faces include flooding, drought, pests, and typhoons. Those which the animal husbandry industry faces include avian flu and food and mouth disease. The risk of the agricultural insurance business is very high. The loss ratio is higher than the safety line. During 1982 to 2002, the average loss ratio is 88%. The loss ratio peaked at 119% in 1991, which was much higher than the break-even point at 79%. There were seven years in which the amount of insurance benefits paid was larger than the amount of premium. Insurance companies continued to suffer loss even with tax exemption.
19. Hereinafter refers to non-insurance financial institutions such as banks.
20. Insurance also transforms unqualified collaterals into qualified ones. For example, Insurance transforms large farm animals from assets with uncertain returns to assets with certain returns to satisfy the requirement of the banks.
21. Mainly recruiting commercial insurance companies as agencies, setting up specialized agricultural insurance companies
22. Special catastrophe risk fund can be founded in China in the following three ways: (1) Through fiscal subsidies and financial allocation. (2) Local governments contribute agricultural capital and relief funds every year. (3) Policy-based insurance companies issue bonds to raise funds.
23. The feature is based on the data presented in The World Bank, 2002.
24. Please refer to Yaron, Benjamin, and Piprek (2002).
25. Usually it is the market savings interest rate after the adjustment of the reserve and taking into account the administration cost of managing extra savings.
26. For example, national subsidies or total operating cost.
27. Same as note 24.
28. This feature is based on Chen Yulu and Zhao Wei, "Learning from international experience to improve agricultural insurance," *Qiushi* 7 (2007).

References

Chinese works:

Cai Fang 蔡昉. 2002. *Zhongguo renkou yu laodong wenti baogao* 中國人口與勞動問題報告 (Report on Population and Labor Force in China). Beijing: Social Sciences Academic Press.

Cai Fang 蔡昉 and Yang Tao 楊濤. 2000. "Chengxiang shouru chaju de zhengzhijingjixue" 城鄉收入差距的政治經濟學 ("Political economics of the urban-rural income gap"). *Zhonguo shehui kexue zazhi she* 中國社會科學雜誌社 (Social Sciences in China) 4:11 – 22.

Cao Yuanzheng 曹遠征. 2004. "Zhongguo nongcun jinrong gaige lujing ji nengli fenxi" 中國農村金融改革路徑及能力分析 ("Analysis of China's rural financial reform path and ability"). 2004 Zhongguo jinrong luntan gongzuo lunwen 2004中國金融論壇 (Working paper of 2004 China Finance Forum).

Chen Jianbo 陳劍波. 2007. "Dangqian nongcun caichan zhidu fangai yinhang xinyong kuoda" 當前農村財產制度妨礙銀行信用擴大 ("Current system of rural property hinders the expansion of bank credit") (April 30). http://www.sina.com.cn.

Chen Yulu 陳雨露. 2008. "Fangtan guanyu tigao nongcun shouru shuiping he xiaofeinengli" 訪談關於提高農村收入水準和消費能力 ("Interview on raising the rural income level and consumption ability") (December 11). http://finance.cctv.com/program/jjxxlb/20081211/109268.shtml.

Chen Yulu 陳雨露 and Ma Yong 馬勇. 2009. *Xiandai jinrong tixi xia de zhongguo jinrongye hunye: Lujing, fengxian yu jianguan tixi* 現代金融體系下的中國金融業混業經營：路徑，風險與監管體系 (China's Financial Mixed Operations Under the Modern Financial System: Path, Risk, and Monitoring System). Beijing: China Renmin University Press.

Chen Yulu 陳雨露 and Zhao Wei 趙巍. 2007. "Xuexi guoji xianjin jingyan zuohao nongyebaoxian gongzuo" 學習國際先進經驗做好農業保險工作 ("Learning from international experience to improve agricultural insurance"). *Qiushi* 求是 (Quishi Journal) 7:57 – 59.

Cheng Siwei 成思危. 2005. *Gaige yu fazhan: Tuijin zhongguo de nongcun jinrong* 改革與發展：推進中國的農村金融 (Reform and Development: Promoting China's Rural Finance). Beijing: Economic Science Press.

Fan Jianyong 範劍勇 and Zhu Guolin 朱國林. 2002. "Zhongguo diqu chaju yanbian ji qijiegou fenxi" 中國地區差距演變及其結構分析 ("Variation of China's regional gap and analysis of its structure"). *Guanli shijie* 管理世界 (Management World) 7:37 – 44.

References

Fei Xiaotong 費孝通. 1985. *Xiangtu zhongguo* 鄉土中國 (Rural China). Shanghai: Shanghai Joint Publishing.

Feng Hefa 馮和法. 1934. *Nongcun shehuixue dagang* 農村社會學大綱 (Outline of Rural Sociology). Shanghai: Niming Books.

Feng Xiaohong 馮小紅. 2004. "Zhongguo xiaonong jingji de pingpan chidu: Ping Huang Zhong zhi de 'guomihua' lilun" 中國小農經濟的評判尺度——評黃宗智的"過密化"理論 ("Evaluation of China's small farm economy: Review of Philip Huang's theory of agricultural involution"). *Zhongguo nongshi* 中國農史 (Agricultural History of China) 2:78 – 84.

Feng Xingyuan 馮興元, He Mengbi 何夢筆, and He Guangwen 何廣文. 2004. "Lun Zhongguo nongcun jinrong de duoyuanhua" 論中國農村金融的多元化 ("Diversity of China's rural finance"). *Zhongguo nongcun guancha* 中國農村觀察 (China Rural Survey) 5:17–29.

Gao Debu 高德步 and Lü Zhiwen 吕致文. 2005. "Xinxing gongyehua dui woguo weilai jiuye de yingxiang" 新型工業化對我國未來就業的影響 ("Influence of new industrialization on China's future employment"). *Jingji lilun yu jingji guanli* 經濟理論與經濟管理 (Economic Theory and Business Management) 2:5 – 11.

Gao Fan 高帆 and Qin Jianxin 秦占欣. 2003. "Eryuan jingji fancha: Yige xinxing gudian jingjixue de jieshi" 二元經濟反差：一個新興古典經濟學的解釋 ("Contrast of dual economy in neoclassical economics"). *Jingji kexue* 經濟科學 (Journal of Economic Sciences) 1:97 – 103.

Guo Wenjie 郭文傑 and Yu Ruixiang 餘瑞祥. 2004. "Guanyu gaibian chengxiang eryuan jingji jiegou de duice yanjiu" 關於改變城鄉二元經濟結構的對策研究 ("Research on the countermeasures against the dual economic structure"). *Jingji wenti tansuo* 經濟問題探索 (Inquiry into Economic Issues) 8:7 – 9.

Han Jun 韓俊. 1998. "Guanyu nongcun jiti jingji yu hezuo jingji de ruogan lilun yu zhengce wenti" 關於農村集體經濟與合作經濟的若干理論與政策問題 ("Theories and policies of rural collective economy and cooperative economy"). *Zhongguo nongcun jingji* 中國農村經濟 (Chinese Rural Economy) 12:11 – 19.

Hao Fang 郝芳. 2006. "Nongcun xindai de sikao—Lianbao daikuan de quexian yu chuangxin" 農村信貸的思考——聯保貸款的缺陷與創新 ("Thinking on rural credit—Defects and innovations of group lending"). *Jiazhi gongcheng* 價值工程 (Value Engineering) 10.

He Dexu 何德旭 and Rao Ming 饒明. 2008. "Woguo nongcun jinrong shichang gongqiu guanxi shiheng de chengyin fenxi: Jinrong paichi shijiao" 我國農村金融市場供求關係失衡的成因分析：金融排斥性視角 ("Analysis of the disequilibrium of demand and supply in China's rural financial market from the perspective of financial exclusion"). *Jingji shehui tizhi bijiao* 經濟社會體制比較 (Comparative Economic and Social Systems) 2:108 - 114.

He Dexu 何德旭 and Yao Zhanqi 姚戰琪. 2005. "Zhengcexing jinrong yu xibu dakaifa" 政策性金融與西部大開發 ("Policy-based finance and China western development"). *Jinrong yanjiu* 金融研究 (Journal of Financial Research) 6:17 - 32.

He Guangwen 何廣文. 2001. "Zhongguo nongcun jinrong gongqiu tezheng ji junheng gongji de lujing xuanze" 中國農村金融供求特徵及均衡供給的路徑選擇 ("Characteristics of China's rural financial demand and supply and the selection of equilibrium supply"). *Zhongguo nongcun jingji* 中國農村經濟 (China Rural Economy) 10:40 - 45.

He Guangwen 何廣文, Feng Xingyuan 馮興元, and Li Lili 李莉莉. 2003. "Nongcun xinyongshe zhidu chuangxin moshi pingxi" 農村信用社制度創新模式評析 ("Evaluation of the innovation in the system of rural credit cooperatives"). Database of the Universities Service Centre for China Studies at The Chinese University of Hong Kong:37 - 43.

He Guangwen 何廣文 and Li Lili 李莉莉. 2005. "Guizhou Tongren diqu nonghu jinrong suiqiu yanjiu"貴州銅仁地區農戶金融需求研究 ("Research on the rural financial demand in Tongren in Guizhou Province"). Consultants' report of Asian Development Bank.

He Mingsheng 何明生 and Shuai Xu 帥旭. 2008. "Rongzi yuesuxia de nonghu xindai suiqiu ji qi juekou yanjiu" 融資約束下的農戶信貸需求及其缺口研究 ("Research on rural households' credit demand and its gap under financing constraints"). *Jinrong yanjiu* 金融研究 (Journal of Financial Research) 7:66 - 79.

Hong Zheng 洪正. 2006. "Lun yinhang ye gongsi zhili de teshu xing" 論銀行業公司治理的特殊性 ("Discussions on the particularity of corporate governance in the banking industry"). *Jingji pinglun* 經濟評論 (Economic Review) 6.

Hu Yijing 胡一莉. 2003. "Minjian jinrong yu defang jingji fazhan—Wenzhou rongzi moshi de qishi" 民間金融與地方經濟發展——溫州融資模式的啟示 ("Non-governmental finance and regional economic development—Lessons from Wenzhou financing mode"). *Nanfang jingji* 南方經濟 (South China Journal of Economics) 3.

Huang Guangguo 黄光國. 1988. *Zhongguo ren de quanli youxi* 中國人的權力遊戲 (Power Game of Chinese). Taipei: Juliu Publishing Company.

Huang, Philip C. C. 黄宗智. 1994. *Zhongguo yanjiu de guifan renshi weiji* 中國研究的規範認識危機 (The Paradigmatic Crisis in Chinese Studies). Hong Kong: Oxford University Press.

References

Huang, Philip C. C. 黄宗智. 2000. *Zhangjiangsanjiaozhou xiaonong jiating yu xiangcun fazhan* 長江三角洲小農家庭與鄉村發展 (Development of Small Farm Households and Rural Areas in Yangtze River Delta). Beijing: Zhonghua Book Company.

Huang, Philip C. C. 黄宗智. 2002 *Huabei de xiaonong jingji yu shehui bianqian* 華北的小農經濟與社會變遷 (Transformation of Small Farm Economy and Society in North China). Beijing: Zhonghua Book Company.

Joint Research Group of the Research Group of the Development of China's Rural Labor Resources of the Development Centre of the State Council 國務院發展研究中心/中國農村勞動力資源開發研究會聯合課題組. 2005. "Woguo zouchu chengxiang eryuanjingji jiegou zhanlüe yanjiu" 我國走出城鄉二元經濟結構戰略研究 ("Research on the tactics to resolving China's dual economic structure"). *Jingji yanjiu cankao* 經濟研究參考 (Review of Economic Research) 9:2 – 48.

Joint Research Group of Renmin University of China and China Development Bank中國人民大學與國家開發銀行聯合課題組. 2006. *Kaifa xing jinrong lungang* 開發性金融論綱 (Development Finance). Beijing: China Renmin University Press.

Kuang Jianguo 匡建國. 2005. "Wanshan jinrong shengtai falü zhidu de sikao" 完善金融生態法律制度的思考 ("Thoughts on refining the legal system in financial ecology"). *Jinrong yanjiu* 金融研究 (Journal of Financial Research) 8:37 – 43.

Kuang Yuanpei 匡元培 and Li Ruifen 李瑞芬. 2004. "Hezuozhi yu woguo nongcun xinyongshe de gaige yanjiu" 合作制與我國農村信用社的改革研究 ("Research on the cooperative system and the reform of China's rural credit cooperatives"). *Beijing nongxueyuan xuebao* 北京農學院學報 (Journal of Beijing University of Agriculture) 4:16 – 19.

Li Lianshui 李廉水 and Song Lewei 宋樂偉. 2003. "Xinxing gongyehua daolu de tezheng fenxi" 新型工業化道路的特徵分析 ("Analysis of the characteristics of the road to new industrialization"). *Zhongguo ruan kexue* 中國軟科學 (China Soft Science Magazine) 9:38 – 42.

Li Rui 李銳 and Li Ninghui 李寧輝. 2004. "Nonghu jiedai xingwei ji qi fuli xiaoguo fenxi" 農戶借貸行為及其福利效果分析 ("Analysis of the borrowing behavior of rural households and its welfare effects"). *Jingji yanjiu* 經濟研究 (Economic Research Journal) 12:96 – 104.

Li Shi 李實 and Yue Ximing 嶽希明. 2004. "Zhongguo chengxiang shouru chaju diaocha" 中國城鄉收入差距調查 ("Survey on China's urban-rural income gap"). *Caijing* 財經 (Caijing Magazine) 3.

Li Yan 李焰. 1999. "Lilü yu jumin chuxu guanxi tantao" 利率與居民儲蓄關係探討 ("Discussions on the relationship between china household savings and interest rates"). *Jingji Yanjiu* 經濟研究 (Economic Research Journey) 11.

Li Yang 李揚. 2006. "Guojia mubiao, zhengfu xinyong, shichang yunzuo: Woguo zhengcexing jnrong jigou gaige tantao" 國家目標，政府信用，市場運作——我國政策性金融機構改革探討 ("The nation's goal, the government's credit, and market operations: An investigation into the reform of China's policy-based financial institutions"). *Jingji shehui tizhi bijiao* 經濟社會體制比較 (Comparative Economic and Social Systems) 1:14 – 19.

Li Yang 李揚, Wang Guogang 王國剛, and Liu Yuhui 劉煜輝. 2005. *Zhongguo chengshi jinrong shengtai huanjing pingjia* 中國城市金融生態環境評價 (Evaluation of the Environment of China's Urban Financial Ecology). Beijing: People Publishing House.

Li Yang 李揚, Wang Guogang 王國剛, and Liu Yuhui 劉煜輝. 2007. *Zhongguo chengshi jinrong shengtai huanjing pingjia (2006–2007)* 中國城市金融生態環境評價（2006 – 2007） (Evaluation of the Environment of China's Urban Financial Ecology, 2006–2007). Beijing: China Financial Publishing House.

Lin Wanglong 林萬龍, Zhong Ling 鐘玲, and Lu Hanwen 陸漢文. 2008. "Hezuo xing fan pinkun lilun yu yilong de shijian" 合作型反貧困理論與儀隴的實踐 ("Cooperative anti-poverty theory and the practice in Yilong County"). *Nongcun jingji wenti* 農業經濟問題 (Issues in Agricultural Economy) 11.

Lin Yifu 林毅夫. 2000. *Zai lun zhidu, jishu yu zhongguo nongye fazhan* 再論制度、技術與中國農業發展 (Re-discuss the Institution, Technology and China's Agricultural Development). Beijing: Peking University Press.

Lin Yifu 林毅夫. 2002. "Fazhan zhanlue, zisheng nengli he jingji shoulian" 發展戰略、自生能力和經濟收斂 ("Development strategy, viability, and economic convergence"). *Jingji xue* (Ji Kan) 經濟學（季刊） (Economics [Quarterly]) 2:269–300.

Lin Yifu 林毅夫. 2003. "Jinrong gaige he nongcun jingji fazhan"金融改革和農村經濟發展 ("Financial reform and rural economic development"). Working paper (no. C2003026), China Center for Economic Research.

Lin Yifu 林毅夫. 2004. "Zhengce xing fudan, daode fengxian yu yusuan ruan yuesu" 政策性負擔、道德風險與預算軟約束 ("Policy burden, moral hazard, and soft budget constraint"). *Jingji yanjiu* 經濟研究 (Economic Research Journal) 2:17–27.

Lin Yifu 林毅夫. 2005. *Zhidu, jishu yu Zhongguo nongye fazhan* 制度、技術與中國農業發展 (Revisiting Institution, Technology, and China's Agricultural Development). Shanghai: Shanghai Joint Publishing.

References

Lin Yifu 林毅夫, G. Feder, Lau Juen-yee 劉遵義, and Luo Xiaopeng 羅小朋. 1989. "Zhongguo de nongye xindai yu nongchang jixiao" 中國的農業信貸與農場績效 ("Performance of China's agricultural credit and farms"). *Bijiao jingjixue zazhi* 比較經濟學雜誌 (Journal of Comparative Economics) 13.

Lin Yifu 林毅夫 and Liu Peilin 劉培林. 2003. "Zhongguo de jingji fazhan zhanlve yu diqu shouru chaju" 中國的經濟發展戰略與地區收入差距 ("China's economic development strategies and the regional income gap"). *Jingji yanjiu* 經濟研究 (Economic Research Journal) 3:19 – 25.

Lin Yifu 林毅夫 and Sun Xifang 孫希芳. 2005. "Xinshi, feizhenggui jinrong yu zhongxiao qiye rongzi" 資訊，非正規金融與中小企業融資 ("Signals, informal finance, and financing of small and medium-sized enterprises"). *Jingji yanjiu* 經濟研究 (Economic Research Journal) 7:35 – 44.

Lin Yongjun 林永軍. 2005. "Jinrong shengtai jianshe: Yige jiyu xitong de fenxi" 金融生態建設:一個基於系統論的分析 ("Building financial ecology: An analysis based on system theory"). *Jinrong yanjiu* 金融研究 (Journal of Financial Research) 8:44 – 52.

Liu Mingkang 劉明康. 2007. "Nuli xiaochu xianzhi nongcun jinrong fazhan de qishixing zhengce" 努力消除限制農村金融發展的歧視性政策 ("Eliminating the discriminatory policies which constrain rural financial development"). *Jinrong shibao* 金融時報 (Financial Times) (January 8).

Liu Minquan 劉民權. 2006. *Zhongguo nongcun jinrong shichang yanjiu* 中國農村金融市場研究 (Research on China's Rural Financial Market). Beijing: China Renmin University Press.

Liu Yuanchun 劉元春, and Luo Yübo 羅玉波. 2003. "Wo guo weilai jingji zengzhang de zhidu jichu" 我國未來經濟增長的制度基礎 ("Institutional basis for China's future economic growth"). *Renmin daxue xuebao* 人民大學學報 (Journal of Renmin University of China) 2:34–41.

Lu Lei 陸磊 and Ding Junfeng 丁俊峰. 2006. "Zhongguo nongcun hezuo jinrong zhuanxing de lilun fenxi" 中國農村合作金融轉型的理論分析 ("Theoretical analysis of the transformation of China's rural cooperative finance"). *Jinrong yanjiu* 金融研究 (Journal of Financial Research) 6:1 – 14.

Ma Junlu 馬君潞, Tian Gang 田崗, and Jin Tieying 金鐵鷹. 2003. "Liyi buyizhi yu nongcun xinyongshe de fazhan he gaige" 利益不一致與農村信用社的發展和改革 ("Conflicting interest and the development and reform of rural credit cooperatives"). *Nankai jingji yanjiu* 南開經濟研究 (Nankai Economic Studies) 3:70 – 77.

Pi Tianlei 皮天雷. 2006. "Jinrong shengtai de falü zhidu yanjiu: Jiyu xingzhidujingjixue de fenxi" 金融生態的法律制度研究.基於新制度經濟學的分析 ("Analysis of the legal system in financial ecology in new institutional economics"). *Jinrong lilun yu shijian* 金融理論與實踐 (Financial Theory and Practice) 2:7 – 11.

Qian Shuitu 錢水土. 2006. "Xianyu jingji fazhan zhong de xianyu jinrong tixi chonggou: Zhejiang anli" 縣域經濟發展中的縣域金融體系重構： 浙江案例 ("Restructuring the financial system in the county financial development: A case study of Zhejing Province"). *Jinrong yanjiu* 金融研究 (Journal of Financial Research) 9:148–157.

Qian Shuitu 錢水土 and Lu Hui 陸會. 2008. "Noncun feizhenggui de fazhan yu nonghu rongzi weixing yanjiu" 農村非正規金融的發展與農戶融資行為研究 ("Research on the development of informal rural finance and the financing behavior of rural households"). *Jinrong yanjiu* 金融研究 (Journal of Financial Research) 10:174 – 186.

Qiu Jianxin 邱建新 and Tong Xing 童星. 2006. "Cong minjian huzhu jinrong huodong de wajie kan shehui zhuanxingqi de chengxin weiji" 從民間互助金融活動的瓦解看社會轉型期的誠信危機 ("Collapse of private mutual-aid finance and credibility crisis in social transition"). *Dangdai zhongguo yanjiu* 當代中國研究 (Modern China Studies) (spring).

Research Group of the Institute of Finance and Banking of the Chinese Academy of Social Sciences 中國社科院金融研究所課題組. 2008. "Difang zhengfu xingwei moshi ji qi dui diqu jinrong shengtai de yingxiang" 地方政府行為模式及其對地區金融生態的影響 ("Patterns of behavior of local governments and their influence on regional financial ecology"). *Xin jinrong* 新金融 (New Finance) 3:47 – 48.

Research Group of the Research Center of The Chinese Banker 銀行家研究中心課題組. 2007. "Chuantong nongqu jinrong xuqiu yu jigou buju diaoyan baogao" 傳統農區金融需求與機構佈局調研報告 ("Research report of financial demand and institutional layout in the traditional agricultural area"). *Yinghang jia* 銀行家 (The Chinese Banker) 7:100–115.

Sheng Yongwei 盛勇煒. 2001. "Chengshixing haishi nongcunxing: Nongcun xinyongshe de yunheng tezhen he gaige de lixing xuanze" 城市性還是農村性.農村信用社的運行特徵和改革的理性選擇 ("Urban or rural: Characteristics and decisions on reform of the operation of rural credit cooperatives"). *Jinrong yanjiu* 金融研究 (Journal of Financial Research) 5:119 – 127.

Shi Jianping 史建平. 2004. "Nongcun xinyongshe chanquan zhidu gaige: Lilun, jixiao yu chulu" 農村信用社產權制度改革：理論，績效與出路 ("Reform of property rights of rural financial cooperatives: Theories, performance and solutions"). *Zhongyang caijing daxue xuebao* 中央財經大學學報 (Journal of Central University of Finance and Economics) 1:21 – 26.

Shi Qinghua 史清華. 2002. "Nonghu jiating chuxu yu jiedai xingwei ji yanbian qushi yanjiu" 農戶家庭儲蓄與借貸行為及演變趨勢研究 ("Research on the trends of saving and borrowing behavior of rural households"). *Zhongguo jingji wenti* 中國經濟問題 (Economic Issues in China) 6:66 – 78.

Shi Qinghua 史清華 and Chen Kai 陳凱. 2002. "Qianfada diqu nongmin jiedai xingwei de shizheng fenxi" 欠發達地區農民借貸行為的實證分析 ("Empirical analysis of the borrowing behavior of rural households in less developed areas"). *Nongye jingji wenti* 農業經濟問題 (Issues in Agricultural Economy) 10:29 – 35.

Su Ning 蘇寧. 2005. "Youhua jinrong huanjing, gaishan jinrong shengtai" 優化金融環境，改善金融生態 ("Optimization of financial environment and improvement of financial ecology"). *Jinrong shibao* 金融時報 (Financial Times) (July 13).

Sun Liping 孫立平. 2003. *Duanlie: Ershi shiji jiushi niandai yilai de zhongguo shehui* 斷裂：20世紀90年代以來的中國社會 (Fracture: The Chinese Society since the 1990s). Beijing: Social Sciences Academic Press.

Sun Liping 孫立平. 2004. *Shiheng: Duanlie shehui de yunzuo luoji* 失衡：斷裂社會的運作邏輯 (Disequilibrium: The Operation Logic of Fractured Society). Beijing: Social Sciences Academic Press.

Sun Liping 孫立平. 2006. *Boyi: Duanlie shehui de liyi chongtu yu hexie* 博弈：斷裂社會的利益衝突與和諧 (Gaming: Conflicts of Interest and Harmony in Fractured Society). Beijing: Social Sciences Academic Press.

Tan Ying 譚英, Wang Dehai 王德海, and Xie Yongcai 謝詠才. 2004. "Pinkun diqu nonghu xinshi huoqu qudao yu qingxiangxing yanjiu" 貧困地區農戶資訊獲取管道與傾向性研究 ("Research on the information channels and tendency of rural households in impoverished areas"). *Nongye jishu yanjiu* 農業技術研究 (Journal of Agritechnical Economics) 2:28 – 33.

Tang Min 湯敏. 2006. "Nongcun jinrong wanquan keyi shangye hua" 農村金融完全可以商業化 ("Rural finance definitely could be commercialized"). *Chongguo jingji baogao* 中國經濟報告 (China Economic Report). http://finance.sina.com.cn/economist/jingjixueren/20060427/16272536388.shtml.

Tao Ran 陶然, Liu Mingxing 劉明興, and Zhang Qi 章奇. 2003. "Zhongguo nongcun shuifei futan: Yige zhengzhijingjixue de fenxi" 中國農村稅費負擔: 一個政治經濟學的分析 ("Tax burden in China's rural areas: Analysis in political economics"). *Zhongguo shehui kexue pinglun* 中國社會科學評論 (Chinese Social Sciences Today) 1.

Wang Jiangui 王檢貴. 2002. *Laodong yu ziben shuangchong guosheng xia de jingji fazhan* 勞動與資本雙重過剩下的經濟發展 (Economic Development Under the Double Surpluses of Labor and Capital). Shanghai: Shanghai Renmin Chubanshe.

Wang Shaoping 王少平, and Li Zinai 李子奈. 2001. "Hekeman yu maikefadeng de kexue gongxian—Jiedu 2000 nian nuobeier jiangjixue jiang" 赫克曼與麥克法登的科學貢獻——解讀2000年諾貝爾經濟學獎 ("Scientific contributions of Heckman and McFadden—Interpreting the 2000 Nobel Prize in Economics"). *Tongji yanjiu* 統計研究 (Statistical Research) (4).

Wang Shuguang 王曙光. 2006. *Nongcun jinrong yu xinnongcun jianshe* 農村金融與新農村建設 (Rural Finance and New Rural Construction). Beijing: Huaxia Publishing House.

Wang Shuguang 王曙光. 2008. "Nongxinshe gaige: Ying zunxun de ba da yuanze yu weilai gaige fangxiang tantao" 農信社改革：應遵循的八大原則與未來改革方向探討 ("Reform of rural credit cooperatives: Eight principles and future reform orientation"). *Zhongguo nongcun xinyong hezuo* 中國農村信用合作 (Rural Credit Cooperative of China) 9.

Wen Tao 溫濤, Ran Guanghe 冉光和, and Hong Deping 熊德平. 2005. "Zhongguo jinrong fazhan yu nongmin shouru zengzhang" 中國金融發展與農民收入增長 ("Development of China's rural finance and rural income growth"). *Jingji yanjiu* 經濟研究 (Economic Research Journal) 9:30 – 43.

Wen Tiejun 溫鐵軍. 1994. "Nongcun hezuo jingrong gaige shiyan yanjiu baogao" 農村合作金融改革試驗研究報告 ("Research report on the pilot reform of rural cooperative finance"). *Zhongguo nongcun jingji* 中國農村經濟 (China Rural Economy) 1:40 – 46.

Wen Tiejun 溫鐵軍. 2001. "Nonghu xinyong yu minjian jiedai yanjiu (Zhu baogao)" 農戶信用與民間借貸研究（主報告）("Research on rural households' credibility and private lending [Main report]"). *Zhongguo jingji xinxi wang 50 ren luntan* 中國經濟信息網50人論壇 (50 forum, China Economic Information Network) (June 7).

Wen Tiejun 溫鐵軍. 2004. "Nongcun de zhen wenti shi shenme?" 農村的真問題是什麼？("What's the real question in the rural area?"). http://www.sdny.gov.cn/art/2004/9/7/art_1794_31277.html.

Wu Guobao 吳國寶. 1997. "Fupin tieshi daikuan zhengce taolun" 扶貧貼息貸款政策討論 ("Discussion on the policies of poverty-relief discount loans"). *Zhongguo nongcun guancha* 中國農村觀察 (China Rural Survey) 4:7 – 13.

Wu Xiaobei 吳小北. 2009. "Zhurou shichang duanqi jiage buodong qushi: Bu junhengde liyilian dui zhurou shichang wending xing de yiangxiang" 豬肉市場短期價格波動趨勢：不均衡的利益鏈對豬肉市場穩定性的影響 ("Analysis on the trend of the short-term fluctuations of the market price of pork: The effect of an imbalanced chain of interest on the stability of the hog industry"). Zhongguo renmin yinhang Chengdu fenghang gongzuo wenjian 中國人民銀行成都分行工作文件 (Working Paper of People's Bank of China Chendu Branch).

Wu Zhong 吳忠, Cao Hongmin 曹洪民, and Lin Wanlong et al. 林萬龍 等. 2008. *Fupin huzhu zijin yilong moshi yu xin shiqi nongcun fan pinkun* 扶貧互助資金儀隴模

式與新時期農村反貧困 (Yilong County Mode of Poverty Alleviation Funds and the Anti-Poverty of the New Century). Beijing: China Agriculture Press.

Xie Ping 謝平. 2001. "Zhongguo nongcun xinyong hezuoshe tizhi gaige de zenglun" 中國農村信用合作社體制改革的爭論 ("Debate about the reform of the systems of China's rural credit cooperatives"). *Jinrong yanjiu* 金融研究 (Journal of Financial Research) 1:1 – 13.

Xie Ping 謝平, Xu Zhong 徐忠, Cheng Zhongjiang 程總江, and Shen Minggao 沈明高. 2005. "Jianli kechixu de nongcun jinrong kuangjia—Zhongguo nongcun jinrong xuqiu yu gongji yanjiu" 建立可持續的農村金融框架——中國農村金融需求與供給研究 ("Establishing a Sustainable Framework for Rural Finance: China's Rural Financial Demand and Supply"). Yazhou kaifa yinhang yanjiu baogao 亞洲開發銀行研究報告 (Report of Asian Development Bank) (April).

Xie Ping 謝平, Xu Zhong 徐忠, and Shen Mingao 沈明高. 2005. "Nongxinshe gaige deshi diaocha" 農信社改革得失調查 ("Research on reform of rural credit cooperatives"). *Caijing* 財經 (Caijing) 25.

Xie Taifeng 謝太峰. 2006. "Guanyu jinrong shengtai neihan yu pingjia biaozhun de xikao" 關於金融生態內涵與評價標準的思考 ("Thoughts on the evaluation standards of financial ecology"). *Jinrong lilun yu shijian* 金融理論與實踐 (Financial Theory and Practice) 4:26 – 28.

Xu Nojin 徐諾金. 2005. "Lun woguo de jintong shengtai wenti" 論我國的金融生態問題 ("Discussion on issues of China's financial ecology"). *Jinrong yanjiu* 金融研究 (Journal of Financial Research) 2:35 – 45.

Xu Zhong 徐忠 and Cheng Enjiang 程恩江. 2004. "Lilü zhengce, nongcun jinrong jigou xinwei yu nongcun xindai duanque" 利率政策，農村金融機構行為與農村信貸短缺 ("Interest rate policies, behavior of rural financial institutions, and shortage of rural credit"). *Jinrong yanjiu* 金融研究 (Journal of Financial Research) 12:34 – 44.

Ye Jianliang 葉建亮. 2003. "Jingjixue shiyeli de xinyong: Yi ge wenxian zongshu" 經濟學視野裡的信用.一個文獻綜述 ("A literature review of credit in economics"). *Zhongguo shehui kexue pinglun* 中國社會科學評論 (Chinese Social Sciences Review) 2.

Ye Jingzhong 葉敬忠. 2004. "Shehuixue shijiao de nonghu jinrong suiqiu yu nongcun jinrong gongji" 社會學視角的農戶金融需求與農村金融供給 ("Rural financial demand and supply in sociology"). *Zhongguo nongcun jingji* 中國農村經濟 (Chinese Rural Economy) 8:31 – 37.

Yi Xiangrong 易憲容 and Lu Ting 盧婷. 2006. "Jichuxing zhidu shi jinrong shenfdai de hexin" 基礎性制度是金融生態的核心 ("The basic system is at the core of financial ecology"). *Jingji tizhi gaige* 經濟體制改革 (Reform of the Economic System) 2:47 – 54.

Zeng Yinchu 曾寅初. 2004. "Nongcun laodongli de zhuanyi yu jngji jiegou taiozheng" 農村勞動力的轉移與經濟結構調整 ("Transfer of labor force and adjustments of the economic structure in rural areas"). In *Zhongguo renmin daxue zhongguo jingji fazhan baogao* 中國人民大學中國經濟發展報告 (Report of Renmin University of China on China's economic development), edited by Ji Baocheng and Yang Ruilong. Beijing: China Renmin University Press.

Zeng Yinchu 曾寅初. 2005. "Jiasu fazhanzhong de nongcun shengyu laodongli zhuanyi yu eryuan jingji zhuanxing" 加速發展中的農村剩餘勞動力轉移與二元經濟轉型 ("Acceleration of the transfer of surplus rural labor forces and the transformation of the dual economy"). In *Zhongguo renmin daxue zhongguo jingji fazhan baogao* 中國人民大學中國經濟發展報告 (Report of Renmin University of China on China's economic development), edited by Ji Baocheng and Yang Ruilong. Beijing: China Renmin University Press.

Zeng Yinchu 曾寅初. 2006. *Zhongguo renmin daxue zhongguo jingji fazhan yanjiu baogao* 中國人民大學中國經濟發展研究報告 (Research Report of China's Economic Development by Renmin University of China). Beijing: Renmin University of China.

Zhang Changyong 張常勇. 2004. "Huang Zongzhi 'guomihua' lilun tantao shuping" 黃宗智"過密化"理論探討述評 ("Review of Philip Huang's theory of agricultural involution"). *Zhongguo nongshi* 中國農史 (Agricultural History of China) 1:113 – 118.

Zhang Jianghua 張江華. 2004. "Gongfenzhixia xiaonong de jingji xingwei: Dui Qiayanofu jiaoshuo de yanzheng yu buchong" 工分制下小農的經濟行為：對恰亞諾夫假說的驗證與補充 ("Small farmer's behavior under the work-point system: Examination of Chayanov's hypothesis"). *Shehuixue ynajiu* 社會學研究 (Sociological Studies) 6.

Zhang Jie 張傑. 1998. "Erchong jiegou yu zhidu yanjin: Dui Zhongguo jingjishi de yizhong xin dechangshixing jieshi" 二重結構與制度演進:對中國經濟史的一種新的嘗試性解釋 ("Evolution of the dual structure and system: A new attempt at explanation of China's economic history"). *Shehui kexue zhanxian* 社會科學戰線 (Social Science Front) 6:12 – 25.

Zhang Jie 張傑. 2000. "Minying jingji de jinrong kunjing yu rongzi cixu" 民營經濟的金融困境與融資次序 ("English financial difficulties and financing sequences of private economy"). *Jingji yanjiu* 經濟研究 (Economic Research Journey) 4.

Zhang Jie 張傑. 2003. *Zhongguo nongcun jinrong zhidu, jiegou, bianqian, yu Zhengce* 中國農村金融制度,結構,變遷與政策 (Financial Institution of Rural China: Structure, Change, and Policy). Beijing: China Renmin University Press.

Zhang Jie 張傑. 2004. "Jiedu zhongguo nongdai zhidu" 解讀中國農貸制度 ("On China's rural credit system"). *Jinrong yanjiu* 金融研究 (Journal of Financial Research) 2.

Zhang Jie 張傑. 2005a. "Nonghu, guojia yu zhongguo nongdai zhidu: Yige zhangqi shijiao" 農戶、國家與中國農貸制度：一個長期視角 ("Rural households, the state, and the agricultural loan system: A long-term perspective"). *Jinrong yanjiu* 金融研究 (Journal of Financial Research) 2:1 – 12.

Zhang Jie 張傑. 2005b. "Jiujing shi shenmo juedingle yiguo yinhang zhidu de xuanze" 究竟是什麼決定了一國銀行制度的選擇 ("What determine the banking system of a nation?"). *Huobi jinrong pinglun* 貨幣金融評論 (Money and Finance Review) 7,8:1 – 18.

Zhang Jie 張傑. 2006. "Zhuzi boyi yu zhongguo nongxinshe gaige" 注資博弈與中國農信社改革 ("Game in capital injection and reform of rural credit union System). *Jinrong yanjiu* 金融研究 (Journal of Financial Research) 3.

Zhang Jie 張傑. 2007. *Zhongguo nongcun jinrong zhidu tiaozheng de jixiao: Jinrong xuqiu shijiao* 中國農村金融制度調整的績效：金融需求視角 (Performance of the Financial System Adjustment in Rural China: Demand Perspective). Beijing: China Renmin University Press.

Zhang Jie 張傑 and Gao Xiaohong 高曉紅. 2006. "Zhuzi boyi yu zhongguo nongxinshe gaige" 注資博弈與中國農信社改革的邏輯 ("Game in capital injection and reform of rural credit union system). *Jinrong yanjiu* 金融研究 (Journal of Financial Research) 3.

Zhang Jie 張傑, Xie Xiaoxue 謝曉雪, and Zhang Shumin 張淑敏. 2005. "Zhongguo nongcun jinrong fuwu: Jinrong suiqiu yu zhidu gongji" 中國農村金融服務：金融需求與制度供給 ("China's rural financial services: Financial demand and system supply"). Zhongguo renmin dauxe caizheng jinrong zhengce yanjiu zhongxin gongzuo lunwen 中國人民大學財政金融政策研究中心工作論文 (Working paper of China Financial policy Research Center of Renmin University of China).

Zhang Jun 張軍. 1997. "Gaigehou zhongguo nongcun de fei zhenggui jinrong bumen: Wenzhou anli" 改革後中國農村的非正規金融部門：溫州案例 ("The informal financial sector after reform: A case study of Wenzhou"). *Zhongguo shehui kexue* (Qiuji) 中國社會科學（秋季） (Social Sciences in China [autumn]).

Zhang Jun 張軍. 2005. "Jinrong gaige yu nongcun jinrong shichang fazhan" 金融改革與農村金融市場發展 ("Financial reform and development of the rural financial market"). *Zhongguo fazhan* 中國發展 (China Development) 2:59 – 69.

Zhang Qi et al. 章奇 等. 2004. "Zhongguo jinrong zhongjie yu chengxiang shouru chaju" 中國的金融仲介發展與城鄉收入差距 ("Development of financial intermediaries and the urban-rural income gap"). *Zhongguo jinrongxue zazhi* 中國金融學雜誌 (China Journal of Finance) 3:62–76.

Zhang Weiying 張維迎. 2003. *Xinshi, xinren yu falü* 資訊，信任與法律 (Signals, Trust, and the Law). Shanghai: Shanghai Joint Publishing.

Zhang Weiying 張維迎. 2004. *Boyilun yu xinshijingjixue* 博弈論與資訊經濟學 (Game Theory and Information Economics). Shanghai: Shanghai People's Publishing House.

Zhang Weiying 張維迎 and Ke Rongzhu 柯榮住. 2002. "Xinren ji qi jieshi: Laizi Zhongguo de kuasheng diaocha fenxi" 信任及其解釋：來自中國的跨省調查分析 (Trust and its explanation: A survey across provinces in China). *Jingji yanjiu* 經濟研究 (Economic Research Journal) 10:59 – 70.

Zhao Gang 趙岡. 2005. "Shengchan hanshu yu nongshi yanjiu—Ping Peng Huang dabianlun"生產函數與農史研究——評彭黃大辯論 ("Production function and research on agricultural history—Review on the debate between Peng Mulan and Philip Huang"). *Zhongguo shehui jingji shi yanjiu* 中國社會經濟史研究 (The Journal of Chinese Social and Economic History) 1:34 – 37.

Zheng Guiyang 鄭桂楊. 2007. "Dui ningde shi nonghu lianbao daikuan qingkuang de diaocha yu sikao" 對寧德市農戶聯保貸款情況的調查與思考 ("Survey and reflection on households' group lending in Ningde"). *Fujian jinrong* 福建金融 (Fujian Finance) 12.

Zheng Yefu 鄭也夫. 2001. *Xinren Lun* 信任論 (Trust Theory). Beijing: China Radio and Television Publishing House.

Zheng Yafu 鄭也夫. 2003. *Zhongguo shehuizhong de xinren* 中國社會中的信任 (Trust in Chinese Society). Beijing: China City Press.

Zhong Hanxiao 鐘含笑 and Tang Li 湯荔. 2003. "Xinxi moxing: Nongcun jinrong jigou shousuo yingxiang de youxiao jieshi" 資訊模型：農村金融機構收縮影響的有效解釋 (Information model: Effective explanations to the shrink of rural financial institutions"). *Zhongguo jinrong jia* 中國金融家 (China Financialyst) 1.

Zhou Xiaochuan 周小川. 2004. "Wanshan falü zhidu, gaijin jinrong shengtai" 完善法律制度，改進金融生態 ("Refining the legal system and improving financial ecology"). http://www.pbc.gov.cn/.

Zhou Xiaochuan 周小川. 2005. "Dazao jiankang de jinrong shengtai huanjing" 打造健康的金融生態環境 ("Building a healthy environment in financial ecology"). http://www.pbc.gov.cn/.

Zhu Shouyin 朱守銀. 2003. "Zhongguo nongcun jinrong shichang gongji yu suiqiu" 中國農村金融市場供給與需求 ("China's rural financial demand and supply"). *Guanli shijie* 管理世界 (Management World) 3:88 – 95.

Zhuo Kai 卓凱. 2001. "Zhongguo jinrong fazhan yu jingji zengzhang" 中國金融發展與經濟增長 ("China's financial development and economic growth"). Working paper. http://old.cenet.ccer.edu.cn/fencai/xinganxian/child.

Translated works:

Baker, G. S. 1998. *Jiating lun* 家庭論 (A Treatise on the Family). Trans. Wang Xiansheng and Wang Yu. Beijing: The Commercial Press.

Duara, Prasenjit. 2004. *Wenhua, quanli yu guojia* 文化、權力與國家 (Culture, Power, and the State: Rural North China, 1900 – 1942). Trans. Wang Fuming. Jiangsu: Jiangsu People's Publishing House.

Ellis, F. 2006. *Nongminjingjixu—Nongmin jiating nongye he nongye fazhan* 農民經濟學—農民家庭農業和農業發展 (Peasant Economics: Farm Households in Agrarian Development). Trans. Hu Jingbei. Shanghai: People's Publishing House.

Fukuyama, F. 2001. *Xinren: Shehui meide yu chuangzao jingji fanrong* 信任：社會美德與創造經濟繁榮 (Trust: The Social Virtues and the Creation of Prosperity). Trans. Peng Zhihua. Hainan: Hainan Publishing House.

Hayami, Yujiro. 2003. *Fazhanjingjixue—Cong pinkun dao fuyu* 發展經濟學—從貧困到富裕 (Development Economics: From the Poverty to the Wealth of Nations). Trans. Li Zhou. Beijing: Social Sciences Academic Press (China).

Johnson, D. G. 2004. *Jingji fazhanzhong de nongye, nongcun, nongmin wenti* 經濟發展中的農業、農村、農民問題 (Economic Development Issues in the Agricultural and Rural Farmers). Trans. Lin Yifu. Beijing: The Commercial Press.

McKinnon, R. I. 1998. *Jingji fazhanzhnog de huobi he ziben* 經濟發展中的貨幣與資本 (Money and Capital in Economic Development). Trans. Lu Cong. Shanghai: Shanghai Joint Publishing.

McKinnon, R. I. 2006. *Jingji fazhan zhong de huobi yu ziben* 經濟發展中的貨幣與資本 (Money and Capital in Economic Development). Trans. Li Yao, Lu Liping, and Chen Yulu. Beijing: China Financial Publishing House.

Myers, R. H. 1999. *Zhongguo nongmin jingji: Hebei he Shandong de nongye fazha* 中國農民經濟:河北和山東的農業發展 (The Chinese Peasant Economy: Agricultural Development in Hopei and Shantung. Trans. Shi Jianyun. Jiangsu: Jiangsu People's Publishing House.

Schultz, T. 1987. *Gaizao chuantong nongye* 改造傳統農業 (Transforming Traditional Agriculture). Trans. Liang Xiaomin. Beijing: The Commercial Press.

Scott, J. C. 2001. *Nongmin de daoyijingjixue: Dongnanya de fanpan yu shengcun* 農民的道義經濟學：東南亞的反叛與生存 (Moral Economy of the Peasant: Rebellion and Subsistence in South East Asia). Trans. Cheng Lixian and Liu Jian. Jiangsu: Yilin Press.

Skinner, G. W. 1998. *Zhongguo nongcun de shichang he shehui jiegou* 中國農村的市場和社會結構 (Marketing and Social Structure in Rural China). Trans. Shi Jianyun. Beijing: China Social Science Press.

The World Bank (Yaron, J., Benjamin, M. P., and Piprek, G.). 2002. "Noncun jinrong: Wenti, sheji he zuijie zuofa" 農村金融：問題、設計和最佳做法 ("Rural finance: Issues, designs, and best practices"). Reading materials in China's Rural Finance Seminar.

Weber, Max. 2003. *Zhongguo de zongjiao: Yujiao yu daojiao* 中國的宗教：儒教與道教 (The Religion of China: Confucianism and Taoism). Trans. Hong Tianfu. Jiangsu People's Publishing House.

English works:

Abiad, A. G. 1988. "Borrowing Transaction Costs and Credit Rationing in Rural Financial Markets: The Philippine Case." Working Paper Series of Philippine Institution for Development Studies, No.88–117.

Aerderson, D., and F. Khambata. 1985. "Financing Small-scale Industry and Agriculture in Developing Countries: The Metrits and Limitations of 'Commercial' Policy." *Economic Development and Cultural Change* 33:349–371.

Arrow, K. J. 1962. "The Economic Implications of Learning by-Doing." *The Review of Economic Studies* 29(3):155–73.

Asian Development Bank. 2000. ADB Annual Report. http://www.adb.org/documents/series/adb-annual-reports.

Bardhan, P. K., and C. Udry. 1999. *Development Microeconomics*. New York: Oxford University Press.

Barro, R. J. and Sala-i-Martin, X. 1991. "Convergence across States and Regions." Brooking Papers on Economic Activity, 1:107–182.

Barro, R. J. and Sala-i-Martin, X. 1992. "Convergence." *Journal of Political Economy* 100 (2):223–251.

Becker, G. S. 1981. *A Treatise on the Family*. Cambridge, MA: Harvard University Press.

Bell, C. 1990. "Interactions between Institutional and Informal Credit Agencies in Rural India." *The World bank Economic Review* 4(3):297 – 327.

Besley, Timothy. 1994. "How Do Market Failures Justify Interventions in Rural Credit Markets." *World Bank Research Observer* 9(1):27 – 47.

Bhattacharyya, S. 2005. "Interest Rates, Collateral and De-Interlinkage: A Micro-Study of Rural Credit in West Bengal." *Cambridge Journal of Economics* 29:439–62.

References

Binswanger, H. P. 1980. "Attitudes toward Risk: Experimental Measurement in Rural India." *American Journal of Agricultural Economics* 62:395–407.

Bohnet, I., and Zeckhauser, R. 2004. "Trust, Risk and Betrayal." *Journal of Economic Behavior and Organization* 55:467–484.

Bose, P. 1998. "Formal-informal Sector Interaction in Rural Credit Markets." *Journal of Development Economics* 56:265–80.

Brandt, L., A. Park, and Wang Sangui. 2001. "Are China's Financial Reforms Leaving The Poor Behind?" Praper presented at the conference on Financial Sector Reform in China (Sep11–13).

Braverman, A. 1981. "Credit and Sharecropping in Agrarain Societies." *Journal of Development Economics* 9:289–312.

Braverman, A. 1986. "Rural Credit Markets and Institution in Development Countries: Lessons for Policy Analysis from Practice and Modern Theory." *World Development* 14:1253–1267.

Braverman, A. 1989. *Institutional Analysis of Credit Cooperatives: The Economics Theory of Agrarian Institutions.* New York: Oxford University Press.

Carpenter, J. P., A. G. Daniere, and L. M. Takahashi. 2004. "Cooperation, trust, and social capital in Southeast Asian urban slums." *Journal of Economic Behavior and Organization* 55:533–551.

Caselli, F. and W. J. Coleman. 2001. "The U.S. Structural Transformation and Regional Convergence: A Reinterpretation." *Journal of Political Economy* 109:587–616.

Chayanov, A. V. 1986. *The Theory of Peasant Economy.* Madison: University of Wisconsin Press.

Cohen, W. 1990. "An analysis of Representation Shift in Concept Learning." Proc. Seventh International Conference on Machine Learning, Austin, Texas, 104–112.

Cull, R. 2000. "Bureaucrats, State Banks, and the Efficiency of Credit Allocation: The Experience of Chinese State-Owned Enterprises." *Journal of Comparative Economics* 28:1 - 31.

Darrat, A. F. 1998. "Tax and Spend, or Spend and Tax? An Inquiry into the Turkish Budgetary Process." *Southern Economic Journal* 64(4):940–956.

Davis, J. R. 1999. "Rural Finance and Private Farming in Romania." *Europe-Asia Studies* 51:843 - 869.

Diagne, A. 2000. "Empirical Measurement of Households Access to Credit and Credit Constraints in Developing Countries: Methodological Issues and Evidence." FCND Discussion Paper No.90.

Diamond, D. W. 1984. "Financial Intermediation and Delegated Monitoring." *Review of Economics Studies* 51:393 - 414.

Diamond, D. W. 1989. "Reputation Acquisition in Debt Markets." *Journal of Political Economy* 97:828–862.

Duara, Prasenjit. 1988. *Culture, Power, and the State: Rural North China, 1900-1942.* California: Stanford University Press.

Ellinger, P. N., and D. L. Neff. 1993. "Issues and Approaches in Efficiency Analysis of Agricultural Banks." *Agriculture Financial Review* 53:82–99.

Engle, R. F. 1987. "Cointegration and Error-Correction: Representation, Estimation, and Testing." *Econometrica* 55:251–276.

Fei, J. C. H., and G. Ranis. 1964. *Development of the Labor Surplus Economy: Theory and Policy.* Homewood, IL: Richard D. Irwin.

Fukuyama, F. 1995. *Trust: The Social Virtues and the Creation of Prosperity.* New York: Simon and Schuster.

Geertz, C. 1963. *Agriculture Involution: The Process of Ecological Change in Indonesia.* Berkeley: University of California Press.

Gertler, M. 1988. "Financial Structure and Aggregate Economics Activity: An Overview." *Journal of Money, Credit, and Banking* 20:559–88.

Giovanni, A., and M. De Melo. 1993. "Government Revenue from Financial Repression." *American Economic Review* 83(4):953–963.

Glaeser, E. L., D. I. Laibson, J. A. Scheinkman, and C. L. Soutter. 2002. "Measuring Trust." *Quarterly Journal of Economics* 115(3):811–846.

Goetz, A. M. and R. Sen Gupta. 1996. "Who Takes the Credit? Gender, Power, and Control over Loan Use in Rural Credit Programmes in Bangladesh." *World Development* 24(1):45–63.

Grabowski, R. 1989. "The Effect of Deregulation on the Efficiency of US Banking Firm." *Journal of Economics and Business* 46:39–54.

Greenwald, B. and J. E. Stiglitz. 1986. "Externalities in Economies with Imperfect Information and Incomplete Markets." *Quarterly Journal of Economics* 101:229–264.

Gupta, M. R., and S .Chaudhuri. 1997. "Formal Credit, Corruption and the Informal Credit Market in Agriculture: A theoretical Analysis." *Economica* 64.

Harrist, J. R., and M. P. Todaro. 1970. "Migration, Unemployment and Development: A Two Sector Analysis." *American Economic Review* 60.

Harveys, S., and J. R. James. 2002. "The Trust Paradox: A Survey of Economic Inquiries into the Nature of Trust and Trustworthiness." *Journal of Economic Behavior and Organization* 47:291–307.

Hayek, F.A. von. 1989. "The Pretense of Knowledge." *American Economic Review* 79(6):3–7.

Heckman, J. J. 1974. "Shadow Prices, Market Wages, and Labor Supply." *Econometrica* 42(4):679–694.

Heckman, J. J. 1979. "Sample Selection Bias as a Specification Error." *Econometrica* 47:153–161.

Hoff, K. and J. E. Stiglitz. 1993. "Moneylenders and Bankers: A model of Fragmented Credit Markets with Monopolistic Competition." Paper presented at the Econometric Society Meetings, Anaheim.

Holden, P., and V. Prokopenko. 2001. "Financial Development and Poverty Alleviation: Issues and Policy Implications for Developing and Transition Countries." IMF Working Paper.

Huang, Philip C.C. 1985. *The Peasant Economy and Social Change in North China.* Stanford, California: Stanford University Press.

Hulme, D., and P. Mosley. 1996. *Finance against Poverty.* London, UK: Routledge.

IFAD. 2002. "Double-edged Sword? Efficiency vs. Equity in Lending to the Poor." IFAD's thematic study on rural finance in China. Evaluation Profile, No.3.34 (April).

IFAD. 2001. "Rural Financial Services in China." Thematic Study Vol.I—Main Report No.1147-CN Rev. (December).

International Monetary Fund. 2001. "Structural Conditionality in Fund-Supported Programs" (February 16). http://www.imf.org.

Jones, E. C. 2004. "Wealth-Based Trust and the Development of Collective Action." *World Development* 32(4):691–711.

Jorgenson, D. W. 1967. "Surplus Agricultural Labor and the Development of a Dual Economy." *Oxford Economic Papers* 19.

Kay, N. M. 1996. "The Economics of Trust." *International Journal of the Economics of Business* 3(2):249–261.

Keeley, M. C. 1990. "Deposit Insurance, Risk, and Market Power in Banking." *American Economic Review* 80:1182–1200.

Khandler, S. R. 1988. *Fighting Poverty.* London: Routledge.

King, Robert G, and Ross Levine. 1993. "Finance and Growth: Schumpeter Might Be Right." *The Quarterly Journal of Economics* 108(3):717–737.

Knack, S., and P. Keefer. 1997. "Does Social Capital Have an Economic Payoff?—A Cross-Country Investigation." *Quarterly Journal of Economics* 112(4):1251–1288.

Kochar, A. 1997a. "Does Lack of Access to Formal Credit Constrain Agriculture Production? Evidence from the Land Tenancy Market in Rural India." *American Journal Agriculture of Economics* 8:754–63.

Kochar, A. 1997b. "An Empirical Investigation of Rationing Constraints in Rural Credit Markets in India." *Journal of Development Economics* 53:339–371.

Kornai, J. 2003. "Honesty and Trust in the Light of the Post-Socialist Transition." *Voprosy Economiki* 9.

Levine, R. 1992. "A Sensitivity Analysis of Cross-Country Growth Regressions." *American Economics Review* 82:942–63.

Levine, R. 1993. "Finance and Growth: Schumpeter Might Be Right." *Quarterly Journal Eeconomics* 3:717–37.

Levine, R. 1998. "Stock Markets Banks and Economic Growth." *American Economics Review* 88:537–58.

Levine, R. 2000. "Financial Intermediation and Growth: Causality and Causes." *Journal of Monetary Economics* 46:31–77.

Lewis, W. A. 1954. "Economic Development with Unlimited Supply of Labor." *The Manchester School of Economic and Social Studies* 22:139–191.

Lucas, R. E. Jr. 1988. "On the Mechanics of Economic Development." *Journal of Monetary Economics* 22:3–42.

McIntosh, J. 1975. "Growth and Dualism in Less Developed Countries." *Review of Economic Studies* 42:421–33.

Mckinnon, R. I. 1973. *Money and Capital in Economic Development*. Washington DC: The Brooking Institution.

Murata, Y. 2002. "Rural-urban Interdependence and Industrialization." *Journal of Development Economics* 68:1-34.

Myers, R. H. 1970. *The Chinese Peasant Economy: Agricultural Development in Hopei and Shantung, 1890-1949*. Cambridge, MA: Harvard University Press.

Newbery, D., and J. Stiglitz. 1979. *Sharecropping, Risk Sharing and the Imperfect Information, in Risk, Uncertainty and Agricultural Development*. Eds. by Roumassset, J., J. M. Boussard, and I. J. Singh. New York: Agricultural Development Council.

Osborne, T. 2006. "Credit and Risk in Rural Developing Economies." *Journal of Economic Dynamics and Control* 30:541–68.

Owoye, O. 1995. "The Causal Relationship Between Taxes and Expenditures in the G7 Countries: Cointegration and Error-Correction Models." *Applied Economics Letters* 2:19 - 22.

P. Sal. 2002. "Household Sectoral Choice and Effective Demand for Rural Credit in India." *Applied Economics* 14:1743–55.

Pasinetti, L. L. 1993. *Structural Economic Dynamics—A Theory of the Economic Consequences of Human Learning*. Cambridge, U.K.: Cambridge University Press.

Polanyi, K., C. M. Arensberg, and H. W. Pearson, eds. 1957. *Trade and Market in the Early Empires: Economies in History and Theory*. Glencoe, I11: Free Press.

Popkin, S. 1979. *The Rational Peasant: The Political Economy of Rural Society in Vietnam.* Berkeley: University of California Press.

Raiser, M., A. Rousso, S. Franklin, and U. Teksoz. 2003. "Trust in Transition: Cross-Country and Firm Evidence, European Bank for Reconstruction and Development." Working Paper No.82.

Ravallion, Martin. 1999. "Is More Targeting Consistent with Less Spending?" *International Tax and Public Finance* 6:411–419.

Romer, P. M. 1986. "Increasing Returns and Long Run Growth." *Journal of Political Economics* 94:1002–1037.

Romer, P. M. 1990. "Endogenous Technological Change." *Journal of Political Economy* 98:71–102.

Rousseau, D. M. 1990. "New Hire Perceptions of Their Own and Their Employer's Obligations: A Study of Psychological Contracts." *Journal of Organizational Behavior* 11:389 - 400.

Rousseau, P. L. 1998. "Financial Intermediation and Economic Performance: Historical Evidence from Five Industrial Countries." *Journal of Money, Credit, and Banking* 30:657–78.

Schiff, Maurice and Alberto Valdés. 1992. *A Synthesis of the Economics in Developing Countries.* Vol.4 of *The Political Economy of Agricultural Pricing Policy,* (A World Bank Comparative Study). Baltimore and London: Johns Hopkins University Press for the World Bank.

Scholtens, B. 2000. "A Critique on the Theory of Financial Intermediation." *Journal of Banking and Finance* 24:1243–51.

Schultz, Theodore W. 1950. "Reflections on Poverty within Agriculture." *Journal of Political Economy* 58.

Schultz, Theodore W. 1964. *Transforming Traditional Agriculture.* New Haven, CT: Yale University Press.

Scott, William G. 1976. *Organization Theory: A Structural and Behavioral Analysis.* Homewood, IL: R.D. Irwin.

Shaw, E. S. 1973. *Financial Deepening in Economic Development.* New York: Oxford University Press.

Shi, Xinzheng. 2002. "Empirical Research on Urban-Rural Income Differentials: The Case of China." Forthcoming, China Center for Economic Research, Beijing University.

Siamwalla, A. 1990. "The Thai Rural Credit System: Public Subsidies, Private Information and Segmented Markets." *The World Bank Economic Review* 4:271–95.

Silverman, B. W. 1986. *Density Estimation for Statistics and Data Analysis.* New York: Chapman and Hall.

Skinner, B. F. 1972. *Cumulative Record: A Selection of Papers*. New York: Appleton-Century-Crofts.

Skinner, G. W. 1964–1965. "Marketing and Social Structure in Rural China." *Journal of Asian Studies* 24(1):3–44; 24(2):195–228; 24(3):363–99.

Smith, A. 1976. *An Inquiry into the Nature and Causes of the Wealth of Nations*. Reprint, Eds. Cannan, E. Chicago: University of Chicago Press.

Solow, R. M. 1956. "A Contribution to the Theory of Economic Growth." *Quarterly Journal of Economics* 39:312–20.

Stiglitz, J. 1981. "Credit Rationing in Market with Imperfect Information." *American Economic Review* 71:339–410.

Stiglitz, J., and A. Weiss. 1981. "Credit Rationing in Markets with Imperfect Competition." *American Economic Review* 71(3):393–410.

Stiglitz, J. E. 1990. "Peer Monitoring and Credit Markets." *World Bank Economic Review* 3:351–366.

Stiglitz, J. 1993. *The Economics of Rural Organization: Theory, Practice, and Policy*. Eds. K. Hoff and A. Braverman. New York: Oxford University Press.

Swinnen, J. F. M., and S. Rozelle. 2006. *From Marx and Mao to the Market: The Economics and Politics of Agricultural Transition*. Oxford: Oxford University Press.

Tansley, A.G. 1935. "The Use and Abuse of Vegetational Concepts and Terms." *Ecology* 16:284–307.

The World Bank. 1989. World Development Report 1989.

The World Bank. 1995. World Development Report 1995.

Todaro, M. P. 1969. "A model of Labor Migration and Urban Unemployment in Less Developed Countries." *American Economic Review* (March) 59.

Tsai, K. S. 1999. "Financing Private Enterprises in China: A Political Economic View from Below." Paper presented at the 1999 Association for Asian Studies annual meeting, Boston.

Tsai, K. S. 2004. "Imperfect Substitutes: The Local Political Economy of Informal Finance and Microfinance in Rural and India." *World Development* 32:1478–1507.

Udry, C. 1994. "Risk and Insurance in a Rural Credit Market: A Empirical Investigation in Northern Nigeria." *Review of Economic Studies* 61:495–526.

Vamvoukas, G. 1997. "Budget Expenditures and Revenues: An Application of the Error Correction Modeling." *Public Finance* 52(1):139–143.

Verghese, A. 2005. "Bank-Moneylender Linkage as an Alternative to Bank Competition in Rural Credit Markets." Oxford Economic Paper 57:315–35.

Villas-Boas J. M., and U. Schmidt-Mohr. 1999. "Oligopoly with Asymmetric Information: Differentiation in Credit Markets." *The RAND Journal of Economics* 30(3):375–96.

Virmani, A. 1982. "The Nature of Credit Markets in Developing Countries: A Framework for Policy Analysis." World Bank Staff Working Paper 524. Washington, D. C.

Watson, A. 1998. "Conflicts of Interest: Reform of the Rural Credit Cooperatives in China." *MOCT-MOST: Economic Policy in Transitional Economies* 8(3):23–40.

Yang, D. T. 1999. "Urban-Biased Policies and Rising Income Inequality in China." *American Economic Review* 89(2):306–310.

Yang, Dennis Tao and Hao Zhou. 1999. "Rural-Urban Disparity and Sectoral Labor Allocation in China." *Journal of Development Studies* 35(3):105–133.

Yaron, J. 1992. "Rural Finance in Developing Countries." Policy Research Working Papers (WPs 875), Agriculture and Rural Development Department, World Bank, Washington, D. C.

Yaron, J., M. P. Benjamin, and G.L. Piprek. 1997. *Rural Finance: Issues, Design, and Best Practices*. Washington, D.C.: World Bank.

Yaron, J., M. P. Benjamin, and S. Charitonenko. 1998. "Promoting Efficient Rural Financial Intermediation." *The World Bank Research Observer* 13:147–70.

Young, A. A. 1928. "Increasing Returns and Economic Progress." *The Economic Journal* 38:527–42.

Zak, P. J., and Knack, S. 2001. "Trust and Growth." *The Economic Journal* 111 (April):295–321.

Zaman, H. 2004. "The Scaling-Up of Microfinance in Bangladesh: Determinants, Impact, and Lessons." Working Paper.

Index

agricultural development 6-7, 96, 107, 118, 120-1, 126, 128, 261, 280, 288
agricultural insurance 277-9, 287-92
agricultural loan market 96-7, 99, 101, 103-5, 107-9, 111, 113, 115, 117, 119, 129-31, 133-5, 141, 232-3, 241-4
agricultural loans 28-9, 36, 39, 50, 56-61, 70, 86, 88, 100, 102, 105, 138, 158, 249-50, 252-4
agricultural production 25-6, 32, 35, 41, 51, 55-6, 58-9, 63, 87, 235, 241, 247-8, 250-1, 279, 289
agricultural sector 2-3, 12, 19-20, 23-4, 26, 29, 275
  traditional 2
agricultural technology 55, 57-61, 86, 100-1, 103-4, 247-8, 250-1, 253
agriculture
  added-value of 126-8
  gross output value of 121, 126-8
agriculture sector 19
annual income of rural households 121, 127-8, 253
arable land per capita index 100, 248, 250-1, 253

balance 136-7, 153, 200, 285
behavior of rural households 234, 244
borrow money 19, 43, 45, 49-50, 59, 67, 72-4, 101-2, 104, 220, 234, 239, 241, 249, 283
borrowers 36-7, 94, 203, 239

capital
  material 80, 88
  potential 240, 255
  source of 30, 86, 88, 116, 242
  supply of 26, 110
capital accumulation 13, 24, 26, 43, 240, 243-4
capital deposit 41, 55, 107, 140, 236-8, 240, 243, 248
capital gap 243
capital mechanism 11, 25-7, 244, 255
commercial banks, state-owned 14-15
commercial insurance 288-9
commercial loans 34, 37, 42, 44, 205, 240
comparative labor productivity 3-7
contract 50-1, 75, 85, 87, 175, 257, 259, 278, 291
contract credit 85-7
credibility 32, 61, 71-3, 75, 82-8, 96, 98, 105, 129, 232-3, 235, 241
credit
  contractual 51
  informal 62-3, 67
  social 121, 125-6, 271
credit balance 136-7
credit constraints 40, 65, 99, 255-6, 261-2, 264-5, 269
credit demand 53, 255-6, 259, 262-3, 267
credit differentiation 259-60, 266
credit expansion 256, 263-4
credit guidance 29
credit insurance, agricultural 263-4, 269, 278
credit limit 16, 40, 261-5
credit market 53, 63, 69, 87, 239, 245-6
credit rationing 19, 110, 157, 257, 259
credit risk 91-2
credit subsidies 29
credit supply 274, 278

Index

dependence, strong 78-9
depositors 184-6, 216
development trap 24-6
dual, urban-rural 5-6
dual structure 3-4, 6-9, 11
duality 5-7, 11, 19, 26, 101

economic activities 53, 66, 72
economic development 2-3, 7, 11, 23, 25-6, 28, 56, 64, 66, 85, 247, 272, 275, 279
economic structure 2-6, 8-12, 18-19, 24-6, 96, 275
economics, neoclassical 96-7, 145
educational level 36, 55-6, 58-61, 100-4, 247-8, 250-1, 253-4
effect, demonstration 81-2, 138-9
effect of capital mechanism 25-6

financial ecology 118, 130-1
financial layout 233, 235, 237, 239, 241, 243, 245, 247, 249, 251, 253, 255, 257, 259, 261
formal credit 30, 46, 62-8, 70, 246

GDP, agricultural 9, 29
government
  central 12, 14, 79
  township 79
government dominance 120-1, 124-5, 128, 130
government intervention 146, 148, 153, 157, 241, 275

household savings 13-14
human capital 42, 44, 55-6, 80, 86, 242, 248

income gap 3, 98
income level 57, 91, 124-5, 130, 247-8, 252, 254
income of agricultural production 55-6, 58-9, 100, 102, 247-8, 250-1
income of rural households 65, 121, 124, 248, 271, 280
industrial sector 2, 7, 19-20, 22, 24, 26
industrialization, agricultural 6, 8-9, 26, 273, 275, 279, 281
informal loans 34, 38, 169-70
information asymmetry 72, 131, 156, 219, 239-40, 246, 256, 259-60, 263-4, 269, 276
institutions, agricultural reinsurance 290
insurance companies, private 287-8, 291
insurance system, agricultural 278, 287
interest, chain of 226-9
interest rate 12-14, 16, 18-19, 29, 34-5, 37, 40, 50, 92, 99, 108-11, 114-18, 157, 266-7, 285
investment, agricultural 262, 265
investment preference 53, 55-6, 58-61, 100, 102-3, 105, 247, 249-50, 252, 254
investment tendency 55, 61

kinship credit 85, 87

labor, excess 20
loan interest rate 49-50, 87
loan preference 56, 58, 60-1, 100, 102-3, 105, 245, 249-50
loan rate 38, 197, 201, 203, 215, 220, 238, 261-2, 264-5, 268, 285-6
loans
  discount 282-3, 285
  formal 38, 46
loans interest rate 13-14
local government 79, 130, 172

marginal productivity 2, 263
marginal return 235-9, 242-3
market price 16, 228, 275
market segmentation 115-16
marketization 43, 67, 234, 272, 274, 288
microcredit 43-4, 62-3, 69, 91, 181, 196-7, 202-4, 206-8, 272, 274
mutual aid cooperatives 270, 273

national agricultural loans 63, 80, 86, 162-3, 165-6, 172, 245-6

operation quality of economy 122-3, 125-6

personal credit 71-2, 74, 85-8
policy loans 17, 80, 86, 242, 276
    discount 86, 88
postal savings banks 15-16
poverty trap 234, 236-7, 239-43
private loans 34, 36, 38, 43-4, 55, 59, 61, 112, 114-15
production functions 19-20, 166, 174
production loans 36, 38-42
    non-agricultural 252, 254
products, agricultural 16, 20, 28, 149, 287, 289-90

ratio, non-performing loan 16, 135-7
rational small farmers 53-4, 170-1, 232-3, 242-4, 246, 255
RCCs (rural credit cooperatives) 15-16, 37, 40, 45-6, 55, 57, 59, 77, 86, 110-11, 172, 174, 254, 270-1, 273
regional economy 102-3, 129-30, 133, 253, 263-4, 269
relational loans 46, 50, 87, 245-6
relationship credibility 72, 85-6, 141, 272
return, rate of 24, 235-6, 238, 262, 264-5, 267-9
risk, natural 36, 41, 43, 289
risk preference 70-1, 86
rural credit 52, 62-4, 66-70, 104, 242-4, 246, 254, 265
rural credit foundations 34-5
rural households
    disadvantaged 65
    general 41-4, 270
    marketized 41, 43
rural households' behavior 33, 35, 37, 39, 41, 43, 45, 47, 49, 51, 53, 55, 57, 59, 61
rural Issues 8, 25, 27, 232-3
rural microcredit 16, 133-4, 136-7

savings, urban-rural 13-14
sectors
    modern 2, 10
    rural 12, 25-6, 129
    urban 7, 12-13, 16, 25, 129
small farmers 57, 66-7, 80, 170-1, 232-3, 244, 281
social capital 37, 71, 74, 241-2, 254
    ethical 72, 74
social relationship capital 56-8, 60-1, 100, 249
social structure 78, 80, 84, 86
social trust 75-6, 84-6, 88
surplus labor 2
surviving small farmers 233-4, 242-6, 255
sustainability 10, 219, 282, 284

Total assets index 100-1, 103-4, 248, 250-1, 253
transformation, dynamic 25-6, 242, 245, 281

transformation of rural households 87-8, 233, 235, 237, 239, 241, 243-5, 247, 249, 251, 253, 271, 273-5, 279, 281

urban-biased policies 28-9
usury 18, 33, 42, 67, 109, 113, 237-41, 243
utility, national 65-7, 70

village cadres 37, 57, 247, 249-50, 252-4